Freedom, Fatalism, and Foreknowledge

Freedom, Fatalism, and Foreknowledge

Edited by John Martin Fischer
and
Patrick Todd

OXFORD
UNIVERSITY PRESS

OXFORD
UNIVERSITY PRESS

Oxford University Press is a department of the University of
Oxford. It furthers the University's objective of excellence in research,
scholarship, and education by publishing worldwide.

Oxford   New York

Auckland   Cape Town   Dar es Salaam   Hong Kong   Karachi
Kuala Lumpur   Madrid   Melbourne   Mexico City   Nairobi
New Delhi   Shanghai   Taipei   Toronto

With offices in

Argentina   Austria   Brazil   Chile   Czech Republic   France   Greece
Guatemala   Hungary   Italy   Japan   Poland   Portugal   Singapore
South Korea   Switzerland   Thailand   Turkey   Ukraine   Vietnam

Oxford is a registered trademark of Oxford University Press
in the UK and certain other countries.

Published in the United States of America by
Oxford University Press
198 Madison Avenue, New York, NY 10016

© Oxford University Press 2015

Library of Congress Cataloging-in-Publication Data
Freedom, fatalism, and foreknowledge / edited by John Martin Fischer and Patrick Todd.
pages cm
Includes bibliographical references and index.
ISBN 978-0-19-994239-8 (cloth: alk. paper)—ISBN 978-0-19-994241-1 (pbk.: alk. paper)
1. Free will and determinism.   2. Fate and fatalism.   I. Fischer, John Martin, 1952–editor.
II. Todd, Patrick, 1983–editor.
BJ1461.F79 2015
149'.8—dc23
2014034145

1 3 5 7 9 8 6 4 2
Printed in the United States of America
on acid-free paper

CONTENTS

ACKNOWLEDGMENTS

We are very grateful to the following for their insightful and helpful comments on versions of the introductory essay: Andrew Bailey, Michael Rea, Sven Rosenkranz, and Neal Tognazzini. Publication of this book was in part supported by a grant from the Big Questions on Free Will Project at Florida State University, supported by the John Templeton Foundation. We wish to thank Al Mele and the John Templeton Foundation.

Permission to reprint the following articles is hereby acknowledged:

"Fate," in Richard Taylor, *Metaphysics* (Englewood Cliffs, N.J.: Prentice Hall, 1963): 54–69.

"Fatalism," in Peter van Inwagen, *An Essay on Free Will* (Oxford: Clarendon Press, 1983): 23–54.

"Truth and Freedom," *The Philosophical Review* Vol. 118, No. 1 (2009): 29–57.

"The Truth about Freedom: A Reply to Merricks," *The Philosophical Review* Vol. 120, No. 1 (2011): 97–115.

"Fatalism, Incompatibilism, and the Power to Do Otherwise," *Noûs* Vol. 37, No. 4 (2003): 672–89.

"Presentism and Fatalism," *Australasian Journal of Philosophy* Vol. 84, No. 4 (2006): 511–24.

"Compatibilist Options," in J. Campbell, M. O'Rourke, and D. Shier (eds.), *Freedom and Determinism* (Cambridge: MIT Press, 2004): 231–54.

"Omniscience and the Arrow of Time," *Faith and Philosophy* Vol. 19, No. 4 (2002): 503–19.

"Troubles With Ockhamism," *Journal of Philosophy* Vol. 87, No. 9 (1990): 462–80.

"Presentism and Ockham's Way Out," in *Oxford Studies in Philosophy of Religion* Vol. I, Jonathan L. Kvanvig, ed., (Oxford: Oxford University Press, 2008): 1–17.

"Geachianism," in *Oxford Studies in Philosophy of Religion* Vol. III, Jonathan L. Kvanvig, ed. (Oxford: Oxford University Press, 2011): 222–51.

"On Augustine's Way Out," *Faith and Philosophy* Vol. 16, No. 1 (1999): 245–55.

"The Meaning of 'Is Going to Be,'" *Mind* Vol. 74, No. 293 (1965): 46–58.

"It Was to Be," in P. T. Geach and A. J. P. Kenny (eds), *Papers in Logic and Ethics* (London: Duckworth, 1976): 97–108.

"Future Contingents and Relative Truth," *The Philosophical Quarterly* Vol. 53, No. 212 (2003): 321–36.

"In Defence of Ockhamism," *Philosophia* Vol. 40, No. 3 (2012): 617–31.

LIST OF CONTRIBUTORS

Alicia Finch, Associate Professor of Philosophy, Northern Illinois University

John Martin Fischer, Distinguished Professor of Philosophy, University of California, Riverside

Charles Hartshorne (1917–2000), his last position was Professor of Philosophy, University of Texas, Austin

David P. Hunt, Professor of Philosophy, Whittier College

John MacFarlane, Professor of Philosophy, University of California, Berkeley

Penelope Mackie, Associate Professor and Reader in Philosophy, University of Nottingham

Trenton Merricks, Professor of Philosophy, University of Virginia

John Perry, Emeritus Professor of Philosophy, Stanford University; Emeritus Professor of Philosophy, University of California, Riverside

A.N. Prior (1914–69), his last position was Fellow and Tutor in Philosophy at Balliol College, Oxford

Michael C. Rea, Professor of Philosophy and Director of the Center for Philosophy of Religion, University of Notre Dame

Sven Rosenkranz, Research Professor, ICREA and University of Barcelona

Richard Taylor (1919–2003), his last position was Professor of Philosophy, University of Rochester

Patrick Todd, Chancellor's Fellow, University of Edinburgh

Peter van Inwagen, John Cardinal O'Hara Professor of Philosophy, University of Notre Dame

David Widerker, Professor of Philosophy, Bar-Ilan University

Linda Zagzebski, George Lynn Cross Research Professor, and Kingfisher College Chair of the Philosophy of Religion and Ethics, University of Oklahoma

PREFACE

Congratulations! You are the proud new owner—or borrower, or anyway temporary possessor—of this book. If you purchased it, we certainly hope that you will not come to regret your decision. But one thing we are rather certain of is this: if you do, then you'll just have to live with your regret (sorry to say). Or at least you'll have to hope that the seller who sold you the book has a permissive return policy. At any rate, one thing that is certain—or seems certain—is that it is now too late never to have bought the book in the first place. You no longer have any choice about *that*. You *did* buy the book, and not even *God* (should God exist) can do anything about that much. In general, we may regret the past, or remember it fondly, or be ignorant of it entirely, but it is not something any of us could possibly do anything about. The past, as philosophers sometimes like to say, is fixed.

That the past is fixed may at first blush seem like an innocent triviality. In fact, however, the idea that the past is fixed has been the intuitive engine driving several millennia's worth of philosophical reflection (and anxiety) concerning the possibility that we might lack *free will*, understood as the ability to do otherwise than what we actually do. There is, unfortunately, disturbing reason to think that our lack of power over the past might somehow transmute—or transmogrify—into a lack of power over *anything*. After all, there may be certain connections between things in the past and things in the present—and if we can't do anything about the former, it might turn out that we can't do anything about the latter, either. The question whether the fixity of the past indeed does threaten free will in this way—and how to avoid the threat if it does—has given rise to a cluster of interrelated philosophical problems that have occupied the attention of philosophers from the time of Aristotle to the present day, problems having to do with time, free will, truth, causation, explanation, and much else. This interrelated set of problems is the topic of this book. Not every essay in this book addresses the fixity of the past directly, but each addresses some aspect of the problems to which it gives rise.

The (alleged) threat to free will from the fixity of the past stems from at least three different sources, two of which are the special focus of this book; these two sources are pinpointed in arguments provided by those who have come to be called *fatalists*. First, consider again your purchase (or temporary acquisition) of this book. Now, from the fact that you purchased the book, it can seem to follow that it was true 1,000 years ago (or at any arbitrary past time) that you would purchase it. There seems to be, then, a connection (a necessary connection) between a truth in the distant past—over which you seemingly have no control—and your present actions. But if you have no choice about one thing, and there is a necessary connection between that thing and another, how could you have a choice about the second thing? It might appear that you couldn't. The conclusion? Given the relevant truth in the past regarding your future decision to buy the book, you really couldn't have done anything else than buy it.

Are you worried yet? Perhaps you aren't. Arguments of this type—arguments that move, roughly, from *truths* in the past regarding future decisions to the conclusion that those decisions are unavoidable, and hence unfree—are those advanced by so-called *logical fatalists*. And nearly every philosopher who has considered such arguments has failed to be persuaded by them. What is curious, however, is the widespread disagreement about just where such arguments go wrong. As we'll see, some say that they misapply (or overextend) the intuitive notion that the past is fixed. Others question the idea that it really was (or must have been) true 1,000 years ago that you would purchase the book. (Still others question whether it even makes sense to talk of what was true "1,000 years ago.") Here, then, we encounter the problem of *future contingents* (propositions of a certain sort about the future). For if it wasn't true 1,000 years ago that you would purchase the book, what was it—false? But how could *that* be? Or was it simply neither true nor false? Classical logic, however, seems to demand that any proposition be either true or false. Then again, what could have *made* any such proposition true or false? These sorts of questions are the focus of the essays in Part 3 of this book.

Perhaps you aren't yet convinced that we've encountered a genuine threat to free will. But there are perhaps more troubling arguments in the neighborhood, arguments that arise most prominently within the context of Western theism—and here we come to the second historical source of anxiety about free will arising from the fixity of the past, a source associated with a different type of fatalistic argument. Above we remarked that not even *God* could have a choice about the past. In fact, introducing God into the picture creates a whole range of new and difficult problems. For instance, even if the intuitive notion of the fixity of the past *doesn't* apply to *prior truths* about what we do (contra the *logical* fatalist), it may indeed apply to *prior beliefs* about what we do. However, God is (or at least has been taken to be) essentially omniscient, in such a way that would imply that, for any truth at all, God believes (and, indeed, knows) that truth. So suppose that God believed 1,000 years ago that you would purchase this book. If you had the power to refrain from purchasing it, wouldn't that have to be the power to make God *wrong* for having believed that you would purchase it? But you couldn't have the power to make God wrong. Consequently, you couldn't have the power to avoid purchasing this book, if God indeed believed beforehand that you would purchase it. Here we have, then, at least one way of putting the ancient problem of divine foreknowledge and human freedom. This problem has in fact been one of the primary historical motivations of discussions of (and theories about) the fixity of the past and future contingents. This book thus treats the two sorts of arguments—those provided by the logical fatalist and theological fatalist—together. The arguments are deeply parallel in certain crucial respects, and (as we hope will become clear), thinking about both together can be mutually illuminating.

We aim in our introductory essay to set out these different "fatalistic" arguments (and the corresponding problem of future contingents) in a more rigorous way, and to indicate the main ways of replying to these arguments. The result, we hope, is a picture of the "state of play" in the contemporary debate about these issues. The essays are grouped according to theme, but these groupings are of course far from perfect, and a paper in one part may go on at length concerning the topic of a different section. As we try to explain in our introductory essay, any one of these issues is intimately bound up with both of the others.

To help the reader find his or her way around this book and the themes it addresses, in what follows next we provide brief descriptions of the contents of the relevant articles. Then in the Introduction we will abstract away from some of the "surface structure" of the articles and seek to provide an analytical framework within which they arguably fit.

RICHARD TAYLOR, "FATE"

This is a chapter from Taylor's introductory text, *Metaphysics*. It is a classic presentation of the worries raised by "fatalism" (here understood as the unavoidability of what happens) and the different sources or reasons for these worries (including causal determinism, the prior truth of statements about the future, and God's foreknowledge). (The threat posed by causal determinism is the third source of worries arising for free will from the fixity of the past, as mentioned above.) Taylor offers his famous "Story of Osmo" to highlight the fatalistic concerns. Taylor's sympathetic treatment of fatalism has received considerable attention over the years.

PETER VAN INWAGEN, "FATALISM"

This excerpt from van Inwagen's important book, *An Essay on Free Will*, presents a critical discussion of fatalistic arguments, including a version of the argument offered in the work of his teacher, Richard Taylor. (The argument is not explicitly articulated in "Fate" above, but it is a regimentation of the worries presented in that piece.) Van Inwagen contends that there are logical infelicities in salient arguments for fatalism. He will go on to argue in *An Essay on Free Will* that the argument for the incompatibility of causal determinism and human freedom (which he dubs the "Consequence Argument") is crucially different from these arguments for fatalism and thus not subject to the logical objections. Van Inwagen's development of the argument from causal determinism highlights the role the fixity of the past (the commonsense idea that the past is now out of our control) plays in both arguments.

TRENTON MERRICKS, "TRUTH AND FREEDOM"

In this article, published in *The Philosophical Review*, Merricks argues that various fatalistic arguments (including arguments from prior truth values and God's foreknowledge) "beg the question." He employs what he dubs a "truism": "a claim or statement or belief or proposition is true because things are how that claim (or statement) represents things as being—and not the other way around." Adopting a strategy that can be traced back to Molina, Merricks argues that (say) God's prior belief depends on an individual's subsequent behavior, rather than the other way around. Merricks exploits this relation of asymmetric dependence to seek to defuse the fatalistic arguments. This article represents an important shift in emphasis in contemporary discussions of fatalistic arguments in giving pride of place to issues surrounding dependence.

JOHN MARTIN FISCHER AND PATRICK TODD, "THE TRUTH ABOUT FREEDOM: A REPLY TO MERRICKS"

In this paper, also published in *The Philosophical Review*, Fischer and Todd argue (against Merricks) that the fatalistic arguments in question do not beg the question. They argue that the truism about dependence, in itself and without further elaboration, does not establish that the arguments are question-begging. This article raises issues about the role and interpretation of dependence as well as the fixity of the past.

PENELOPE MACKIE, "FATALISM, INCOMPATIBILISM, AND THE POWER TO DO OTHERWISE"

This article, published in *Noûs*, highlights certain "striking" similarities between the "Consequence Argument" (the argument that causal determinism rules out freedom to do otherwise) and an argument for what Mackie calls "logical fatalism." This is in a tradition of noting similarities between the arguments issuing from the various "sources" of fatalistic worries; but whereas Taylor thinks that the arguments are sound, Mackie thinks they are similarly problematic. She contends that resources employed by compatibilists about causal determinism and human freedom can be applied fruitfully at parallel points in the logical fatalist's argument.

MICHAEL C. REA, "PRESENTISM AND FATALISM"

Rea argues (in this piece published in *Australasian Journal of Philosophy*) that a presentist about time must choose between the principle of bivalence and libertarianism. (He takes this to be a "cost" of presentism.) Presentism is the doctrine that only the present moment exists, so that "there are no actual but non-present objects." (This doctrine is in opposition to "eternalism" about time, according to which all temporal moments exist "equally" and are thus on an ontological par.) This is a significant article, in part because it makes connections between the arguments about free will and fundamental issues in the philosophy of time. As with Merricks's contribution (above), Rea is connecting the discussion of issues about free will with other areas of metaphysics (including the philosophy of time), thus providing illumination of both sets of issues (free will and fundamental metaphysics). This represents a salient analytic turn in recent discussions of free will.

JOHN PERRY, "COMPATIBILIST OPTIONS"

In this paper, published in *Freedom and Determinism* (proceedings of an *Inland Northwest Philosophy Conference*) John Perry closely examines the Consequence Argument (for the incompatibility of causal determinism and human freedom), especially as developed by Peter van Inwagen in *An Essay on Free Will* and other venues. Perry develops a novel approach to responding to it on behalf of the compatibilist. As with Mackie's contribution, this kind of reply can also be applied to the logical fatalist's argument(s). The pieces collected in the anthology thus far illustrate that an analysis of the fatalistic arguments can be enhanced by comparing such arguments issuing from different sources, for example, causal determinism, God's foreknowledge, and prior truth values, as well as invoking resources from fundamental metaphysics and philosophy of time.

LINDA ZAGZEBSKI, "OMNISCIENCE AND THE ARROW OF TIME"

This paper, originally published in *Faith and Philosophy*, explores in a novel way the relationships between the fatalistic arguments that issue from the various sources: prior truths, God's foreknowledge, and causal determination. As with other authors in this book (Taylor, Perry, and Mackie), Zagzebski contends that the arguments can be illuminated by reflecting on their common deep structure. She contends that underlying the argument from divine foreknowledge (as well as the other arguments) is a deeper tension between certain fundamental metaphysical assumptions. Again, this is an instance of a "turn" in the analysis of the arguments about free will; as with Merricks and Rea, Zagzebski is pointing to connections between the evaluation of the arguments about free will and issues in basic metaphysics.

DAVID WIDERKER, "TROUBLES WITH OCKHAMISM"

In this paper, published in *The Journal of Philosophy*, Widerker focuses on "Ockhamism" in the sense stemming from Nelson Pike in which there is a distinctive reply to the argument for fatalism arising from God's foreknowledge. In this sense of "Ockhamism," it is important to distinguish "hard" (temporally intrinsic) from "soft" (temporally extrinsic) facts about the past; further, an Ockhamist in this sense might also hold that God's prior beliefs are mere soft facts about the past and thus not within the purview of the commonsense notion of the fixity of the past. Widerker articulates various problems with this Ockhamist strategy. The paper is noteworthy for (among other things) a critique of the "entailment view" of soft facthood (endorsed famously by Alvin Plantinga).

ALICIA FINCH AND MICHAEL REA, "PRESENTISM AND OCKHAM'S WAY OUT"

Published in *Oxford Studies in Philosophy of Religion*, this paper builds on Rea's previous contribution in building additional bridges between the evaluation of the fatalistic arguments (from various sources) and views in philosophy of time. Finch and Rea contend that Ockhamism (in the sense of Pike and the distinction between hard and soft facts) is incompatible with presentism; indeed they argue that Ockhamism presupposes eternalism. They conclude that "the response that some consider the best response [to the fatalistic argument stemming from God's foreknowledge] is unavailable to the presentist." This provides what they take to be a further cost of presentism (in addition to the cost identified in the article by Rea above).

PATRICK TODD, "GEACHIANISM"

This paper, first published in *Oxford Studies in Philosophy of Religion*, develops a position originally suggested by P. T. Geach but not hitherto given a detailed articulation. The view offers a novel way of responding to the fatalistic arguments from prior truth values and God's foreknowledge. On this Geach-inspired view, the future is "mutable" in the following sense. It can literally and unqualifiedly be true at time *T1* that a given plane will crash at *T3* and then become literally and unqualifiedly true at *T2* that the plane will not crash at *T3*. Todd lays out this under-theorized view as at least an option worth considering in seeking to respond to the fatalistic arguments.

DAVID HUNT, "ON AUGUSTINE'S WAY OUT"

This paper, which appeared in *Faith and Philosophy*, argues that we can illuminate the fatalistic arguments by distinguishing between different senses (or implications) of "free will." Free will may imply freedom to do otherwise; but it may simply imply acting freely (without the [arguably] further requirement for freedom to do otherwise or access to alternative possibilities). Hunt contends that a proper interpretation of Augustine would have it that we can act freely without being free to do otherwise. This is the key, according to Hunt, to replying to the fatalist argument issuing from God's foreknowledge. Hunt contends that this "Augustinian" strategy is preferable to those of Boethius and Aquinas (positing an atemporal God) and Ockham (employing in a certain way the distinction between hard and soft facts). This strategy resonates with the "actual-sequence" approach to moral responsibility advocated by philosophers such as Harry Frankfurt and John Martin Fischer. Here illumination of the fatalistic arguments is sought not so much through connections to basic metaphysics or philosophy of time, but normative theory.

CHARLES HARTSHORNE, "THE MEANING OF 'IS GOING TO BE'"

Published in *Mind*, this pathbreaking paper develops the view that "will" and "will not" are *contraries*, not *contradictories*, thus opening up a novel way to be an open-futurist beyond the traditional "Aristotelian" way of denying bivalence concerning future contingents. According to this approach (developed more fully by Prior and then by Todd in more recent work), future contingents are all false. This paper contains a response to what is perhaps the main objection to this view: the "prediction problem." This problem stems from the fact that when a predicted event comes to pass, it seems natural to say that the prediction turned out true. Thus, it seems that the relevant future contingent was true. Hartshorne suggests a reply.

A. N. PRIOR, "IT WAS TO BE"

In this paper (originally published in a collection, *Papers in Logic and Ethics*), Prior helpfully distinguishes and compares different usages of (and semantics for) the future-tense "will". On his preferred semantics, future contingents are all false (rather than indeterminate in truth value). This paper also contains an interesting discussion of the prediction problem.

JOHN MACFARLANE, "FUTURE CONTINGENTS AND RELATIVE TRUTH"

This article, published in *The Philosophical Quarterly*, argues for a novel and nuanced semantics for future contingents. MacFarlane argues that we need to relativize utterance-truth to a context of assessment, and sentence-truth to both a context of utterance and a context of assessment. As he puts it, "This amounts to recognizing a new kind of linguistic context-sensitivity." In addition to providing the theoretical framework for a more nuanced assessment of the fatalistic arguments, this article provides a new way of responding to the prediction problem.

SVEN ROSENKRANZ, "IN DEFENSE OF OCKHAMISM"

This paper, which appeared in *Philosophia*, defends what Prior calls an "Ockhamistic" tense-logic, according to which truths about the future need not be grounded in deterministic present causal tendencies. "Ockhamism" is used in (at least) two salient ways. In this way, it refers to the view that truths about the future need not rest on causal determination. In another usage (see the contributions from Finch/ Rea, Widerker, Hunt, and Fischer/Todd in this anthology), "Ockhamism" is a distinctive reply to the argument for theological fatalism that invokes a distinction between "hard" (temporally intrinsic) and "soft" (temporally extrinsic) facts about the past. The first usage stems from Arthur Prior, and the second from Nelson Pike. Ockhamism, in the sense in question in this paper by Rosenkranz, accepts the "thin red line" (also discussed by MacFarlane)—namely, a privileged future of those that remain causally possible.

Freedom, Fatalism, and Foreknowledge

INTRODUCTION

Patrick Todd and John Martin Fischer

This Introduction has three sections, on "logical fatalism," "theological fatalism," and the problem of future contingents, respectively.

1. LOGICAL FATALISM

The logical fatalist argues—in a particular sort of way—that no one has free will, understood as the ability to do otherwise than what one actually does. Though there are perhaps various ways of arguing that ought to make one a "logical fatalist," there is one particular recurring *pattern* of argument that we shall explicitly focus on in this Introduction (and that also recurs in many of the essays in this book). This is, we think, the *best* argument that moves from time, truth, and logic to the conclusion that no one has free will.[1] We find it helpful to separate two aspects of the fatalist's overall argument that no one is free. First, the fatalist argues—in a particular way—that "prior truths" specifying what we will do in the future are incompatible with our having free will. According to this argument, if it was true already, 1,000 years ago (say), that you would purchase this book, then you could not have done otherwise than purchase the book. Second, the fatalist claims that, as a matter of logic, or as a matter of common sense, or as a matter of something else, we will have to say that for

---

[1]This raises a difficult question: what is it that makes one a "logical fatalist"? There is, unfortunately, no generally agreed upon definition of this term. Minimally, the logical fatalist argues that necessarily, no human being has free will. But not just *any* way of arguing that, necessarily, no one has free will makes one a logical fatalist. We (tentatively) suggest that what makes one a fatalist is that one argues that, necessarily, no one has free will *without* explicitly invoking any thesis about *causation* or causal determinism. There is, of course, a venerable argument—sometimes discussed in the essays of this book (especially in the essays of Perry and Mackie)—that causal determinism is incompatible with free will. But proponents of this argument are not now generally taken to be supporting the cause of "fatalism" or "the fatalist"—even in combination with an argument that determinism is *true* (or even necessarily true). The logical fatalist thinks we can show that no one has free will with more minimal resources.

anything that happens, it always was the case that it would happen. If it is happening, this implies that there was indeed a "prior truth" specifying that it was going to. The fatalist concludes that we are never able to do otherwise than what we in fact do.[2]

At the most general level, responses to the logical fatalist divide according to whether one rejects the fatalist's argument for the *incompatibility* of "prior truths" and free will, or instead the argument that there are (or were) such truths in the first place. Broadly, denials of the argument for "prior truths" are most commonly associated with the thesis of the "open future," which we shall define as the thesis that future contingent propositions—roughly, propositions saying of undetermined events that they will happen—systematically fail to be true. (We discuss these positions in more detail in Section 3.) Our focus in the remainder of this section instead concerns by far the most popular way of responding to the fatalist: denying her argument for incompatibilism. According to this response, the mere fact that it was true 1,000 years ago that you would purchase this book does not, in itself, tell us that you could not have done otherwise than purchase it. At the outset, however, it is important to note that not all who endorse the fatalist's argument for incompatibilism need themselves be fatalists. For one might endorse the fatalist's argument for incompatibilism about prior truths and free will, but *not* the fatalist's argument (or any other) for prior truths. Indeed, some have taken the strength of the fatalist's argument for incompatibilism to be strong reason to *deny* that there were the relevant prior truths—thereby preserving free will.

1.1. The Logical Fatalist's Argument for Incompatibilism

You purchased this book. (Thanks!) Could you have refrained from doing so? If it was true 1,000 years ago that you would purchase it, apparently not. For consider the following argument:

(1) You had no choice about: it was true 1,000 years ago that you would purchase the book at *t*.
(2) Necessarily, if it was true 1,000 years ago that you would purchase the book at *t*, then you purchase the book at *t*. So,
(3) You had no choice about: purchasing the book at *t*.

---

[2] Not everyone is comfortable with talking about "prior truths" in this way; some deny that it makes sense to talk about what *was* true *at a time* in the first place. See, for instance, van Inwagen's essay in this volume—and see Merricks's essay for a reply. With Merricks, we believe that the basic argument at issue here can be reformulated without employing the notion of truth at a time. However, for simplicity, we will continue talking about "prior truths" in the indicated way.

This is the fatalist's argument for incompatibilism, which we shall simply call "the incompatibilist's argument." (More particularly, it is a token of an argument *schema*—a method of argumentation that we could apply to any candidate free human action—but we set this point aside.) The central idea here is simple. You have no choice about what necessarily follows from what you have no choice about. But since you had no choice about what was true 1,000 years ago, before you were ever even born, you had no choice about what necessarily follows from what was true 1,000 years ago, namely, that you purchase this book.

Or we could put the point this way. By the time you were purchasing the book, it was too late to prevent its having been the case 1,000 years ago that you would purchase it. In particular, it was 1,000 years too late for that. But what necessarily follows from what is too late to prevent is similarly too late to prevent. Consequently, you had no power to prevent your purchase of this book.

Premise (2) of the argument embodies the commonplace idea that it cannot both be the case that it was true 1,000 years ago that you would purchase the book, and yet you don't in fact purchase it. So premise (2) seems indisputable.[3] There are, then, two crucial points of interest concerning the argument: premise (1), and the "transfer principle" licensing the move from (1) and (2) to (3)—the principle that says that you have no choice about what necessarily follows from what you have no choice about. A denial of the transfer principle would maintain that the mere fact that *q* is entailed by a proposition one has no choice about does not *in itself* give us good reason to conclude that one has no choice about *q*.[4] And, indeed, some have called the transfer principle into question. However, the principle does seem plausible, and few are inclined to reject it.[5]

---

[3]Understood in a certain way, Geachianism (discussed in Todd's essay in this volume) denies this thesis. Since Geachianism is such an extreme minority (even if interesting and neglected) view, we shall set this view aside.

[4]Note: here one needs to be careful concerning the modal implications of a rejection of the transfer principle. It is tempting to say that someone who rejects this principle maintains that *it is possible that* though S does not have a choice about *p*, and though *p* obtains and entails *q*, S *does* have a choice about whether *q* obtains. Such a "rejection" would, of course, automatically commit one to the thesis that free will is possible. But this is too quick: one who rejects the transfer principle could think that free will is impossible, but for reasons independent of the validity of the transfer principle. A more cautious way of putting a rejection of the transfer principle is thus the following: the *mere fact* that S does not have a choice about *p* and *p* entails *q* does not *by itself* give us *good reason* to conclude that S has no choice about *q*. That is, *arguments* employing the transfer principle are (to the extent that they do so) bad arguments, even if the conclusions of those arguments are true, and, indeed, even if those arguments are valid (in the sense that it is impossible that the premises of the arguments be true while the conclusions are false).

[5]For discussion of the transfer principle, see the essays from Perry, Mackie, and Zagzebski in this volume. See also Kapitan 1996.

Our focus instead is on the most popular way of disputing the incompatibilist's argument: rejecting premise (1). Why believe premise (1)? Clearly, the thought here has something to do with the nature of the past and the nature of what we could plausibly have a choice about. That is, the incompatibilist recommends that we accept premise (1) on the basis that it is an instance of a more general thesis concerning our lack of power over the past; this is the thesis of *the fixity of the past*. You could have no choice about what was fashionable (or wasn't) 1,000 years ago. You could have no choice about who was king (or not) 1,000 years ago. (Or so it seems.) So why think you could have a choice about what was true 1,000 years ago? If something *was* true 1,000 years ago, how could one *now* prevent its *having been* true 1,000 years ago? Isn't it simply *too late* to prevent its having been true? More generally, isn't it simply too late to prevent anything's having been . . . anything? We prevent things from *becoming* things—people from becoming new business partners, say, or propositions from becoming true. But we don't prevent people from *having been* business partners, or proposition's *having been* true.

It is often alleged that the incompatibilist's argument is simply a non-starter or just obviously defective.[6] We think this is a mistake. There is something puzzling about a denial of the transfer principle. And there is also something puzzling about a denial of premise (1). Rejections of premise (1) therefore consist in ways of making (or trying to make) what can seem so puzzling about a rejection of (1) less puzzling.

There are, again, various ways of denying premise (1). What is common to all such ways is that they each employ, in their own particular way, the notion of *dependence*. Those who deny premise (1) will (in general) emphasize the following sort of point: what was true 1,000 years ago concerning what you do at t depends on what you do at t. Since what was true 1,000 years ago concerning what you do at t depends on what you do at t, this points to the possibility that you, even now, have a choice about what was true 1,000 years ago. Look at it this way. Suppose that, prior to considering the fatalist's argument, it seems that there is no problem in saying that what you do at t is fully up to you. That is, no one is coercing you, you aren't under some strange spell or hypnosis, no one has implanted a chip in your brain that controls what you do, and so on. Thus, it seems unproblematic, so far, to assume that what you do at t is up to you. Shouldn't we go on to say, then, that anything that *depends* on what you do at t is similarly up to you? If it initially seems "OK" to say that what

---

[6]No doubt some fatalistic arguments *are* obviously defective. It is common, for instance, for certain fatalistic arguments to be dismissed on grounds that they employ a modal fallacy, e.g. that they confuse the "necessity of the consequent" and the "necessity of the consequence". But no such confusion is present in the argument considered here. Merricks has a short discussion of some obviously defective such arguments in chapter 3. See also van Inwagen, chapter 2.

you do is up to you, then just by "adding in" something that *depends* on what you do, we shouldn't deny that what you do is up to you. Rather, it should similarly seem "OK" to say that you have a choice about whatever it is that depends on what you do.

This, we think, is the core strategy employed by those who seek to deny premise (1). However, whereas this sort of strategy is, we believe, *implicit* in a great many discussions of the fatalist's argument, the precise sort of dependence at issue—and the role it is meant to play—has not always been given the detailed attention it would seem to deserve. Recently, however, the notion of "dependence" has begun to receive greater attention, both within the debates concerning fatalistic arguments and in metaphysics more generally. What does it mean to say that what was true 1,000 years ago concerning what happens today *depends on* what happens today? Depends in what sense? What is the nature of this sort of dependence? What sort of picture of time does it presuppose? What does it presuppose concerning the relationship between truth and "the world"? These sorts of questions have begun to be more explicitly treated within the literature on fatalistic arguments.[7] Here we aim to continue this development by putting the notion of dependence front and center (in the place it arguably deserves).

We suggest (and now aim to develop the idea) that different ways of denying premise (1) involve differences regarding dependence. Again, *all* denials of premise (1) will maintain (as a first approximation) that the relevant truths in the past in some sense depend on "what you do." (The rationale for the scare quotes will become evident in what follows.) But, as we will see, such truths might depend on "what you do" in different ways—some being stronger than others. For instance, there is *counterfactual* dependence, the dependence at issue in *entailment*, and more besides. The question of what sort of dependence is the *relevant* sort of dependence has, as we will see, important ramifications for the fatalist's argument. Call the relevant sort of dependence "dependence with a capital 'd'": Dependence. More particularly, let us say that Dependence is such that those things that do *not* Depend on what you do are outside the range of things you might have a choice about. And it is such that those things that *do* Depend on what you do are inside that range—anyway, so long as nothing *else* is blocking your free will. That is, Dependence is such that if something Depends on what you do, we have no reason to deny that you have a choice about that thing, again, so long as no *other* threats to your free will are yet on the table. The point, then, is that if one can establish that the relevant prior truths Depend on what one does, one will have defused the fatalist's argument.

---

[7]In addition to the articles in this book, see, for example, McCall 2011 and Westphal 2011. For a reply to these papers, see Fischer and Tognazzini 2014.

We could also specify the nature of Dependence in the following way. Suppose we ask what must be *held fixed* when evaluating what an agent can do at a given time *t*. Intuitively, anything that needn't be *held fixed* when evaluating what you can do at *t* is something that we have no reason to deny that you have a choice about at *t* (and vice versa).[8] The incompatibilist's contention can thus be put as follows: insofar as what was true in the distant past is now unpreventable and over-and-done-with, when evaluating what Jones can do at *t*, we must hold fixed what was true in the distant past relative to *t* (even regarding what Jones himself would do at *t*). Those who reject the relevant instance of premise (1), on the other hand, say the following: when evaluating what Jones can do at *t*, we needn't hold fixed prior truths about what Jones will do at *t*. Rather, we can let those truths vary. More specifically, those who reject premise (1) maintain that we can let those truths vary because those truths *depend on* what Jones does at *t*. Dependence, then, is such that, when evaluating what a person can do at *t*, we must hold fixed everything that does not Depend on what that person does at *t*, and nothing that does.

We proceed as follows. We identify five different (progressively stronger) accounts of Dependence. The accounts are progressively "stronger" in this sense: that the sort of dependence at issue in a prior account holds does not entail that the sort of dependence at issue in any later account also holds, whereas if the given sort of dependence in a later account holds, this entails that the sort of dependence at issue in any earlier account will also hold. (There will, however, be doubts concerning whether the dependence at issue in the fifth account indeed entails the sort at issue in the fourth.) As we will see, the first two accounts are relatively "weak"—but their failures are nevertheless instructive. We then consider three further accounts: the account suggested by Trenton Merricks (in this volume), (our development of) Ockhamism, and the account suggested by Finch and Rea (in this volume). And we suggest (though certainly do not fully defend) the following thesis: the sort of dependence identified by Merricks is too weak, whereas the sort required by Finch and Rea is too strong. (That is, Finch and Rea [arguably] require too much, whereas

---

[8]Note: we cannot say that anything that needn't be held fixed when evaluating what you can do at *t* (that is, that Depends on what you do at *t*) is something you *do* have a choice about at *t*. Perhaps the fact that it was true 1,000 years ago that you would purchase this book at *t* needn't be held fixed when evaluating what you were able to have done at *t*. But this fact, in itself, certainly doesn't tell us that you *did* have a choice about this truth 1,000 years ago—for perhaps your purchase was the result of clandestine CIA manipulation, or perhaps it was otherwise causally determined by factors beyond your control. In this case, though the truth 1,000 years ago Depends on what you do at *t*, you (plausibly) *still* do not have a choice about that truth at *t*. The point remains, however: since the prior truth Depends on what you do at *t*, in itself it tells us nothing concerning what you were able to have done at *t*.

Merricks [arguably] does not require enough.) The sort required by Ockhamism, however, is just right—anyway, *if* premise (1) is to be rejected in the first place.

Counterfactual Dependence

Suppose Jones hadn't sat at *t*. Well, then it never would have been true 1,000 years ago that he *would* sit at *t*. In that sense, then, what was true 1,000 years ago depends on what he does—namely, it counterfactually depends on what he does in just the indicated way. Accordingly, one might say: if X counterfactually depends on what you do at *t*, then X, in itself, is no threat to your ability to do otherwise than what you do at *t*, and needn't be held fixed when evaluating what you can do at *t*.

Is counterfactual dependence the right sort of dependence? Arguably it isn't. Circumstances may be such that, had Jones stood at *t*, he wouldn't have been locked up in chains (as he was) just prior to *t*. But this would hardly show that Jones had a choice about whether he was locked up in chains. The mere fact that, *had* Jones stood, he *wouldn't* have been locked up does not thereby tell us that his having been locked up was no threat to his ability to have stood. In other words, suppose I suggest that Jones had no choice about whether to sit or to stand, since he was in chains, and these chains prevented him from standing. I will hardly be moved by the observation that had Jones in fact stood, those chains never would have been there in the first place. Intuitively, when evaluating what Jones could have done at *t*, we *do* need to hold fixed that Jones was in chains just prior to *t*—*even if* he wouldn't have been had he done otherwise. So counterfactual dependence is (plausibly) too weak to be dependence (and thus license a rejection of premise (1)).

Entailment

Necessarily, it was true that Jones would sit at *t* only if Jones sits at *t*. So, not only is it the case that, had Jones not sat, it would not have been true that he would sit, it is *necessarily* the case that, had he not sat, it never would have been true that he would sit. In the "chains" case, perhaps it is true that had Jones not sat, he would *as a matter of fact* never been in chains, but it is not *necessary* that had he not sat, he never would have been in chains. It is metaphysically possible that, though he was in chains, Jones nevertheless did not sit, insofar as it is metaphysically possible (say) that Jones should have suddenly acquired superhuman powers, or that a miracle occur, or the like. So though Jones's standing up at *t* would *imply* (in the circumstances) that he was never in chains, Jones's standing at *t* does not *entail* that he was never in chains. But Jones's standing at *t* *does* entail that it was never true that he would sit at *t*.

So the suggestion is this: when evaluating what Jones could have done at *t*, we needn't hold fixed anything that entailed that Jones would in fact sit at *t*. For anything that entails that Jones shall sit at *t* depends on his sitting at *t*, and anything that so depends on what Jones does at *t* is, in itself, no threat to Jones's ability to do otherwise than sit at *t*. Is this suggestion plausible? We think it is deeply problematic. Consider, first, the doctrine of *causal determinism*. On causal determinism, the (temporally intrinsic; we return to this crucial notion shortly) state of the world in the distant past, together with the laws of nature, entailed that Jones sits at *t*. More generally, for anything anyone ever does, the past and the laws entail that one does those things. The suggestion here, then, would immediately imply that causal determinism is no threat to free will. For insofar as the past and the laws *entail* what you do, they therefore *depend* on what you do (on the current account), and accordingly needn't be held fixed when evaluating *what* you can do. However, it is at least very plausible that, when evaluating what you can do at *t*, we *do* need to hold fixed the past and the laws relative to *t*. (Classical compatibilists about free will and determinism, however, will disagree.[9]) Insofar as the current suggestion would imply that causal determinism is no threat to free will, we think many will find this suggestion problematic.

Or consider a case involving divine decrees. Suppose God decrees that Jones shall sit at *t*. Necessarily, God's decrees always come to pass. So God's decree *entails* that Jones shall sit at *t*. Intuitively, a divine decree that one shall do a given thing certainly calls into question one's ability to refrain from doing that thing. But, on this suggestion, it does not. For insofar as the decree *entails* what you do, it *depends* on what you do, and accordingly needn't be held fixed when evaluating *what* you can do. But this suggestion seems implausible. When evaluating what Jones is free to do at *t*, arguably we should take into account (and hold fixed) any divine decrees concerning what Jones does at *t*. So, again, mere entailment would not seem to be the right sort of dependence.[10] Indeed, that the past and the laws and the divine decrees (and the prior truths) *entail* what you do seems to be the *problem*—so how could the mere recognition of this fact be the solution?[11]

The Simple Because (Trenton Merricks)

So both counterfactual dependence and entailment seem too weak, insofar as both are susceptible to counterexamples involving causal determinism and divine decrees. And upon reflection the problem with these accounts seems clear: they

---

[9]For more on this issue, see John Perry's essay in this volume. See also Mackie, chapter 5.

[10]There is a development of this point in relation to the Ockhamist reply to the theological fatalist in Widerker's essay in this volume. See also Todd 2013a.

[11]David Hunt makes a similar point in assessing the Ockhamist reply to the theological fatalist (and the "entailment" criterion of soft-facthood) in his essay in this volume.

do not imply anything about the *order of explanation*. From the mere fact that X entails Y, for instance, we cannot conclude that X obtains *because* Y does. Indeed, as the decrees case brings out, X might entail Y, and Y obtain because X does. That is, intuitively, it seems clear that, if God decreed that Jones shall sit, Jones sat because of God's decree, and not the other way around. Further, on determinism, it seems clear that you do what you *because* the past and the laws were the given way—and it is not the case that the past and the laws were that way because of what you do. The lesson, then, would appear to be this: we don't need simple *dependence*, but *explanatory dependence* of some kind. We need the proper order of explanation.[12]

Enter Trenton Merricks. In his paper, "Truth and Freedom," Merricks emphasizes the following point: truth depends on the world, and does so in the following ("trivial") sort of way:

> It is true that grass is green because grass is green.
> It is true that there are no hobbits because there are no hobbits.

Now we apply this sort of dependence to "prior truths" about what we will do. Suppose it is true that Jones will sit. Then, Merricks notes, we can say the following:

> It is true that Jones will sit because Jones will sit.

---

[12]A similar point has been widely recognized within the literature on ontological dependence. Suppose we consider what it is for one object to exist *in virtue of* another object's existence, and thereby depend for its existence on that object. Following Kit Fine's 1994 paper "Essence and Modality," it has been widely accepted that this relationship cannot be captured in purely modal terms (in terms of necessity and possibility)—for example, by saying that one object could exist without the other, but not the other way around. For consider the example (provided by Fine) of sets and their members. Intuitively, singleton Socrates (the set consisting solely of Socrates) depends for its existence on Socrates, and not the other way around. However, Socrates could *not* exist without singleton Socrates, since, necessarily, whenever anything exists, so does the singleton set of that thing. The general upshot of this sort of example seems to be that the relationship in question—what it is for one thing to exist in virtue of another—cannot be captured modally. A similar sort of point (or perhaps the recognition of this point) seems to be emerging in the literature on fatalistic arguments. (Todd 2013a explicitly draws comparisons between the literature on ontological dependence and the literature on fatalism and free will.) That is, it seems clear that the relevant relationship must be sensitive to the proper order of explanation—and therefore cannot be purely modal in character (as is the notion of entailment). However, just as there are substantive disputes in general metaphysics concerning how this (admittedly not purely modal) relationship should be further characterized, so there are substantive disputes (as we shall see) concerning how the sort of dependence relevant to responding to the fatalist should be characterized. These issues are thus deeply continuous with a recent "trend" in contemporary metaphysics that focuses on the related notions of truthmaking, grounding, fundamentality, and dependence. The literature on these topics is enormous; see Lowe 1998 (ch. 6) Armstrong 2004, and Schaffer 2008 for a (small) start.

And, looking backwards, we can say that it *was* true that Jones *would* sit because Jones would sit. Call the sort of dependence at issue in these examples "M-dependence." Is M-dependence Dependence? The (rough) suggestion is this. When evaluating whether S could have refrained from doing A at t, we do not need to hold fixed anything that was the way it was (or existed, or obtained, or . . .) because S would do A at t. Everything else, however, must be held fixed.[13]

We believe that M-dependence is our first real contender for being Dependence. But there is, we think, substantial reason to worry that it is not. In particular, one might worry about the claim that we do not need to hold fixed anything that M-depends on what you do at t, when evaluating what you can do at t. Perhaps something may M-depend on what you do in this sense, but *still* must be held fixed. Accordingly, one might worry that M-dependence (like counterfactual dependence and entailment) is still too weak (is insufficient). Consider, first, a case involving divine beliefs. Suppose God believes that Jones will sit at t. On standard assumptions (viz., that God cannot be mistaken), this entails that Jones will sit at t. But suppose we add: God believes that Jones will sit at t because Jones will sit at t. Does this imply that God's prior belief tells us nothing about Jones's ability to refrain from sitting at t, and that we have no reason to deny that Jones has a choice about whether God held that prior belief? It is hard to say. For it is substantially mysterious how Jones *now* could have any choice at all about whether God (or anyone else) had or lacked a certain belief in the past.[14] As Linda Zagzebski notes in this context, there is no use crying over spilled milk. And past beliefs seem as much like spilled milk as anything could be.[15] So it is certainly not immediately evident that M-dependence gives us the right result in this case.

It would, however, be contentious to suggest the case of God's beliefs as a straightforward *counterexample* to the sufficiency of M-dependence. For, as readers of Merricks's paper will discover, Merricks argues that this precise fact—that God believes that Jones will sit at t because Jones will sit at t—serves to reconcile divine foreknowledge with human freedom. So consider instead someone who believes in divine *prepunishment*. (Typically, of course, punishment for a crime *follows* the crime. In a case of prepunishment, however, one is punished for committing a crime *before* one commits the crime.) Suppose this person maintains the following: in

[13]This is our *reconstruction* of Merricks's view, or our statement of a "Merricks-inspired" view—but Merricks himself does not put his points precisely in these terms.
[14]It is also hard to say for the following reason: it isn't clear what it is for God to believe that p "because p," as in Merricks's constructions. For more on this issue, see Todd and Fischer 2013.
[15]Zagzebski 1991: 84.

general, God prepunishes someone for committing a given crime because he or she will, in fact, commit it, and not the other way around. Intuitively, this mirrors precisely what we have just been saying about the prior truths and God's beliefs. Now, the question is this. Is there still a good *argument* that such divine prepunishment would be inconsistent with the freedom of those prepunished? Insofar as one thinks that there still is available such an argument, one should think that M-dependence is insufficient to license a rejection of premise (1). We find it at least very plausible that we *should* be able cogently to argue that divine prepunishment would be inconsistent with the freedom of those prepunished. If M-dependence is Dependence, however, then no such argument will be available, for the proponent of divine prepunishment can maintain that God's prepunishments M-depend "on what we do," and therefore needn't be held fixed when evaluating what we can do. However, when evaluating whether Jones can refrain from sitting at *t*, arguably we *should* hold fixed that God prepunished him for doing so, insofar as this fact is now totally in the past and beyond anyone's subsequent control. However, if we *do* hold *God's* prepunishment fixed, then Jones's "alternatives" will be reduced to *one*, since there is only one "alternative" regarding what Jones does at *t* that is consistent with God's having prepunished him for sitting at *t*.[16] So, again, it is not clear that M-Dependence is in fact Dependence.[17]

Determination and the Intrinsic/Extrinsic (Hard/Soft Fact) Distinction (Ockhamism)

Here, then, we come to "Ockhamism"—or at any rate, *our* construal of Ockhamism. We should begin by noting that the term "Ockhamism" has been used in various different ways in various different contexts to refer to sometimes subtly different theses and positions. Of course, what matters most is that, however we use our terms, we are clear about how we are using them. And we aim to be clear about how we shall use the term "Ockhamism." We intend our usage to be both descriptive *and* prescriptive. On the one hand, we believe that our usage is most faithful (insofar as

---

[16]For an extensive development of the argument that divine prepunishment would be incompatible with the freedom of those prepunished, see Todd 2013b; see also Todd and Fischer 2013. In a word, the problem can be put as follows. Suppose that we (the authors) believe that you will do something wrong tomorrow, and prepunish you for doing it. It would seem that your only hope for innocence is that you can prove us wrong for having prepunished you for a crime you never in fact commit. But when *God* is the prepunisher, this possibility evaporates—and with it your freedom.

[17]For more, see Todd and Fischer 2013.

any such usage can be) to the tradition of usage of this term in the literature regarding fatalism in the last 50 years. However, given recent developments, we further intend to *recommend* this usage—that is, we maintain that, in order to forestall confusion, the term *should* be used in this way (to refer to the position we now aim to describe).[18]

Suppose that, instead of putting the problem in terms of true propositions about what someone will do in the future, we put it in terms of true *predictions* about what someone will do in the future. Suppose Jones just sat down a few minutes ago, at *t*. Now, we're asked: could Jones have refrained from sitting? Of course, that depends. But suppose someone points out: Smith predicted yesterday that Jones would sit today at *t*. Accordingly, Jones did precisely what Smith predicted he would do. Thus, not only did Smith predict what Jones would do, Smith *truly* predicted what Jones would do. However, that Smith had already *truly predicted* what Jones would do is a fact about the past (relative to Jones's sitting at *t*)—and thus a fact over which Jones lacked subsequent control. Accordingly, it must be held fixed when evaluating what Jones was able to do at *t*. Holding fixed that Smith had already *truly predicted* that Jones would sit at *t*, Jones could not have refrained from sitting at *t*.

Now, the Ockhamist says the following. Of course, when evaluating what Jones could have done at *t*, we must hold fixed the fact that Smith had already *predicted* that he would sit at *t*. *That much* seems "over and done with" and beyond Jones's subsequent control. But we *need not* hold fixed the fact that Smith had *truly* predicted that Jones would sit at *t*. Indeed, absent any further reasons to doubt Jones's freedom, we can say that Jones, at *t*, had a choice about whether Smith's prediction *was right* or *was wrong*. That is, whether Smith had *truly* predicted that he would sit at *t* was up to Jones at *t*.

The Ockhamist's account of these facts is as follows. That Smith had already *predicted* that Jones would sit at *t* was part of the past (relative to *t*) *intrinsically considered*, whereas that Smith had *truly* predicted that Jones would sit at *t* was only "part of the past" considered *extrinsically*. More particularly, the Ockhamist's contention is this. When evaluating what an agent can do at *t*, we must hold fixed everything

---

[18]"Who are you to tell us how to define our terms?" This is a good question that we propose to ignore. Note: we ourselves have not always followed our own advice. In our reply to Trenton Merricks in this volume, we suggest that Merricks could take up the mantle of Ockhamism, and maintain that what we call "M-dependence" is the sort of dependence at issue in soft-facthood (which is the core notion employed by the Ockhamist). Subsequent reflection has led us to think instead that the particular sort of dependence we develop here (the sort of determination at issue in the intrinsic/extrinsic distinction) is *essential* to Ockhamism, and that Merricks's approach should be *distinguished* from Ockhamism precisely because it does not employ this sort of dependence, but instead the weaker "M-dependence."

about the past relative to *t*, *intrinsically considered*. However, we do *not* need to hold fixed "everything about the past," considered extrinsically. Or we could put the point this way. If an agent's performing a certain action at *t* would require an *intrinsic change* in the past relative to *t*—that is, would require the past to have been intrinsically different than how it actually was—then the agent *cannot* perform that action at *t*. However, that an agent's performing an action at *t* would require an *extrinsic change* in the past relative to *t* tells us nothing, in itself, concerning whether the agent can refrain from performing that action at *t*. In this case, however, Jones's doing otherwise than sitting at *t* despite Smith's *true prediction* that he would sit at *t* would not require an *intrinsic* change in the past, but only an *extrinsic* ("mere Cambridge") change—it would only require that Smith's prediction should have lacked a certain extrinsic property it actually did have, viz. the property of being a *correct* prediction.[19] For whether a current prediction about what you will do counts as correct is at least in part *determined by* whether you will do that thing. Accordingly, we have not yet encountered any clear obstacle to saying that Smith could have refrained from sitting at *t*, despite Smith's true prediction that he would.

The Ockhamist thus makes a distinction between two sorts of facts about the past: facts that report how the past was *intrinsically* at a given time, and facts that report (at least in part) how the past was *extrinsically* at a given time. In the literature, this distinction is called the distinction between "hard facts" about the past (or at times) and "soft facts" about the past (or at times).[20] Given the variety of frameworks one

---

[19]Note: it is crucial to see that the Ockhamist *does not* contend that we can change—even Cambridge-change—the past. Rather, the Ockhamist (who thinks we have free will) contends that we can act in ways that would *require* such changes.

[20]We don't mean to suggest that everyone who has used the "hard/soft fact" terminology has done so in this precise way. The distinction has been "glossed" in many ways in the literature, including as

- the distinction between those facts that are "solely about" a given time and those "at least in part about the future" relative to that time
- the distinction between those facts that are "over and done with" as of a given time, and those that are not
- the distinction between those facts at a time that do not depend on or hold in virtue of the future relative to that time, and those that do (without paying explicit attention to the kind or manner of the dependence here invoked)
- the distinction between those facts relevant to determining which possible worlds "share the same past as" another given possible world (the hard facts being relevant, and the soft facts being irrelevant)
- ostensively, as the distinction that correctly explains "the difference" between such facts as (1)–(3) and (1*)–(3*), noted below

All of these usages are, we think, at least somewhat "legitimate," insofar as it is no longer clear (if it ever was) who "owns" the soft/hard terminology, and all pick up on results it is meant to capture. (The terminology was first introduced by Nelson Pike in Pike's 1966 reply to Saunders.) Still, we maintain that the *best* way to use the distinction, if one is going to use the terminology at all, is

might have about times, facts, and propositions (and the like), there never emerged any "canonical" way of expressing the hard/soft fact distinction. But consider some examples:

(1) John F. Kennedy was being shot in Dallas in 1963.
(2) Smith predicted yesterday at $t1$ that Jones would sit tomorrow at $t3$.
(3) Smith believed yesterday at $t1$ that Jones would sit tomorrow at $t3$.

Intuitively, (1)–(3) report how the past was *intrinsically* at the relevant times. They thus are (or report) "hard facts" about the past. Consider, however, the following:

(1*) John F. Kennedy was being shot in Dallas in 1963, 50 years prior to our writing this essay in 2013.
(2*) Smith correctly predicted yesterday at $t1$ that Jones would sit tomorrow at $t3$.
(3*) Smith truly believed yesterday at $t1$ that Jones would sit tomorrow at $t3$.

Intuitively, (1*)–(3*) do not simply report how the past was intrinsically at the relevant times, but also how it was extrinsically. They thus are (or report) "soft facts" about the past. For instance, whether an event is taking place 50 years prior to when another event will take place is not an *intrinsic* feature of that event, but an extrinsic feature—viz., a feature the first event has in virtue of the fact that another event will take place 50 years later. And whether a prediction or a belief counts as *correct* or *true* is not an *intrinsic* feature of that prediction or belief, but an extrinsic feature.

simply to *identify* it with the temporally intrinsic/extrinsic distinction. This "gloss" would then leave open various further ways of *analyzing* the distinction.

The main constraint we would wish to insist on is only that the distinction, in itself, should *not* be stated in a way as to analytically entail any results about agency or free will. That is, it is (unfortunately) very common for writers employing this distinction to mistakenly claim that "soft facts" are those facts about the past that someone has or may have a choice about, whereas "hard facts" are those facts about the past that no one has or could have a choice about. This is *not* a legitimate usage of or "gloss on" the hard/soft distinction. The distinction itself is *neutral* on this score—indeed, the distinction was drawn (at least in part) in order to help us *resolve* such questions (though it is need for other purposes as well, such as defining the doctrine of causal determinism) so cannot be *defined* in terms of them. (For a similar point, see Zagzebski 1991: 67.) In particular, there will be, on *any* view, any number of soft facts about the past that no one has a choice about—and it is not *analytic* that no one has a choice about the hard facts about the past. Some may—and some have—maintained that even some *hard* facts about the past needn't be held fixed when evaluating what agents can do at later times. (See Fischer 1994.) Indeed, Trenton Merricks's view, insofar as Merricks admits (Merrick 2011) that God's beliefs are hard facts at times, is precisely such a view. (For more on this issue, see our reply to Trenton Merricks in this volume.)

Thus, the sort of dependence the Ockhamist appeals to—the sort they say is Dependence—is the sort at issue in the intrinsic/extrinsic distinction. It is the sort at issue in cases like these (which all come out on the "extrinsic" side of the distinction):

- whether one *counts* as being an uncle is (at least in part) *determined by* whether one's sibling has a child
- whether one's punishment *counts* as just is (at least in part) *determined by* whether one commits the given crime
- whether one's belief *counts as* knowledge is (at least in part) *determined by* whether that belief is true
- whether that mark on Jones's skin *counts* as a mosquito bite is (at least in part) *determined by* whether it was produced by a mosquito

And now we apply this sort of "determination" to the cases at issue:[21]

- whether a prediction about what you will do *counts* as true is (at least in part) *determined by* whether you will do that thing
- whether a proposition about what you do *counts* as true is (at least in part) *determined by* whether you will do that thing

Thus, according to the Ockhamist, the fact that someone had already truly predicted what Jones would do at *t* (or that it was already true that he would perform a certain action at *t*) needn't be held fixed when evaluating what Jones was able to have done at *t*. The logical fatalist's argument is thereby defused.

Note: it is crucial to our understanding of "Ockhamism" that Ockhamism is *not* committed to any particular thesis about which further facts about the past (beyond the sort of facts just mentioned) are indeed "soft." That is, as we are conceiving it, Ockhamism is itself *neutral* as concerns which further facts about the past are "intrinsic" or "extrinsic" (in the relevant way). It is thus an additional question to which further cases the Ockhamist strategy *applies*. As we discuss in the next section (on "theological fatalism"), some have sought to apply the Ockhamist strategy even to God's past beliefs about the future; that is, some have maintained that the

---

[21]We are open to the suggestion that the sort of determination at issue in these examples can be found in cases that do not involve the intrinsic/extrinsic property distinction. That is, though it seems that all cases involving the intrinsic/extrinsic distinction will exhibit this sort of "determination," perhaps not all cases of this sort of "determination" are also cases involving the intrinsic/extrinsic distinction. In any case, it is this sort of "determination" that, on our view, the Ockhamist says is Dependence.

Ockhamist strategy developed above will apply in this case as well, since, roughly, God's past beliefs (on the appropriate construal of God's past beliefs) are soft facts about the past. (Indeed, for many readers, "Ockhamism" may be a term that refers primarily to a way of attempting to reconcile divine foreknowledge and human freedom by means of the "hard/soft" distinction.) However, it is crucial to see that the core Ockhamist strategy itself is *neutral* on this score. One might endorse this core strategy, but *not* the application of this strategy to the argument of the theological fatalist, for one might contend that it is implausible that God's past beliefs are soft facts about the past. Ockhamism *itself* is just fine, one may think—but not the application of Ockhamism to this further case.

Thus, we can note the following. The Ockhamist strategy, in itself, is *not* automatically susceptible to worries arising from divine beliefs and divine prepunishments. (Recall that a central worry for Merricks's approach is that it might be thought precipitously to reconcile divine foreknowledge and divine prepunishment with human freedom. That is, the worry for Merricks's approach was that M-dependence is, in this sense, too weak.) Someone employing the Ockhamist strategy *could* say the following. If God believes that Jones will sit at t, then Jones's refraining from sitting at t would not merely require an *extrinsic* change in the past, but an *intrinsic* change—it would require that God should never have even *believed* that Jones would sit at t. For whether someone—even God—counts as *believing* that one will perform a given action is *not* even in part *determined by* whether one will perform that action. (This claim, however, will be denied by those who seek to apply the Ockhamist strategy [as we have developed it] to God's past beliefs.) Similarly, if God (per impossible, perhaps) has *prepunished* Jones for sitting at t, then Jones's refraining from sitting would require an *intrinsic* change in the past—it would require that Jones should never have been punished by God at all. For whether one counts as being *punished* (unlike *justly* punished) for committing a given crime is not even in part determined by whether one will ever in fact commit that crime. In other words, someone employing the Ockhamist strategy could maintain that the relevant facts (that God had believed that Jones would sit at t or had prepunished Jones for sitting at t) are *hard facts* about the past relative to t. Accordingly, they must be held fixed when evaluating what he can do at t.

Is Ockhamism plausible? We believe it is (so construed). We believe that it captures the intuitive thought that our freedom—if we have freedom at all—is the freedom to *extend the actual past* one way or another. That is, in the words of Carl Ginet, our freedom is the freedom to *add to the given past*.[22] But not simply anything gets to go into a statement of the "given past" relevant to this thesis. Rather,

---

[22]Ginet 1990: 102–03.

what seems intuitively very plausible is that our freedom is the freedom to add to what has *really happened* in the basic sense—to add to the real history of the world, intrinsically considered. We will, however, consider a challenge to the *sufficiency* of the Ockhamist's sort of dependence in the next section (that is, that the fact that this sort of dependence holds is sufficient to license a rejection of premise (1)). And, as we've seen, Merricks would of course wish to challenge its *necessity* (that the holding of this sort of dependence is necessary to license a rejection of premise (1)). Merricks will contend that this sort of dependence does not *need* to hold in order to license a rejection of premise (1), because Merricks will contend that even some things (in particular, God's past beliefs about what you will do) do not display this sort of dependence on what you do, but nevertheless, according to Merricks, needn't be held fixed when evaluating what you can do. Whether one here sides with Merricks or with the Ockhamist would seem to be a matter (at least in part) of where one stands on the cases of divine belief and divine prepunishment—but this is a matter we cannot here further aim to resolve.

"Because of" (Finch and Rea)

From the fact that it is true that Jones will sit because Jones will sit, it does not follow that it is true that Jones will sit *because of Jones's sitting.* And from the fact that whether the proposition that Jones will sit counts as true is determined by whether Jones will sit, it similarly does not follow that that proposition is now true (if it is) *because of Jones's sitting.* For we should distinguish between two things: the fact that Jones will sit, on the one hand, and Jones's sitting, on the other. This is not an essay on fundamental ontology, and we will not sketch any sort of theory about the ontological distinctions between propositions, facts, states of affairs, and events. These are complicated questions. Still, there would seem to be ample room to treat "Jones's sitting" as an *event*—a concrete event. And from the fact that something now depends on the fact that a concrete event *will* come to exist, it does not follow that anything now depends on the existence of that concrete event. For to suppose that a concrete event *will* exist is not—many will maintain—thereby to suppose that any such event *does* exist. So here we come to the rationale for the scare quotes concerning the phrase "what we do at t" (and the like). For such a phrase is ambiguous between two readings: "what we do at t" could refer to (something like) the *fact* that we will perform some action at t, or it could refer to the concrete event of our performing that action at t. And these are importantly different things.

It is tempting to write—and we have as a matter of fact written—that on Merricks's approach, the relevant prior truths (and God's beliefs/prepunishments) "M-depend on what we do." It is also tempting to write that, on Merricks's approach, the truth that Jones will sit at *t* "M-depends on Jones's sitting at *t*." But here we must be careful—for arguably these constructions are misleading. Suppose we grant to Merricks the claim that it is true that Jones will sit at *t* because Jones will sit at *t*. Do we *thereby* grant that this truth in any sense depends on "Jones's sitting at *t*", where Jones's sitting at *t* is construed as a concrete event? No. And some will contend that precisely this sort of dependence is the sort that is required. That is, some will contend that, if the relevant prior truths are to be no threat to Jones's free will, then Jones's very action—that concrete event—must in some sense be "explanatorily prior to" or otherwise "ground" those prior truths. Accordingly, M-dependence and the Ockhamist's "determination" are not the relevant sort of dependence. They are not Dependence.

In their paper in this volume, Alicia Finch and Michael Rea suggest (in a somewhat different guise) precisely this sort of view, and thereby connect these issues with an important and related set of issues within the philosophy of time.[23] More particularly, Finch and Rea maintain that whereas it is clear how *eternalists* can capture the right sort of dependence, it is far from clear how *presentists* or *growing-block theorists* might attempt to do so. We certainly cannot here engage in an extended discussion concerning presentism, growing-block theory, and eternalism. Roughly, however, presentists maintain that only present objects exist (nothing exists at a temporal distance from the present), growing-block theorists maintain that past and present (but no future) objects exist, and eternalists maintain that past, present, and future objects are all on an ontological par.[24] Now, Finch and Rea point out that, prospectively at least, eternalists can give a more robust account of the relevant sort of dependence than their presentist and growing-block counterparts. Eternalists are in a position to say, whereas presentists and growing-blocks theorists are not, that *Jones's very action* (construed concretely) was itself *ontologically* (though of course not *temporally*) prior to its being true that he would perform that action. Non-eternalists, however, can tell no such story. Suppose it is true now, at *t1*, that Jones will sit at some future time *t10*. According to the presentist/growing block theorist, there simply *is no such thing* as the concrete event of "Jones's sitting at *t10*." But insofar as no such action *exists* at *t1*, if it is *true* at *t1* that Jones will sit

---

[23]They do so in the name of calling into question whether presentists can be *Ockhamists*—that is, whether presentists can employ the Ockhamist strategy of responding to the arguments of the logical and theological fatalists. They thus construe "Ockhamism" more broadly than we do in this essay. On their construal, *any* response to these arguments that employs the notion of "explanatory dependence" is a version of Ockhamism. As we have it here, the Ockhamist does not "own" the point about dependence—only a particular *version* thereof. In our favored framework, then, their point can be put as follows: the sort of dependence the Ockhamist appeals to is insufficient; a more robust sort is required.

[24]For more, see Rea's essay in this volume.

at $t10$, then this truth at $t1$ is *not* now "grounded in" or true "because of" the concrete (future) event of Jones's sitting at $t10$.

We do not have any particular *name* for (or further way of characterizing) the sort of dependence Finch and Rea take to be Dependence. This is, as they admit, a difficult question about which we can remain neutral. Their main point, we take it, is that the dependence must hold between the *right sorts of entities*. We can thus interpret their suggestion to be the following. When evaluating what an agent can do at t, one need not hold fixed anything that held (or existed, or obtained . . .) *because of* that agent's concrete action at t. Anything else, however, must be held fixed. Accordingly, eternalists can reject the logical fatalist's argument. Presentists and growing-block theorists, however, cannot. We could also put the point this way. According to Finch and Rea, eternalism is necessary for the relevant sort of dependence to hold. Insofar as presentists and growing-block theorists can appeal to the sort of dependence at issue in (our developments of) M-dependence and Ockhamism, these sorts are therefore insufficient to license a rejection of premise (1). (Presentists can say that it is true that something will happen because that thing will happen; presentists are also seemingly entitled to the distinction between what is intrinsic to a time and what is not.)[25]

We shall not here take issue with the *sufficiency* of Finch and Rea's sort of dependence (for licensing a rejection of premise (1)). The problem with this account, plausibly, is not that the relevant sort of dependence (like counterfactual dependence and entailment) is too weak. Rather, we wish to question its *necessity* (for licensing a rejection of premise (1)). The problem with the account, arguably, is that it requires too much—it requires that one's very action be "ontologically prior" to the relevant past truth, and thus the truth of eternalism. But is this really required? It is hard to know how to settle this question. But we suggest the following. It seems that the Ockhamist's story *in itself* is sufficient to make it intuitively plausible that the given past truths needn't be held fixed. That is, insofar as it *is* intuitively plausible that, say, Jones *now* might have a choice about whether Smith's prior prediction was (then)

---

[25]Earlier we remarked that the five accounts are progressively stronger in the sense that if the sort of dependence at issue in a latter account holds, this entails that the sort at issue in any previous account will also hold. And we noted that there will be doubts that the sort of dependence at issue in the fifth account—the one we are now considering—indeed entails the sort at issue in the fourth, namely, Ockhamism. And perhaps we can now see why this might be so. Certainly someone sympathetic to Finch and Rea's position might maintain that God's prior belief is somehow "grounded in" one's concrete future action, without also wishing to maintain that God's prior belief is somehow extrinsic or relationally determined (that is, that the fact that God holds this belief at this time is a soft fact at or about this time). Whether this strategy can succeed depends on whether we can make sense of the idea that a current belief is "grounded in" a concrete future action.

right or (then) wrong, this is plausible because *whether* it was then right or wrong was *then* determined by whether Jones will in fact sit—and whether Jones will in fact sit is, in turn, determined by Jones himself (or so we might suppose). No appeal is made in this account to *Jones's very action* (construed concretely). So, again, we suggest that, even on eternalism, what makes it the case that such prior truths needn't be held fixed is nothing uniquely licensed by eternalism itself. It is not, one might suggest, the eternalist-qua-eternalist that can block the fatalist's argument, but the eternalist-qua-Ockhamist.

Summary

We hope the preceding discussion has brought out the subtlety, complexity, and *difficulty* of the issues here at stake. The most popular way of rejecting the fatalist's argument for incompatibilism is to reject the premise that we could have no choice about what was true in the distant past. Those who reject this premise reject it because, they think, what was true in the distant past regarding what we will do (in some sense or other) depends on our doing those very things. We have suggested that rejections of the fatalist's premise (1) should be individuated according to the nature of the dependence here invoked. And we have further argued that it is not immediately obvious precisely what sort of dependence is *necessary* to license a rejection of (1), nor what sort is *sufficient* to license that rejection. Counterfactual dependence and mere entailment, we think, are too weak. But once we move to Merricks's account, and other accounts that are explicitly sensitive to the "order of explanation," matters become substantially more difficult. Nevertheless, we have suggested that Merricks's sort of dependence is insufficient, whereas the sort required by Finch and Rea is not necessary. But certainly we have not here resolved this question, and part of the aim of this book is to put this issue at the front and center of the debate.

Here ends our discussion of the logical fatalist's argument for the incompatibility of "prior truths" and free will. Before moving on, we wish to note that most think (for good reasons or not) that the fatalist's argument is a failure. But here we must be very careful in stating our conclusion. It is *tempting* to add: "That is, most think that prior truths about what you do are perfectly compatible with your ability to do otherwise." But this would be a dangerous addition, and indeed a gratuitous and unjustified *leap* from the failure of the fatalist's argument. From the fact that the logical fatalist does not succeed in showing that prior truths are incompatible with free will, it does not follow that they indeed *are compatible* with free will. For they might be incompatible for a different reason—a reason the logical fatalist's argument for incompatibilism fails to bring out. For instance, they might be incompatible with free will because prior truths require deterministic grounds—a position advocated, for instance, by Hartshorne's essay in this volume (and rejected by Rosenkranz's)—and determinism is incompatible with free will. (We discuss this position further in Section 3.) Or prior truths might be incompatible with free will because God necessarily exists and is essentially omniscient. On this view, *p* will be logically equivalent to *God believes p*. Thus, if there is a good argument that such prior divine *beliefs* would be incompatible with free will, one would have a good argument that prior truths in turn are incompatible with free will, for anything incompatible with *p* is incompatible with anything logically equivalent to *p*.[26] Whether there is indeed a good such argument is the topic of the next section.

[26]This point is crucial in seeing what is problematic with the following argument:

> Everyone agrees that the logical fatalist's argument is a failure: everyone agrees that prior truths about what you do are compatible with your ability to do otherwise than what you do. But anything compatible with *p* is compatible with anything logically equivalent to *p*. But, if God necessarily exists and is essentially omniscient, then a truth such as that you would purchase this book is logically equivalent to God's having believed that you would purchase it: *God believes p* is logically equivalent to *p*. So God's having believed that you would purchase the book is in turn compatible with your ability to do otherwise than purchase it. So divine foreknowledge is compatible with freedom.

This is not a compelling argument. And it is not compelling at least in part due to the following: one cannot move from "the fatalist's argument is a failure" to "prior truths about what you do are compatible with your ability to do otherwise than what you do." Someone could easily—and with no shred of implausibility, we think—maintain the following. The logical fatalist's argument is an unconvincing failure. However, prior truths about what you do are nevertheless *inconsistent* with your ability to do otherwise, since God necessarily exists and is necessarily omniscient, and the *theological* fatalist's argument (to be discussed shortly) is *not* a failure. That is, one might maintain that "adding in" a divine prior *belief* to the argument makes the argument importantly different—and importantly better—in virtue of introducing a genuinely hard, temporally intrinsic fact about the past that entails what you do. If one thinks that God necessarily exists and is essentially omniscient, one would then reason as follows. There is no "possible world" in which both (1) it is true that one will perform some action and (2) one can refrain from performing that action. For in any world in which it is true that one will perform an action, God believes that you will perform it. And since you cannot so act that God would have been mistaken, you cannot do otherwise than perform it. One might attempt to ridicule proponents of this position by saying that "They think that prior truths are inconsistent with free will! But who thinks that?" What would be important to keep in mind, however, is that the proponent of this view is *not* thereby saddled with defending the logical fatalist's argument. Prior truths are indeed inconsistent with freedom, but the *reason* for endorsing this inconsistency is indirect: it goes *via* the *theological* fatalist's argument and the necessary equivalence of *p* and *God believes p*. For more on these topics, see Warfield 1997 (the argument of which, if not identical to the one provided above, anyway inspired it), Hasker 1998, Brueckner 2000, Warfield 2000, Speaks 2011, and Hunt's essay in this volume.

2. "THEOLOGICAL FATALISM"

Return to the logical fatalist's argument discussed above. You purchased this book. Could you have refrained from doing so? If it was true 1,000 years ago that you would purchase it, apparently not. After all:

(1) You had no choice about: it was true 1,000 years ago that you would purchase the book at *t*.

(2) Necessarily, if it was true 1,000 years ago that you would purchase the book at *t*, then you purchase the book at *t*. So,

(3) You had no choice about: purchasing the book at *t*.

And recall: the most popular way of responding to this argument is to deny (or say that we have no reason to accept) the relevant instance of premise (1). Once we see, many suppose, that the given truth in the past *depends on* what you do (in the relevant way), we'll see that we have no reason to accept (without further argument) that you had no choice about that truth. Consider, now, a parallel argument, an argument that moves not from prior *truths* about what you do, but from prior divine *beliefs* about what you do. This is the argument of the *theological* fatalist. Accordingly, suppose that God's beliefs cannot be mistaken, and suppose that God believed 1,000 years ago that you would purchase this book. Could you have refrained from doing so? Apparently not. After all:

(1*) You had no choice about: God believed 1,000 years ago that you would purchase the book at *t*.

(2*) Necessarily, if God believed 1,000 years ago that you would purchase the book at *t*, then you purchase the book at *t*. So,

(3) You had no choice about: purchasing the book at *t*.

Now, nearly everyone agrees that *this* argument (for the incompatibility of prior divine beliefs and free will) is importantly better than the parallel argument of the logical fatalist for the incompatibility of prior truths and free will. And this is because, on reflection, (1*) seems more plausible than (1). That is, it can seem clearer that there is nothing you could now do about someone's having had a *belief* in the past than it is that there is nothing you could now do about something's "having been true" in the past. That someone once had a certain belief seems to be a *real feature* of the past in some important way in which something's "having been true" in the past does not. Or we can look at it this way. Suppose someone now believes that you will perform some given action tomorrow. That this person has this belief would now seem to be part of the concrete circumstances in which you are operating. The question, then, is simply whether you can prove this person wrong for having had the relevant belief. When God is the believer, however, this possibility evaporates—and with it your freedom. For you cannot prove God wrong for having believed that you would perform an action you do not, in fact, perform.

How might one seek to reply to such an argument? Recall the strategy for denying premise (1) in the logical fatalist's argument: maintain that the given truths *depend* on what we do. One might seek to employ the same strategy with respect to God's beliefs: God's beliefs *depend* on what we do, and therefore needn't be held fixed in evaluating *what* we can do. Other things being equal, then, we may have a choice about God's having had the given beliefs. Above we considered five different accounts of the relevant sort of dependence ("Dependence") as applied to prior truths about what we do, the latter three of which seemed particularly promising. Here we briefly sketch how these accounts may be applied to God's past beliefs. Note: we here take some liberties in considering what Merricks and Finch and Rea would say in these contexts—these are, in any case, positions *inspired by* their essays in this volume.

M-dependence (Merricks)

If God believes (say) that Jones will sit at *t*, God believes that Jones will sit at *t* because Jones will sit at *t*. Anything that depends on what Jones does in this sense needn't be held fixed when evaluating what Jones is able to do at *t*. Accordingly, God's prior belief that Jones would sit at *t* does not tell us that Jones cannot do otherwise than sit at *t*. True, Jones's *refraining* from sitting at *t* would require that the past have been intrinsically different from how it actually was, viz., it would require that God should have never held the relevant belief, and that would amount to an intrinsic difference in the past.[27] However, so long as the thing that would have to be different in the past *depends* (in the indicated way) on Jones's sitting at *t*, it is no problem that the past would have to be different in that way, in order for Jones not to sit at *t*.

Ockhamism (as Applied to God's Past Beliefs)

The trouble with Merricks's account is his admission that, if God believed that Jones would sit at *t*, Jones's refraining from sitting at *t* would in fact require an intrinsic difference in the past relative to *t*. Whereas Jones's refraining would require that

---

[27]Merricks admits that God's beliefs are hard facts about the past (in this sense) in Merricks 2011.

God should never have held the relevant belief, this is not an *intrinsic* difference in the past, but rather merely an extrinsic difference. For on the best account of God's beliefs, and the distinction between what goes into a statement of the past, intrinsically considered, and what does not, that God held the relevant beliefs will not belong in such a statement. Rather, God's past beliefs are "soft" facts at or about past times. Accordingly, those past beliefs may depend on what we do in the sense relevant to soft-facthood, and needn't be held fixed when evaluating what we can do at later times. In a word, they do not belong in a statement of the "circumstances" in which one is now operating. The Ockhamist strategy as developed above will *also* apply to God's past beliefs.[28]

Finch and Rea

The trouble with "Ockhamism" (as characterized in this Introductory essay) as applied to God's past beliefs is that it is implausible that, given God's past belief that he would sit at *t*, Jones's refraining from sitting would not require an intrinsic difference in the past relative to *t*. Of course it would. God's beliefs are hard facts about the past in this sense. However, Merricks's basic insight is correct: when even a "hard fact" about the past depends in the relevant way on the future, and in particular on the future actions of agents, this fact about the past needn't be held fixed when evaluating what such agents are able to do at later times. The problem with Merricks's account, however, is simply that he has the wrong sort of dependence. In particular, Merricks's account says nothing concerning whether *Jones's very action* is explanatorily or ontologically prior to God's prior belief that he would perform that action. However, if Jones's very action *is* prior to God's belief in the indicated way, it needn't be held fixed when evaluating what Jones is able to do at *t*.[29]

We believe that each of these accounts faces significant problems. The central problem for Ockhamism (as applied to God's past beliefs), as noted, is that it is hard to see how Jones's refraining from sitting, given God's belief, *would not* require an intrinsic difference in the past. The central problem for the other accounts, however, is that they maintain that we can act in ways that would in fact require such

---

[28]See Widerker's and Hunt's essays in this volume for further discussion of this position. For interesting recent discussions of Ockhamism (as applied to God's past beliefs), see Pendergraft and Coates 2014 and Arnold forthcoming.

[29]This is a big "if," one might say. We believe that it is substantially mysterious how God's present belief could be held "because of" or be "grounded in" some future event, even on eternalism. For presumably that (future) event does not *cause* God's prior belief: this would be to invoke widespread backwards causation.

differences. They thus must give up what seems like a compelling principle: that freedom is the freedom to *add to the given past*. This is the principle of the fixity of the past. Anything you *can* do at *t* must be consistent with the given past relative to *t*—the past, intrinsically considered. Why believe the fixity of the past, so construed? It is hard to say what would *justify* the fixity of the past, as this would take us far beyond the scope of this Introduction. Nevertheless, the principle does seem plausible. As we noted in Section 1, it seems to capture part of common sense: the scenarios that represent possibilities for us are scenarios that *branch off* from our actual past. Those and only those scenarios are the ones we may now have it within our power to actualize.

At this stage, we wish to consider a somewhat conciliatory line of thought that might be pursued by those sympathetic to the thesis that divine foreknowledge is compatible with human free will. Initially, the fixity of the past does seem very plausible. We naturally arrive at the fixity of the past via consideration of ordinary contexts: if, say, someone already believes that you will commit a given crime tomorrow, the question whether you can avoid committing the crime is pretty clearly the question whether you can prove this person wrong. And now we consider the case of divine foreknowledge, or divine forebelief. Now, we (the authors) are seeming to suggest that we should simply *keep applying* the natural, common sense idea that the past is fixed, and so to arrive at the conclusion that, given God's belief, you cannot avoid performing the action God believes you will perform, since you can't prove God wrong.

But now the complaint. Aren't we simply failing to give *any credit* to the thought that this is *God* we're talking about? Doesn't introducing *God* into the picture—a person with, we might grant, an entirely different mode of knowing than our own—*count* for something? Doesn't introducing God into the story here call into question the propriety of continuing to apply a principle arrived at via reflection on *ordinary* contexts in which no foreknowing God is presumed to be present? But introducing God into the picture introduces an *extraordinary* context—akin to introducing a crystal ball. And why, then, should the fixity of the past still apply? On reflection, then, yes: maintaining that divine foreknowledge and human free will are consistent requires a denial of the thesis of the fixity of the past. But this is acceptable, and further, just what we should expect, at least in certain cases, given the truth of theism: we should expect that, given theism, the structure of reality will sometimes not be as it seems to us to be. Why shouldn't the existence of a foreknowing God imply that the structure of time and agency are perhaps not what they might initially appear to be?

We don't know what to say, precisely, to this line of thought. Indeed, the resolution of these questions appears to implicate an entire metaphysics. Instead, we should simply like to suggest that this is, in part, where the debate concerning divine foreknowledge might make progress. What justifies the fixity of the past? Or what is it in virtue of which the past is fixed, if it is? And what would justify rejecting it? Perhaps, until such questions are further resolved, we should simply be agnostics concerning the compatibility of foreknowledge and freedom. For now, however, we set these issues aside. If one *were* confident, however, that the past is fixed, and that divine foreknowledge is thus incompatible with free will, one might wish to seek a way to avoid the conclusion that, given God's existence, we are not, in fact, free. We now turn to one such strategy.

2.1. OPEN THEISM

Just as there are two aspects to the logical fatalist's overall argument that no one is free, there are two aspects to the theological fatalist's argument that no one is free. The first is that, for anything we do, God always knew (and believed) that we would do that thing. And the second is that (as is shown by the argument above) God's having had such beliefs is incompatible with our having free will. One strategy of responding to the theological fatalist that has become more popular recently is to reject this *first* aspect of the theological fatalist's overall argument. On this view, it does not follow from the fact that you bought this book that God always knew that you would buy it.[30] To reject the first aspect of the theological fatalist's argument is to endorse *open theism*. There are, however, two importantly different ways of being an open theist. The first is to maintain that though it was true 1,000 years ago (say) that you would purchase this book, this was simply a truth God did not then know or believe. We might call this view "limited foreknowledge open theism."[31] On this sort of view, though some future contingent propositions are in fact true, these are not truths that God knows. The second is to maintain that there was no such truth 1,000 years ago in the first place, given that you freely purchased this book; this view endorses the "open future" view to be discussed in the next section, according to which all future contingents fail to be true. And God, of course, fails to believe what isn't true. We might call this view "open future open theism."[32]

---

[30]Strictly speaking, views that maintain that God is "outside time" also endorse this thesis, insofar as they deny that God (strictly speaking) "foreknows" anything at all. This view is, of course, one of the historically most prominent ways of "dissolving" the problem of freedom and foreknowledge. For some contemporary developments of this sort of view, see Pike 1970, Leftow 1991, and Stump and Kretzmann 1981. We assume in this section that God is not "outside time."
[31]For defenses of this version of open theism, see Swinburne 1977, Hasker 1989, and van Inwagen 2008.
[32]For defenses of this version of open theism, see Prior 1962, Lucas 1989, Rhoda et al. 2006, Rhoda 2007, Tuggy 2007, and Todd 2014.

Perhaps the primary challenge for limited foreknowledge open theism is to explain *why* God fails to know (and believe) the relevant propositions, when they are, in fact, true. Perhaps the most natural thought for the limited foreknowledge open theist would be this: though *truth itself* concerning the future does not require deterministic grounds, *infallible belief* about the future nevertheless does. That is, on this sort of view, it needn't be the case that something *now* causally determines that a given event will occur in order for it to be *true* that that event will occur.[33] However, in order for anyone—including God—now to *infallibly believe* that an event will occur, there would have to be something about *now* that grounds that belief—that is, there would have to be deterministic *evidence* now accessible to God that the event will occur. In the case of a future *contingent*, however, *ex hypothesi* there is no such evidence. So, we might imagine, even though it was true 1,000 years ago that you would purchase this book, this was not something God then believed—and *not* because of any epistemic (or other) defect in God, but instead precisely because of God's epistemic perfection. Not even God could "just see" that a future contingent proposition is true, if in fact it is.[34]

We set aside the question of whether this is a plausible picture of God's beliefs and future contingents. What about the difficulties attending open future open theism? The chief *philosophical* difficulties for the open future open theist are simply those facing open futurism more generally. Such problems are the topic of Section 3 below (on the problem of future contingents).

2.2. HUNT AND AUGUSTINE'S WAY OUT

Before moving on to the problem of future contingents, we wish to consider a different sort of reply to the arguments of the logical and theological fatalist. One might simply concede that one or both of the relevant arguments show that we lack free will in the sense at issue—that is, that we lack the ability to do otherwise than what we actually do. One might contend, however, that free will (so construed) is not necessary for what we typically *care* about when we care about "free will." What matters is that we have the sort of control with respect to our behavior that is necessary for *moral responsibility*. (The connection between the ability to do otherwise and moral

---

[33]Skipping ahead: the limited foreknowledge open theist thus endorses what is called "Ockhamism" in the *next* section (according to which there can be truths about the undetermined future), though *not* what was called "Ockhamism" in the *previous* section as applied to God's past beliefs: the limited foreknowledge open theist will typically contend that God's past beliefs are "hard facts" about the past.

[34]Todd suggests this account on behalf of the limited foreknowledge open theist in Todd 2014.

responsibility is one of the main reasons the issues of this book have taken on such historical importance.) But having the ability to do otherwise is *not* necessary for moral responsibility. Accordingly, one could be "free" in the sense we care about, but lack the sort of free will targeted by the fatalist's arguments.

This is precisely the strategy pursued by David Hunt in his essay in this volume ("On Augustine's Way Out")—a strategy Hunt finds in the writings of Augustine on this topic.[35] Needless to say, this sort of position has various attractive features, one of which is that it is not committed to finding fault with any of the fatalistic arguments we have considered. We wish, however, to mention at least one difficulty with Hunt's own development of this sort of position. It is crucial to Hunt's "Augustinian" solution to the problem that though God's prior beliefs imply that one's future actions are *unavoidable*, they do *not* do so because God's prior beliefs imply that one's future actions are causally determined. In the contemporary parlance of the "free will" debate, Hunt wishes to be a so-called "source incompatibilist." That is, Hunt wants to maintain that though the ability to do otherwise is not necessary for moral responsibility, nevertheless *causal determinism* is still incompatible with moral responsibility, because causal determinism is incompatible with one's being the proper "source" of one's behavior. Thus, since Hunt wishes to maintain moral responsibility, Hunt *cannot* maintain that the ultimate reason divine foreknowledge implies that one lacks free will (the ability to do otherwise) is that it implies that one's actions are causally determined. For Hunt, divine foreknowledge *in itself* rules out one's free will, even though one's actions remain causally undetermined. Nothing at all causally determines you to do what you do—nevertheless, you lack the ability to do otherwise than what you actually do.

Upon reflection, there can seem to be something puzzling about Hunt's position here—something that raises a crucial set of issues often ignored in discussions of fatalistic arguments. Hunt's position, again, is that, given God's foreknowledge, though nothing causally determines you to do what you do, you nevertheless lack the ability to do otherwise than what you do. But the question here is simple. How could God's foreknowledge, in itself, have any such effect? That is, how could God's foreknowledge, in itself, make you unable to do otherwise than what you actually do, if it neither causes what you do nor implies that something *else* causes

---

[35]Hunt thus follows in a tradition that has emerged in discussions of free will in the wake of Harry Frankfurt's famous 1969 attack on the "principle of alternate possibilities," according to which one is morally responsible for performing a certain action only if one could have done otherwise. For more on this important topic, and for a defense of Frankfurt's strategy, see Fischer 1994, Fischer and Ravizza 1998, and Fischer 2012.

what you do?[36] On this latter score, one strategy for a theological fatalist would be to maintain that though God's foreknowledge *shows* (via the argument considered above) that you lack the ability to do otherwise, such foreknowledge is not itself what *makes* you unable to do otherwise. Rather, what *makes* you unable to do otherwise are the causal conditions that would have to be in place in order for God to have such infallible foreknowledge in the first place.[37] On this sort of picture, God's foreknowledge and one's own actions are both (though in different ways) effects of a common cause: it is the presence of the relevant causal factors that explain both God's foreknowledge of your actions and your actions themselves. That is, on this picture, though the fatalistic argument considered above provides good *epistemic reason* to conclude that divine foreknowledge is incompatible with free will, the *metaphysical account* of this incompatibility is that divine foreknowledge would ultimately have to be explained by deterministic causes.

But this is *not* a position available to proponents of Hunt's Augustinian solution. Again, Hunt must maintain that God's foreknowledge, in itself, could *make* one's actions unavoidable, even if it doesn't (and nothing else does) causally determine those actions. But again we can ask: how could it have any such effect? If no *causal* factor makes one unable to do otherwise than what one does, precisely what sort of factor *does* accomplish this result? Are we to believe in some sort of "metaphysical force field" that makes one unable to do otherwise than what one does? But what could *that* be? We do not claim that this problem (as developed thus far) is decisive against Hunt's position. However, we do think these issues raise a crucial question for those sympathetic to fatalistic arguments. If prior truths or prior divine beliefs are incompatible with free will, *how* are they incompatible with free will? What, if anything, does the work in *making* us unfree, given such truths or such beliefs? What is the *relationship* between such truths or beliefs and our unfreedom? Do such truths and beliefs themselves *make* us unfree, or do they merely *show* that something else makes us unfree? If the latter, what is it that they show makes us unfree? And is it plausible that the given truths or beliefs have this sort of

---

[36]This is a question Hunt explicitly considers concerning the freedom required to be morally responsible—but *not* considering the ability to do otherwise. That is, Hunt maintains that it is mysterious how God's prior belief could "transform" an action that might otherwise be a perfect candidate for a free, morally responsible action into one that is not free (in that sense) at all. But Hunt seemingly does *not* find it mysterious how God's prior belief, in itself, could render one's future actions unavoidable (i.e., could make one lack the freedom to do otherwise). Our point here is that the question Hunt addresses (namely, how God's beliefs could have the relevant result) *also* arises for the sort of free will Hunt *does* think is ruled out by God's foreknowledge.

[37]This is a possibility considered by Trenton Merricks (inspired by Jonathan Edwards) in his essay in this volume. For more on this topic, see Craig 1987, Anderson and Watson 2010, Byerly 2012, Byerly 2014, and Todd 2014.

consequence? These are deep questions proponents of fatalistic arguments seemingly must further address.

3. THE PROBLEM OF FUTURE CONTINGENTS

We turn now to the *problem of future contingents*. Future contingent propositions are propositions saying of contingent, presently undetermined events that they will happen.[38] (The events must be neither determined to occur, nor determined *not* to occur.) The problem of future contingents arises from the following conflict. On the one hand, we have what we might call *the grounding problem*. If nothing about present reality—and the laws governing how reality unfolds over time—settles it that the relevant events will happen, how and why is it *true* that they will happen? What, in short, accounts for the truth of future contingent propositions? Or if nothing *does* account for their truth, how are they nevertheless true? On the other hand, we have what we might call *the logical problem* and *the prediction problem*. If, instead, such propositions are never true, what are they—neither true nor false? But then we seem to be denying classical logic. Or are they simply false? But how could *that* be? This is the logical problem. Further, if such propositions are never true, how are we to make sense of the common practice of retrospectively predicating truth to predictions that in fact come to pass? If you predict that a horse will win a race, and then that horse does win, we will typically say that "you were right." If future contingents are never true, however, then it is not clear how this practice can make sense. This is the prediction problem.[39]

As we shall use the terms, "open futurists" deny that future contingents can ever be true, and thus face the logical problem and the prediction problem.[40] "Ockhamists" maintain that there can be truths about the undetermined future, and thus face the grounding problem.[41] Here, however, we must pause to discuss

---

[38]No doubt a more rigorous definition could be provided. See, e.g., Rosenkranz, chapter 16.

[39]Richard Taylor presses both the logical problem and the prediction problem in his essay in this volume.

[40]We don't mean to suggest that only "open futurists" (so defined) can capture the familiar, pre-theoretical idea that the future is "open" to our agency in a sense in which the past is not. Whether "open futurism" (as defined by us) is indeed required to account for this intuition is a substantive, controversial matter.

[41]As we are defining Ockhamism here, the Ockhamist is committed to the possible truth of indeterminism. However, one might think this result to be problematic, if one thought that Ockhamism itself has nothing to do with this issue. For our purposes, however, it will be easier simply to say that Ockhamism is the view that it is jointly possible that it be true that an event will occur and it be undetermined that that event will occur.

how Ockhamism—so defined—relates to the "Ockhamism" discussed in the previous sections on the arguments of the fatalists. As Sven Rosenkranz's chapter in this book makes clear, there is a usage of the term "Ockhamism" to refer simply to the thesis that there can be truths about the undetermined future. So construed, Ockhamism is simply a thesis about the status of future contingent propositions, and *in itself* says nothing about free will, the fixity of the past, or anything concerning agency at all. In particular, you could be an Ockhamist in this sense, *without* endorsing what we called the "Ockhamist" reply to the fatalist's argument for the incompatibility of "prior truths" and free will discussed above. For instance, one might instead endorse Merricks's response to that argument; for that matter, one might think that though there can be truths about the undetermined future, nevertheless the fatalist's argument for the incompatibility of such truths and *free will* is successful. On this view, the truth of future contingents would be compatible with indeterminism, but nevertheless *not* with freedom.

Before moving on, it will be helpful to state another way one might characterize the difference between Ockhamism and open futurism, a way that employs a familiar way of *modeling* our thought and talk about time and the future. Assume indeterminism. Intuitively, on indeterminism, there are many distinct (maximal and complete) "ways" things could go from a given time t, consistently with the past (relative to t) and the laws of nature. These are the causally possible futures at t. Now, on open futurism, all we have, so to speak, are the various futures—but what we do not have, on this model, is a *privileged* future, the one that is "going to obtain." On Ockhamism, however, not so. According to the Ockhamist, when we're assessing whether a future contingent such as "It will be the case that p" is true, we simply need to go forward along the privileged "branch" (or look at the "actual" future of those that remain causally possible) and see whether that branch (or future) features p. Both Ockhamism and open futurism allow for various causally possible futures, but only the Ockhamist allows the further claim that one such future is now-privileged—lit up, as it were, with "the thin red line."[42]

Looked at from this point of view, those who press the "grounding problem" maintain that the existence of a "thin red line" marking a privileged future would be ungrounded—unacceptably arbitrary or brute. However, as Ockhamists may point out, without a "thin red line," we face the logical problem and the prediction problem. We turn first to the logical problem and the prediction problem. We then consider the grounding problem for Ockhamism.

---

[42]This terminology was introduced in Belnap and Green 1994.

3.1. THE LOGICAL PROBLEM

There are, as far as we are aware, two different potential open futurist responses to the logical problem. The first is to maintain that though future contingents are neither true nor false, and though we must therefore deny classical logic, denying classical logic in the requisite way is not, in the end, an unacceptable result. This response to the logical problem has a long, venerable pedigree, going all the way back to Aristotle's famous discussion of the sea-battle tomorrow in *On Interpretation* 9.[43] It has been developed with considerable sophistication by logicians such as Jan Łukasiewicz and A. N. Prior.[44] This response has also been developed in connection with issues concerning *vagueness* and compared to so-called *supervaluationist* positions on that topic.[45]

Here, and in this volume, we wish instead to highlight a different (and relatively unknown) response to the logical problem, one that seeks to *preserve* classical logic: this response does not maintain that future contingents are neither true nor false, but that they are simply *false*. As far as we are able to determine, the view at issue was first articulated and defended in 1941 by Charles Hartshorne, who later further developed the view in his 1965 *Mind* paper, "The Meaning of 'Is Going to Be'," reprinted in this volume.[46] The view was also (it seems independently) developed (though not explicitly endorsed) by the founder of tense logic himself, A. N. Prior, in the 1950s and '60s.[47] Prior's only non-technical discussion of this view, in his posthumously (and somewhat obscurely) published essay "It Was to Be" is also reprinted in this volume. Part of our aim in publishing these essays here is to draw increased attention to this view, which we feel has been unjustly neglected in the vast literature on free will, fatalism, and future contingents.

But what is the view? In brief, if we say that something *will* happen if and only if that thing is *determined* to happen, and that something *will not* happen if and only if that thing is determined *not* to happen, then future contingents will all turn out false. After all, a future contingent says of an event that is neither determined to happen nor determined *not* to happen that it *will* happen. In this case, however, it is false that the event *will* happen (since it is false that it is determined to happen), and it is false that the event *will not* happen (since it is false that it is determined *not* to happen). On this view, then, "will" and "will not" are *contraries* (both can be false,

---

[43]For an excellent discussion of the history of this topic during the medieval period, see Knuuttila 2011.
[44]See Łukasiewicz 1957 and 1967 and Prior 1957 and 1967.
[45]See Thomason 1970. For a helpful overview, see Øhrstrøm and Hasle 2011.
[46]See Hartshorne 1941: 100–01.
[47]See Prior 1957 and 1967.

but both can't be true) rather than contradictories. Thus, a statement such as that "It will be the case that *p*, or it will not be the case that *p*" is not an instance of *p* v ~*p*. This is because one cannot move from "It is not the case that it will be the case that *p*" to "It will not be the case that *p*", for the same reason as one cannot move from "It is not the case that X is determined to happen" to "X is determined *not* to happen". This latter move is, of course, plainly illegitimate (an event could be, as yet, undetermined to happen either way)—and consequently, according to this view, so is the former.

Despite the seeming elegance of this view, many writers on future contingents (and related matters) do not seem to be aware of it. For instance, in his essay in this volume (which, we hasten to add, has many compensating virtues), Michael Rea maintains, roughly, that "presentists" cannot adequately respond to the logical fatalist's argument for the incompatibility of prior truths and free will, and accordingly must either give up such truths by denying bivalence, or instead give up free will. In fact, however, what Rea's argument shows, if it succeeds, is not that presentists who maintain free will must deny bivalence, but that they must deny bivalence *or* adopt the "all false" view of future contingents.[48] That is, Rea writes as if there is only one option in regard to maintaining that future contingents are never true: that they are neither true nor false. There is, however, also the view developed by Hartshorne and Prior (and others): that they are simply false.

At this point, we will leave the Hartshornean/Priorean development of the "all false" view to Hartshorne and Prior.[49] Before moving on, however, we wish briefly to note that there is a yet further, distinct way of getting to the "all false" view of future contingents, a way recently developed by one of the current authors (Todd).[50] Instead of defining "will" to mean "determined", this view takes its cue from the famous debate between Russell and Strawson concerning bivalence and "the present King of France." According to the Strawsonian view, "The present King of France is bald" is neither true nor false, whereas, on the Russellian view, that proposition is simply false, since its logical form (roughly) is "There *exists* a present King of France, and that person is bald", and there does not exist any such king. Now, on the relevant "Ockhamist" semantics for "will", something "will" happen (as a first approximation) if and only if "the unique actual future" features the

---

[48]Seymour also makes this point in (manuscript).

[49]The most thorough discussion and defense of Hartshorne's views concerning future contingents is the excellent Shields and Viney 2003. Hartshorne's writings on this topic have not attracted much attention, but see this essay for a defense of Hartshorne's view against criticisms in Cahn 1967 and Clark 1969; see further Shields 1988 and Viney 1989. Rhoda et al. defend a similar "all false" view in their 2006, as does Seymour (manuscript).

[50]For an extensive development of this view, see Todd forthcoming.

thing happening—the privileged future of those that remain causally possible. But if there is no such privileged future (no "thin red line"), as open futurists contend, then (on a Russellian analysis) such a proposition simply comes out false, for precisely the same reason as that "The present King of France is bald" comes out false, according to Russell. In short, the sense of "will" at stake—the sense Ockhamists claim that the Hartshornean/Priorean semantics is failing to capture—implicitly quantifies over a privileged future. But, if Russell is right, in the absence of a privileged future, such a proposition simply comes out false. This, anyway, is the very basic idea. If successful, we arrive at the "all false" view (and thereby preserve classical logic) without (implausibly, it seems) simply *defining* "X will happen" to mean "X is determined to happen."

3.2. THE PREDICTION PROBLEM

So much for the logical problem for open futurists. We turn now to the *prediction problem* for open futurists. Prior expresses the problem nicely in his essay in this volume:

> Nevertheless, the way of talking that I have just sketched [on which future contingents all come out false] shares with the three-valued way of talking [on which they are neither true nor false] one big disadvantage, namely that it is grossly at variance with the ways in which even non-determinists ordinarily appraise or assign truth-values to predictions, bets, and guesses. Suppose at the beginning of a race I bet you that Phar Lap will win, and then he does win, and I come to claim my bet. You might then ask me, "Why, do you think this victory was unpreventable when you made your bet?" I admit that I don't, so you say, "Well I'm not paying up then—when you said Phar Lap would win, what you said wasn't true—on the three-valued view, it was merely neuter: on this other view of yours, it was even false. So I'm sticking to the money." And I must admit that if anyone treated a bet of mine like that I would feel aggrieved; that just isn't the way this game is played. (Prior, this volume, chapter 14)

This problem is widely regarded to be the most difficult problem facing open futurists. One strategy for dealing with it is explored at length in John MacFarlane's essay in this book. Roughly, according to MacFarlane, relative to the context of utterance, one's prediction that Phar Lap will win is neither true nor false; relative, however, to the context of assessment (now, once Phar Lap has won), one's prediction is true. MacFarlane's "relativist" solution to the prediction problem is ingenious—and controversial. Certainly the jury on MacFarlane's solution is still out.[51]

[51]For criticism of MacFarlane's relativism, see, e.g., Heck 2006 and Moruzzi and Wright 2009. MacFarlane develops his view further in his 2014.

If one does not go in for MacFarlane's relativism, however, then how should one respond to the prediction problem? It isn't clear, and certainly there is no canonical open futurist response to the difficulty at hand. Hartshorne addresses this problem in his essay in this volume, though how successfully we leave an open question. There are, however, at least two avenues of reply that we wish briefly to suggest as worthy of further development.

First, the open futurist might insist that we pay close attention to *another* thing we are liable to say in contexts of prediction. One thing we say is that "you were right." Another thing we say, however, is that "what you said *came true*." And the open futurist might see in this latter construction an opening for her position. After all, on this construction, we do not say that what you said *was* true, but that it *came* true—and what *that* seems to mean is simply that the thing one predicted to happen in fact ended up happening. But certainly the open futurist is entitled to "what you predicted would happen in fact happened." If, however, the open futurist is entitled to "what you predicted to happen in fact happened," then, arguably, she is entitled to "what you predicted came true." And if she is entitled to "what you predicted came true," then she can plausibly argue that, though we do say, "you were right," this commits us to nothing over and above what we're committed to in saying (or *just is* a way of saying) that "what you predicted came true," which, we just saw, is something the open futurist can happily accept. One sometimes sees open futurists making this sort of point (or a similar one) in the literature, but, to our knowledge, no one has developed it with the sort of care it would seem to deserve.

Second, though we aren't aware of anyone who has done so, the open futurist might seek to employ the resources of a (relatively) new area of metaphysics and philosophy of language to the prediction problem: fictionalism.[52] Broadly speaking, fictionalism regarding a range of discourse maintains that claims made within that discourse are best regarded as engaging in a fiction, not as aiming at the literal truth. Fictionalism, roughly, is a way of maintaining that although we may *say* a great many things that appear to commit us to some problematic entities, we are not *really* committed to those entities, since, when we are engaged in such talk, we are engaged in talk about a fiction. In short, it is a way of escaping certain unwelcome ontological commitments. In general, one can apply the fictionalist strategy whenever: (a) one has some folk claims that seem to be true; (b) their truth seems to entail the existence of an object or objects of a given type; and (c) the existence of objects of that type seems metaphysically extravagant (or otherwise problematic).[53]

---

[52]For more on fictionalism, see Eklund 2011.
[53]We thank Mark Balauger for this construal of the fictionalist strategy.

So construed, fictionalism would seem to have a natural application to the problem of future contingents. First, we have some folk claims that seem to be true, claims such as that "you were right." Second, their truth seems to entail the existence of an object (broadly construed) of a certain type: namely, a metaphysically privileged future of those that were causally possible, or a so-called "thin red line." Third, the existence of a "thin red line" seems—anyway to some—to be metaphysically extravagant. Accordingly, it would seem that the fictionalist strategy should be on the table. On this approach, one interprets "you were right" as something like, "According to the fiction of the thin red line, you were right." That is, when, looking backwards, we engage in such talk, we are engaged in a fiction; we take up a point of view on which there existed a fictional "thin red line," and assess matters from that point of view. It is, of course, perfectly natural, and perfectly understandable, that this practice should arise; it is, equally, perfectly natural to see it as imbued with less than full ontological seriousness. Needless to say, we have only hinted at how to develop this sort of proposal; however, given the similarities between this context and other contexts in which fictionalist strategies have been applied, we believe that these connections deserve more attention than they have received. And, regarding the prediction problem, it isn't as if the open futurist already has a wealth of other plausible options on the table.

3.3. THE GROUNDING PROBLEM

As we've just seen, open futurism faces problems—the logical problem and the prediction problem. What, then, motivates the view? As we saw in Section 1, one set of motivations is "indirect," going *via* the fatalist's argument for the incompatibility of the truth of future contingents and free will. But another is "direct," and this is simply that the alternative view, Ockhamism, seems to face a serious *grounding problem*. What accounts for the truth of future contingent propositions?

One way to press the grounding problem for Ockhamism is to invoke some version of "truthmaker theory." According to "truthmaker maximalism," every truth has a truthmaker—roughly, some feature of the world that *makes* the relevant proposition true.[54] According to this line of thought, future contingents would lack truthmakers: there is no feature of the world that would *make* such propositions true. For instance, one could not cite current causal conditions and laws as truthmakers for the relevant truths, for *ex hypothesi* such conditions and laws fail to secure the given outcomes. Another way to develop this objection would be to invoke the

---

[54]For a defense of truthmaker maximalism, see Armstrong 2004.

related thesis that "truth supervenes on being," the thesis that, for any true proposition, if that proposition were instead false, there would have to be some difference somewhere in reality.[55] Intuitively, however, true future contingents would seem to fail to supervene on reality. If some true future contingent were instead false, this would seem to require no difference at all in the "facts on the ground," so to speak: such facts could be just as they are, and yet that proposition be false instead of true. For instance, suppose it is a true future contingent that Hillary Clinton will be the next president of the United States. The objector says: the facts on the ground could be *just as they actually are*, given indeterminism, and yet it be *false* that Hillary will become president. The falsity of the future contingent would not require any discernible difference in the way things are. The objection is thus that the truth that Hillary will become the next president seems problematically "disconnected" from reality: it "floats free" of reality in some allegedly objectionable way.

Of course, these objections are only as good as the principles that truths require truthmakers and that truth supervenes on being. And they are only as good as the argument that, given indeterminism, we cannot provide "truthmakers" for future contingents or say that truth supervenes on being. Another way to press the grounding objection, however, is to pay attention to the *model* of the future (or our discourse about the future) that Ockhamists must endorse. Return to the theme noted above: in addition to the causally possible futures at *t*, the Ockhamist also maintains that there exists a *privileged* future of those that remain causally possible—a "thin red line." But now we can ask: whence comes the privilege? As John MacFarlane notes in his chapter in this volume, don't symmetry considerations push strongly in favor of the conclusion that no such future is now-privileged? After all, whatever one such future could "say" (so to speak) concerning why *it* is the privileged future, any other such future could also say. That is, all such futures would have, *ex hypothesi*, an "equal claim" on being "how things go from here." Wouldn't it be simply arbitrary if one such way *just were* the way things *will* go from here?

There is one final way we could put the grounding objection to Ockhamism—a way that serves helpfully to unite the themes of this book. Assume indeterminism. And assume that there are some true future contingents. Now we ask: how could God *know* that any such propositions are true? How could God know, in advance, the outcome of a genuinely indeterministic process? Intuitively, there would be *nothing at all* about the world that God has created on the basis of which God could come to know that the event will occur. In order to know that it will occur, then, it seems that God will have to have some mystical insight into the truth itself: God will have

---

[55]For an overview of truthmaker theory and the thesis that "truth supervenes on being," see MacBride 2013.

to know what will happen by being immediately and directly acquainted with the truth.[56] The Ockhamist, then, is seemingly committed to the following: either God can have this sort of mysterious access to the truth—or instead there is a "metaphysical gap" between what even a *perfect knower* could know, on the one hand, and what is true, on the other. And it is precisely this sort of "metaphysical gap" that strikes many who press the grounding objection to be so problematic. Neither option thus seems altogether comfortable—though, with respect to the former, one might say that greater mysteries have been associated with God. In this respect, it is perhaps fitting that we should conclude with a quote from Ockham himself, an ardent defender of the compatibility of divine foreknowledge and human free will: "It is impossible to express clearly the way in which God knows future contingent events."[57]

[56]For an excellent discussion of this position, see Mavrodes 1988.
[57]Ockham in Adams and Kretzmann 1969: 50.

PART I

The Arguments for Fatalism

1

FATE

Richard Taylor

We all, at certain moments of pain, threat, or bereavement, are apt to entertain the idea of fatalism, the thought that what is happening at a particular moment is unavoidable, that we are powerless to prevent it. Sometimes we find ourselves in circumstances not of our own making, in which our very being and destinies are so thoroughly anchored that the thought of fatalism can be quite overwhelming, and sometimes consoling. One feels that whatever then happens, however good or ill, will be what those circumstances yield, and we are helpless. Soldiers, it is said, are sometimes possessed by such thoughts. Perhaps all men would feel more inclined to them if they paused once in a while to think of how little they ever had to do with bringing themselves to wherever they have arrived in life, how much of their fortunes and destinies were decided for them by sheer circumstance, and how the entire course of their lives is often set, once and for all, by the most trivial incidents, which they did not produce and could not even have foreseen. If we are free to work out our destinies at all, which is doubtful, we have a freedom that is at best exercised within exceedingly narrow paths. All the important things—when we are born, of what parents, into what culture, whether we are loved or rejected, whether we are male or female, our temperament, our intelligence or stupidity, indeed everything that makes for the bulk of our happiness and misery—all these are decided for us by the most casual and indifferent circumstances, by sheer coincidences, chance encounters, and seemingly insignificant fortuities. One can see this in retrospect if he searches, but few search. The fate that has given us our very being has given us also our pride and conceit, and has thereby formed us so that, being human, we congratulate ourselves on our blessings, which we call our achievements, blame the world for our blunders, which we call our misfortunes, and scarcely give a thought to that impersonal fate which arbitrarily dispenses both.

FATALISM AND DETERMINISM

Determinism, it will be recalled, is the theory that all events are rendered unavoidable by their causes. The attempt is sometimes made to distinguish this from fatalism by saying that, according to the fatalist, certain events are going to happen *no matter what*, or in other words, regardless of causes. But this is enormously contrived. It would be hard to find in the whole history of thought a single fatalist, on that conception of it.

Fatalism is the belief that whatever happens is unavoidable. That is the clearest expression of the doctrine, and provides the basis of the attitude of calm acceptance that the fatalist is thought, quite correctly, to embody. One who endorses the claim of universal causation, then, and the theory of the causal determination of all human behavior, is a kind of fatalist—or at least he should be, if he is consistent. For that theory, as we have seen, once it is clearly spelled out and not hedged about with unresolved "ifs", does entail that whatever happens is rendered inevitable by the causal conditions preceding it, and is therefore unavoidable. One can indeed think of verbal formulas for distinguishing the two theories, but if we think of a fatalist as one who has a certain attitude, we find it to be the attitude that a thoroughgoing determinist should, in consistency, assume. That some philosophical determinists are not fatalists does not so much illustrate a great difference between fatalism and determinism, but rather the humiliation to one's pride that a fatalist position can deliver, and the comfort that can sometimes be found in evasion.

FATALISM WITH RESPECT
TO THE FUTURE AND THE PAST

A fatalist, then, is someone who believes that whatever happens is and always was unavoidable. He thinks it is not up to him what will happen a thousand years hence, next year, tomorrow, or the very next moment. Of course he does not pretend always to *know* what is going to happen. Hence, he might try sometimes to read signs and portents, as meteorologists and astrologers do, or to contemplate the effects upon him of the various things that might, for all he knows, be fated to occur. But he does not suppose that whatever happens could ever have really been avoidable.

A fatalist thus thinks of the future in the way we all think of the past, for all men are fatalists as they look *back* on things. To a large extent we know what has happened—some of it we can even remember—whereas the future is still obscure to us, and we are therefore tempted to invest it, in our imagination, with all sorts of "possibilities". The fatalist resists this temptation, knowing that mere ignorance can hardly give rise to any genuine possibility in things. He thinks of both past and future "under the aspect of eternity," the way God is supposed to view them. We all think of the past this way, as something settled and fixed, to be taken for what it is. We are never in the least tempted to try to modify it. It is not in the least up to us what happened last year, yesterday, or even a moment ago, any more than are the motions of the heavens or the political developments in Tibet. If we are not fatalists, then we might think that past things once *were* up to us, to bring about or prevent, as long as they were still future—but this expresses our attitude toward the future, not the past.

Such is surely our conception of the whole past, whether near or remote. But the consistent fatalist thinks of the future in the same way. We say of past things that they are no longer within our power. The fatalist says they never were.

THE SOURCES OF FATALISM

A fatalistic way of thinking most often arises from theological ideas, or from what are generally thought to be certain presuppositions of science and logic. Thus, if God is really all-knowing and all-powerful, it is not hard to suppose that He has arranged for everything to happen just as it is going to happen, that He already knows every detail of the whole future course of the world, and there is nothing left for you and me to do except watch things unfold, in the here or hereafter. But without bringing God into the picture, it is not hard to suppose, as we have seen, that everything that happens is wholly determined by what went before it, and hence that whatever happens at any future time is the only thing that can then happen, given what precedes it. Or even disregarding that, it seems natural to suppose that there is a body of truth concerning what the future holds, just as there is such truth concerning what is contained in the past, whether or not it is known to any man or even to God, and hence, that everything asserted in that body of truth will assuredly happen, in the fullness of time, precisely as it is described therein.

No one needs to be convinced that fatalism is the only proper way to view the past. That it is also the proper way to view the future is less obvious, due in part, perhaps, to our vastly greater ignorance of what the future holds. The consequences of holding such fatalism are obviously momentous. To say nothing of the consolation of fatalism, which enables a person to view all things as they arise with the same undisturbed mind with which he contemplates even the most revolting of history's horrors, the fatalist teaching also relieves one of all tendency toward both blame and approbation of others and of both guilt and conceit in himself. It promises that a perfect understanding is possible, and removes the temptation to view things in terms of human wickedness and moral responsibility. This thought alone, once firmly grasped, yields a sublime acceptance of all that life and nature offer, whether to oneself or one's fellows; and although it thereby reduces one's pride, it simultaneously enhances the feelings, opens the heart, and expands the understanding.

DIVINE OMNISCIENCE

Suppose for the moment, just for the purpose of discussion, that God exists and is omniscient. To say that God is omniscient means that He knows everything that is true. He cannot, of course, know that which is false. Concerning any falsehood, an omniscient being can know that it is false; but then it is a truth that is known, namely, the truth that the thing in question *is* a falsehood. So if it is false that the moon is a cube, then God can, like you or me, know that this is false; but He cannot know the falsehood itself, that the moon is a cube.

Thus, if God is omniscient He knows, as you probably do, the date of your birth. He also knows, as you may not, the hour of your birth. Furthermore, God knows, as you assuredly do not, the date, and indeed the moment, of your conception—for there is such a truth, and we are supposing that God knows every truth. Moreover, He knows, as you surely do not, the date of your death, and even the exact moment, and the circumstances thereof—whether at that moment, known already to Him, you die as the result of accident, a fatal malady, suicide, murder, whatever. And, still assuming God exists and knows everything, He knows whether any ant walked across my desk last night, and if so, what ant it was, where it came from, how long it was on the desk, how it came to be there, and so on, to every truth about this insect that there is. Similarly, of course, He knows when some ant will again appear on my desk, if ever. He knows the number of hairs on my head, notes the fall of every sparrow, knows why it fell, and why it was going to fall. These are simply a few of the consequences of the omniscience that we are for the moment assuming. A more precise way of expressing all this is to say that God knows, concerning any statement whatever that anyone could formulate, that it is true, in case it is, and otherwise, that it is false. And let us suppose that God, at some time or other, or perhaps from time to time, vouchsafes some of his knowledge to men, or perhaps to certain chosen men. Thus prophets arise, proclaiming the coming of certain events, and things do then happen as they have foretold. Of course it is not surprising that they should, on the supposition we are making; namely, that the foreknowledge of these things comes from God, who is omniscient.

THE STORY OF OSMO

Now then, let us make one further supposition, which will get us squarely into the philosophical issue these ideas are intended to introduce. Let us suppose that God has revealed a particular set of facts to a chosen scribe who, believing (correctly) that they came from God, wrote them all down. The facts in question then turned out to be all the more or less significant episodes in the life of some perfectly ordinary man named Osmo. Osmo was entirely unknown to the scribe, and in fact to just about everyone, but there was no doubt concerning whom all these facts were about, for the very first thing received by the scribe from God, was: "He of whom I speak is called Osmo." When the revelations reached a fairly voluminous bulk and appeared to be completed, the scribe arranged them in chronological order and assembled them into a book. He at first gave it the title *The Life of Osmo, as Given by God*, but thinking that people would take this to be some sort of joke, he dropped the reference to God.

The book was published, but attracted no attention whatsoever, because it appeared to be nothing more than a record of the dull life of a very plain man named Osmo. The scribe wondered, in fact, why God had chosen to convey such a mass of seemingly pointless trivia.

The book eventually found its way into various libraries, where it gathered dust until one day a high school teacher in Indiana, who rejoiced under the name of Osmo, saw a copy on the shelf. The title caught his eye. Curiously picking it up and blowing the dust off, he was thunderstruck by the opening sentence: "Osmo is born in Mercy Hospital in Auburn, Indiana, on June 6, 1942, of Finnish parentage, and after nearly losing his life from an attack of pneumonia at the age of five, he is enrolled in the St. James school there." Osmo turned pale. The book nearly fell from his hands. He thumbed back in excitement to discover who had written it. Nothing was given of its authorship nor, for that matter, of its publisher. His questions of the librarian produced no further information, he being as ignorant as Osmo of how the book came to be there.

So Osmo, with the book pressed tightly under his arm, dashed across the street for some coffee, thinking to compose himself and then examine this book with care. Meanwhile he glanced at a few more of its opening remarks, at the things said there about his difficulties with his younger sister, how he was slow in learning to read, of the summer on Mackinac Island, and so on. His emotions now somewhat quieted, Osmo began a close reading. He noticed that everything was expressed in the present tense, the way newspaper headlines are written. For example, the text read, "Osmo is born in Mercy Hospital," instead of saying he *was* born there, and it recorded that he quarrels with his sister, is a slow student, is fitted with dental braces at age eight, and so on, all in the journalistic present tense. But the text itself made quite clear approximately when all these various things happened, for everything was in chronological order, and in any case each year of its subject's life constituted a separate chapter, and was so titled—"Osmo's Seventh Year," "Osmo's Eighth Year," and so on through the book.

Osmo became absolutely engrossed, to the extent that he forgot his original astonishment, bordering on panic, and for a while even lost his curiosity concerning authorship. He sat drinking coffee and reliving his childhood, much of which he had all but forgotten until the memories were revived by the book now before him. He had almost forgotten about the kitten, for example, and had entirely forgotten its name, until he read, in the chapter called "Osmo's Seventh Year," this observation: "Sobbing, Osmo takes Fluffy, now quite dead, to the garden, and buries her next to the rose bush." Ah yes! And then there was Louise, who sat next to him in the eighth grade—it was all right there. And how he got caught smoking one day. And how he felt when his father died. On and on. Osmo became so absorbed that he quite forgot the business of the day, until it occurred to him to turn to Chapter 26, to see what might be said there, he having just recently turned twenty-six. He had no sooner done so than his panic returned, for lo! what the book said was *true!* That it rains on his birthday for example, that his wife fails to give him the binoculars he had hinted he would like, that he receives a raise in salary shortly thereafter, and so on. Now how in God's name, Osmo pondered, could anyone know that, apparently before it had happened? For these were quite recent events, and the book had dust on it. Quickly moving on, Osmo came to this: "Sitting and reading in the coffee shop across from the library, Osmo, perspiring copiously, entirely forgets, until it is too late, that he is supposed to collect his wife at the hairdresser's at four." Oh my god! He had forgotten all about that. Yanking out his watch, Osmo discovered that it was nearly five o'clock—too late. She would be on her way home by now, and in a very sour mood.

Osmo's anguish at this discovery was nothing, though, compared to what the rest of the day held for him. He poured more coffee, and it now occurred to him to check the number of chapters in this amazing book. Only twenty-nine! But surely, he thought, that doesn't mean anything. How anyone could have gotten all this stuff down so far was puzzling enough, to be sure, but no one on God's earth could possibly know in advance how long this or that man is going to live. (Only God could know that sort of thing, Osmo reflected.) So he read along, though not without considerable uneasiness and even depression, for the remaining three chapters were on the whole discouraging. He thought he had gotten that ulcer under control, for example. And he didn't see any reason to suppose his job was going to turn out that badly, or that he was really going to break a leg skiing; after all, he could just give up skiing. But then the book ended on a terribly dismal note. It said: "And Osmo, having taken Northwest flight 569 from O'Hare, perishes when the aircraft crashes on the runway at Fort Wayne, with considerable loss of life, a tragedy rendered the more calamitous by the fact that Osmo had neglected to renew his life insurance before the expiration of the grace period." And that was all. That was the end of the book.

So *that's* why it had only twenty-nine chapters. Some idiot thought he was going to get killed in a plane crash. But, Osmo thought, he just wouldn't get on that plane. And this would also remind him to keep his insurance in force.

(About three years later our hero, having boarded a flight for St. Paul, went berserk when the pilot announced they were going to land at Fort Wayne instead. According to one of the stewardesses, he tried to hijack the aircraft and divert it to another airfield. The Civil Aeronautics Board cited the resulting disruptions as contributing to the crash that followed as the plane tried to land.)

FOUR QUESTIONS

Osmo's extraordinary circumstances led him to embrace the doctrine of fatalism. Not quite completely, perhaps, for there he was, right up to the end, trying vainly to buck his fate—trying, in effect, to make a fool of God, though he did not know this, because he had no idea of the book's source. Still, he had the overwhelming evidence of his whole past life to make him think that everything was going to work out exactly as described in the book. It always had. It was, in fact, precisely this conviction that terrified him so.

But now let us ask these questions, in order to make Osmo's experiences more relevant to our own. First, why did he become, or nearly become, a fatalist? Second, just what did his fatalism amount to? Third, was his belief justified in terms of the evidence he had? And finally, is that belief justified in terms of the evidence *we* have—or in other words, should we be fatalists too?

This last, of course, is the important metaphysical question, but we have to approach it through the others.

Why did Osmo become a fatalist? Osmo became a fatalist because there existed a set of true statements about the details of his life, both past and future, and he came to know what some of these statements were and to believe them, including many concerning his future. That is the whole of it.

No theological ideas entered into his conviction, nor any presuppositions about causal determinism, the coercion of his actions, by causes, or anything of this sort. The foundations of Osmo's fatalism were entirely in logic and epistemology, having only to do with truth and knowledge. Ideas about God did not enter in, for he never suspected that God was the ultimate source of those statements. And at no point did he think God was *making* him do what he did. All he was concerned about was that someone seemed somehow to *know* what he had done and was going to do.

What, then, did Osmo believe? He did not, it should be noted, believe that certain things were going to happen to him, *no matter what*. That does not express a logically coherent belief. He did not think he was in danger of perishing in an airplane crash even in case he did not get into any airplane, for example, or that he was going to break his leg skiing, whether he went skiing or not. No one believes what he considers to be plainly impossible. If anyone believes that a given event is going to happen, he does not doubt that those things necessary for its occurrence are going to happen too. The expression "no matter what", by means of which some philosophers have sought an easy and even childish refutation of fatalism, is accordingly highly inappropriate in any description of the fatalist conviction.

Osmo's fatalism was simply the realization that the things described in the book were unavoidable.

Of course we are all fatalists in this sense about some things, and the metaphysical question is whether this familiar attitude should not be extended to everything. We know the sun will rise tomorrow, for example, and there is nothing we can do about it. Each of us knows he is sooner or later going to die, too, and there is nothing to be done about that either. We normally do not know just when, of course, but it is mercifully so! For otherwise we would simply sit checking off the days as they passed, with growing despair, like a man condemned to the gallows and knowing the hour set for his execution. The tides ebb and flow, and heavens revolve, the seasons follow in order, generations arise and pass, and no one speaks of taking preventive measures. With respect to those things each of us recognizes as beyond his control, we are of necessity fatalists.

The question of fatalism is simply: Of all the things that happen in the world, which, if any, are avoidable? And the philosophical fatalist replies: None of them. They never were. Some of them only seemed so.

Was Osmo's fatalism justified? Of course it was. When he could sit right there and read a true description of those parts of his life that had not yet been lived, it would be idle to suggest to him that his future might, nonetheless, contain alternative possibilities. The only doubts Osmo had were whether those statements could really be true. But here he had the proof of his own experience, as one by one they were tested. Whenever he tried to prevent what was set forth, he of course failed. Such failure, over and over, of even the most herculean efforts, with never a single success, must surely suggest, sooner or later, that he was *destined* to fail. Even to the end, when Osmo tried so desperately to save himself from the destruction described in the book, his effort was totally in vain—as he should have realized it was going to be had he really known that what was said there was true. No power in heaven or earth can render false a statement that is true. It has never been done, and never will be.

Is the doctrine of fatalism, then, true? This amounts to asking whether our circumstances are significantly different from Osmo's. Of course we cannot read our own biographies the way he could. Only men who become famous ever have their lives recorded, and even so, it is always in retrospect. This is unfortunate. It is too bad that someone with sufficient knowledge—God, for example—cannot set down the lives of great men in advance, so that their achievements can be appreciated better by their contemporaries, and indeed, by their predecessors—their parents, for instance. But mortals do not have the requisite knowledge, and if there is any god who does, he seems to keep it to himself.

None of this matters, as far as our own fatalism is concerned. For the important thing to note is that, of the two considerations that explain Osmo's fatalism, only one of them was philosophically relevant, and that one applies to us no less than to him. The two considerations were: (1) there existed a set of true statements about his life, both past and future, and (2) he came to know what those statements were and to believe them. Now the second of these two considerations explains why, as a matter of psychological fact, Osmo became fatalistic, but it has nothing to do with the validity of that point of view. Its validity is assured by (1) alone. It was not the fact that the statements happened to be written down that rendered the things they described unavoidable: that had nothing to do with it at all. Nor was it the fact that, because they had been written, Osmo could read them. His reading them and coming to believe them likewise had nothing to do with the inevitability of what they described. This was ensured simply by there being such a set of statements, whether written or not, whether read by anyone or not, and whether or not known to be true. All that is required is that they should *be* true.

Each of us has but one possible past, described by that totality of statements about us in the past tense, each of which happens to be true. No one ever thinks of rearranging things there; it is simply accepted as given. But so also, each of us has but one possible future, described by that totality of statements about oneself in the future tense, each of which happens to be true. The sum of these constitutes one's biography. Part of it has been lived. The main outlines of it can still be seen, in retrospect, though most of its details are obscure. The other part has not been lived, though it most assuredly is going to be, in exact accordance with that set of statements just referred so. Some of its outlines can already be seen, in prospect, but it is on the whole more obscure than the part belonging to the past. We have at best only premonitory glimpses of it. It is no doubt for this reason that not all of this part, the part that awaits us, is perceived as given, and men do sometimes speak absurdly of altering it—as though what the future holds, as identified by any true statement in the future tense, might after all *not* hold.

Osmo's biography was all expressed in the present tense because all that mattered was that the things referred to were real events; it did not matter to what part of time they belonged. His past consisted of those things that preceded his reading of the book, and he simply accepted it as given. He was not tempted to revise what was said there, for he was sure it was true. But it took the book to make him realize that his future was also something given. It was equally pointless for him to try to revise what was said there, for it, too, was true. As the past contains what has happened, the future contains what will happen, and neither contains, in addition to these things, various other things that did not and will not happen.

Of course we know relatively little of what the future contains. Some things we know. We know the sun will go on rising and setting, for example, that taxes will be levied and wars rage, that men will continue to be callous and greedy, and that people will be murdered and robbed. It is just the details that remain to be discovered. But the same is true of the past; it is only a matter of degree. When I meet a total stranger I do not know, and will probably never know, what his past has been, beyond certain obvious things—that he had a mother, and things of this sort. I know nothing of the particulars of that vast realm of fact that is unique to his past. And the same for his future, with only this difference—that *all* men are strangers to me as far as their futures are concerned, and here I am even a stranger to myself.

Yet there is one thing I know concerning any stranger's past and the past of everything under the sun; namely, that whatever it might hold, there is nothing anyone can do about it now. What has happened cannot be undone. The mere fact that it has happened guarantees this.

And so it is, by the same token, of the future of everything under the sun. Whatever the future might hold, there is nothing anyone can do about it now. What will happen cannot be altered. The mere fact that it is going to happen guarantees this.

THE LAW OF EXCLUDED MIDDLE

The presupposition of fatalism is therefore nothing but the commonest presupposition of all logic and inquiry; namely, that there is such a thing as truth, and that this has nothing at all to do with the passage of time. Nothing *becomes* true or *ceases* to be true; whatever is true at all simply *is* true.

It comes to the same thing, and is perhaps more precise, to say that every meaningful statement, whether about oneself or anything else, is either true or else it is false; that is, its denial is true. There is no middle ground. The principle is thus appropriately called the law of excluded middle. It has nothing to do with what tense a statement happens to express, nor with the question of whether anyone, man or god, happens to know whether it is true or false.

Thus no one knows whether there was an ant on my desk last night, and no one ever will. But we do know that either this statement is true or else its denial is true—there is no third alternative. If we say it *might* be true, we mean only that we do not happen to know. Similarly, no one knows whether or not there is going to be an ant there tonight, but we do know that either it will or else it will not be there.

In a similar way we can distinguish two mutually exclusive but exhaustive classes of statements about any man; namely, the class of all those that are true, and the class of all that are false. There are no others in addition to these. Included in each are statements never asserted or even considered by anyone, but such that, if anyone were to formulate one of them, it would either be a true statement or else a false one.

Consider, then, that class of statements about some particular person—yourself, let us suppose—each of which happens to be true. Their totality constitutes your biography. One combination of such statements describes the time, place, and circumstances of your birth. Another combination describes the time, place, and circumstances of your death. Others describe in detail the rises and falls of your fortunes, your achievements and failures, your joys and sorrows—absolutely everything that is true of you.

Some of these things you have already experienced, others await you. But the entire biography is there. It is not written, and probably never will be; but it is nevertheless there, all of it. If, like Osmo, you had some way of discovering those statements in advance, then like him you could hardly help becoming a fatalist. But foreknowledge of the truth would not create any truth, nor invest your philosophy with truth, nor add anything to the philosophical foundations of the fatalism that would then be so apparent to you. It would only serve to make it apparent.

OBJECTIONS

This thought, and the sense of its force, have tormented and frightened men from antiquity, and thinkers whose pride sometimes exceeds their acumen and their reverence for truth have attempted every means imaginable to demolish it. There are few articles of faith upon which virtually all men can agree, but one of them is certainly the belief in their cherished free will. Any argument in opposition to the doctrine of fate, however feeble, is immediately and uncritically embraced, as though the refutation of fatalism required only the denial of it, supported by reasons that would hardly do credit to a child. It will be worthwhile, therefore, to look briefly at some of the arguments most commonly heard.

1. One can neither foresee the future nor prove that there is any god, or even if there is, that he could know in advance the free actions of men.

   The reply to this is that it is irrelevant. The thesis of fatalism rests on no theory of divination and on no theology. These ideas were introduced only illustratively.

2. True statements are not the causes of anything. Statements only entail; they do not cause, and hence threaten no man's freedom.

But this, too, is irrelevant, for the claim here denied is not one that has been made.

3. The whole argument just conflates fact and necessity into one and the same thing, treating as unavoidable that which is merely true. The fact that a given thing is going to happen implies only that it is *going* to happen, not that it *has* to. Someone might still be able to prevent it—though of course no one will. For example, President Kennedy was murdered. This means it was true that he was going to be murdered. But it does not mean his death at that time and place was unavoidable. Someone *could* have rendered that statement false; though of course no one did.

That is probably the commonest "refutation" of fatalism ever offered. But how strong is the claim that something *can* be done, when in fact it never *has* been done in the whole history of the universe, in spite, sometimes, of the most strenuous efforts? No one has ever rendered false a statement that was true, however hard some men have tried. When an attempt, perhaps a heroic attempt, is made to avoid a given calamity, and the thing in question happens anyway, at just the moment and in just the way it was going to happen, we have reason to doubt that it could have been avoided. And in fact great effort was made to save President Kennedy, for example, from the destruction toward which he was heading on that fatal day, a whole legion of bodyguards having no other mission. And it failed. True, we can say that *if* more strenuous precautions had been taken, the event would not have happened. But to this we must add, *true*, they were not taken, and hence *true* they were not going to be taken—and we have on our hands again a true statement of the kind that no man has ever had the slightest degree of success in rendering false.

4. The fatalist argument just rests on a "confusion of modalities". The fact that something is true entails only that its denial is false, not that its denial is impossible. All that is impossible is that both should be true, or both false. Thus, if the president is going to be murdered, it is certainly false that he is not—but not impossible. What is impossible is that he will be both murdered and spared.

Here again we have only a distracting irrelevancy, similar to the point just made. The fatalist argument has nothing to do with impossibility in those senses familiar to logic. It has to do with unavoidability. It is, in other words, concerned with human abilities. The fact that a statement is true does not, to be sure, entail that it is necessary, nor do all false statements express impossibilities. Nonetheless, no man is able to avoid what is truly described, however contingently, in any statement, nor to bring about what is thus falsely described. Nor can anyone convert the one to the other, making suddenly true that which was false, or vice versa. It has never been done, and it never will be. It would be a conceit indeed for someone now to suggest that he, alone among men, might be able to accomplish that feat. This inability goes far beyond the obvious impossibility of making something both true and false at once. No metaphysics turns on that simple point.

5. Perhaps it would be best, then, to discard the presupposition underlying the whole fatalist philosophy; namely, the idea that statements are true in advance of the things they describe. The future is the realm of possibilities, concerning any of which we should neither say it is true that it will happen, nor that it is false.

But, in reply, this desperate move is nothing but arbitrary fiction, resorted to for no other reason than to be rid of the detested doctrine of fatalism. What is at issue here is the very law of excluded middle, which, it is suggested, we shall be allowed to affirm only up to that point at which it threatens something dear. We shall permit it to hold for one part of time, but suddenly retract it in speaking of another, even though the future is continuously being converted to the past through sheer temporal passage.

Most surely, if the statement, made now, that President Kennedy has been murdered is a true one, then the prediction, made before the event, that he was going to be murdered, was true too. The two statements have exactly the same content, and are in fact one and the same statement, except for the variation of tense. The fact that this statement is more easily known in retrospect than in prospect casts no doubt on its truth, but only illustrates a familiar fact of epistemology. A prediction, to be sure, must await fulfillment, but it does not thereupon for the first time acquire its truth. Indeed, had it not been true from the start, it could not have been fulfilled, nor its author congratulated for having it right. Fulfillment is nothing but the occurrence of what is correctly predicted.

The law of excluded middle is not like a blank check, into which we can write whatever values we please, according to our preferences. We can no more make ourselves metaphysically free and masters of our destinies by adding qualifications to this law than a poor man can make himself rich just by adding figures to his bankbook. That law pronounces every meaningful statement true, or, if not true, then false. It leaves no handy peg between these two on which one may hang his beloved freedom of will for safekeeping, nor does it say anything whatever about time.

Every single philosophical argument against the teaching of fatalism rests upon the assumption that we are free to pursue and realize various alternative future possibilities—the very thing, of course, that is at issue. When some of these possibilities have become realized and moved on into the past, the supposed alternative possibilities usually appear to have been less real than they had seemed; but this somehow does not destroy the fond notion that they were there. Metaphysics and logic are weak indeed in the face of an opinion nourished by invincible pride, and most men would sooner lose their very souls than be divested of that dignity which they imagine rests upon their freedom of will.

INVINCIBLE FATE

We shall say, therefore, of whatever happens, that it was going to be that way. And this is a comfort, both in fortune and in adversity. We shall say of him who turns out bad and mean, that he was going to; of him who turns out happy and blessed, that he was going to; neither praising nor berating fortune, crying over what has been, lamenting what was going to be, or passing moral judgments.

Shall we, then, sit idly by, passively observing the changing scene without participation, never testing our strength and our goodness, having no hand in what happens, or in making things come out as they should? This is a question for which each will find his own answer. Some men do little or nothing with their lives, and might as well never have lived, they make such waste of it. Others do much, and the lives of a few even shine like the stars. But we knew this before we ever began talking about fate. In time we will all know of which sort we were destined to be.

2

FATALISM

Peter van Inwagen

2.1 Fatalism, as I shall use the term, is the thesis that it is a logical or conceptual truth that no one is able to act otherwise than he in fact does; that the very idea of an agent to whom alternative courses of action are open is self-contradictory.[1] The word "fatalism" is used in philosophy in at least two other senses: it is used (i) for the thesis that what is going to happen is *inevitable*, and (ii) for the thesis that no one is able to act otherwise than he in fact does. (This latter thesis is entailed by but does not entail what I am calling fatalism.) So long as it is understood that neither of these theses is what *I* mean by "fatalism", no confusion will result from this plurality of senses. But the idea of the inevitability of what is going to happen is so commonly associated with the word "fatalism" that I feel I should say something about it.

2.2 Suppose a witch predicts that I shall drown within the next twenty-four hours. She also predicts that I shall attempt to evade this fate, and that my efforts will be in vain. Here are two stories about how her prediction might come true.

(a) I determine to spend the next twenty-four hours at the top of a high hill. But as I leave the witch's hovel, I am overpowered by three assailants in the employ of an enemy of mine, who, despite my struggles, carry me to a nearby pond and hold me under water till I am dead.

(b) I determine to spend the next twenty-four hours at the top of a high hill. While climbing the hill, I fall into a hidden well and drown. Moreover, if I had simply gone

---

[1] C. D. Broad was a fatalist by the terms of this definition. The argument of his inaugural lecture, "Determinism, Indeterminism and Libertarianism" (in *Ethics and the History of Philosophy*, New York: 1952), might be summarized as follows: free will is incompatible with both determinism and indeterminism and is therefore impossible (though this bald summary does not do justice to Broad's beautifully finished lecture). In this present chapter we shall be concerned with fatalistic arguments in a narrow sense (I resist the temptation to pun): those arguments that depend on the notions of time and truth. The question of the compatibility of free will with determinism and indeterminism will be considered in chapters III and IV.

about my business and done nothing in particular to avoid drowning, I should not have drowned.

In each of these stories, the witch's prediction, that my efforts to avoid drowning would be in vain, came true. But there is an important difference between them. In story (a), I should have drowned no matter what I had done, and this is not a feature of story (b). And yet story (b) produces—in me at any rate—the sort of feeling one might express by saying, "Yes, that's what inescapable fate means." How is this feeling produced? Let us examine a more artful story of the same kind.

SHEPPY: I wish now I'd gone down to the Isle of Sheppey when the doctor advised it. You wouldn't 'ave thought of looking for me there.

DEATH: There was a merchant in Bagdad who sent his servant to market to buy provisions and in a little while the servant came back, white and trembling, and said, Master, just now when I was in the marketplace I was jostled by a woman in the crowd and when I turned I saw it was death that jostled me. She looked at me and made a threatening gesture; now, lend me your horse, and I will ride away from this city and avoid my fate. I will go to Samarra and there death will not find me. The merchant lent him his horse, and the servant mounted it, and he dug his spurs in its flanks and as fast as the horse could gallop he went. Then the merchant went down to the market-place and he saw me standing in the crowd and he came to me and said, Why did you make a threatening gesture to my servant when you saw him this morning? That was not a threatening gesture, I said, it was only a start of surprise. I was astonished to see him in Bagdad, for I had an appointment with him to-night in Samarra.

SHEPPY: [With a shudder.] D'you mean there's no escaping you?

DEATH: No.[2]

Death seems to imply that she and the merchant's servant would have met that very night, no matter what he had done. But this is false. They would not have met that night if he had remained in Bagdad. (Otherwise, the point of the story is lost.) But then why does Death's story have the effect on us of making her seem inescapable? Well, because her story leads us to believe that whatever one attempts to do to avoid her will be just the wrong thing. In this sense, she is inescapable. But notice that the fact that there's no escaping her depends on our inevitable ignorance of what she has got written down in her little (presumably black) book. Such stories as story

[2]The Collected Plays of W. Somerset Maugham, (London: 1931), 298–9. The quotation is from "Sheppy," Act III.

(b) above and Death's story and the story of Oedipus depend for their effect on the ignorance of their protagonist about the way in which a prediction will come true. Story (a) does not depend on the ignorance of its protagonist. Even if the witch in story (a) had told me exactly how I should be drowned, this would not have enabled me to escape drowning.

Let us introduce some philosophical jargon. Let us say of a certain future event (an event that is in fact going to happen) that it is *strongly inevitable for me* if it would happen no matter what I did.[3] Similarly, a future *state of affairs* is strongly inevitable for me if it would *obtain* no matter what I did. Let us say that a future event, or state of affairs, is *weakly inevitable for me* if both of the following conditions hold: (i) it is not strongly inevitable, and (ii) if I tried to take measures to prevent it, then I should choose the wrong measures out of ignorance, and it is strongly inevitable for me that I should be ignorant of the right measures.

In story (a), my death by drowning at a certain moment was strongly inevitable for me at the time of the witch's prediction. In story (b), my death by drowning at a certain moment was weakly inevitable for me at the time of the witch's prediction, at least assuming that nothing I might have done there-after would have been sufficient for getting a more detailed prediction from the witch. In Death's story, it was weakly inevitable for the servant that he should meet her in Samarra that night, at least assuming that nothing he might have done before arriving in Samarra would have been sufficient for discovering that it was "Samarra" and not "Bagdad" that was written beside his name in her appointment book. (The "effect" of these stories, their "atmosphere" of inescapable fate, is not due solely to the fact that they are stories about men whose death at a certain moment is weakly inevitable. These literary qualities also owe a great deal to the fact that their protagonists' incomplete fore-knowledge has magical or supernatural sources, to the fact that their protagonists

---

[3]There is a problem about defining *no matter what I do* (*he does*, etc.). Suppose you were to say "She would have died no matter what he had done", and a carping critic replied "That's not true! She wouldn't have died if he'd prevented her death, made an effective medicine out of the materials at hand, transported a doctor to her bedside by magic, or if he'd done any of a great variety of things." The obvious way of dealing with this critic is to stipulate that "no matter what one does" means "no matter *which of the things one can do* one does". But if we accept this stipulation, then it will follow from fatalism that the man who delayed seeing a doctor about his cough till it was too late would have died of the disease the cough signaled *no matter what he had done* (since, according to fatalism, what he could have done and what he did coincide). And, in general, if we accepted this stipulation, it would be a consequence of fatalism that all events are strongly inevitable for everyone. That this is a consequence of fatalism is a thesis that one of the most prominent contemporary authorities on fatalism has been at pains to deny. (See Steven Cahn, *Fate, Logic, and Time*, New Haven and London: 1967, ch. 2, *passim*.) It would hardly do, therefore, to make this thesis true by definition. Perhaps the solution to this problem is to stipulate that *no matter what one does* means *no matter what choices or decisions one makes*.

in fact attempt to escape death, and to the fact that the very measures their protagonists take to escape death contribute to their deaths.)

It is obviously possible, magical or supernatural prediction aside, that *some* events be strongly inevitable, and possible that *some* events be weakly inevitable. It is, for example, strongly inevitable for me and for anyone else that the sun rise tomorrow. As to weak inevitability, suppose I am in a burning building—I do not yet realize it is burning, but shall in a moment—from which there are exactly two possible exits. And suppose that all the following propositions are true:

(i) if I do not try to leave the building, I shall be burned to death;
(ii) if I try to leave by the nearer exit, I shall be burned to death;
(iii) if I try to leave by the more remote exit, I shall succeed and save my life;
(iv) I have no reason to think that either exit is more likely to lead to safety than the other, and have no way of finding out if either exit is preferable;
(v) if I believed I were in danger and saw two routes of possible escape, I should always choose the nearer unless I had some good reason to regard the more distant as preferable.

If (i)–(v) are true, then my death by burning is now weakly inevitable for me.

But if it is possible that some events be inevitable, in either sense, for someone, could it be that all events are inevitable, in either sense, for anyone or everyone? Let us first consider weak inevitability. Taken literally, this question must be answered "No": it is certainly not weakly inevitable for me that I shall continue writing for at least the next five minutes, though, unless I am very much mistaken, I *shall* in fact do this. A more interesting question is whether some important subclass of the class of future events is weakly inevitable for everyone. For example, everyone will die at some particular moment; could it be that, for every living person, there is some future moment such that it is weakly inevitable for him that he shall die at that moment?

Let us look carefully at this question. Consider the class of people who will die at noon tomorrow. Many of these people, unfortunately, are in excellent health, and no one could now predict any of the fires, bathing accidents, acts of political terrorism, and so on, that will cause their deaths. But this is not sufficient for the weak inevitability of any of their deaths. It seems enormously likely that at least one of these people is such that *if* now, contrary to fact, he were to come to think that there was good reason to believe he should die tomorrow at noon, then he would *not* die tomorrow at noon. Consider, for example, Mergendus, who will die in a boating accident at noon tomorrow. Suppose, contrary to fact, that you or I were to predict in Mergendus's hearing that he should die at noon tomorrow, and that

Mergendus—he is a superstitious man—took our prediction seriously enough to believe that his life was in danger, and that he had better take care. What would happen? What I should *expect* would happen is that Mergendus would refuse to leave his house tomorrow (much less, go boating) and that, owing to this precaution, he would *not* die at noon tomorrow. But, of course, there is no intrinsic absurdity in supposing that what would happen is that Mergendus would refuse to leave his house tomorrow and would be killed in his own bed by a meteorite at just the moment at which he would have drowned if he had gone boating. In fact, *someone* or other has probably been in just this doubly unfortunate position: even if he had taken steps sufficient to avoid whatever it was that in fact caused his death at a certain moment, he would, none the less, have died at just that same moment because, to speak theromorphically, another death was lying in wait for him.

There seems to be no conceptual absurdity in supposing that this is *always* the case: it is conceptually possible that, for every person, there is a moment such that he will die at that moment and such that his death at that moment is weakly inevitable for him if it is not strongly inevitable. But we cannot take seriously any suggestion that this conceptual possibility is in fact realized. If it were realized, this would either be simply an enormous, meaningless multiple accident, an accident of more than astronomical improbability, or else the result of the manipulations of some cosmic "puppet-master" like Death or Death's employers in Maugham's play. And surely a belief in a personified Death or Fate, or whatever one might want to call a cosmic puppet-master, is a belief for which "superstition" is, if anything, too flattering a word.[4]

Let us turn now to strong inevitability. Is there any reason to think that all future events, or some important and interesting class of future events, are strongly inevitable for us? To believe this is to believe that the future would be the way it is in fact going to be, even if we should choose to behave differently and no matter *how* we should choose to behave. To affirm this thesis is simply to deny the reality of cause and effect. Thus baldly stated, the thesis that all future events (or all those of some important kind) are strongly inevitable has nothing whatever to recommend it. It is therefore not surprising that there exist philosophical arguments for it. I offer the reader two. One is a chestnut, and one is, as the White Knight would say, my own invention. It may be regarded as a generalization of the first.

It's no good summoning a physician if you are ill, for a physician can't help you. For either you're going to recover or you aren't. If you aren't going to recover, the

[4]To believe that God plays the role of a cosmic puppet-master would be to have a superstitious belief about God.

physician can't help you. If you are going to recover, the physician can't help you, since you don't need help.[5]

Let E be any event that might happen. Consider the theorem of logic "$(q \supset p) \vee (r \supset {\sim} p)$". In virtue of this theorem, one or the other of the following two propositions must be true:

If I try, by any means whatever, to prevent E, E will happen;

If I try, by any means whatever, to bring about E, E will not happen.

Therefore, either E or the non-occurrence of E is strongly inevitable for me.

Each of these arguments is sheerest sophistry. (I leave them to the reader to expose.) And, so far as I know, there is no reason for thinking that all events, or all events of some important kind, are strongly inevitable always and for everyone, other than the reasons, such as they are, that are supplied by sophistical arguments like these.

We may summarize our conclusions about the "inevitability of what is going to happen" as follows. If one's belief that what is going to happen is inevitable is a belief in the *weak* inevitability of all, or all of some important class of, future events, then one's belief is a belief in an accidental, meaningless, and staggeringly improbable aggregation of circumstances, or else mere superstition. If one's belief is a belief in the *strong* inevitability of all, or all of some important class of, future events, then one's belief, if it is founded upon anything at all, is founded upon sophistry.

2.3 Let us now turn to fatalism proper. The fatalist is not an "inevitabilist", strong or weak. The strong inevitabilist affirms the counter-factual conditional

If Caesar had taken ship for Spain on March 14, Caesar would have been murdered on March 15

but neither the fatalist nor the weak inevitabilist affirms this proposition. (Perhaps they don't *deny* it either; after all, for all anyone knows, if Caesar had suddenly decided to leave for Spain on March 14, a storm would have forced his ship back to port, and the assassination would have gone through as planned. But the fatalist and the weak inevitabilist see no particular *reason* to affirm this proposition.) The weak inevitabilist affirms the counter-factual conditional

If Caesar had taken seriously the soothsayer's warning, Caesar would have been murdered on March 15 and the fatalist does not affirm this proposition, though perhaps he doesn't *deny* it; he simply sees no particular reason to think it's true. What the fatalist does believe is that, since Caesar *didn't* take ship for Spain on March 14, he *couldn't* have done this. And since Caesar didn't in fact take the sooth-sayer's warning seriously, he *couldn't* have. And, of course, he believes this not because he thinks he knows some special facts about Caesar, but as an instance of a general thesis: it is a logical or conceptual truth that if an agent in fact does some particular thing, then that thing is the *only* thing the agent is able to do. And, as regards the future, the fatalist believes that if an agent is in fact going to do some particular thing, then that thing is the only thing he can do, the only thing it is open to him to do.

Now if there is any good reason to think that fatalism is true, it is a very important thesis. It seems to be a feature of our concept of moral responsibility that we hold a person morally responsible for the way he has acted only if we believe he could have acted otherwise. And it seems to be a feature of our concept of deliberation that we can deliberate about which of various mutually exclusive courses of action to pursue only if we believe that each of these courses of action is open to us. Therefore, anyone who accepts fatalism must regard all ascriptions of moral responsibility as incorrect, and must, on pain of self-contradiction, refrain from deliberating about future courses of action.[6] But deliberation and the ascription of moral responsibility are extremely important; in fact it is hard to imagine what human life would be like without them. But these very facts that show that fatalism is extremely important if there is any reason to think it true, also seem to show that there could not be any reason to think it true. If fatalism is true, then the ideas expressed by sentences like "he alone is to blame for the accident" and "I am trying to decide whether to have my father declared mentally incompetent" are conceptually defective. The former is, if fatalism is true, a straightforward conceptual falsehood, like "he alone has trisected the angle". The second, while it could be used to express a truth even if fatalism were true, would be like "I am trying to devise a method for trisecting the angle": these sentences could be used to express a truth only by one who *believed* a conceptual falsehood.

I think it is incoherent to suppose that any thesis could be true that has the consequence of rendering conceptually defective sentences so utterly *basic* to human life as the sentences about blame and deliberation mentioned above. But I shall not argue for this thesis. It could not, I think, be adequately argued for in print: philosophers who disagree about such deep matters as these can hope to resolve their disagreement, if at all, only in conversation. In any case, this is not a book of

---

[6]For a detailed treatment of these issues, see Chapter V.

metaphilosophy but of metaphysics. In such a book as this, the wisest course is to look at various arguments for fatalism and see what can be made of them. It will probably not surprise the reader to discover that I think that the arguments we shall examine are houses built upon sand. But I shall not claim to show that fatalism is false, since, for all I shall show, there may be arguments for fatalism that are not open to the objections I shall raise. Unless I am mistaken, however, most arguments for fatalism depend upon premises that are among or are variants on the premises of the two arguments I shall discuss.[7] Therefore, what I shall say will be directly relevant to, if it does not actually refute, just about any argument for fatalism.

I shall not examine directly the classical sources of fatalism. The meaning of Aristotle's famous passage (*De Interpretatione*, IX) is in dispute; the very structure of the Master Argument of Diodorus is a matter of scholarly conjecture. I, who am no historian, do not propose to undertake an investigation of what these philosophers may have meant. If any of the blunders I shall doubtless make in the sequel could have been avoided by more careful attention to Aristotle, Cicero, Epictetus, or their modern commentators, I expect someone will be good enough to point this out.

2.4 Fatalistic arguments typically depend on the notions of truth and falsity. But what are truth and falsity? Truth and falsity are properties. But properties of what? They are properties of propositions. I do not mean anything mysterious by "proposition". I use this word as a general term for the things people *assent to, reject, find doubtful, accept for the sake of argument, attempt to verify, deduce things from*, and so on.[8] (Some of the phrases in this list take more than one sort of object. One may, for example, reject not only propositions but bribes. I hope no one is going to be difficult about this.) We have plenty of "specialized" words for propositions in the language of everyday life, just as we have plenty of specialized words for human beings. On various occasions we call propositions "doctrines", "theses", "theories", "premises", "conclusions", "theorems", "views", "positions", "conjectures", "statements", "hypotheses", "dogmas", "beliefs", and "heresies", just as, on various occasions we

---

[7]The one exception I know of is "Time, Truth, and Modalities" by "Diodorus Cronus" (Steven Cahn and Richard Taylor), *Analysis* (1965).

[8]This is true in the same sense as that in which it is true that I use "cardinal number" as a general term for the things people count with. But, of course, most numbers are too large for us to count with, and—in my view—most propositions are too complex for us to entertain. It would be more accurate, therefore, to say that I use *proposition* as a term for a certain class of objects, some of the simpler members of which are the things people *assent to*, etc. If anyone finds the "further" or "unentertainable" propositions mysterious, I ask him to lay aside his objections for the moment. Unentertainable propositions will play no role in the argument of the present chapter, though they will figure in our attempts to define determinism in Chapter III

call human beings "women", "babies", "thieves", "Trotskyites", "Australians", and "Catholics".

It is thus uncontroversial that there are propositions. The only question that could arise is: "What *are* propositions?" Many philosophers apparently think propositions are sentences, since they think sentences are what are true or false. But I can make no sense of the suggestion that propositions are sentences, and I shall not discuss it further. It is true that I am willing on occasion to speak of sentences being true or false, but this is only shorthand. When I say that a given sentence is *true*, I mean that the proposition—a non-sentence—that that sentence expresses is true. (To say that an English sentence *expresses* a given proposition is to say, roughly, that the result of concatenating "the proposition that" and that sentence *denotes* that proposition.) Similarly, when I say that a name is *honorable*, I mean that the individual or family that bears that name is honorable. I can no more understand the suggestion that a sentence might be true otherwise than in virtue of its expressing a true proposition than I can understand the suggestion that a name might be honorable otherwise than in virtue of its being borne by an honorable individual or family.

There are philosophers who will demand at this point that I state a "principle of identity" for propositions. I will not do this. When one attempts to give a general way of determining whether two predicates applying to propositions are coextensive, a number of vexed questions arise. What I want to say about fatalism can be said without answering most of them. But there is one sort of question about propositional identity that we must be able to answer. We might call questions of this sort, "questions about propositions expressed by sentences containing indexical expressions". Suppose a madman says, "I am Napoleon", and that a second madman, perhaps at another time and in another place, speaks these same words. Do these madmen assert or express the same thing?—what we might call the "proposition that one is Napoleon". Or, again, suppose that at a certain moment I believe I am about to die and that at another moment, years later, I believe I am about to die. Do I believe the same thing to be true on these two occasions ("the proposition that one is about to die"), or two different things?

It seems to me that only one answer is possible: the madmen say, and I believe, different things.[9] Take the former case. Suppose, to simplify the argument, that one

---

[9]For the sake of convenience, I shall frequently use "believe" and "say" transitively when talking about the relations people bear to propositions, despite the fact that sentences of the form "S says p" and "S believes p" are usually too odd-sounding for me to feel at all comfortable about them, except for the case in which "p" is replaced by certain "wh"-nominalizations. For example, we certainly can't say "John said Newtons's First Law of Motion" and *my* ear doesn't much care for "John believes Newtons's First Law of Motion"—but "John believes Newton postulated about motion" is perfectly all right.

of the madmen *was* Napoleon. Then what one said was true and what the other said was false, and, therefore, by the non-identity of discernibles, what one said was not what the other said. (If we had supposed neither of the madmen to be Napoleon, then what each said would have been false; but this would not have changed matters essentially, since they would none the less have been in *disagreement* about the identity of Napoleon, and therefore saying distinct things.) More or less the same argument can be given in respect of the two occasions on which I believe I am about to die: there are possible circumstances in which what I believe on the earlier occasion is false and what I believe on the later occasion is true. But there are no possible circumstances in which some one thing is both true and false. Of course someone might say that what I believed on the earlier occasion was *then* false but later *became* true. But if that were right, I could say on the later occasion, "When I thought I was about to die twenty years ago I was *then* wrong. But, what I then believed has now become true. When I look at my diary of twenty years ago and see the words "I am about to die," I am comforted in my present affliction by the thought that what I wrote has become true and that, in consequence, nothing said in my diary is *now* false." And this would be an absurd thing to say.

So the two madmen said, and I believed, two different things. That is, in each of our two cases, two numerically distinct propositions are involved. To take a more extreme example, if someone asks me how I feel and I say, "I am tired," and, five seconds later I am again asked how I feel and again say, "I am tired," then I assert or express two distinct propositions: at a certain moment, I express the proposition that I am then tired; five seconds later, I express a distinct proposition, the proposition that I am *then* tired.[10]

This is a very sketchy account of "propositions", but perhaps it will do for our purposes. Truth and falsity are, as we said earlier, properties of propositions. There are, of course, many other properties whose extensions comprise propositions. Propositions, in addition to being true or false, may be empirically verifiable, hard to understand, inexpressible in the tongue of a certain tribe, and so on. But I take it that each of us knows *what* properties truth and falsity are. Any one sufficiently pervicacious to claim *not* to know, may perhaps be helped by two famous passages from Aristotle's *Metaphysics* (Ross's translation):[11]

---

[10]Thus, sentences containing indexical terms can, strictly speaking, be said to express propositions only in or relative to a situation or a "context of utterance", just as denoting phases containing indexicals can be said denote objects only in or relative to a situation or context of utterance. We may therefore say that a sentence containing indexical terms expresses a given proposition in a given context of utterance, provided that the result of concatenating "the proposition that" and that sentence denotes that propositions in that context of utterance.

[11]We: shall return to the topic of truth and falsity in sec. 2.7.

To say of what is that it is not, or of what is not that it is, is false, while to say of what is that it is, and of what is not that it is not, is true ... (Γ , 1011ᵇ.)

It is not because we think truly that you are white that you *are* white but because you are white that we who say this have the truth. (Θ , 105lᵇ.)

Let us now turn to an argument for fatalism.

2.5 The argument we shall now consider turns on the notion of an agent's "ability to render a proposition false". Let us suppose that we have a sufficient intuitive grasp of the schema "*s* can render *p* false" to go on with.

Let us consider some proposition about the future—say the proposition that I shall shave tomorrow morning. This proposition—call it "S", for short—is true if and only if I shall shave during the morning of June 4, 1976. Since I shall shave during this period (I *might* be wrong about this; but then I *might* be wrong about almost anything), S is true. That is, S is true *now*. But it would seem that if a proposition is true at some particular moment then it must be true at every moment. If this were not the case, then the following would be part of a conceivable "history" of S: S was false all through April 1902, but early in May it became true and remained true till Good Friday 1936, after which it was false until V-E day . . .. But this sort of history is not conceivable, and, hence, if S is true, S is unchangeably true. We might put the matter this way: there are possible worlds in which S is always true and possible worlds in which S is always false; but there are no possible worlds in which S is at one time true and at another false. But if S is unchangeably true, then I cannot render S false, for the same reason that, if a certain king is unchangeably powerful, then I cannot render him helpless. But if I cannot render S false, then I cannot refrain from shaving tomorrow morning; for if I could refrain from shaving tomorrow morning, then I could render S false.

Now this argument is sound only if a certain factual claim I have made—that I shall shave tomorrow morning—is true.[12] But even if I am mistaken in thinking I shall shave tomorrow morning, then, though the argument we have been considering is not sound, an essentially identical argument for the conclusion that I cannot shave tomorrow morning *is* sound. Thus, either I cannot refrain from shaving tomorrow morning or else I cannot shave tomorrow morning: my belief that, of two incompatible courses of action, shaving and not shaving, both are open to me, is shown to be false.

---

[12]I use "sound" and "valid" in what have become their usual technical senses: a valid argument is an argument whose conclusion follows from its premisses; a sound argument is valid argument with true premisses.

This reasoning can, of course, be generalized. If it is correct, then for every true proposition about the future there is a similar argument, also sound, for the conclusion that I cannot (nor can anyone else) render that proposition false. That is to say, if anyone is in fact going to act in a certain way then just *that* way is the only way he *can* act. Or, to put our conclusion another way, fatalism is true.

Various philosophers have found this way of arguing compelling. Such philosophers do not usually, at least in modern times, become fatalists. But they do think that this way of arguing forces us to choose between fatalism and some almost equally unattractive alternative, such as the recognition of some third truth-value in addition to truth and falsity. I cannot myself say whether this is the case, for the above paragraphs contain phrases I do not understand.[13] Among them are: "true at some particular moment", "true at every moment", "became true", "remained true", "is unchangeably true", and so on. That is—and we must be very careful about this—I do not see what these phrases mean if they are used as they are used in the above argument for fatalism. If I were to say, "Municipal bonds are a good investment," and someone replied, "That used to be true but it isn't true any more," his words would be a model of lucidity. But if someone were to speak to me as follows:

> Consider the proposition that municipal bonds are a good investment. *This very proposition* used to be true but is no longer true

then I should have grave problems in understanding what he meant. Let us pretend that "T" denotes in our dialect, yours and mine, the moment at which my imagined respondent spoke. When he spoke the words "the proposition that municipal bonds are a good investment," he referred to a proposition that is true if and only if municipal bonds were a good investment at T. (I do not say the proposition he referred to *is* the proposition that municipal bonds were a good investment at T; whether this is the case is one of the questions about identifying propositions that I don't have to answer.) If he had spoken these same words one day earlier, he would have referred to a proposition that is true if and only if municipal bonds were a good investment one day earlier than T. What could he mean by saying of such a proposition that it "was once" true but "is no longer" true? My understanding of the ordinary use of "was once true" and "is no longer true" is of no help to me. Normally, if I utter a certain sentence and am told, "That was once true",[14] my respondent means

---

[13]The remainder of this section owes a great deal to A J Ayer's essay "Fatalism," in *The Concept of a Person* (London: 1963).

[14]I take it that when someone speaks these words, he uses the demonstrative pronoun to refer to the proposition expressed by the sentence the person he is speaking with has uttered, and

something like: "If you had used those same words on a certain *earlier* occasion, then you *would have* said something true" or "The words you have spoken *used* to express a true proposition."

If anyone thinks this an ad hoc description of what "was once true" means, let him consider the following case, which raises exactly analogous difficulties. Suppose I say, "The number of committee members is odd, so the vote won't be a tie," and you, who know of a change in the structure of the committee reply, "It used to be odd, but it isn't any more." You are *not* saying that there is a certain number—twelve, say—that used to be odd but isn't nowadays; rather, you are saying *something* like this: the phrase "the number of committee members" *used* to denote an odd number, but now it denotes a different number, one that isn't odd. I think that most philosophers will agree that we are on the right track in the "used to be odd" case; I think we are also on the right track in the "used to be true" case.

In any event, the analogy between the two cases is instructive. Suppose someone were to say, "There is a number that used to be odd," and I replied, as indeed I should, that I didn't understand what he meant. My failure to understand him might or might not be justified, but, however this might be, clearly I should not be helped toward understanding him by an explanation like this one: "Look, you understand what I mean if I say that the number of committee members used to be odd. But the number of committee members is a number; therefore you understand what it means to say there is a number that used to be odd." Similarly, my difficulties about sentences like "There is a proposition that used to be true" are not going to be cleared up by explanations like: "The proposition that municipal bonds are a good investment used to be true. So it is clear what it means to say that there is a proposition that used to be true."

I have argued that, when, in ordinary speech, we appear to say of a certain proposition that it used to be true, we are in fact saying of a certain propositional name that it used to denote, or of a certain sentence that it used to express, a proposition that is true, just as when we appear to say of a certain number that it used to be odd, we are in fact saying of a certain descriptive phrase that it used to denote a number that is odd. If I am right, then our ordinary use of "used to be true" and similar phrases (of which a parallel account could be given) will not enable us to

---

not to the sentence uttered. To deny this would be like saying that in the following fragment of conversation,

"How many have you invited to the wedding?"
"Four hundred."
"That's too many.",

the demonstrative pronoun refers not to the number four hundred but to the *words* "four hundred".

understand the use made of such phrases in the argument for fatalism that we are considering.

What I have done so far is to argue that temporal qualification of a copula connecting "true" or "false" and a name of a proposition cannot be explained in a certain way, namely, by reference to *apparent* instances of it in ordinary speech. But it may very well be that there is some other way to make sense of such qualification. To make sense of this idea, it would be sufficient to make sense of the open sentence:

(The proposition) x is true at (the moment) t,

since all the other locutions involving temporal qualification of the possession of truth by a proposition that are required by the fatalistic argument we are examining can be defined in terms of this sentence.

I know of only one explanatory paraphrase of this open sentence that is worthy of serious consideration.[15] It is this:

If someone were to assert x and nothing else at t, then what he asserted at t would be true.

Thus, for example, according to the proponents of this explanation, the sentence

The proposition that Queen Victoria died in 1901 was true in 1878

expresses a truth, since, if anyone had said in 1878, "Queen Victoria will die in 1901"—which are words that were suitable in 1878 for asserting the proposition we *now* call "the proposition that Queen Victoria died in 1901"—he would have been right. (This sort of device can be applied in all manner of cases. For example, someone could say, "The number twelve is even in Tibet," and explain

---

[15]This paraphrase, I believe, captures Aristotle's view of truth-at-a-time. At any rate it is suggested by the language he uses in *De Interpretatione*, IX, particularly at 18b. A typical and especially suggestive passage is "... if a thing is white now, it was true before to say that it would be white, so that of anything that has taken place it was always true to say 'it is' or 'it will be'."(W. D. Ross (ed.), *The Works of Aristotle Translated into English*, vol. I (Oxford: 1928), tr. E. M. Edghill.) About twenty lines later, in discussing the alleged necessity of the events referred to in a correct prediction, he says, "... a man may predict an event... and another predict the reverse; that which was truly predicted at the moment in the past will of necessity take place in the fullness of time. Further, it makes no difference whether people have or have not actually made the contradictory statements...". Steven Cahn employs essentially this Aristotelian conception of truth-at-a-time. See his *Fate, Logic, and Time* (cited in note 3), 33 note 15.

these strange words as just another way of saying, "If someone were to refer to the number twelve in Tibet, he would be referring to something even.") Now I do not think that what we have been offered is a good *explanation* of the meaning of "*x* is true at *t*" since I don't think this sentence means anything—just as I don't think "The number twelve is even in Tibet" means anything—and thus I don't think that *anything* is or could be an explanation, good or bad, of its meaning. But perhaps this is not terribly important, since we can always regard what we have been offered as a stipulative definition: it is, after all, a sentence containing the proper variables free, and that is the only formal requirement on the *definiens* of a stipulative definition. That is to say, we may regard "*x* is true at *t*" as simply a convenient abbreviation, without antecedent meaning, for what has mistakenly been offered as an analysis or explanation of "*x* is true at *t*".[16] We now have a way of interpreting (apparent) temporal qualifications of the ascription of truth-values to propositions. Let us return to our argument for fatalism and see whether its premises appear plausible when the temporal qualifications they contain are interpreted in this way.

The crucial premise in this argument seems to be the proposition that S is unchangeably true. The sentence "S is unchangeably true" can, I think, be paraphrased in terms of our "basic" locution "*x* is true at *t*" in this way (by analogy to, e.g., "God is unchangeably powerful"):

$$(\exists x) \,(\text{S is true at } x) \,\,\& \sim \Diamond (\exists x)(\exists y) \,(\text{S is true at } x \,\&\sim \text{S is true at } y)$$

where " $\Diamond$ " abbreviates "it is possible that". Expanding the second conjunct of this sentence in terms of our stipulative definition of "*x* is true at *t*", we obtain:

(a) $\sim \Diamond (\exists x)(\exists y)$ (If someone were to assert S at *x*, then what he asserted at *x* would be true & $\sim$ If someone were to assert S at *y*, then what he asserted at *y* would be true).

Now this sentence seems to express a truth: consider the conjunctive open sentence got by dropping " $\sim \Diamond (\exists x)(\exists y)$ " from it; there is no possible world in which there exists a pair of moments of time that satisfies this open sentence. Have we

---

[16]This definition faces a great many purely technical difficulties. Suppose, for example, that no propositions were asserted in 10,000,000 BC or earlier. Then, it would seem, it was in 10,000,000 BC that no propositions had yet been asserted; or, at least, this would seem to be the right thing to say if the temporal qualification of the possession of truth makes sense. But, of course, if anyone had asserted this proposition in 10,000,000 BC he would have said something false.

then proved fatalism? Not unless we can deduce "I cannot render S false" from "S is unchangeably true". Why should anyone accept this consequence? Earlier I wrote:

> But if S is unchangeably true, then I cannot render S false, for the same reason that, if a certain king is unchangeably powerful, then I cannot render him helpless,

and this appears to be a conclusive argument. But does the analogy really hold? When we say, "Edward III was powerful in 1346," our use of the adverbial phrase "in 1346" is transparent; it does not need to be *given* a meaning. But when we say, "S was true in 1346," the phrase "in 1346" is not transparent; it needs to be given a meaning. Well, we gave it a meaning in the only way in which anything can be given a meaning: by stipulation. Having done this, we proceeded to define "S is unchangeably true" in such a way that this phrase would have the same logical properties as "Edward is unchangeably powerful", *provided* "S is true at *t*" had the same logical properties as "Edward is powerful at *t*". Do they have the same logical properties? The answer to this question is not obvious. After all, the logical properties of, for example, "Edward III was powerful in 1346" are determined by the rules, embedded in our linguistic practice, for the use of the words it contains, and this is not the case with "S was true in 1346": *its* logical properties are determined by the rules for the use of the words contained in its stipulated *definiens*. Perhaps the wisest course we could take would be to refrain from framing our questions in terms of the stipulatively defined sentence "S is unchangeably true" and, instead, frame them in terms of the *definiens* we have provided for this sentence. That is, instead of asking whether "I cannot render S false" follows from "S is unchangeably true", let us ask whether it follows from the conjunction of

$(\exists x)$ (if someone were to assert S at x, then what he asserted at *x* would be true)

with proposition (a). Informally, suppose S has these two features: (i) there is a time such that if anyone were to assert S at that time, his assertion would be true, and (ii) there *could not be* a pair of times such that, if someone were to assert S at one of these times, he would say something true, *and* if someone were to assert S at the other of these times, he would say something false. Does it follow from this supposition that I cannot render S false? Well, perhaps it does; but I don't see any reason to think so. Suppose someone said yesterday (Thursday) that I should shave on Saturday morning, and that what he said on Thursday is true. It is, of course, quite impossible for this to be the case *and* for it to be the case that he should say tonight, "You are going to shave tomorrow morning," and be wrong. Moreover, it is simply not possible that he should have said on Thursday "You are going to shave on Saturday" *and* have

been right *and* it be the case that I shall not shave on Saturday. But, I thin͟
ing of interest about my free will with respect to shaving on Saturday foll͟
argument-form

p S is true
$\sim\Diamond(p \& q)$ It's not possible that (s is true and ~s is ~true)
hence, $\sim\Diamond q$ It's not possible that (~s is true)

is notoriously fallacious. But perhaps clever fatalists do not rely on this fallacious form of reasoning. The clever fatalist may claim to reason as follows:

> Look, you admit that S was true yesterday. But it's not *now* up to you what was the case yesterday: it is not within your power to change the fact that S was true yesterday. And it is a logical consequence of S's having been true yesterday that you will shave tomorrow. Therefore, it is not within your power to change the fact that you will shave tomorrow. If I am making use of any "modal" argument-form, it is this:
>
> $\sim Pp$
>
> the fact that q is a logical consequence of the fact that p
>
> hence, $\sim Pq$,
>
> where "P" abbreviates "it is within one's power to change the fact that".[17]

I am not convinced by this argument. Its proponent says, "But it's not now up to you what was the case yesterday," and this has the ring of an extremely plausible assertion. If the adverb "yesterday" that occurs in "It's not now up to you what was the case yesterday" has its usual sense, then it can hardly be denied that this sentence expresses a truth. But if the argument we are considering is to avoid the fallacy of equivocation, then "yesterday" must be used in the same sense in the argument's first and second sentences. And if its first sentence is to make sense, then "yesterday" must have in that sentence a sense of the sort we have stipulated for temporal adverbs that qualify copulae flanked by "true" or "false" and propositional names, or some other purely stipulative sense. I shall ignore this second possibility, since I do not know what other sense might be given to these adverbs. Therefore, in evaluating this argument we must interpret

It's not *now* up to you what was the case yesterday

---

[17]This argument-form is essentially the principle that will be called "Rule (β)" in the parts of this book that deal with free will and determinism. I have no wish to dispute the validity of this argument-form, for the validity of (β) comes very close to being the single premise upon which the argument of this book is based.

in accordance with our stipulation. And I see no reason to think that this sentence, so interpreted, expresses a truth. In particular, I see no reason to assent to

If S was true yesterday, then it's not now up to me whether S was true yesterday,

though I see every reason to assent to, for example,

If S was believed yesterday, then it's not now up to me whether S was believed yesterday.

In the second of these sentences, "yesterday" has the sense it has in everyday usage; in the first it has a peculiar sense stipulated by the fatalist, just as "in Tibet" has a special sense in "The number twelve is even in Tibet" if this peculiar sentence is interpreted as was suggested earlier.

If we expand the first of these sentences in accordance with our stipulation, we obtain:

If (if someone had asserted S yesterday, then he would have asserted something true), then it's not now up to me whether it is the case that (if someone had asserted S yesterday, then he would have asserted something true).

Now I think the antecedent of this conditional is true. But I see no reason to think that its consequent isn't false. That is, I see no reason to think that the truth-value of

If someone had asserted S yesterday, then he would have asserted something true

isn't now up to me, for it is up to me just in the case that I can shave tomorrow and can refrain from shaving tomorrow. And I see no reason to doubt that both these things are within my power. Moreover, even if I am wrong about this and I am either unable to shave or unable to refrain from shaving, I do not see that the fatalist has ever suggested any *logical* or *conceptual* reason why this might be so. Someone might, I suppose, offer the following argument: "If S was true yesterday and if you have it within your power to render S false, then you have the power to make it the case that S was at one time true and at another time false, which is impossible." But such a consequence doesn't follow. What follows is that it is within my power to make it the case that S was always false. When I say this, I am talking the fatalist's language. If it sounds strange to say that I now have it within my power to make it the case that a certain true proposition was always false, that is the fatalist's fault. It is he, after all, who has invented a strange sense for the word "always", a sense such that, using the word in that sense, I can truly describe my ability to refrain from shaving tomorrow morning as an ability to make it the case that the true proposition S "was always" false.

I realize that neither the fatalist nor the philosopher who feels drawn to fatalism is likely to be convinced by these arguments. Richard Taylor has responded to them in conversation along these lines: "You say you have the ability to render false the proposition that you will shave tomorrow—that is, to make it the case that this proposition has always been false—even though this proposition is in fact true. And you say there are ever so many true propositions about the future that you have this sort of power over. Very well then, let us see you exercise this power that you claim: pick any true proposition about the future, and then so act that this proposition has always been false." But this is an illegitimate demand. I claim to have a certain power and the description I give of this power depends for its application on this power's not being exercised. (The description is "the power to render certain always true propositions always false".) What Taylor demands is that I show that I have such a power by exercising it. If this sort of demand were legitimate, fatalism could be established very easily. Fatalism may be looked upon as the doctrine that the only powers one has are—of logical necessity—powers that one in fact exercises. Suppose I say that fatalism is false since I have powers I never in fact exercise, and the fatalist replies, "Very well then, if you have such powers, *let's see you exercise one.*" This is not perhaps a very convincing argument. In fact, it depends on the same fallacy as an infamous sophistical demand sometimes made by not very able Berkeleians: "You say that objects continue to exist while they're not being observed; very well then, *let's see one.*"

To recapitulate: Either the use that the fatalist makes of "temporal" qualifications of the possession of truth and falsity by a proposition is meaningless, or else this use must be explained by a stipulation like the one I have suggested. If it is explained by such a stipulation, then sentences like "Every proposition is, if true, unchangeably true" express, in *his* usage, truths. (And there is no other usage in which they express anything.) But the proposition expressed by this sentence is quite consistent with its being the case that there are many true propositions about, for example, what will happen tomorrow that I have it within my power to render false. Or, at least, I have never seen any compelling argument for the conclusion that this is not the case.

2.6 Richard Taylor has offered a puzzling and ingenious argument for fatalism.[18] His argument may be put as follows:

Suppose I am a naval commander who is deliberating about whether to issue order O or to refrain from issuing order O. Suppose that, under the conditions that in fact prevail, my issuing O would result in there being a naval battle tomorrow,

---

[18]*Metaphysics* (Englewood Cliffs, NJ: 1963), ch. 5.

while my refraining from issuing O would result in there being *no* naval battle tomorrow.

We shall show that either it is not within my power to issue O, or else it is not within my power to refrain from issuing O.

(i) Suppose no naval battle will occur tomorrow. Then a condition necessary for my issuing O is absent, namely, a naval battle tomorrow. For, since my issuing O is a condition *sufficient* for there being a naval battle tomorrow, then a naval battle tomorrow is a condition *necessary* for my issuing O. If someone feels it is odd to talk of my *now* doing something "in the absence of", for example, a naval battle *tomorrow*, we may agree with him. Let us say that our use of "in the absence of" is an *extension* of normal English usage. We may in our present usage say I am now writing *in the absence of* an earthquake in London tomorrow, provided there will be no earthquake in London tomorrow. As regards the past, we may say I am now writing *in the absence of* a German invasion of the British Isles in 1940. While there is an element of artificiality in this way of speaking, the truth-conditions for assertions that involve it are none the less intelligible enough. The first of our illustrative sentences expresses just the same proposition as, or a proposition necessarily equivalent to, that expressed by

I am now writing and there will be no earthquake in London tomorrow.

The second illustrative sentence expresses the same proposition as, or a proposition necessarily equivalent to, that expressed by

I am now writing and the Germans did not invade the British Isles in 1940.

Now consider the following principle:

(A)   No agent is able to perform an act in the absence of a condition necessary for its accomplishment.

Taylor says of this principle, "This is no law of logic, and in fact cannot be expressed even in the contemporary modal logics, but it is nonetheless manifestly true" (p. 58). It follows from (A) and from what we have already established—that a condition necessary for my issuing O is absent—that I cannot issue O.

(ii) Suppose a naval battle will occur tomorrow. Then a condition necessary for my refraining from issuing O is absent: namely, the non-occurrence of a naval battle tomorrow. But then, by principle (A), I cannot refrain from issuing O.

Therefore, either I cannot issue O or else I cannot refrain from issuing O. That is to say, it is not up to me whether I issue O. This argument, of course, can be generalized. If it is sound, then, for any case of an agent who is deliberating about which of various courses of action to pursue, we can show by a similar argument that at most *one* of these courses of action is open to him; that at most one is such that he can pursue it; that it is not up to him which if any of these courses he shall pursue.

The crucial premise in Taylor's argument is Principle (A). If we accept this principle, then we can derive fatalism by a much simpler argument than Taylor's. For it is obvious that whenever I am *not* performing a certain act, then there is absent a condition necessary for my performing it: namely, my performing it.[19] And, of course, whenever I am performing a certain act, there is absent a certain condition necessary for my *not* performing it: my not performing it.[20] Thus, Principle (A) leads *directly* to the collapse of the distinction between what one does and what one can do: one who accepts Principle (A) has already got fatalism in his pocket and need not shop for it in Taylor's elaborate naval bazaar, diverting though the wares offered there may be.

Is Principle (A) true? The question is complex, for Principle (A) is ambiguous. We shall see that there are two ways it might be interpreted. Interpreted in one of these ways, it is obviously true but does not yield Taylor's conclusion; interpreted in the other way, it indeed yields Taylor's conclusion, though there is no reason to think it is true.

Let us call an *ability-sentence* a complete, grammatical, declarative sentence that consists of a subject term that denotes or purports to denote a person (I; "Richard Taylor"), followed by an "ability-copula" such as "can", "am able to", or "has it within his power to", followed by any string of words.

---

[19] Note that this point does not depend on our artificially extended sense of *in the absence of*. It therefore seems unlikely that Taylor's argument is defective owing to some incoherency in the notion of one's performing an act "in the absence of" conditions that, if they obtained, would obtain at times different from the time at which one performs the act.

[20] Taylor has told me that he intended Principle (A) to apply only in the case of conditions causally but not logically necessary for one's acts. But what is the point of this restriction? Surely if it's plausible to suppose that I can't do a thing in the absence of a condition causally necessary for my doing it, then it's even more plausible to suppose that I can't do a thing in the absence of a condition logically necessary for my doing it. That is to say, if there were any good reason to reject the principle

No agent is able to perform an act in the absence of a condition logically necessary for its accomplishment,

that reason would be an even better reason for rejecting the principle

No agent is able to perform an act in the absence of a condition causally but not logically necessary for its accomplishment.

Ability-sentences containing adverbs or adverbial phrases are often ambiguous. Consider:

I can refrain from talking at any time.

Does the adverbial phrase "at any time" modify the verb-phrase "refrain from talking" or does it modify "can"? In the former case, the sentence means something like "It is within my power to keep a vow of perpetual silence"; in the latter case, something like "At any given moment, I can at that moment refrain from talking."

In normal English usage, this ambiguity is usually not very important. It is resolved by such factors as intonation or one of the syntactically possible interpretations being wildly inappropriate. If there were some real possibility of confusion, the speaker might reposition the adverbial phrase:

I can, at any time, refrain from talking.

It will be convenient for us to introduce a more explicit device than these for the disambiguation of ability-sentences. Let us use round brackets in this fashion:

I can (refrain from talking) at any time;
I can (refrain from talking at any time).

The import of the round brackets is this: in the first of these sentences, "at any time" must modify "can", since both "can" and "at any time" are outside the brackets; in the second sentence, "at any time" must modify "refrain from talking", since both these phrases are inside the brackets. Roughly speaking, the presence of a pair of disambiguating brackets in an ability-sentence "forces" an adverb or adverbial phrase to modify a verb or verb-phrase that is on the "same side" of the pair of brackets.

Or, if the reader is willing to include in his ontology abstract entities called "acts" and is willing to recognize "refraining from talking" and "refraining from talking at any time" as phrases naming acts, then he may regard the round brackets as marking the boundaries of names of acts. Thus, on this way of looking at matters, the above pair of sentences may be read:

I can perform the act *refraining from talking* at any time;
I can perform the act *refraining from talking at any time.*

Perhaps even the reader whose ontology is not so copious as to include such acts will regard this explanation as intuitively useful if ontologically dubious, like an explanation of the derivative as a quotient of infinitesimal quantities.

A third way of looking at this pair of sentences is to regard them as marking the same distinction as:

> I can obey the command "Refrain from talking" at any time;
> I can obey the command "Refrain from talking at any time".

But this is not quite satisfactory, since the propositions expressed by these sentences seem to have unwanted entailments, as, for example, that I can understand English. Let us, therefore, regard our first explanation of our use of brackets as official, and the second and third explanations as being offered for the sake of such intuitive value as they may have.

Let us now return to principle (A). Let us look at some instances of this principle. First a "trivial" instance:

(a) I cannot move my finger when my finger is not moving.

This sentence may be disambiguated as follows:

(b) I cannot (move my finger) when my finger is not moving;
(c) I cannot (move my finger when my finger is not moving).

If an English speaker were to utter sentence (a), he would most naturally be taken to mean (c). But (b) is *a possible* reading of (a), though what is expressed by (b) would normally be expressed by "Whenever my finger is not moving, I lack the ability to move my finger". Obviously, if someone uttered sentence (c), or uttered (a) *meaning* (c), he would be right. But what about (b)? Could a person utter this sentence and say something true? Well, consider the following case. My finger is paralyzed, but it is important to me that it move, so I am continuously straining to move it. During intermittent and unpredictable intervals I become able to move my finger and then, of course, it begins to move; then it again becomes paralyzed and ceases to move. In that case, if I were to utter (b), I should say something true. There is therefore a semantic difference between (b) and (c); sentence (a) is not merely syntactically ambiguous. But if (a) is an instance of (A), then it would seem to follow that (A) is ambiguous. Is it (b) or (c) that is an instance of (A)?

A similar point can be made about

(d) I cannot issue O in the absence of a naval battle tomorrow.

Does Taylor intend this sentence to mean (e) or (f)?

(e) I cannot (issue O) in the absence of a naval battle tomorrow.
(f) I cannot (issue O in the absence of a naval battle tomorrow).

Which of these sentences is an instance of (A)? Obviously this question has no answer. For (A) itself is ambiguous. We must distinguish between:

(A)1 No agent is able to (perform an act) in the absence of a condition necessary for its accomplishment,

and

(A)2 No agent is able to (perform an act in the absence of a condition necessary for its accomplishment).

In which of these ways shall we read (A)? Let us try it both ways. Suppose (A) means A(2). From A(2) we may deduce (f), though there seems to be no reason to think we can deduce (e). Does it follow from (f) together with the proposition that there will be no naval battle tomorrow that I cannot issue O? I see no reason to think it follows. Certainly not just any inference of this *form* can convincingly claim to be valid. For example, the inference

I cannot (move my finger in the absence of my finger's moving);
My finger is not moving;
hence, I cannot move my finger

does not *seem* to be valid. In fact, it seems to be invalid. For its premises are true, but its conclusion certainly seems to be false. As one philosopher (an unlooked-for ally) has put the matter:

The statement "I can move my finger," as well as the statement "I can hold my finger still," are both true (though their joint truth obviously does not entail that I can do both at once). This I take to be quite certain . . . if there is any philosophical theory implying that one or the other of these statements must be false, then that theory is doubtful.[21]

Is there then some special reason, some reason having to do with naval battles and orders, to suppose that the proposition that I cannot issue O follows from (f)? This would be hard to maintain. Proposition (f) is the same proposition as, or, at least, is entailed by, the proposition that I cannot issue O without a naval battle tomorrow resulting. And the following inference hardly seems valid:

> I cannot issue O without a naval battle tomorrow resulting;
> There will be no naval battle tomorrow;
> *hence*, I cannot issue O.

Of course, if fatalism is true, then this inference *is* valid, as is the inference about the movement of my finger we looked at earlier. But I am not arguing that fatalism is false; rather that a certain argument does not show that it is true.

It seems, therefore, that, while A(2) is true, there is no reason to think that it can be used to prove fatalism. What about A(1)? A(1) does indeed entail (e), and hence fatalism. But is there any reason to think that A(1) is true? I see none. The only argument Taylor offers in support of (A) does not produce—in me, at any rate—any tendency to accept A(1). His argument consists simply in exhibiting instances of situations in which he is unable to perform some act and in which a condition necessary for his performing that act is absent and in which his inability to perform that act is a result of the absence of that condition:

> I cannot, for example, live without oxygen, or swim five miles without ever having been in water, or read a given page of print without having learned Russian, or win a certain election without having been nominated, and so on. (p. 58.)

But this argument is invalid. Since my being able to perform a certain act is a necessary condition for my performing it, any condition necessary for my being able to perform that act is a condition necessary for my performing it. Therefore, since there are indeed conditions necessary for my being able to perform various acts, there are conditions that are necessary for my performing various acts that are also necessary for my being *able* to perform those acts. What Taylor has done

[21]Richard Taylor, "I Can," *The Philosophical Review* (1960), 81.

is simply to list certain conditions necessary for his being able to perform certain acts, conditions that are *a fortiori* necessary for his performing those acts. But such a list lends no support to A(1). One might as well try to show that one cannot live in America if some condition necessary for one's living in California is absent by arguing:

> I cannot, for example, live in America, if I do not live in the Western Hemisphere, live upon dry land, live north of the Equator . . .

I conclude that Taylor's attempt to establish fatalism is a failure. Principle A is ambiguous. On one interpretation, A(2), it is true but there is no reason to think it entails fatalism; on the other, A(1), it entails fatalism but there is no reason to think it true.

2.7 Discussions of the "Law of the Excluded Middle" bulk large in most treatments of fatalism. But I have not discussed this "law" at all, and it does not appear as a premise in either of the fatalistic arguments we have examined. It would be possible to maintain, however, that these two arguments do make covert use of the Law of the Excluded Middle. My formulation of Taylor's argument, for example, depends for its validity on the validity of the inference-form

$p \supset q$

$\sim p . \supset q$

hence, q

which certainly seems to depend, in some sense, on the Law of the Excluded Middle. And perhaps it is arguable that the argument discussed in 2.5 depends, again "in some sense", on the Law of the Excluded Middle.

But what is the Law of the Excluded Middle (hereinafter "LEM")? Here are three candidates:

(i) If p is any English sentence, then the sentence that results from writing p and then writing "or it is not the case that" and then once more writing p, expresses (as an English sentence) a true proposition;[22]

(ii) Every proposition is either true or false;

(iii) For every proposition, either that proposition is true or its denial is true.

---

[22]This is as close as I can come to making sense of the syntactical *lusus naturae* (or *artis*) "$(p) (p \lor \sim p)$". One might try "Everything is such that either it or it is not the case that it".

Candidate (i) must be provided with some informal qualification if it is even to be plausible. Obviously "sentence" must be understood to mean "declarative sentence", where, one hopes, the class of "declarative" sentences of English is one that can be specified by purely syntactical means. But even if this can be done, a more serious problem remains: (i) seems to be a report of a fact about English that is at best contingently true. And this would be the case even if "true" in (i) were replaced with "necessarily true". After all, "or" and "not" might have meant something other than what they in fact mean. Of course, (i) might be elaborated to meet this difficulty, but the objection might be elaborated, too. On the whole, I think it would be more profitable for us to turn our attention to (ii) and (iii), than to play modification-and-counter-example with (i).

There are two main differences between (ii) and (iii): (ii) contains "false" and (iii) does not, and (iii) contains "denial" and (ii) does not. But what does "false" mean if not "not true"; what is falsehood but the complement of truth in the domain of propositions? And what is the "denial" of a proposition if not the proposition that it is not true? Some philosophers, I know, think that "true" and "false" are like "transparent" and "opaque": just as there are visible objects that are neither transparent nor opaque, so there are propositions that are neither true nor false. It has been argued, for example, that the proposition that the present king of France is bald is neither true nor false. These well-known arguments, however, establish at best that it is not clear whether "the proposition that the present king of France is bald" denotes anything, given the political conditions that actually prevail in France. But if this description does denote something—presumably it denotes the proposition that someone is now the only king of France and is bald, if it denotes anything—what it denotes is, I should think, either true or false; if it denotes nothing, then no counter-example to the thesis that falsehood is, in the domain of propositions, the complement of truth, has been produced. (The thesis that propositions "about the future" are neither true nor false we shall consider presently.)

If, as I have argued, "false" means "not true", and the denial of a proposition is the proposition that it is not true, then (ii) and (iii) come to much the same thing. I shall treat them as equivalent and equally good expressions of LEM.

Is LEM true? Various reasons for saying it is not have been offered. One class of interesting reasons for rejecting LEM arises in physical science, from considerations involving the physical interpretation of the formal mathematical theory of quantum mechanics; another class of reasons arises in pure mathematics from considerations involving non-constructive descriptions of infinite sets. I have nothing interesting to say about these reasons, which are, in any case, of no direct relevance to those questions about LEM that arise in discussions of fatalism. (They may, of course, be of indirect relevance; if they are persuasive, they may lead the erstwhile champion of LEM to mistrust his intuitions concerning the application of this principle even in cases involving only macroscopic objects and constructive predicates.)

What *is* of direct relevance to the problem of fatalism is the question whether LEM "applies" to propositions "about the future". Does this principle give us license to say that, for example, the proposition that I shall one day kill myself (K) is either true or false? Let us say that it does, and then ask whether the principle, so interpreted, is true. It will, I think, be sufficient to ask whether K is either true or false. If K is neither true nor false, then LEM is false; if K is either true or false then—I should think—just any proposition "about the future" is either true or false, at least assuming it involves only assertions about macroscopic objects and properties expressible by means of constructive predicates.

The question whether K is either true or false is just the question whether it is the case that either I shall kill myself or I shall not. For consider the argument:

(1) The proposition that I shall kill myself is true if and only if I shall kill myself
(2) The proposition that I shall kill myself is false if and only if I shall not kill myself
(3) Either I shall kill myself or I shall not
hence, (4) Either the proposition that I shall kill myself is true or it is false.

By way of commentary on this argument: (a) it is formally valid, being an instance of the form " $p \equiv q; r \equiv s; q \vee s;$ *hence* $p \vee r$ ";[23] (b) the sentence displayed to the right of "(1)" is formed by filling the blank in "The proposition that . . . is true if and only if . . . ". Such a sentence expresses—as a sentence of English and relative to a given context of utterance (I shall from now on leave it to the reader to supply such qualification as this)—a *true* proposition provided the sentence that fills the blank expresses *any* proposition. (I shall presently discuss the contention that "I shall kill myself" does not express *any* proposition.) If anyone denies this, I do not understand what he means by "true". The same remarks apply *mutatis mutandis* to the sentence to the right of "(2)". (c) Therefore—leaving aside the question whether "I shall kill myself" and its negation express propositions—(4) is true if (3) is true.

Is (3) true? It is certainly the case that if I were to utter the sentence displayed to the right of "(3)" above, I should say something true. (Or at least this is the case if we suppose I utter this sentence in a context in which my uttering it constitutes my asserting that I either shall or shall not kill myself, and not a mere phonetic exercise.)

---

[23]This argument-form certainly does not in any clear sense "presuppose" LEM.

But such a context is easily imagined: suppose you and I are discussing the advisability of my buying a certain type of life insurance, and I utter this sentence as a preface to an argument by cases.) But if that is the case, then how could (3) be anything but true? Could it be the case that there is a certain sentence *s* such that (i) if I were to utter *s* I should in uttering *s* say something true, and (ii) the proposition expressed by *s* is *not* true? To answer "Yes" to this question is surely to contradict oneself.

Therefore, (4) is true unless "I shall kill myself" fails to express a proposition, unless there *is* no such proposition as the proposition that I shall kill myself, just as there is no such proposition as the proposition about kangaroos I just now asserted. How could there be no such proposition? Surely someone may believe or assert or even know that I shall one day kill myself. But if a sentence can be meaningfully concatenated with "he believes that . . ." or "he knows that . . ." or can be used as the vehicle of an assertion, then that sentence expresses a proposition. That is what it *is* for a sentence to express a proposition.

Perhaps the opponent of LEM will want to protest: "I grant you that it is possible for someone to utter, say, 'he will someday kill himself' and make an assertion. What I am saying is that the assertion he makes, or the proposition he expresses, is neither true nor false." But to say this is simply to grant the premise of my argument—that it is possible to make assertions about the future—and to deny the conclusion: that any such assertion is either true or false. And that would be to deny that my argument is valid without attempting to find a flaw in it.

There is a good deal more that could be said about LEM, but I shall not say it. I have attempted in 2.7 to show that LEM is true because I think it *is* true and because certain writers on fatalism have denied it, thinking that such a denial constitutes the only escape from fatalism. But since there are no known compelling arguments for fatalism, this is not the case. Such writers are like atheists who become Parmenideans in order to deny the premise of St. Thomas's First Way. To enter into an extended debate about LEM would be as profitless an undertaking as writing a treatise proving that some things are in motion.

3

TRUTH AND FREEDOM

Trenton Merricks

1. A TRUISM

Aristotle says:

> If there is a man, the statement whereby we say that there is a man is true, and
> reciprocally—since if the statement whereby we say that there is a man is true,
> there is a man. And whereas the true statement is in no way the cause of the actual
> thing's existence, the actual thing does seem in some way the cause of the state-
> ment's being true: it is because the actual thing exists or does not that the state-
> ment is called true or false. (*Categories* 14b, 15–22 [1984, 22])

Elsewhere, Aristotle adds:

> When is what is called truth or falsity present, and when is it not? We must con-
> sider what we mean by these terms. It is not because we think that you are white,
> that you *are* white, but because you are white we who say this have the truth.
> (*Metaphysics* 9, 1051b, 5–8 [1984, 1661])

I take Aristotle to be endorsing a general point: a claim or statement or belief or
proposition is true because things are how that claim (or statement . . .) represents
things as being—and not the other way around.

Again, Aristotle tells us that what is true depends on what the world is like—but
not vice versa.

The point that truth depends on the world is not the thesis that, for each truth,
there is something in the world to which that truth "corresponds". Nor is it the thesis
that every truth has a "truthmaker". Nor is it even the thesis that there is a *depends on*
relation, or a *because* relation, that holds between each truth and (some part of) the
world. For, as certain negative existentials readily show, every one of these theses is
more controversial than the point that truth depends on the world.

That there are no white ravens is true. Yet it is a matter of controversy whether there is some entity—such as the state of affairs (or, in other words, the event) of *the universe's lacking white ravens*—to which that truth corresponds. Likewise, it is controversial whether that truth has a truthmaker.[1] Similarly, it is controversial whether that truth stands in a *depends on* or a *because* relation to some relatum, a relatum like (again) the state of affairs of *the universe's lacking white ravens*. But even so, it should not be at all controversial that *that there are no white ravens* is true because there are no white ravens. That is, it should not be at all controversial that that truth depends on the world, and in particular on there being no white ravens.[2]

Or suppose, as "deflationists" would have it, that there is no property of *being true*. Suppose, instead, that *that there are no white ravens's* being true amounts to nothing more than there being no white ravens. Even so, we should still recognize that, insofar as it is correct to say "*that there are no white ravens* is true", this is correct because there are no white ravens. And we should still deny that there being no white ravens depends on the truth of *that there are no white ravens*.

Despite the many controversies surrounding truth, it should be uncontroversial that a claim, if true, is true because the world is the way that claim represents the world as being, and not vice versa. Again, it should be uncontroversial that *that there are no white ravens* is true because there are no white ravens, *that dogs bark* is true because dogs bark, *that there were dinosaurs* is true because there were dinosaurs, and so on. Some might complain that this is not only uncontroversial, but also uninteresting. That is, some might complain that the point that truth thus depends on the world is a mere truism. Fair enough. But, as we shall see, this truism about truth undermines a familiar threat to freedom.

2. A FAMILIAR THREAT TO FREEDOM

Suppose that Jones, who is sitting, is worried that he is not sitting *freely*. Perhaps Jones suspects that the CIA is conducting an experiment in mind control, involving, among other things, the agency's causing him to intend to sit. Or, if he is an

---

[1] Elsewhere (Merricks 2007), I argue against both the correspondence theory of truth and the claim that every truth has a truthmaker.

[2] The same point could be made with contingent predications. Consider Fido the brown dog. And consider this uncontroversial claim: *that Fido is brown* is true because Fido is brown. This claim is not the controversial assertion that there is a *because* (or *depends on*) relation holding between two relata. After all, the "Fido is brown" that follows the "because" in this claim does not seem to name an entity, and so does not seem to name a potential relatum. The same goes for the "*that Fido is brown* is true" that occurs before the "because" and, more generally, for every expression of the form "*p* is true".

incompatibilist about freedom and determinism, Jones's worry might come from his suspicion that his sitting is the inevitable result of the laws of nature combined with the state of the distant past.

But whatever Jones ought to think of government conspiracies or determinism, he should not worry that the truth of *that Jones is sitting* keeps his sitting from being free. He should not have this worry even though that truth absolutely necessitates Jones's sitting; that is, even though, necessarily, if (and only if) *that Jones is sitting* is true, then Jones is sitting.

He should not have this worry because everyone, incompatibilists included, should deny that this truth's necessitating Jones's sitting determines his sitting in such a way that his sitting is not free. One reason that everyone should deny this is that such determination would imply a falsehood. It would imply that Jones is sitting because *that Jones is sitting* is true. That false implication is at odds with the point that the way the world is does not depend on what is true, but rather the other way around.

Of course, no one argues that Jones's sitting is not free because of the truth of *that Jones is sitting*. More generally, for all S and all A, no one sees a threat to S's freely doing A—suppose S is doing A right now—in the current truth of *that S does A*. No one sees a threat here even given that, necessarily, if (and only if) *that S does A* is true, then S does A. Even so, some have seen a threat to the freedom of some actions in the truth of certain propositions about those actions.

More specifically, and ever since Aristotle and Diodorus Cronus, some have thought that if certain propositions about *future* actions were true, those actions would not be free.[3] Suppose their idea was that any truth implying the occurrence of a future action would thereby determine that that future action will occur, and moreover that that action's being thus determined rules out its being free. Then we could conclude without further discussion that their idea was mistaken, and we could conclude this no matter what our position on the consistency of free will and determinism. For the idea that truths about the future thus determine the future violates a truth, if not a truism, about truth: truth depends on the world, not the other way around.

But we cannot dismiss arguments for "fatalism" that quickly. To see why not, consider this remark from Jonathan Edwards concerning foreknowledge:

> Whether prescience be the thing that *makes* the event necessary or no, it alters not the case. Infallible foreknowledge may *prove* the necessity of the thing foreknown, and yet not be the thing which *causes* the necessity. (*Freedom of the Will*, pt. 2, sec. 12 [1957, 263])

---

[3] A bit more on Aristotle below; for discussion of Diodorus, see Bobzien 1998, 102–08.

An argument that moves from premises invoking truths about the future to the conclusion that the future is determined, and determined in such a way as to preclude freedom, is not thereby committed to the claim that those truths themselves do that determining. So arguments for fatalism do not automatically violate our truism about truth. Nevertheless, as we shall see, that truism will ultimately undermine the most compelling sort of argument for fatalism.

That truism does not, however, undermine every possible argument for fatalism. But I think that the arguments that it fails to undermine are not particularly compelling to start with. For example, some such arguments seem to conflate what *will happen* with what *must happen*. Consider arguments given by philosophers who correctly note that the truth of *that S will do A* implies that S will do A—but then jump, without argument, from that S will do A to that S must do A. (See, for example, Lukasiewicz 1967, 53; MacFarlane 2003, 325–26; and Ryle 1954, 15.)

Here is another example of an argument for fatalism that is not undermined by our truism, but is uncompelling for other reasons. According to Donald C. Williams (1951, 292) and Susan Haack (1974, 74–81), Aristotle's reasoning in *De Interpretation* 9 is of the following form: suppose that it is now true that Jones will sit tomorrow; necessarily, if it is true that Jones will sit tomorrow, then Jones will sit tomorrow; therefore, necessarily, Jones will sit tomorrow.[4]

If this reasoning were valid, we could conclude that if it is true that Jones will sit tomorrow, then Jones must sit tomorrow. But, while it is a matter of controversy whether Aristotle reasons as Williams and Haack say he does, it is not controversial that such reasoning is invalid. After all, if it were valid, we could easily show that every true claim p was necessarily true, without any recourse to truths about the future: p is true; necessarily, if p is time then p is true; therefore, necessarily, p is true.[5]

3. THE MAIN ARGUMENT

Let time t be just a few minutes in the future from now, and consider the *Main Argument*:

(1) Jones has no choice about: *that Jones sits at t* was true a thousand years ago.

(2) Necessarily, if *that Jones sits at t* was true a thousand years ago, then Jones sits at time t.

[4]Aristotle is standardly read as concluding that contingent propositions about the future lack a truth-value; for a nonstandard reading, see Anscombe 1956.
[5]Aquinas (1975, 224) points out that this sort of reasoning is invalid in *Summa Contra Gentiles* 1.67.10.

Therefore,

(3) Jones has no choice about: Jones's sitting at time *t*.

I shall take (3), the conclusion of the Main Argument, to imply that Jones's sitting at *t* will not be free.[6]

In my opinion, the Main Argument is the strongest argument for fatalism; that is, it is the strongest argument that moves from truths in the past to a present or future lack of freedom. But, as we shall see, the Main Argument fails because of considerations arising from truth's dependence on the world (sections 4–5). We shall also see that every initially compelling argument for fatalism—that is, every argument for fatalism free of obvious flaws like those noted in the preceding section—fails for the same reason.

The first premise of the Main Argument, (1), asserts both that the proposition *that Jones sits at t* was true a thousand years ago and also that Jones has no choice about this proposition's having then been true. Thus (1) entails that a proposition (namely, *that Jones sits at t*) was true a thousand years ago. A. J. Ayer (1963) and Peter van Inwagen (1983, 35) claim that propositions exist "outside time." As a result of existing outside time, so Ayer and van Inwagen argue, propositions are not true at times. So, they would agree, no proposition was true a thousand years ago. So they would say that (1) is false. In fact, Ayer and van Inwagen see the claim that propositions are not true at times as a way to block arguments like the Main Argument.

But I deny that propositions are outside time. Rather, I think that they exist at times, and so are true (or false) at times. After all, it certainly seems that some propositions—for example, *that humans exist*—were true long before I was born, and anything true *before* I was born must exist in time. Moreover, I shall argue that some propositions undergo change in truth-value, and if propositions undergo change of any sort, then propositions exist in time. So let us begin with two claims, which together imply that some propositions undergo change in truth-value.

First, for each way things are, there is a true proposition representing things being that way.[7] For example, suppose that O is F. Then there is the proposition *that O is F*. Second, for some O and some F, O goes from being F to failing to be F. This second claim is not shorthand for the claim that O is, all along, F-at-one-time

---

[6]In the Main Argument, and in the arguments to follow, "Jones has no choice about" could be exchanged for "Jones does not have, never had, and never will have a choice about". This might make it even clearer that the conclusion of these arguments implies a lack of freedom. Indeed, "Jones has no choice about" could even be exchanged for "Jones is not free with respect to".

[7]My argument works with weakened versions of this first claim, just so long as they imply that there are propositions like *that O is F*. But taken "full strength", and assuming that there is a way everything is, this first claim implies that there is a true "maximal" proposition. Thus, at least on one understanding of "possible worlds", this first claim gets us one possible world (in particular,

and not-*F*-at-another-time. Nor is it shorthand for the claim that one temporal part of *O* is always *F* and another temporal part of *O* never was *F* to begin with. Rather, *O* itself goes from simply being *F*, without qualification, to simply lacking that same property, again without qualification (see Merricks 1994; Hinchliff 1996; Crisp 2003).

Some will reject this second claim. And some might reject even the first. Nevertheless, both claims are quite plausible, and I believe that they are both true. Given these two claims, we can conclude that some propositions undergo change in truth-value. For suppose that *O* is *F*. Then *that O is F* is true. Suppose that later *O* is no longer *F*. Then *that O is F* is no longer true. Indeed, *O* changes with respect to being *F* if and only if *that O is F* changes with respect to being true.[8]

Entities that exist outside time do not change. So, since *that O is F* changes, *that O is F* does not exist outside time. So *that O is F* exists at times. So *that O is F* is true (or false) at times. Indeed, *that O is F* is true at every time that *O* is *F*; similarly, whenever *O* is not *F*, *that O is F* is not true.

I assume that either all propositions are outside time, or none are. So I conclude that, since *that O is F* exists at times and is true (or false) at times, all propositions exist at times and are true (or false) at times. This includes even those propositions that cannot change in truth-value, propositions like *that O is F at t* and—to return to the Main Argument—*that Jones sits at t*. So I do not endorse Ayer's and van Inwagen's objection to the first premise of the Main Argument, which premise is:

(1) Jones has no choice about: *that Jones sits at t* was true a thousand years ago.

Besides, there is an argument involving true beliefs—as opposed to true propositions—that parallels the Main Argument (see section 7). Nothing like Ayer's and van Inwagen's objection to (1) can block this parallel argument because, even if propositions are outside time, at least some beliefs exist at, and are true at, times. So even if Ayer's and van Inwagen's objection to (1) is correct, it is a mere stopgap measure.

it gets us the actual world). If for each way everything could be, but is not, there is a proposition representing things being that way, then we get the full panoply of possible worlds.

[8]The idea that (some) propositions undergo change in truth-value seems to be at least as old as Aristotle: "Suppose, for example, that the statement that somebody is sitting is true; after he has got up this same statement will be false. Similarly with beliefs" (*Categories* 4a, 24–26 [1984, 7]). Moreover, those who endorse (the standard way of understanding) Aristotle's views on future contingents say that *that a sea battle occurs at time t* is neither true nor false before *t*, but from *t* onward is true or, instead, false; this, too, would be a change in truth-value.

4. THE MAIN ARGUMENT IS
QUESTION-BEGGING ...

Again, let t be just a few minutes in the future from now. Here is the *Parody of the Main Argument*, which focuses on the future truth (as opposed to the past truth) of *that Jones sits at t*:

(1*) Jones has no choice about: *that Jones sits at t* will be true a thousand years from now.

(2*) Necessarily, if *that Jones sits at t* will be true a thousand years from now, then Jones sits at time t.
Therefore,

(3) Jones has no choice about: Jones's sitting at time t.

I think that everyone will agree that the Parody fails to present a legitimate threat to Jones's freedom. Again, I think that everyone will agree that the Parody is not a good argument for the conclusion that Jones has no choice about his sitting at time t.

Everyone will agree. This includes those who do not believe in free will (for example, Pereboom [2001] and Strawson [1987]). So this includes those who will endorse the first premise of the Parody. And some of these will add not only that the second premise is true, but also that the Parody is valid. But even so, I do not think that they will seize upon the Parody as a new defense of their view. For, as already noted, they will agree that the Parody is not a good argument.

Even those who endorse the Parody's premises and affirm its validity—that is, even those who think that the Parody is sound—should agree that it is not a good argument. So they must find fault with the Parody. But I think that the only fault for them to find is that the Parody begs the question. In particular, they should claim that at least one of the premises of the Parody presupposes that argument's conclusion, and does so in such a way as to render the Parody not a good argument. No other criticism of the Parody should be plausible to those who endorse its soundness.[9]

Clearly, the Parody's second premise, (2*), does not presuppose that argument's conclusion. So the culprit must be (1*), the first premise. That is, those who think

---

[9]For what it is worth, I can think of only two ways a sound argument can fail to be good. First, it can beg the question. Second, its conclusion can be necessarily true and otherwise unrelated to its premises, following only trivially from those premises; here is an example: dogs bark; therefore, there is no greatest prime number. The Parody does not fail in this second way.

that the Parody is sound should say that that premise presupposes—in the sense of "presupposes" relevant to begging the question—(3), the Parody's conclusion.[10]

And it is not only those who take the Parody to be sound who should insist that its first premise presupposes its conclusion. We should all insist on this. For imagine telling Jones that he has no choice about whether he will sit just a few minutes from now, at t. And imagine telling him that he has no such choice because of the following. First, it will be true tomorrow that he sat at t; and, second, he has no choice about that future truth. Jones ought to reply that, because he does have a choice about sitting at t, he does have a choice about whether it will be true tomorrow that he sat then. To deny that he has such a choice about that truth, he ought to insist, is to presuppose that he has no choice about whether he will sit at t.

Look at it this way. If *that Jones sits at t* will be true tomorrow—or in a thousand years—we know why it will then be true. It will then be true because, at t, Jones will sit. That future truth *depends* on Jones's sitting at t. So the claim that he does not have a choice about that future truth presupposes that he does not have a choice about sitting at t, and it presupposes this in such a way that it begs the question with respect to his having a choice about sitting at t. This illustrates a general corollary of truth's dependence on the world. The corollary is that, for all S and all p, S has no choice about p's truth presupposes (in the sense of "presupposes" relevant to begging the question) that S has no choice about what p's truth depends on (in the sense of "depends on" in which truth depends on the world).[11]

With this in mind, reconsider the first premise of the Main Argument:

(1) Jones has no choice about: *that Jones sits at t* was true a thousand years ago.

Suppose that *that Jones sits at t* really was true a thousand years ago. Given truth's dependence on the world, we know why *that Jones sits at t* was then true. It was true because Jones will sit at t. So—recall the corollary of truth's dependence on the world—that Jones has no choice about that truth presupposes that Jones has no choice about his sitting at t. Thus (1), which is the first premise of the Main

---

[10]Throughout this article, I shall use "presuppose" to mean *presuppose in the sense relevant to begging the question*. To grant that a premise of an argument thus presupposes that argument's conclusion is thereby to grant that that argument is question-begging.

[11]This corollary provides new proof that every truth's "truistic" dependence on the world is not the same thing as every truth's having a truthmaker. For a parallel corollary in terms of truthmaking is false, at least given the plausible assumption that if p has a truthmaker x, x is a truthmaker for any disjunction of which p is a disjunct. For example, Jones has no choice about a necessary truth, so Jones has no choice about *either that Jones is sitting or it is false that Jones is sitting*. But this does not presuppose that Jones has no choice about his sitting.

Argument, presupposes the Main Argument's conclusion, which is that Jones has no choice about his sitting at *t*.

The Main Argument's first premise presupposes its conclusion in exactly the same way that the Parody's first premise presupposes its conclusion. Therefore, the Main Argument begs the question in exactly the same way that the Parody begs the question. And so we should conclude that the Main Argument is question-begging.

(The Main Argument closely resembles the "Consequence Argument" for incompatibilism, whose defenders include Carl Ginet (1966), David Wiggins (1973), and Peter van Inwagen (1983). In light of this resemblance, those who take the Consequence Argument to be invalid might suspect that the Main Argument itself is invalid.[12] But such suspicion is misguided. Because (1) presupposes (3), (1) entails (3). As a result, the Main Argument's premises—(1) and (2)—entail its conclusion, (3). And so the Main Argument is valid, just like every other question-begging argument.)[13]

The Main Argument is question-begging, but not because (1) says that the proposition *that Jones sits at t* was true a thousand years ago. Rather, it is question-begging because (1) says that Jones *has no choice* about that proposition's having been true a thousand years ago. So if (1) were replaced with the following, the Main Argument would cease to be question-begging:

(1**)   *That Jones sits at t* was true a thousand years ago.

(1**) begs no questions. But revising the Main Argument by replacing (1) with (1**) renders that argument invalid.

The easiest way to see that the Main Argument, thus revised, would be invalid is to consider a similarly revised—and likewise invalid—version of the Parody:

[12]Van Inwagen's (1983, 94) "Beta Principle" has received the most scrutiny: (N*p* and N(if *p*, then *q*)) entails N*q*, where "N*p*" means "*p* and no one has, ever had, or will have a choice about *p*". The Main Argument's form is not that endorsed by the Beta Principle, but is closer to (N*p* and Necessarily (if *p*, then *q*)) entails N*q*. The counterexamples to the Beta Principle are not counterexamples to the form of the Main Argument. See discussions in Widerker 1987; McKay and Johnson 1996; Kane 1998, chap. 4; Crisp and Warfield 2000; Finch and Warfield 1998; and O'Connor 2000, chap. 1.

[13]More carefully, every argument that begs the question in virtue of one or more of its premises presupposing its conclusion is valid. But an argument might also be deemed to be question-begging if it is, to borrow a phrase from Alston 1993, 15–17, "epistemically circular." An epistemically circular argument's conclusion is presupposed not by that argument's premises, but rather by one's reasons for endorsing one or more of those premises. Not all epistemically circular arguments are valid.

(1***) *That Jones sits at t* will be true a thousand years from now.

(2*) Necessarily, if *that Jones sits at t* will be true a thousand years from now, then Jones sits at time *t*.

Therefore,

(3) Jones has no choice about: Jones's sitting at time *t*.

The revised Parody's form is quite similar to that of the invalid argument that Williams and Haack attribute to Aristotle. And, whatever its similarities to other invalid arguments, the revised Parody is clearly invalid. With this in mind, I conclude that revising the Main Argument by replacing (1) with (1**) renders that argument invalid as well.

5. ... AND ALSO HAS A FALSE PREMISE

The (unrevised and valid) Main Argument is a question-begging failure whether or not any agent ever acts freely. But the Main Argument's failure is of interest primarily to those of us who think we do sometimes act freely. So let us assume that we do. And, to keep our focus on the Main Argument, let us assume that Jones sits freely at *t*. Jones's sitting freely at *t* implies the falsity of (3), which says that Jones has no choice about his sitting at *t*.

Recall the Main Argument's first premise:

(1) Jones has no choice about: *that Jones sits at t* was true a thousand years ago.

As we saw above, (1) presupposes, and so entails, (3). Therefore the falsity of (3) entails the falsity of (1). So I say that (1) is false. ((1)'s falsity is a second failing of the Main Argument, a failing in addition to that argument's begging the question.)

Some might account for the falsity of (1) by denying that *that Jones sits at t* was true a thousand years ago, even though Jones sits at *t*. One way to deny this, we have seen, is to claim that propositions are outside time. And there is another way to deny this. One might reason as follows: a thousand years ago, *that Jones sits at t* existed, but was neither true nor false; so it was not true a thousand years ago; so it was not, a thousand years ago, a true proposition whose truth was something about which Jones now has no choice.

I reject this way of accounting for (1)'s falsity. For I claim that, at every time, each proposition is true or, if not true, then false (cf. Williamson 1994, 188–89). This claim implies that a thousand years ago *that Jones sits at t* was either true or, if not true, then false. But it was not false, since, ex hypothesi, Jones will sit at *t*. So *that*

Jones sits at t was true. So I conclude that Jones has a choice about the truth, a thousand years ago, of *that Jones sits at t*.

Some might find this conclusion unacceptable. In particular, some might object that the past has a special kind of *necessity*. Their idea is not that the past is absolutely metaphysically necessary. Again, their idea is not that there are no "possible worlds" with histories differing from that of the actual world. Nevertheless, some do say that the past is, in some other way, necessary.[14] And, so the objection we are now considering goes, the necessity of the past gives us a reason to deny that Jones now has a choice about what was true a thousand years ago. It gives us a reason to deny this, according to this objection, because the necessity of the past entails that Jones now has no such choice.

My reply to this objection begins by considering three ways one might understand the claim that the past is necessary. First, suppose that that claim is just another way of saying that no one now has (and no one in the future will have) a choice about what the past was like, not even about which propositions were true in the past. If this is all the necessity of the past amounts to, then arguments for Jones's having no choice about sitting at *t* that start with the necessity of the past truth of *that Jones sits at t* just are the Main Argument, put in other words.

And if this is all the necessity of the past amounts to, the objection just considered fails. For that objection takes the assertion that the past is necessary to be a reason for the claim that no one now has a choice about what the past was like. But that claim cannot be a reason for itself. So let us assume that the past's being necessary is not one and the same thing as no one's now having a choice about what the past was like, even though the past's being appropriately necessary is supposed to entail that no one now has such a choice. At least, it must entail this if it is to support the above objection.

Second, suppose that the past's being necessary means only that the past cannot be changed. Because the past cannot be changed, the past is thus necessary. But the claim that the past is thus necessary does not underwrite the above objection. For it does not entail that no one now has a choice about what the past was like.

To see that it fails to have this entailment, suppose that Jones now makes *that Jones sits at t* true a thousand years *in the future*. Then it never was the case to begin with that *that Jones sits at t* will not be true a thousand years from now. But that would have had to have been the case if Jones were to have *changed* the thousand-years-in-the-future truth of *that Jones sits at t*. So Jones did not, and cannot, change the aspect of the thousand-years-hence future that is the truth of that proposition. More generally, the future is unchangeable. But this does not entail that no one now has a choice

---

[14]See Plantinga's (1986, 243) discussion of arguments considered by Aquinas, Ockham, Jonathan Edwards, and Nelson Pike.

about the future. Nor, by parity of reasoning, does the unchangeableness of the past entail that no one now has a choice about the past.[15]

Suppose, finally, that the past's being necessary means only that our present and future actions cannot *cause* events in the past (cf. Plantinga 1986, 258). Then the past's being necessary amounts to there being no "backward" causation. But, like the unchangeableness of the past, the absence of backward causation fails to entail that no one now has a choice about what the past was like. This is because having a choice about the past truth of a proposition does not require backward causation.

It does not require backward causation because the truistic way in which the truth of a proposition depends on the world is not causal. This is why, for example, truth's dependence on the world does not involve the laws of nature or the transfer of energy. Moreover, truth's dependence on the world does not involve a *depends on* relation holding between a truth and some other relatum. (Recall section l's brief discussion of *that there are no white ravens*.) Therefore it does not involve a causal *depends on* relation, relating cause and effect.

Or consider the following: abstract objects cause absolutely nothing. This familiar claim about abstract objects might be false. But it is not shown to be false merely by the truism that *that abstract objects exist* is true (if it is true) because abstract objects exist. That is, that truth's *depending on* abstract objects does not imply that abstract objects cause something; so it does not imply that abstract objects cause that truth to be true (cf. Merricks 2001, 105). Therefore the truistic way in which truth depends on the world is not causal. So even though *that Jones sits at t* was true a thousand years ago *because* Jones sits (or will sit or did sit) at *t*, the "because" here is not causal. And so it is not "backward" causal.[16]

Above we considered an objection to the claim that Jones now has a choice about the truth, a thousand years ago, of *that Jones sits at t*. That objection was that the past is appropriately necessary and that the past's being thus necessary gives us a reason to say that no one now has a choice about what the past was like, not even about which propositions were true in the past. But the ways in which the past is plausibly

---

[15]See Plantinga 1986, 244. Van Inwagen (1983, 92; 2006, 164–65) seems to conflate the (controversial) claim that one cannot have a choice about the past with the (obviously true) claim that one cannot change the past.

[16]Recall that Aristotle says: "the actual thing [a man] does seem in some way the cause of the statement's [*that there is a man*] being true." But I do not think Aristotle claims that a man is (what we would nowadays call) a *bona fide* cause—that is, an Aristotelian efficient cause—of the truth of *that there is a man*. And even with his broad notions of causation, Aristotle hedges, saying that the man "does seem in some way" the cause of the statement's being true. He glosses that way with the unobjectionable: "it is because the actual thing exists or does not that the statement is called true or false."

"necessary" fail to give us a reason to say that no one now has a choice about what the past was like. So this objection fails.

And failed objections to it aside, the claim that Jones even now has a choice about the past truth of *that Jones sits at t*, when *t* is in the future, should not be puzzling. To begin to see why I say this, suppose that *that Jones sits at t* is true right now. Then it is true because of (that is, its truth depends on) Jones's sitting at *t*. Add to this a second corollary of truth's dependence on the world: for all *S* and all *p*, if *S* has a choice about what *p*'s truth depends on, then *S* has a choice about *p*'s truth. Given this addition—plus the assumption that Jones has a choice about sitting at *t*—we should conclude that Jones does have a choice about the truth of *that Jones sits at t*.

This little argument involving a second corollary of truth's dependence on the world did not turn on *when* the proposition in question is true. So this argument can easily be adjusted to show, for example, that Jones now has a choice about the *future* truth of *that Jones sits at t*. And it can also show that, if indeed there are past truths about future actions, Jones now has a choice about that proposition's *past* truth. Moreover, all of this shows that Jones's having a choice about that proposition's past truth is no more or less puzzling than his having a choice about its future truth, which is to say, it is not puzzling at all.

But let us consider one last attempt to make it seem puzzling. So consider this argument: Jones did not exist a thousand years ago; so, a thousand years ago, Jones did not do anything; so, a thousand years ago, he did not exercise control over anything; so, a thousand years ago, he did not exercise control over the truth of *that Jones sits at t*; so Jones has no choice about that proposition's having been true a thousand years ago.[17]

This argument purports to raise worries about whether one has a choice about past truths about one's present and future actions. But a very straightforward adaptation of this argument seems to show something far more striking. The following adaptation seems to rule out one's having a choice about future truths about one's present and future actions.

Jones will not exist a thousand years in the future; so, a thousand years from now, he will not do anything; so, a thousand years from now, he will not exercise control over anything; so, a thousand years from now, he will not exercise control over the

---

[17]This argument is inspired by an argument given by Finch and Rea (2008). Finch and Rea's argument takes aim at Ockhamism, which will be discussed in the following section. But, obviously, the argument I have just offered, which is inspired by their argument, threatens my reply to the Main Argument. Finch and Rea show that their argument can be blocked by "eternalism" about time. (Rea shows the same thing about the argument of Rea 2006, discussed here.) But they think that their argument goes through given "presentism" about time. As we shall see, however, I shall block the argument inspired by their argument without relying on any particular view of time.

truth of *that Jones sits at t*; so Jones has no choice about that proposition's being true a thousand years in the future.

We have the resources to block both of the arguments just considered. *That Jones sits at t* is true, whenever it is true, because Jones sits at *t*. Jones has a choice about that proposition's being true if he has a choice about whether he sits at *t*. Since *t* is a few moments from now, Jones does not need to exist (or exercise control) a thousand years from now to have a choice about his sitting at *t*. Therefore he does not need to exist (or exercise control) a thousand years from now to have a choice about the thousand-years-hence truth of *that Jones sits at t*. For similar reasons, he does not need to have existed (or have exercised control) a thousand years ago to have a choice about the thousand-years-ago truth of *that Jones sits at t*. The arguments just considered go wrong by assuming that Jones must exist (and exercise control) at a particular time if he is to have a choice about whether *that Jones sits at t* is true at that time.[18]

Consider:

(0) The past is appropriately necessary; and, necessarily, if the past is appropriately necessary, then no one now has a choice about what the past was like, not even about which propositions were true in the past.

---

[18]Similarly, Rea 2006, 518, affirms this principle:

(M5) If the truth of a proposition p at a past time t_n was not even partly grounded in the occurrence of any event involving S, or in the agent causal activity of S, then S has never had and will never have a choice about whether p was true at t_n.

Rea concludes that the truth of a proposition at a past time cannot be (even partly) grounded in an event involving S or the agent causal activity of S if S existed only *after* that past time (see Rea 2006, 518–20). But I think that the reasoning that leads Rea to this conclusion ought also to lead him to conclude that the truth of a proposition at a past time cannot be (even partly) grounded in an event involving S or the agent causal activity of S if S existed only *before* that past time. More generally, I think that Rea should add that the truth of a proposition at a time cannot be (even partly) grounded in an event involving S or the agent causal activity of S if S did not exist at that time.

If Rea did add this, then his reasoning would have implications for propositions that are true in the future. For example, Rea's reasoning—combined with (M5)—would imply that if S will not exist a thousand years in the future, then S does not now have a choice about the thousand-years-hence truth of any proposition, including propositions about S's current and future free actions.

But I say, as a result of the arguments of this article, that S can now have a choice about the thousand-years-hence truth of p, even if S will not exist in a thousand years; S can now have such a choice if p's thousand-years-hence truth will appropriately depend on what S is now about to freely do. Similarly, I say that S can now have a choice about the thousand-years-ago truth of p, even if S did not exist a thousand years ago; S now has such a choice if p's thousand-years-ago truth appropriately depended on what S is now about to freely do. So I conclude, at least given what Rea takes to be necessary for grounding, that (M5) is false.

Also, suppose that *that Jones sits at t* was true a thousand years ago. This supposition and (0) together imply the Main Argument's premise (1), which says that Jones has no choice about: *that Jones sits at t* was true a thousand years ago.

Suppose we recast the Main Argument so that it starts with (0), rather than with (1). Then (1) is not an assumption with which that argument begins, but rather an intermediary conclusion. So (1) is not really a premise of that argument. So (1)'s presupposing the Main Argument's conclusion does not render the Main Argument question-begging. And so, one might claim, the Main Argument thus recast, unlike the original version of the Main Argument, is not question-begging (section 4).

But the Main Argument, thus recast, still fails. This failure is one moral of the above discussion of the necessity of the past. For suppose that the past's being necessary amounts to the past's being unchangeable. Or suppose that it amounts to there being no backward causation. Either way, the second clause of (0) is false, and so (0) itself is false.

Of course, we are not yet done with (0). For perhaps the past's being necessary is nothing other than no one's having a choice, from here on out, about anything in the past, not even about the past truth of propositions about present and future actions. This account of the necessity of the past renders the second clause of (0) trivial, and thus secures the truth of that clause.

But I think that this account of the necessity of the past implies the falsity of the first clause of (0), and so the falsity of (0) itself. After all, since truth depends on the world, the past truth of some propositions depended on what will happen. Assuming that we now have a choice about some of what will happen, it follows that—recall our second corollary—we now have a choice about the past truth of some propositions. So if the (alleged) necessity of the past is nothing other than the (alleged) relevant lack of choice, then (0) is false.

Some might resist this argument for (0)'s falsity. In particular, some might deny that we now have a choice about the past truth of some propositions. Of course, in light of the arguments of this article, I think their denial is mistaken. And I have another complaint about their denial. Their denial presupposes (among other things) the truth of (1). (Recall that (1) is the claim that Jones has no choice about the past truth of a certain proposition.) If (0) must be defended, and can be defended only by presupposing (1), then the recast Main Argument loses any advantage, with respect to begging the question, that it may have had over the original Main Argument.

Return to the original version of the Main Argument, the argument beginning with (1). We have seen that that argument fails. And the ways in which the Main Argument fails guarantee the failure of any initially compelling argument that moves from truths about the future to a lack of freedom. For any such argument must assume that we have no choice about the long-ago truth of propositions about our present and future actions. But, as we saw in section 4, that assumption presupposes our present and future lack of freedom. So any such argument will be question-begging. Moreover, that assumption is also false, at least when the proposition in question concerns a present or future free action (section 5).

6. OCKHAMISM

In *Predestination, God's Foreknowledge, and Future Contingents*, William of Ockham claimed that we now have a choice about the past truth of propositions about our present and future actions. So Ockhamists reject this premise of the Main Argument:

(1) Jones has no choice about: *that Jones sits at t* was true a thousand years ago.

That is, Ockhamists reject (1) even given that *that Jones sits at t* was true a thousand years ago. So do I. But this resemblance between us is superficial. For my reasons for rejecting (1) are not the reasons of the Ockhamist. Indeed, there are at least three important ways in which my treatment of the Main Argument differs from Ockhamism.

First, I object that the Main Argument begs the question. But Ockhamists would not thus object to the Main Argument. For Ockhamists do not invoke the idea underlying this objection, the idea that truth depends on the world.

Second, one of my arguments for the falsity of (1), even given the thousand-years-ago truth of *that Jones sits at t*, turned on a corollary of truth's dependence on the world: for all S and all p, if S has a choice about what p's truth depends on, then S has a choice about p's truth. Ockhamists do not rely on this corollary.

Suppose that you reject the first premise of the Main Argument. And suppose you do so because you insist that Jones now has a choice about the truth, a thousand years ago, of *that Jones sits at t*. The obvious question is: *why* does Jones have such a choice? This is the obvious question because Jones lacks a choice about most of what the world was like a thousand years ago. For example, he has no choice about who was king of the Britons a thousand years ago.[19]

The Ockhamists now among us have an answer to this question, which answer drives their objection to (1). It is that the past truth of *that Jones sits at t* is, when t is not itself past, a "soft fact" about the past; because it is a soft fact about the past, someone even now has a choice about it; in this case, that someone is Jones; and so

---

[19]Paul Horwich (1987, 30) would agree with the Ockhamists, and also with me, that Jones now has a choice about the thousand-years-ago truth of *that Jones sits at t*. For, Horwich would argue, it is better to say that Jones has such a choice than to accept fatalism or to reject bivalence—and Horwich says that fatalistic arguments force us to do one of the three.

(1) is false. They would add that if a fact about the past is a "hard fact", no one now has a choice about it (see, e.g., Adams 1967).[20]

Given this answer, these Ockhamists should not define "soft fact" as a fact about which someone even now has a choice. For if they did, the claim that a particular fact about the past is "soft" would be nothing other than—and so could not be a reason for—the conclusion that someone even now has a choice about it.

Nevertheless, these Ockhamists must make sense of the distinction between soft facts and hard facts and must do so in such a way that a fact about the past's being soft implies that someone or other now has (or will have) a choice about it. Moreover, their way of making sense of that distinction had better imply that the thousand-years-ago truth of *that Jones sits at t* is a soft fact. And it had also better imply, for example, that Llywelyn ap Seisyll's being king of the Britons a thousand years ago is a hard fact.

Ockham himself does not use the terms "soft fact" or "hard fact" (or, for that matter, the terms "*factum molle*" or "*factum durum*"). But he does draw a distinction that

---

I think that Horwich needs to tell us why, if we now have a choice about some of what was true in the past, we do not now have a choice about other facets of the past, such as who was king of the Britons. And Horwich seems to have an answer. His answer seems to be that no one now has a choice about the existence (or occurrence) of any past event (1987, 30). Similarly, I assume that Horwich would answer that no one now has a choice about the past exemplification of any property. But I think these answers are not consistent with Horwich's claim that we now have a choice about some of what was true in the past.

They are not consistent because if Jones has a choice about the thousand-years- ago truth of *that Jones sits at t*, Jones thereby has a choice about the past exemplification of a property, namely, the thousand-years-ago exemplification of *being true* by *that Jones sits at t*. And if there are events, Jones thereby has a choice about the existence, a thousand years ago, of the event of *that Jones sits at t's exemplifying being true*. (See section 7 for an argument that Jones has a choice about what God believed in the past.)

Horwich (1998) might respond by denying that a proposition's being true amounts to its exemplifying the property of *being true*. For my defense of the property of *being true*, see Merricks 2007, 187–91.

Consider an argument much like the Main Argument, but which begins with the premise that Jones has no choice about: a thousand years ago, rock *R* exemplified the property of *being such that Jones will sit at t*. I would respond to this argument by denying that rock *R* did exemplify the property of *being such that Jones will sit at t*; I would deny this partly because I doubt that there is any such property at all. One reason that I find the Main Argument more interesting than the parallel argument involving rock *R* is that I think there is a property of *being true*.

[20]Plantinga (1986) seems to be an exception since he seems to think that someone now has a choice about some hard facts about the past. Nevertheless, Plantinga would deny that anyone has a choice about an "accidentally necessary" fact about the past—and the distinction, among contingent facts about the past, between the nonaccidentally necessary and the accidentally necessary does the work for Plantinga that the distinction between soft facts and hard facts does for other Ockhamists.

is similar to—or, perhaps arguably, the same as—the soft fact/hard fact distinction. To get a sense of Ockham's distinction, pretend that it is one thousand years before *t*. Then Ockham would say that *that Jones sits at t* is "about the present as regards [its] wording only and [is] equivalently about the future." Still pretending that it is one thousand years before *t*, I think Ockham would also say that *that Llywelyn ap Seisyll is king of the Britons* is "about the present as regards both [its] wording and [its] subject matter" (Ockham, *Predestination* . . ., Assumption 3 [1983, 46–47]).

Ockham might add that a past truth's being about the past in wording only, and being equivalently about the future, implies that someone or other now has (or will have) a choice about that past truth. And he might further add that a past truth's being about the past as regards both its wording and subject matter implies that no one now has (or ever will have) a choice about that past truth.

All of this highlights a third difference between my approach and Ockhamism. Unlike the Ockhamists, I rely on neither a distinction between "soft facts" and "hard facts" nor on a distinction between what propositions are about with respect to "wording" and about with respect to "subject matter". So I do not have to make sense of these distinctions at all, much less in a way that delivers certain results, results like: for each soft fact about the past, someone or other now has (or will have) a choice about it.[21]

Given that Jones lacks a choice about most of what the world was like a thousand years ago, why does he now have a choice about the truth, a thousand years ago, of *that Jones sits at t*? My answer was given in sections 4 and 5. Jones even now has that choice because, first, truth depends on the world, and, second, he has a choice about sitting at *t*. And note that neither truth's dependence on the world nor anything else I have defended above suggests that someone now has a choice about, for example, who was king of the Britons a thousand years ago.

We have seen three ways in which my approach to the Main Argument differs from Ockhamism. I shall now explain a fourth difference between my approach to the Main Argument and that of at least some Ockhamists.

S has "counterfactual power" over a past event *E* if and only if *S* is able to perform some action *A*, and if *S* were to perform action *A*, *E* would not have occurred. For example, suppose that Jones is now able to refrain from sitting at *t*. In the "nearest possible world" in which he refrains from sitting at *t*, *that Jones sits at t* was not true a thousand years ago. Therefore, Jones now has counterfactual power over whether

---

[21]Fischer (1983; 1989, 32–48) argues that Ockhamists have not articulated, and cannot articulate, an account of soft facts that delivers the relevant results. I assume that he would say the same about Plantinga's (contingent and) nonaccidentally necessary facts about the past and Ockham's past truths that are about the past in wording only, and are equivalently about the future.

the event of *that Jones sits at t*'s being true occurred a thousand years ago, and therefore over whether *that Jones sits at t* was true a thousand years ago.

Some Ockhamists seem to assume that Jones's now having counterfactual power over the past truth of a proposition is sufficient for the past truth of that proposition's being a soft fact. Moreover, and in the parlance of the Main Argument, they seem to treat having counterfactual power over a past truth as sufficient for having a choice about that past truth (see Fischer 1989, 18–23; Plantinga 1974, 69–73; Saunders 1966). But, as we shall see, I think that they are mistaken.

Suppose that I cleaned my house yesterday because my brother is going to visit tomorrow. Suppose that my brother's visiting will be done freely. Suppose that in the "nearest world" in which he does not visit tomorrow, he never intended to visit. And suppose that, in that world, he never told me that he was going to visit. So in that world I did not clean the house yesterday. And so, if my brother were not to visit me tomorrow, I would not have cleaned the house yesterday.

Given these suppositions, my brother is now able to do something (namely, not visit me tomorrow) such that, if he were to do it, I would not have cleaned the house yesterday. That is, my brother has "counterfactual power" over my cleaning the house yesterday. Some might conclude that my brother now has a genuine choice about whether I cleaned the house yesterday. But, for what it is worth, this seems to me to be the wrong conclusion. I conclude, instead, that having counterfactual power over a past event is not sufficient for having a genuine choice about whether that past event occurred.[22]

In debates over freedom, "being able to bring about something" is often treated as if it has at most two disambiguations: having counterfactual power over that something's occurrence and being able to cause that something (cf. Lewis 1981; Fischer 1989, 18–23). With this in mind, one might ask what my claim that Jones has a choice about the thousand-years-ago truth of *that Jones sits at t* amounts to. This is a nice question for two reasons. First, I have just committed myself to the position that his having counterfactual power over that truth is not sufficient for his having such a choice. Second, I deny that his having such a choice involves his being able to (backward) cause that truth (see section 5).

---

[22]My suppositions about the "nearest world" in which my brother fails to visit might be false. But I think that there are at least some true counterfactuals that deliver the result that someone now has counterfactual power over a past event, an event about which he or she seems to lack a genuine choice. See, for example, Plantinga's (1986) argument, on the basis of such counterfactuals, that he might now have counterfactual power over whether Abraham ever existed. Also, Lewis 1981 argues that we have counterfactual power over the laws of nature.

Before answering this question, I want us to suppose that *t* is a few moments from now and that Jones has a genuine choice about whether he will sit at *t*. (Assuming his sitting will be free, this seems to be a paradigm case of having a genuine choice.) Given this supposition, it should be uncontroversial that Jones—before *t*—has a genuine choice about whether *that Jones sits at t* will be true at *t*.

Now for my answer. My claim that Jones has a choice about the thousand-years-ago truth of *that Jones sits at t* amounts to the following. Jones has a choice about that past truth in exactly the same way that he has a choice about the truth, at time *t*, of *that Jones sits at t*. And so he has a genuine choice about that past truth. All of this should bring to mind the second corollary of truth's dependence on the world: if an agent has a choice about performing some action like sitting, and if the truth of a proposition depends on the performance of that action, then the agent has a choice about the truth of that proposition.

7. FOREKNOWLEDGE

Smith once made a lucky guess. Ten years ago, she guessed that Jones would sit at *t*. And, as *t* approaches, Jones is about to sit. With this in mind, consider the *Lucky Guess Argument*:

(4) Jones has no choice about: Smith's belief *that Jones sits at t* was true ten years ago.

(5) Necessarily, if Smith's belief *that Jones sits at t* was true ten years ago, then Jones sits at time *t*.

Therefore,

(3) Jones has no choice about: Jones's sitting at time *t*.

My belief *that there are no white ravens* is true because there are no white ravens. Your belief *that dogs bark* is true because dogs bark. And so on. In general, a belief's truth depends on the world. This dependence has a corollary: for all persons *S* and all beliefs *b*, that *S* has no choice about *b*'s truth presupposes that *S* has no choice about what *b*'s truth depends on. To defend this corollary, simply mimic section 4's defense of the parallel corollary involving propositions. (And if a belief just is a proposition that is believed, this corollary about beliefs is simply an instance of the parallel corollary about propositions.)

This corollary involving beliefs implies that the first premise of the Lucky Guess Argument presupposes (3), that argument's conclusion. Thus, like the Main Argument, the Lucky Guess Argument is question-begging. Moreover, suppose that Jones freely sits at *t*. Then Jones has a choice about what the truth of Smith's belief depended on, which implies that Jones has a choice about whether Smith's belief was true ten years ago. Then the Lucky Guess Argument, again like the Main Argument, has a false first premise.

Start with the Lucky Guess Argument. Replace Smith with God. (And dispense with all talk of "luck" and "guesses".) The resulting argument is merely a variant of the Lucky Guess Argument. So the resulting argument is, like the Lucky Guess Argument, question-begging, and presumably has a false premise.[23]

The Lucky Guess Argument and its variants resemble the Main Argument by making claims about Jones's not having a choice about something's having been true. And they can be shown to fail, like the Main Argument, by focusing on truth's dependence on the world. But an argument that made no mention of truth would not be merely a variant of the Lucky Guess argument (cf. Pike 1965, 40–46). Nor would an argument that made no mention of truth run afoul of truth's dependence on the world. With this in mind, consider the *Divine Foreknowledge Argument*:

(6) Jones has no choice about: God believed *that Jones sits at t* a thousand years ago.[24]

(7) Necessarily, if God believed *that Jones sits at t* a thousand years ago, then Jones sits at time *t*.

Therefore,

(3) Jones has no choice about: Jones's sitting at time *t*

God is essentially omniscient. That is, necessarily, God believes all and only truths. Thus the second premise of the Divine Foreknowledge Argument is true, even though that premise makes no mention of truth, but instead mentions merely what God believed. (A parallel premise regarding merely what Smith believed would be false.)

My objection to this argument builds on an idea that goes back at least to Origen, who says: ". . . it will not be because God knows that an event will occur that it

---

[23]Some philosophers—from Augustine (Ora *Free Choice of the Will*, bk. 3, sec. 4 [1993, 78]) to Ayer (1963, 252)—have treated divine foreknowledge as if it is no more (or less) of a threat to freedom than is human foreknowledge.

[24]Some hold that God is outside time and so, they conclude, God did not believe anything *a thousand years ago* (see Boethius's *Consolation of Philosophy*, and, more recently, Stump and Kretzmann 1991). They would take God's being outside time to undermine the Divine Foreknowledge Argument. But see Plantinga 1986, 240; Wierenga 1991, 430–33; and van Inwagen 2008.

happens; but, because something is going to take place it is known by God before it happens."[25] Similarly, I say that God has certain beliefs about the world because of how the world is, was, or will be—and not vice versa. For example, God believes *that there are no white ravens* because there are no white ravens, and not the other way around. And God believed, a thousand years ago, *that Jones sits at t* because Jones will sit at *t*, and not the other way around.[26]

These observations do not, all by themselves, show that the Divine Foreknowledge Argument fails. For that argument's conclusion is not that Jones sits at *t* because God believed, long ago, *that Jones sits at t*, rather than vice versa. Instead, the Divine Foreknowledge Argument merely moves from foreknowledge as a premise to the relevant lack of choice as a conclusion.

Recall Edwards's remark quoted earlier (section 2): "Infallible foreknowledge may *prove* the necessity of the thing foreknown, and yet not be the thing which *causes* the necessity." Edwards makes this remark while showing that Origen's idea above does not, all by itself, block arguments from foreknowledge to a lack of freedom. So we must say more than did Origen if we are to show that the Divine Foreknowledge Argument fails.

Nevertheless, I begin with Origen's insight: God's beliefs depend on the world. This has a corollary: for all *S* and all God's beliefs *b*, that *S* has no choice about whether God has belief *b* presupposes (in the sense of "presupposes" relevant to begging the question) that *S* has no choice about what God's having belief *b* depends on (in the sense of "depends on" in which God's beliefs depend on the world). We can defend this by mimicking the defense of the similar corollary involving the truth of propositions.

For example, suppose I said that you have no choice about whether you will eat lunch at noon tomorrow. And suppose I added that you have no such choice as a result of the following: first, at noon tomorrow, God will believe (that is, will have

---

[25]*Commentary on the Epistle to the Romans*, bk. 7, chap. 8, sec. 5 [2002, 90]. Molina (*Concordia* 4, disputation 52, sec. 19 [1988, 179]) joins Origen in taking God's beliefs about the future to depend on what will happen, rather than the other way around.

[26]Some might claim that the way the world is depends on God's beliefs, not vice versa. And they might say that Aquinas makes this same claim, citing the *Summa Theologica* (Ia.q14.a8 [1945, 147–48]) and the *Summa Contra Gentiles* (1.67.5 [1975, 222]). But Aquinas's claim has to do with *causal* dependence. And so Aquinas does not deny my thesis that God's beliefs about the future depend on what will happen; more carefully, he does not deny the version of this thesis—articulated at the end of this section—according to which God's beliefs about the future are not caused by what happens in the future. Note also that Aquinas explicitly says that he does not disagree with Origen on this issue (*Summa Theologica* Ia.q.14.a8, reply Obj. 1).

the belief) that you are then eating lunch; and, second, you have no choice about what God will believe at noon tomorrow.

You ought to object as follows: you have a choice about whether you will eat lunch at noon tomorrow; whether God will believe, at noon tomorrow, that you are then eating lunch depends on whether you will be eating lunch then; therefore, you have a choice about whether God will believe, at noon tomorrow, that you are eating lunch then. At the very least, the claim that you do not have a choice about God's believing this at noon tomorrow presupposes that you do not have a choice about eating lunch at noon tomorrow.

Recall the first premise of the Divine Foreknowledge Argument:

(6) Jones has no choice about: God believed *that Jones sits at t* a thousand years ago.

Given the above corollary regarding God's beliefs, we can conclude that this premise presupposes the conclusion of that argument, which is:

(3) Jones has no choice about: Jones's sitting at time *t*.

So I object that the Divine Foreknowledge Argument, like the Main Argument and the Lucky Guess Argument, is question-begging.

The first premise of the Divine Foreknowledge Argument presupposes (and so entails) that argument's conclusion. I assume that this conclusion is false since I assume that Jones will sit freely at *t*. Therefore, I object that the first premise of the Divine Foreknowledge Argument is false. That is, I think it is false even if God really did believe, a thousand years ago, *that Jones sits at t*. I think that Jones, even now, has a choice about what God believed a thousand years ago.

(6)'s presupposing (3) is not the only reason to say that Jones now has such a choice. Another reason is that, first, Jones has a choice about sitting at *t*, and, second, God's having—even a thousand years ago—the belief *that Jones sits at t* depended on Jones's sitting at *t*. This is in all relevant respects just like the case above, in which you have a choice about God's believing, at noon tomorrow, that you are then eating lunch.[27]

Suppose the dependence of God's beliefs on the world implies that the world causes God's beliefs. Suppose, further, that God's beliefs about future events are caused by those future events. Then we have backward causation. Perhaps this sort of backward

---

[27]Ockhamists say that Jones has a choice about what God believed a thousand years ago, but for a reason other than my reasons. They might say, for example, that God's having had a belief a thousand years ago about the present or the future is a soft fact about the past. Of course, neither Ockhamists nor I say that Jones can *change* what God believed (see section 5).

causation is acceptable, even if backward causation takes a miracle, since God's fore-knowledge itself—like everything else about God?—might be miraculous.

But divine foreknowledge does not require backward causation. The first step toward seeing this is to suppose that God believed, a thousand years ago, *that Jones sits at t* because the proposition *that Jones sits at t* was true a thousand years ago. Obviously enough, this claim—a claim about God's believing a proposition at the very time at which that proposition was true—does not invoke backward causation. (Indeed, it need not invoke causation of any sort.)

The second and final step is to suppose that, since truth depends on the world, *that Jones sits at t* was true a thousand years ago because Jones will sit at *t*. The dependence of truth on the world is not causal (section 5). Thus there is no backward causation implied by the claim that *that Jones sits at t* was true a thousand years ago because Jones will sit at *t*.

These two steps deliver a sense of "because" in which God believed, a thousand years ago, *that Jones sits at t* because Jones will sit at *t*. But they do not rely on backward causation at any point. As a result, they deliver a backward-causation-free sense of "because" in which God believed, a thousand years ago, *that Jones sits at t* because Jones will sit at *t*.

ACKNOWLEDGMENTS

Thanks to audiences at the Australian National University, the University of Auckland, the University of Notre Dame, the University of Michigan, the University of St. Andrews, Georgetown University, and Wake Forest University, and to the Rutgers Philosophy of Religion Reading Group. Thanks also to Mike Bergmann, Jim Cargile, Tom Crisp, Joungbin Lim, Brannon McDaniel, Mark Murphy, Paul Nedelisky, Al Plantinga, Mike Rea, Donald Smith, Charlie Tanksley, Nick Wolterstorff, and Dean Zimmerman.

REFERENCES

Adams, Marilyn McCord. 1967. "Is the Existence of God a 'Hard' Fact?" *Philosophical Review* 76: 492–503.

Alston, William. 1993. *The Reliability of Sense Perception*. Ithaca, NY: Cornell University Press.

Anscombe, G. E. M. 1956. "Aristotle and the Sea Battle." *Mind* 65: 1–15.

Aquinas, Thomas. 1945. *Basic Writings of Saint Thomas Aquinas*, ed. A. C. Pegis. New York: Random House.

——.1975. *Summa Contra Gentiles*, trans. and ed. A. C. Pegis. Notre Dame, IN: University of Notre Dame Press.

Aristotle. 1984. *The Complete Works of Aristotle: The Revised Oxford Translation*, vols. 1–2, ed. Jonathan Barnes. Princeton, NJ: Princeton University Press.

Augustine. 1993. *On Free Choice of the Will*, trans. and ed. Thomas Williams. Indianapolis, IN: Hackett.

Ayer, A. J. 1963. "Fatalism." In *The Concept of a Person and Other Essays*, 235–68. New York: St. Martin's.

Bobzien, Susanne. 1998. *Determinism and Freedom in Stoic Philosophy*. Oxford: Oxford University Press.

Boethius. 1918. *The Theological Tractates and the Consolation of Philosophy*, trans. H. F. Stewart, E. K. Rand, and S. J. Tester. Cambridge, MA: Harvard University Press.

Crisp, Thomas M. 2003. "Presentism." In *The Oxford Handbook of Metaphysics*, ed. Michael J. Loux and Dean Zimmerman, 211–45. Oxford: Oxford University Press.

Crisp, Thomas M., and Ted A. Warfield. 2000. "The Irrelevance of Indeterministic Counterexamples to Principle Beta." *Philosophy and Phenomenological Research* 61: 173–84.

Edwards, Jonathan. 1957. *Freedom of the Will*, ed. Paul Ramsey. New Haven, CT: Yale University Press.

Finch, Alicia, and Michael C. Rea. 2008. "Presentism and Ockham's Way Out." In *Oxford Studies in Philosophy of Religion*, ed. Jonathan Kvanvig, 1–17. Oxford: Oxford University Press.

Finch, Alicia, and Ted A. Warfield. 1998. "The *Mind* Argument and Libertarianism." *Mind* 107: 515–28.

Fischer, John Martin. 1983. "Freedom and Foreknowledge." *Philosophical Review* 112: 67–79.

——. 1989. "Introduction: God and Freedom." In *God, Foreknowledge, and Freedom*, 1–36. Stanford, CA: Stanford University Press.

Ginet, Carl. 1966. "Might We Have No Choice?" In *Freedom and Determinism*, ed. Keith Lehrer, 87–104. New York: Random House.

Haack, Susan. 1974. *Deviant Logic: Some Philosophical Issues*. Cambridge: Cambridge University Press.

Hinchliff, Mark. 1996. "The Puzzle of Change." In *Philosophical Perspectives.*, vol. 10, *Metaphysics*, ed. James E. Tomberlin, 119–36. Oxford: Blackwell.

Horwich, Paul. 1987. *Asymmetries in Time: Problems in the Philosophy of Science*. Cambridge, MA: MIT Press.

——.1998. *Truth*. 2nd ed. Oxford: Clarendon.

Kane, Robert. 1998. *The Significance of Free Will*. New York: Oxford University Press.

Lewis, David. 1981. "Are We Free to Break the Laws?" *Theoria* 47: 113–21.

Lukasiewicz, Jan. 1967. "Philosophical Remarks on Many-Valued Systems of Propositional Logic." In *Polish Logic 1920–1939*, ed. Storrs McCall, 40–65. Oxford: Clarendon.

MacFarlane, John. 2003. "Future Contingents and Relative Truth." *Philosophical Quarterly* 53: 321–36.

McKay, Thomas, and David Johnson. 1996. "A Reconsideration of an Argument against Compatibilism." *Philosophical Topics* 24: 113–22.

Merricks, Trenton. 1994. "Endurance and Indiscernibility." *Journal of Philosophy* 91: 165–84.

—— 2001. *Objects and Persons*. Oxford: Clarendon.

—— 2007. *Truth and Ontology*. Oxford: Clarendon.

Molina, Luis de. 1988. *On Divine Foreknowledge: Part IV of the Concordia*, trans. and ed. Alfred J. Freddoso. Ithaca, NY: Cornell University Press.

Ockham, William. 1983. *Predestination, God's Foreknowledge, and Future Contingents*, trans. and ed. Marilyn McCord Adams and Norman Kretzmann. Indianapolis, IN: Hackett.

O'Connor, Timothy. 2000. *Persons and Causes: The Metaphysics of Free Will*. Oxford: Oxford University Press.

Origen. 2002. *Commentary on the Epistle to the Romans, Books 6–10*, trans. T. P. Scheck. Washington, DC: Catholic University of America Press.

Pereboom, Derk. 2001. *Living without Free Will*. Cambridge: Cambridge University Press.

Pike, Nelson. 1965. "Divine Omniscience and Voluntary Action." *Philosophical Review* 74: 27–46.

Plantinga, Alvin. 1974. *God, Freedom, and Evil*. New York: Harper and Row.

——. 1986. "On Ockham's Way Out." *Faith and Philosophy* 3: 235–69.

Rea, Michael C. 2006. "Presentism and Fatalism." *Australasian Journal of Philosophy* 84: 511–24.

Ryle, Gilbert. 1954. *Dilemmas*. Cambridge: Cambridge University Press.

Saunders, John Turk. 1966. "Of God and Freedom." *Philosophical Review* 75: 219–25.

Strawson, Galen. 1987. *Freedom and Belief*. Oxford: Clarendon.

Stump, Eleonore, and Norman Kretzmann. 1991. "Prophecy, Past Truth, and Eternity." In *Philosophical Perspectives*, vol. 5: *Philosophy of Religion*, ed. James Tomberlin, 395–424. Atascadero, CA: Ridgeview.

Van Inwagen, Peter. 1983. *An Essay on Free Will*. Oxford: Clarendon.

——. 2006. *The Problem of Evil: The Gifford Lectures Delivered in the University of St Andrews in 2003*. Oxford: Clarendon.

——. 2008. "What Does an Omniscient Being Know about the Future?" In *Oxford Studies in Philosophy of Religion*, ed. Jonathan Kvanvig, 216–30. Oxford: Oxford University Press.

Widerker, David. 1987. "On an Argument for Incompatibilism." *Analysis* 47: 37–41.

Wierenga, Edward. 1991. "Prophecy, Freedom, and the Necessity of the Past." In *Philosophical Perspectives*, vol. 5: *Philosophy of Religion*, ed. James Tomberlin, 425–45. Atascadero, CA: Ridgeview.

Wiggins, David. 1973. "Towards a Reasonable Libertarianism." In *Essays on Freedom of Action*, ed. Ted Honderich, 31–62. London: Routledge and Kegan Paul.

Williams, Donald C. 1951. "The Sea Fight Tomorrow." In *Structure, Method, and Meaning: Essays in Honor of Henry M. Sheffer*, ed. P. Henle, H. M. Kalen, and S. K. Langer, 282–306. New York: Liberal Arts.

Williamson, Timothy. 1994. *Vagueness*. London: Roudedge.

4

THE TRUTH ABOUT FREEDOM
A REPLY TO MERRICKS

John Martin Fischer and Patrick Todd

1. INTRODUCTION

In "Truth and Freedom," Trenton Merricks articulates a truism: "a claim or statement or belief or proposition is true because things are how that claim (or statement . . .) represents things as being—and not the other way around."[1] Merricks argues that this truism—that truth depends on the world—can help us to see that various arguments for "fatalism" (by which he means to include incompatibilism about God's foreknowledge and human freedom) are problematic. Indeed, he contends that a proper application of the truism shows that the most plausible arguments for fatalism are question-begging.

In this reply, we argue that mere invocation of the truism, even together with other considerations, does *not* show that the arguments under consideration are question-begging. At most, the truism helps us to see—what we should in any case have seen before—that the arguments, as regimented by Merricks, are *incomplete*. But the truism in no way establishes or even suggests that the relevant arguments cannot be supplemented by additional resources that render the arguments at least plausible. Supplemented suitably, the arguments are *not* question-begging, although they are admittedly controversial in various ways.

2. MERRICKS'S ARGUMENT

Here is the *Main Argument* and Merricks's initial reflections on it:

Let time *t* be just a few minutes in the future from now, and consider the *Main Argument*:

---

[1] Trenton Merricks, "Truth and Freedom," *Philosophical Review* 118 (2009): 29–57; the quotation is on p. 29.

(1) Jones has no choice about: *that Jones sits at t* was true a thousand years ago.

(2) Necessarily, if *that Jones sits at t* was true a thousand years ago, then Jones sits at time *t*.

Therefore,

(3) Jones has no choice about: Jones's sitting at time *t*.

In my opinion, the Main Argument is the strongest argument for fatalism; that is, it is the strongest argument that moves from truths in the past to a present or future lack of freedom. But, as we shall see, the Main Argument fails because of considerations arising from truth's dependence on the world. . . . We shall also see that every initially compelling argument for fatalism—that is, every argument for fatalism free of obvious flaws . . . —fails for the same reason.[2]

Merricks says that the truism helps us to see that it is question-begging to assume (1). Suppose Jones does in fact sit at *t*. The truism purports to tell us that *that Jones sits at t* was true a thousand years ago *because* Jones sits at *t*, that is, the truth of *that Jones sits at t* depends on Jones's sitting at *t*.[3] Further, Merricks articulates the following corollary of truth's dependence on the world: "for all *S* and all *p*, *S* has no choice about *p*'s truth presupposes . . . that *S* has no choice about what *p*'s truth depends on (in the sense of "depends on" in which truth depends on the world)."[4] So to suppose that (1) is true, that is, to suppose that Jones has no choice about the truth of *that Jones sits at t*, appears to presuppose precisely what is at issue, namely, that Jones has no choice about sitting at *t*.

Merricks also contends that the standard argument for the incompatibility of God's foreknowledge and human freedom is question-begging in a way that is similar to the way in which the Main Argument is (allegedly) question-begging. He considers what he calls the *Divine Foreknowledge Argument*:

(6) Jones has no choice about: God believed *that Jones sits at t* a thousand years ago.

(7) Necessarily, if God believed *that Jones sits at t* a thousand years ago, then Jones sits at time *t*.

Therefore,

(3) Jones has no choice about: Jones's sitting at time *t*.[5]

---

[2]Ibid., 33.
[3]We return to a critical evaluation of this contention below.
[4]Ibid., 37.
[5]Ibid., 51–52.

About this argument Merricks says:

> My objection to this argument builds on an idea that goes back at least to Origen, who says: "it will not be because God knows that an event will occur that it happens; but, because something is going to take place it is known by God before it happens." [Merricks refers here to *Commentary on the Epistle to the Romans*, bk. 7, chap. 8, sec. 5; also he says, "Molina (*Concordia* 4, disputation 52, sec. 19) joins Origen in taking God's beliefs about the future to depend on what will happen, rather than the other way around."] Similarly, I say that God has certain beliefs about the world because of how the world is, was, or will be—and not vice versa. For example, God believes *that there are no white ravens* because there are no white ravens, and not the other way around. And God believed, a thousand years ago, *that Jones sits at t* because Jones will sit at *t*, and not the other way around.[6]

Admitting that these considerations do not "all by themselves" show that the Divine Foreknowledge Argument fails, nevertheless Merricks builds on what he takes to be "Origen's insight", namely, that God's beliefs depend on the world. He then articulates the following corollary: "For all *S* and all God's beliefs *b*, that *S* has no choice about whether God has belief *b* presupposes (in the sense of "presupposes" relevant to begging the question) that *S* has no choice about what God's having belief *b* depends on (in the sense of "depends on" in which God's beliefs depend on the world)." Now Merricks goes on to say:

Recall the first premise of the Divine Foreknowledge Argument:

> (6) Jones has no choice about: God believed *that Jones sits at t* a thousand years ago.

Given the above corollary regarding God's beliefs, we can conclude that this premise presupposes the conclusion of that argument, which is:

> (3) Jones has no choice about: Jones's sitting at time *t*.

So I object that the Divine Foreknowledge Argument, like the Main Argument . . . is question-begging.[7]

---

[6]Ibid., 52.
[7]Ibid., 53.

3. CRITIQUE OF MERRICKS: THE DIVINE FOREKNOWLEDGE ARGUMENT

We begin by considering Merricks's critique of the Divine Foreknowledge Argument, given our belief that it, more clearly than the Main Argument, does *not* beg the question.[8] We shall go on to consider whether the resources we employ in our defense of the Divine Foreknowledge Argument can be applied similarly to the Main Argument. We agree that it would indeed be dialectically infelicitous simply to announce that (say) premise (6) is true without any defense of it. But this would not be the typical approach of the proponent of the Divine Foreknowledge Argument (or similar arguments).[9] Rather, the proponent of the incompatibility of God's foreknowledge and human freedom (in the sense of "freedom to do otherwise") would contend that (6) is an instance of the very plausible general thesis that the past is "fixed". If (6) is an instance of the fixity (sometimes also called the "necessity") of the past, then (6) would not be question-begging.

But what exactly is the commonsense notion of the fixity of the past? And how does it apply to premise (6)? Merricks himself explores the possibility that considerations pertinent to the "necessity of the past" might help to establish a premise such as (6).[10] Below we shall return to Merricks's discussion, but before doing so, we shall seek to give a plausible account of the fixity of the past and its relationship to premise (6).

We start with what appears to be a bit of common sense: we have no choice about the past. For instance, we have no choice about the fact that John F. Kennedy was shot in Dallas in 1963. We have no choice about the fact that Caesar crossed the Rubicon. These facts seem "fixed" or out of our control, and it is simply too late to do anything about them now. As a first approximation, the claim that the past is fixed—the fixity of the past—is just the claim that we have no choice about such facts. But there are various ways one might wish to "regiment" the claim that we have no choice about the past. One promising way to do so, and the way we shall employ in this essay, uses the notion of possible worlds.

---

[8]Perhaps we should note that the whole notion of "begging the question" is quite vexed. The epithet "question-begging" is invoked to point to a range of dialectical infelicities. Here we shall follow Merricks in using the term (and not seeking to define it), and we shall assume that we have a tolerably clear idea of the sort of dialectical impropriety under consideration.

[9]John Martin Fischer, "Recent Work on God and Freedom," *American Philosophical Quarterly* 29 (1992): 91–109; and John Martin Fischer, ed., *God, Foreknowledge, and Freedom* (Stanford: Stanford University Press, 1989).

[10]Merricks, "Truth and Freedom," 40–42.

It is widely agreed that an agent *can* perform a given action only if there is a possible world suitably related to (and thus "accessible from") the actual world in which the agent *does* perform the action. While this much is uncontroversial, exactly which worlds *are* accessible from the actual world is highly contentious. Incompatibilists about the freedom to do otherwise and causal determinism, for instance, contend that an agent can do otherwise at a given time only if there exists a possible world with the *same past* as the actual world (up to the given time) in which the agent performs the action. In other words, according to the incompatibilist, the only accessible worlds are worlds with the same past as the actual world; the actual past must be *held fixed* when assessing a can-claim. If a fact obtains in every possible world accessible to one from the actual world, then that fact *is fixed* for one.[11] The fixity of the past, then, is the thesis (to be qualified shortly) that all facts about the past are fixed.

Of course, it is beyond the scope of this essay to attempt to *justify* the thesis of the fixity of the past. However, we think this thesis has considerable plausibility. The fixity of the past says that one can do something only if there is a possible world with the same past as the actual world in which one does it. If there is not such a world, then it will be a requirement on one's performing the given action that the past have been different. Plausibly, however, it's now too late for the past to have been different, and thus one cannot perform the action in question. In other words, if it is a *requirement* (or a *necessary condition*) on one's performing some action that some fact about the past—the fact, say, that Kennedy was shot in Dallas in 1963—not have obtained, then it is plausible that one cannot perform the action. For Kennedy *was* shot, and, plausibly, any possible world now "accessible" to one will include this fact. Intuitively, this notion nicely captures the idea that we have no choice about Kennedy's having been shot: in virtue of being a fact about the past, this fact will obtain in all possible worlds now accessible to us. It thus enjoys a certain sort of necessity.

---

[11]Although it is perhaps somewhat unusual to think of possible worlds as accessible to *agents* (rather than other possible worlds), there is an established tradition of allowing for an accessibility relation between agents and possible worlds in the literature on possible-worlds approaches to "can". For example, Keith Lehrer says, "The crux of the foregoing is that when we say that a person could have done something he did not do, we should not, and I believe do not, thereby affirm that every antecedent necessary condition of his performing the action is fulfilled. It is enough that there be some possible world minimally different from the actual world restricted in an appropriate way so that the person performs the action and those conditions are fulfilled. We may speak of worlds restricted in the appropriate way as possible worlds that are *accessible* to the agent from the actual world." Keith Lehrer, " 'Can' in Theory and Practice: A Possible Worlds Approach," in *Action Theory*, ed. Myles Brand and Douglas Walton (Dordrecht: Reidel, 1976) 241–70, esp. 253–54.

Before we can give a fully perspicuous account of the fixity of the past, however, we must make the crucial distinction between so-called "hard" and "soft" facts about the past. The distinction between hard and soft facts (although not the terminology) traces back to William of Ockham.[12] Ockham employed this distinction to give a certain sort of *response* to the Divine Foreknowledge Argument, but the distinction is crucial also in providing a proper interpretation of the argument itself. Hard facts are (in some way that is hard to characterize precisely) temporally non-relational as regards the future (relative to the time they are about). More specifically, a hard fact about some time *t* is genuinely about *t* and not also genuinely about some time after *t*. In contrast, a soft fact is temporally relational as regards the future (relative to the time it is about); that is, a soft fact about some time *t* is at least in part genuinely about some time after *t*.

For instance, it is a hard fact about 1963 that John F. Kennedy was then shot in Dallas. However, from the fact that we are presently writing this essay, standard assumptions have it that it was true in 1963 that we would write it. Thus, it follows that Kennedy's assassination had the property of taking place (roughly) forty-six years prior to our writing this essay. But this is plainly a soft feature of Kennedy's assassination; it has this feature simply in virtue of its temporal relationship to a future time, namely, the present time at which we are writing this essay. So, whereas it is a hard fact about the past relative to now that Kennedy was assassinated in 1963, it is a soft fact about the past relative to now that Kennedy was assassinated forty-six years prior to our writing our essay.

Now, as a first approximation, the defender of the Divine Foreknowledge Argument merely wishes to defend the claim that all hard facts about the past are fixed, but he or she grants (or may grant) that some soft facts are not fixed. Here, it is important to note that if all soft facts about the past are fixed, then (given our assumptions) logical fatalism would immediately follow. On our assumptions, from the fact that we are writing this essay, it follows that it is a fact about the past that Kennedy was shot forty-six years prior to our writing the essay. But suppose this fact was (prior to our writing the essay) fixed for us. Then any possible world accessible to us included this fact. Thus, any possible world accessible to us included our actually writing the essay, and hence we could not have done anything else than write it. Generalizing, we can never do other than what we actually do. While this result clearly follows from the claim that all soft facts are fixed, it does not follow from the

[12]William of Ockham, *Predestination, God's Foreknowledge, and Future Contingents*, trans. and ed. Marilyn McCord Adams and Norman Kretzmann (Indianapolis: Hackett), esp. 46–47. For discussions of Ockham's views and contemporary versions of Ockhamism, see Fischer, *God, Foreknowledge, and Freedom* and Fischer, "Recent Work."

weaker (and more plausible) claim that all *hard* facts are fixed. And, as we will see, this is arguably all the proponent of the Foreknowledge Argument needs.

With the distinction between hard and soft facts under our belts, we can now state the thesis of the fixity of the past slightly more carefully as follows:

(FP)   For any action Y, agent S, and time t, S can perform Y at t only if there is a possible world with the same "hard" past up to t as the actual world in which S does Y at t.[13]

We contend that (FP) is both plausible and captures the intuitive idea that the past is beyond our control. And we are now in a position to see why the Divine Foreknowledge Argument is not in fact question-begging. As we said above, it would be incomplete if it were left as developed by Merricks, unsupplemented by further considerations. But that is not the best way to understand the argument. Rather, the proponent of the Divine Foreknowledge Argument should (and typically would) invoke the fixity of the past to support the crucial premise (6).

That is, the proponent of the argument would first contend that the fact that God had a belief a thousand years ago that Jones will sit at t is a hard (temporally nonrelational) fact about a thousand years ago. The thought here is just this: God's being in a certain mental state at a time does not exhibit the temporal relationality essential to soft facthood. God's being in such a mental state at a time is a temporally intrinsic, hard feature of that time. That is, it is not relevantly similar to Kennedy's having been shot forty-six years prior to our writing this essay. Rather, God's having a certain belief at a time is relevantly similar simply to Kennedy's having been shot.

Next, given the above claim about God's beliefs, the proponent of the Divine Foreknowledge Argument would point out that it follows from (FP) that Jones can do otherwise than sit at t only if there is a world with the same "hard" past as the actual world—in particular, a world in which God believed a thousand years ago that he (Jones) sits at t—in which he does not sit at t. However, there is no such world since, given God's essential omniscience, there is no world in which God believes that Jones will sit at t and in which Jones does not in fact sit at t. In other words, given God's past belief, it is a necessary condition of Jones's doing otherwise that some hard fact about the past have been otherwise. Plausibly, then, Jones cannot do otherwise than sit at t. Thus, considerations pertaining to the intuitive and commonsense notion of the fixity of the past—as regimented by (FP)—provide the

---

[13]See, for example, John Martin Fischer, *The Metaphysics of Free Will: An Essay on Control* (Cambridge: Blackwell, 1994), 90.

requisite support for premise (6). This shows that, whatever its flaws, the Divine Foreknowledge Argument is *not* question-begging.

Now manifestly it does not follow from an argument's not being question-begging that it is uncontroversially sound! Ockhamists, for instance, will call into question the contention that God's prior beliefs are hard facts about the past; indeed, the point of Ockham's introduction of the distinction between hard and soft facts was to argue that God's beliefs are *soft* facts about the relevant times. (As we emphasized above, the distinction *itself* is not "owned" by the Ockhamist, and it is needed in order to formulate the Divine Foreknowledge Argument in a plausible way. What is distinctive to Ockhamism is the *categorization* of God's prior beliefs as *soft* facts about the relevant times.) We certainly do not wish to argue here that the Divine Foreknowledge Argument can in the end be defended against the Ockhamist objection (and others). We simply seek to show that, *contra* Merricks, the argument (properly interpreted) is not *question-begging*.

Merricks does in fact consider whether the Main Argument (and also presumably the Divine Foreknowledge Argument) might rely on the notion of the fixity of the past. He considers three ways one might understand the claim that the past is necessary (or fixed). One is to say that there cannot be "backward causation". Another is to say that the past cannot be changed. We agree with Merricks that these notions do not capture what it is for the past to be fixed, though those claims certainly are *prerequisites*, so to speak, of the past being fixed.[14] Merricks presents—and criticizes—a third interpretation of the necessity of the past as follows:

Suppose that that claim [the necessity of the past] is just another way of saying that no one now has (and no one in the future will have) a choice about what the past was like, not even about which propositions were true in the past. If this is all the necessity of the past amounts to, then arguments for Jones's having no choice about sitting at *t* that start with the necessity of the past truth of *that Jones sits at t* just are the Main Argument, put in other words.

And if this is all the necessity of the past amounts to, the objection just considered [that the past is necessary] fails. For that objection takes the assertion that the past is necessary to be a reason for the claim that no one now has a choice about what the past was like. But that claim cannot be a reason for itself.[15]

---

[14]In other words, if we can causally affect the past or directly change it, this would certainly call (FP) into question.

[15]Merricks, "Truth and Freedom," 40.

Above, we contended that the necessity (or fixity) of the past amounts to no one's having a choice about *hard* facts about the past—that such facts obtain in all worlds accessible to us. Note that Merricks saddles the proponent of the fixity of the past with the claim that we have no choice about what propositions (quite generally) were true in the past. But proponents of the fixity of the past are in no way committed to this general claim since such propositions may have expressed soft facts about the past.

Moreover, Merricks contends that the claim that the past is necessary (or fixed) is supposed to be a *reason* for the claim that no one now has a choice about what the past was like. But this response is confused. For, as we have noted, the claim that the past is fixed—(FP)—*just is* this claim (as applied to hard facts). However, while *what it is* for the past to be fixed is for us to have no choice about hard facts about the past, one may *support* (FP) by invoking considerations having to do with the temporal nonrelationality of hard facts, and their attendant lack of dependence on what we now do, or by some other means. That is, arguably (FP) *follows* from deeper facts about our powers, time, and dependence. (Again, it is beyond the scope of this essay to give a full defense of (FP)). On this picture of the structure of the dialectic, (FP) is not supposed to be a *reason* for thinking we have no choice about the past but is meant to *capture* this claim.

To summarize, we can interpret the proponent of the Divine Foreknowledge Argument as first arguing for (FP) itself. Next, he or she contends that facts about God's beliefs a thousand years ago are hard facts about a thousand years ago. He or she concludes that the fact that God held a given belief a thousand years ago is now fixed; no one has any choice about this fact now. None of the steps of this more extended argument appears question-begging. Many—including the present authors—think the arguments on behalf of (FP) are persuasive. At any rate, we do not see in Merricks's argumentation any reason to conclude that (FP) is unmotivated, implausible, or that its invocation by itself begs the question.[16] Indeed, we

---

[16]We think Merricks has perhaps missed the force of considerations arising from the fixity of God's past beliefs due to a subtle shift in what the relevant fact about the past is supposed to be. Note: there is an important distinction between *God's having believed p*, on the one hand, and *what God believed* (namely, *p*), on the other. According to the proponent of the Foreknowledge Argument, what is fixed is the former thing—that is, it is fixed for Jones at *t* that God believed thus and so a thousand years prior. It is God's having been in a certain *mental state* that is over and done with and a putative hard fact about the past. It is *not* (in the first instance, at least) *what God believed* that is the putative hard fact. But we note that Merricks seems to have missed this distinction. In stating that he takes it that the Foreknowledge Argument has a false premise, for instance, Merricks ("Truth and Freedom," 54) says, "I think [premise one] is false even if God really did believe, a thousand years ago, *that Jones sits at t*. I think that Jones, even now, has a choice about what God believed a thousand years ago." But the proponent of the Foreknowledge Argument ought to complain that Merricks has unfairly shifted the dialectic here. For it is more

wish to point out that (FP) (along with a similar premise concerning the fixity of the natural laws) is a linchpin in the importantly parallel argument for the incompatibility of causal determinism and freedom to do otherwise, and is thus widely accepted among incompatibilists. It would thus come as some surprise if employing (FP) begs the question. Of course, as above, one could (with Ockhamists) object to the contention that God's past beliefs are hard.[17] But we fail to see how the contention that they *are* hard begs any pertinent questions (we return to this claim below). So we fail to see how Merricks has established that the Divine Foreknowledge Argument begs the question.

4. CRITIQUE OF MERRICKS: OCKHAMISM AND DEPENDENCE

Before considering whether the Main Argument can be saved from Merricks's objections, we wish to highlight our belief that Merricks has fundamentally misunderstood Ockhamism, both with respect to its technical details and its very heart and soul. Merricks wishes to distinguish his own views from those of Ockhamists. He says,

> Unlike the Ockhamists, I rely on neither a distinction between "soft facts" and "hard facts" nor on a distinction between what propositions are about with respect to "wording" and about with respect to "subject matter." So I do not have to make sense of these distinctions at all, much less in a way that delivers certain results, results like: for each soft fact about the past, someone or other now has (or will have) a choice about it.[18]

counterintuitive to suppose that Jones could have a choice about *God's having believed p* than it is to suppose that he could have a choice about the *content* of God's belief, namely, that he sits at *t*. It is, in other words, comparatively easy to see how one could have a choice about sitting at *t*, but much harder to see how one could have a choice about someone's having believed something a long time ago. Indeed, how *could* one have a choice about something like that? For some discussions of this issue, see John Martin Fischer, "Freedom and Foreknowledge," *Philosophical Review* 92 (1983): 67–79, reprinted in Fischer, *God, Foreknowledge, and Freedom*, 86–96; and Eddy Zemach and David Widerker, "Facts, Freedom, and Foreknowledge," *Religious Studies* 23 (1988): 19–28, reprinted in Fischer, *God, Foreknowledge, and Freedom*, 111–22.

[17]For some such Ockhamist arguments, see, for example, Marilyn McCord Adams, "Is the Existence of God a 'Hard' Fact?," *Philosophical Review* 76 (1967): 492–503, reprinted in Fischer, *God, Foreknowledge, and Freedom*, 74—85; Joshua Hoffman and Gary Rosenkrantz, "Hard and Soft Facts," *Philosophical Review* 93 (1984): 419–34, reprinted in Fischer, *God, Foreknowledge, and Freedom*, 123–35; and Alfred J. Freddoso, "Accidental Necessity and Logical Determinism," *Journal of Philosophy* 80 (1983): 257–78, reprinted in Fischer, *God, Foreknowledge, and Freedom*, 136–58.

[18]Merricks, "Truth and Freedom," 48.

But the Ockhamist does *not* hold that for each soft fact about the past, someone or other now has (or will have) a choice about it. For example, it is a soft fact about early this morning that the sun rose twenty-four hours prior to another sunrise, but presumably no one now has a choice about this fact since no one can prevent the sun's rising tomorrow. This fact is thus fixed now, although it is not fixed in virtue of the fixity of the *past*. It is best to draw a bright line between the two distinctions: hard versus soft facts and fixed versus nonfixed facts. The Ockhamist (as opposed to the Multiple-Pasts Compatibilist) argues that all hard facts about the past are now fixed, whereas *some* soft facts about the past are *not* now fixed.[19] An Ockhamist does *not* assert that *all* soft facts about the past fail to be fixed now—just those that depend on our free decisions.

We think Merricks has misunderstood Ockhamism at an even deeper level. He says,

> I object that the Main Argument begs the question. But Ockhamists would not thus object to the Main Argument. For Ockhamists do not invoke the idea underlying this objection, the idea that truth depends on the world.[20]

But we believe that Ockhamists do indeed invoke the idea that truth depends on the world. At any rate, Merricks's claim that they do not is at best superficial. For, as we now wish to argue, precisely what makes the difference for the Ockhamist between soft and hard facts about the past is that soft facts—the paradigmatic instances of which are facts incorporating past *truths* about the future—are (in a particular way) dependent on the future, and thus (sometimes) within our control. That is, those soft facts about the past that we have a choice about are precisely those that depend on our free decisions. Thus, we think the central contentions that have motivated Merricks are (perhaps ironically) fundamentally the same as those that have been motivating Ockhamists all along.

Note that Ockham himself says, concerning what are now called soft facts, "Other propositions are about the present as regards their wording only and are equivalently about the future, since their truth depends on the truth of propositions about the future."[21] Consider also, for example, Alfred Freddoso's way of putting the point:

---

[19]The Multiple Pasts Compatibilist replies to the "Consequence Argument" for the incompatibility of causal determinism and freedom to do otherwise by contending that even hard facts about the past need not be fixed now. For a development of the Consequence Argument, see Peter van Inwagen, *An Essay on Free Will* (Oxford: Clarendon Press, 1983). For a discussion, including an evaluation of Multiple Pasts Compatibilism, see Fischer, *Metaphysics of Free Will*.

[20]Merricks, "Truth and Freedom," 46.

[21]William of Ockham, *Predestination*, 46–47. Indeed, Merricks quotes this passage from Ockham on p. 49 of "Truth and Freedom," and, arguably, this amounts to precisely what Merricks wants.

Although, as we shall see, the detailed articulation of this position [Ockhamism] is rather complicated, the intuition which grounds it is the familiar, but often mis-understood, claim that a future-tense proposition is true now *because* the appro-priate present-tense proposition or propositions will be true in the future.[22]

Indeed, Freddoso explicitly invokes the notion of dependence in order to motivate his Ockhamism.

Recall the Ockhamist's basic contention: whereas all hard facts about the past are fixed, some such soft facts are not. Now, according to the Ockhamist, what grounds this distinction with respect to fixity? Why is it, in other words, that cer-tain temporally relational facts about the past needn't be held fixed when evaluating a "can-claim"? After all, given that the relevant soft facts about the past entail our future decisions, it will be a necessary condition on our doing otherwise that these soft facts were different. Why is this no threat to our freedom? Although we cannot fully defend this claim here, we think the Ockhamist literature clearly supports the claim that (on their view) such facts needn't be fixed because they held *in virtue of* our free decisions.

Consider again the soft fact about the past that Kennedy was shot forty-six years prior to our writing this essay. On Ockhamism, this was a fact in 1963 *because of* or *in virtue of* our writing our essay. According to the Ockhamist, then, to suppose that we had no choice (just prior to writing our essay) about the obtaining of this fact in 1963 would be to suppose that we had no choice about what this fact depended on, namely, our writing the essay. Intuitively, however, according to the Ockhamist, since (apart from any convincing skeptical argument) we did have a choice about writing this essay, we had a choice about whatever facts (past, present, or future) depended on our writing it. In other words, the ultimate rationale the Ockhamist would wish to provide for the lack of fixity of such temporally relational, soft facts about the past is that—as suggested by Merricks—they *depend* on what we do.[23]

Given this fact, we think Merricks would have been better served casting his objection to the Divine Foreknowledge Argument in a different way. For, as we have been arguing, the hallmark of a soft fact is that it *depends* on the future—and, in the case of the relevant soft facts, that they depend on our free decisions. Indeed, given the above construal of Ockhamism, perhaps Merricks would wish to adopt

---

[22]Freddoso, "Accidental Necessity," in Fischer, *God, Foreknowledge, and Freedom*, 143.

[23]For discussion of the manner in which Ockhamists rely on the notion of dependence, see John Martin Fischer, Patrick Todd, and Neal Tognazzini, "Engaging with Pike: God, Freedom, and Time," *Philosophical Papers* 38 (2009): 247–70. See also Alicia Finch and Michael Rea, "Presentism and Ockham's Way Out," in *Oxford Studies in Philosophy of Religion*, vol. 1, ed. Jonathan Kvanvig (New York: Oxford University Press, 2008), 1–17.

the mantle of Ockhamism and argue that a proper application of the truism shows that God's relevant past beliefs *are soft*.

It should come as no surprise, however, that Ockhamism cannot be so easily vindicated. For while it is the hallmark of a soft fact that it depends on the future, dependence comes in different sorts (as many philosophers have recently argued),[24] and it is not at all obvious that the sort of dependence facts about God's past beliefs exhibit on the future is the sort relevant to soft facthood. In other words, it is not enough that the fact that God has a certain belief about the future *in some sense* depends on the future. This fact must depend on the future *in the right way*.

We can begin to see the challenge of specifying the relevant notion of dependence as follows. Some philosophers working on the notion of ontological dependence have suggested that the notion be analyzed in terms of a primitive relationship of *objective explanation*.[25] Similarly, Merricks has repeatedly insisted that God had the relevant beliefs *because* of what we do. Thus, perhaps we should try:

(BC)   A fact F about at a time t is soft if and only if it is a fact at t because of how the future is relative to t.

(BC) certainly seems to be on the right track. But consider a well-known story from Alvin Plantinga:

Let us suppose that a colony of carpenter ants moved into Paul's yard last Saturday. Since this colony has not yet had a chance to get properly established, its new home is still a bit fragile. In particular, if the ants were to remain and Paul were to mow his lawn this afternoon, the colony would be destroyed. Although nothing remarkable about these ants is visible to the naked eye, God, for reasons of his own, intends that it be preserved. Now as a matter of fact, Paul will not mow his lawn this afternoon. God, who is essentially omniscient, knew in advance, of course, that Paul will not mow his lawn this afternoon; but if he had foreknown instead that Paul *would* mow this afternoon, then he would have prevented the ants from moving in.[26]

---

[24]See, for example, Kit Fine, "Ontological Dependence," *Proceedings of the Aristotelian Society* 95 (1995): 269–90; E. J. Lowe, *The Possibility of Metaphysics* (Oxford: Oxford University Press, 1998), 136–53; and Fabrice Correia, *Existential Dependence and Cognate Notions* (Munich: Philosophia Verlag, 2005).

[25]See Correia, *Existential Dependence*; and Benjamin Schnieder, "A Certain Kind of Trinity: Dependence, Substance, Explanation," *Philosophical Studies* 129 (2006): 393–419.

[26]Alvin Plantinga, "Ockham's Way Out," in Fischer, *God, Foreknowledge, and Freedom*, 201.

Now, in the context of the above story, consider:

(1) That colony of carpenter ants moved into Paul's yard last Saturday.

The problem (1) poses for (BC) is that (1) is, on Plantinga's story, a fact because of how the future was relative to last Saturday. More particularly, the fact that there are ants in Paul's yard on Saturday is a fact because of how the future is relative to that time—in particular, it is a fact because Paul will not mow his lawn this afternoon.[27] However, (1) is plainly a hard fact about last Saturday—as Plantinga says, (1) is "about as good a candidate for being an exemplification of [hard facthood] as we can easily think of."[28]

Given Plantinga's story, (1) arguably constitutes a counterexample to (BC). More generally, given God's presence as an agent who intervenes in the world on the basis of his foreknowledge, it seems that a hard fact can obtain at a time because of how the future is relative to that time. This will be the case whenever God arranges the past relative to a time on the basis of foreknowing that something will happen at that time. Again, in that case, those features of the past will be the way they are because of how the future is.

The lesson here is that any proper account of the hard/soft fact distinction must thread the needle between the fact that (in the story) ants moved into Paul's yard last Saturday and a fact such as that John F. Kennedy was assassinated forty-six years prior to our writing this essay. Both facts are facts in virtue of, or because of, how the future is. Yet only one—the latter—is soft. Thus, we still need a sense in which the JFK fact depends on the future but (1) doesn't. Both depend on (or hold because of) the future *somehow*, but only one is soft. Notably, the failure of (BC) would show that one cannot simply invoke the idea that God has the relevant beliefs because of

---

[27]If anyone is concerned that the fact that Paul will not do something is not a proper fact about the future, we could change the story so that the relevant fact is that Paul *will* do something; for example, that God had ants move in because he knew that Paul was going to take a nap today.

[28]Plantinga, "Ockham's Way Out," in Fischer, *God, Foreknowledge, and Freedom*, 201. Plantinga goes on to say that Paul *can* mow his lawn, and if he were to do so, the ants would not have been in his yard last Saturday. Thus, Plantinga denies *one* way some sought to capture the fixity of the past, namely, that "can-claims" are incompatible with the truth of such backtracking counterfactuals. That is, Plantinga denies:

(FPC) For any action Y, agent S, and time t, if it is true that if S were to do Y at t, then some hard fact about the past (relative to t) would not have been a fact, then S cannot do Y at t.

However, it is crucial to note that the denial of (FPC) is entirely compatible with the *acceptance* of (FP). For more on the distinction between (FP) and (FPC) and how one might deny the former but accept the latter, see Fischer, *Metaphysics of Free Will*, 87–110; and Patrick Todd, "A New Approach to Ockhamism" (unpublished manuscript).

what we do in order to show that these facts do not fall under the fixity of the past (as regimented by (FP)).

In this section, we have first pointed out that, despite his statements to the contrary, Merricks relies on the same ideas about dependence as those that have been motivating Ockhamists all along. Our discussion also shows that it is not at all easy to specify the sort of dependence relevant to soft facthood. It is, of course, comparatively much easier simply to *say* that God's beliefs depend on our decisions, as does Merricks, without wading into the difficulties surrounding in just what sense God's beliefs so depend and whether this sense is intuitively relevant to fixity. Our point here has not been to argue that God's past beliefs are *not* dependent in the right sort of way on the future. Nor have we offered any particular account of the sort of dependence relevant to softness.[29] Further, we believe that it is not obvious that God's beliefs *do* depend on the future in the right way. Thus, unsurprisingly, it turns out that the mere invocation of a truism does not lay to rest the Divine Foreknowledge Argument.

To be a bit more explicit, we have argued that despite Merricks's claim that it is a virtue of his account that it avoids the hard/soft fact distinction, at a deep level he is committed to precisely this distinction (albeit under a different name or guise). This is because Merricks is committed to the distinction between those facts that depend on the future (in a certain way) and those that do not; the facts that exhibit the distinctive dependence on the future are soft, whereas the facts that do not are hard. Merricks is thus subject to exactly the same difficulties as the Ockhamist's distinction; as the problems with (BC) indicate, he must say more about what the relevant kind of dependence on the future consists in.

5. CRITIQUE OF MERRICKS: THE MAIN ARGUMENT

Thus far we have sought primarily to argue that invocation of Merricks's "truism" does not circumvent the thrust of the Divine Foreknowledge Argument. Here we briefly consider whether it nevertheless *does* circumvent the thrust of the Main Argument. It is often thought that the relevant premise of the Divine Foreknowledge Argument,

(6) Jones has no choice about: God believed *that Jones sits at t* a thousand years ago,

---

[29] However, for an account of the soft/hard distinction, see Patrick Todd, "Soft Facts and Ontological Dependence," *Philosophical Studies* 164 (1) (May 2013): 189–203.

is more plausible than the parallel premise in the Main Argument,

(1) Jones has no choice about: *that Jones sits at t* was true a thousand years ago.

That is, some have thought that the embedded clause in (6) arguably, at least, expresses a hard fact about a thousand years ago, whereas in (1) it does not.[30] But some philosophers would argue that the status of (1) is not significantly—or relevantly—different from that of (6). Such philosophers would begin by arguing that "truths require truthmakers". They would further argue that if it was true a thousand years ago that Jones would sit at *t*, then there must have been some temporally nonrelational truthmaker that existed a thousand years ago in virtue of which this was true, the existence of which entails that Jones sits at *t*. Given this claim, it can be argued that (1) is indeed supported by the fixity of the past. For Jones's ability to do otherwise than sit at *t* requires that the relevant truthmaker not have existed

---

[30]We have said that it is at least arguable that a fact such as that God believed a thousand years ago that Jones will sit at *t* is hard, whereas it is plausible that a fact such as that it was true a thousand years ago that Jones will sit at *t* is soft. But if God is necessarily existent and essentially omniscient, then the two facts would be logically equivalent. But how then could it even be possible that one fact be hard and the other soft? (We thank an anonymous referee for the *Philosophical Review* for this question.) For the sake of simplicity, we can think of facts as true propositions (although nothing in our essay or in this part of it depends on this particular construal of facts). Now note that it does not follow from two propositions' being logically equivalent that they are the same proposition. For example, the proposition that two plus two equals four and the proposition that three plus three equals six are logically equivalent, but it is at least plausible that they are different propositions. Thus, there would be no reason to suppose that they must have all the same properties. Similarly, the proposition about God's belief and the proposition about the prior truth in question are logically equivalent, but it does not follow that they are the *same* proposition. Thus, there would be no reason to suppose that they have all the same properties. More specifically, it would not follow from their logical equivalence that if one is hard, the other must also be hard. Similar considerations would apply, mutatis mutandis, on other construals of the nature of facts.

On our view, then, one can have pairs of propositions that are logically equivalent but in which one but not the other of the pair displays the distinctive temporal relationality of soft facts. We believe that the pair of facts above might be just such a pair: whereas the fact that it was true a thousand years ago that Jones would sit at *t* might display the characteristic dependence on the future, a fact such as that God believed a thousand years ago that Jones would sit at *t* nevertheless might not. Similarly, whereas the fact that it was true a thousand years ago that Jones would sit at *t* might display the signature dependence on the future, a fact such as that God decreed a thousand years ago that Jones would sit at *t* presumably does not. Whereas (on certain assumptions about God) the two propositions are logically equivalent, they arguably, at least, differ with respect to the relevant kind of dependence on the future. After all, intuitively it is clear that God's decrees about the future do not depend on the future events' taking place; rather, the dependence is the other way around. There is a development of this sort of example and a discussion of its implications for the hard/soft fact distinction in Todd, "Soft Facts and Ontological Dependence."

a thousand years ago, and the fact that it did exist then is a hard fact about the past relative to t.[31]

Of course, it must be admitted that the above argument relies on a further controversial premise in addition to the mere premise that truths require truthmakers. It relies on the premise that truth at a time is made true by the world at that time. That is, it relies on the claim that if *that Jones sits at t* was true a thousand years ago, then there must have been something temporally nonrelational about the world *a thousand years ago* in virtue of which this was true. We do not here seek to *argue for* this premise. And we note that Merricks has denied that truths require truthmakers in the way envisaged in the argument.[32] However, it is enough for our purposes to note that these theses have considerable plausibility and cannot be dismissed out of hand. Given these points, it would seem that one could not dismiss the Main Argument without considering precisely the same sorts of issues concerning the fixity of the past one must address when evaluating the Divine Foreknowledge Argument.

Merricks invokes the truism that truth depends on the world in an attempt to undermine the fatalist arguments. But the fatalist will in no way contest the truism. Rather, he or she will point out that the truism has to be *properly applied*: if we are to be free, truths about what we do must not only depend on the world but must depend on the *right part* of the world—a part of the world under our control. But if the thousand-years-ago truth of *that Jones sits at t* was made true by a hard feature of the world a thousand years ago, then whereas this truth depended on the world, it depended on a part of the world outside Jones's control at t, namely, how the world was a thousand years prior! Thus, features of the world beyond Jones's control entail what he does. Arguably, in this way he is rendered unable to do otherwise.[33]

6. CONCLUSION

We have sought to argue that the truism invoked by Merricks does not yield significant benefits in the analysis of the Main Argument and the Divine Foreknowledge

---

[31]Some philosophers have rejected a truthmaker approach and have instead adopted the thesis that truth supervenes on being. Exactly the same analysis would apply to a supervenience view; nothing in our critique depends on accepting a truthmaker view as opposed to a supervenience view.

[32]Trenton Merricks, *Truth and Ontology* (Oxford: Clarendon Press, 2007).

[33]Indeed, it would seem as if the truism is a driving force behind the intuitive *appeal* of fatalism. For when a fatalist hears that it was true a thousand years ago that he or she would sit at t, he or she applies the truism: truth depends on the world. Thus, something about the world a thousand years ago already settled his or her sitting at t. And how does he or she have a choice about what the world was like a thousand years ago?

Argument. One can fully accept the truism compatibly with acknowledging the force of the parallel arguments; this force is imparted by considerations of the fixity of the past. That is, one can accept that truth depends on the world but still believe that one never has a choice about hard facts about the past.

We have pointed out that the Main Argument and Divine Foreknowledge Argument both depend (in different specific ways) on considerations of the fixity of the past. We have not attempted to argue *for* the claim that God's beliefs are hard facts about the times at which they are held or the claim that truth at t depends on the world at t. These are contentious claims. In order to offer decisive support for the Main Argument and the Divine Foreknowledge Argument, one would need to provide arguments for these claims. But here our project has been different. Here we have shown, *contra* Merricks, that mere invocation of the truism does *not* show that the arguments are question-begging. It is thus necessary for a critic of the parallel arguments to address the vexing traditional questions about the fixity of the past—many of which have been explored at some length in the pages of this journal.

ACKNOWLEDGMENTS

We are very grateful for comments from Neal Tognazzini, Derk Pereboom, Philip Swenson, and an anonymous referee for the *Philosophical Review.*

5

FATALISM, INCOMPATIBILISM, AND THE POWER TO DO OTHERWISE

Penelope Mackie

Compatibilists about free will and causal determinism face a challenge from versions of what is known as "the consequence argument" for incompatibilism.[1] Nevertheless, compatibilists have been resourceful in responding to this challenge, and it seems fair to say that the consequence argument is not generally regarded as a refutation of compatibilism. As I shall show, there is a striking similarity between the consequence argument for incompatibilism and a standard argument for (logical) fatalism. However, what does not appear to have been noticed is that if the compatibilist responses to the consequence argument are effective, they yield parallel solutions to the problem of fatalism, solutions that are, moreover, quite distinct from those presented in the literature as the standard responses to fatalism. It follows that we must choose between two possibilities. One is that these compatibilist responses to the problem of free will and causal determinism are, despite their popularity, untenable. The other is that they are tenable, but that they have, as their analogues, a pair of hitherto surprisingly neglected solutions to the problem of fatalism.

§ 1. THE FATALIST ARGUMENT

Consider the following argument, concerning some action A (e.g., playing tennis) that I actually perform later today:

Argument 1

(1L) It was true yesterday that I would do A today. (*Antecedent truth*)

---

[1] See van Inwagen 1975 and 1983. Cf. Ginet 1966, Lamb 1977, Wiggins 1973. The term "consequence argument" was introduced by van Inwagen (1983).

(2L) Necessarily, if it was true yesterday that I would do A today, then I shall do A today.

(3L) I am, today, unable to affect whether it was true yesterday that I would do A today. (*One cannot affect the past*)

Therefore:

(4L) I am (today) unable to avoid doing A today. (*No power to do otherwise*)

One who accepts "logical fatalism"—henceforth "fatalism"—holds that Argument 1 is valid, and also that, in the case of any action A that I actually perform today, (1L), (2L), and (3L) are all true, and hence (4L) is also true.[2] Generalizing, the fatalist concludes that one *never* has the ability to avoid doing anything that one actually does. Very few philosophers accept fatalism.[3] Yet those who have considered the matter appear to agree that Argument 1 is valid, and hence that, if the fatalist conclusion is to be avoided, any case in which (4L) is false must be a case in which at least one of (1L)–(3L) is false. Since (2L) is undeniable,[4] these opponents of fatalism have concluded either that if I actually do A today, it need not be the case that it was true yesterday that I would do so (denial of (1L)) or, alternatively, that the past truth of propositions such as the proposition that I would play tennis later today represents an exception to the general rule that one cannot affect the past (denial of (3L)).

The first of these responses (the denial of "antecedent truth", and hence of (1L)) takes two distinct forms. There are those who adopt the view, traditionally ascribed to Aristotle, that the principle of bivalence does not apply to propositions about future contingents, and hence that it was, yesterday, neither true nor false that I would play tennis today.[5] In addition, however, some theories that attempt to avoid fatalism by appeal to the "timelessness of truth" may be regarded as denying (1L).

---

[2]Fatalism in this sense must be distinguished from the view (sometimes labeled "popular fatalism") that is associated with the slogan "what will be will be, regardless of what I do", and implies that my actions are causally irrelevant to what comes about. The logical fatalist claim that I never have the power to do other than I actually do (e.g., that if I do not go to the air raid shelter, it is not in my power to go there) must be distinguished from the (absurd) claim that if I *were* to do something different (e.g., go to the air raid shelter), this would make no difference to the outcome (e.g., to whether or not I am killed by a bomb).

[3]Richard Taylor is perhaps the only prominent philosopher to have defended logical fatalism in recent times. See Taylor 1963–1992.

[4]Undeniable, that is, when taken to express the logical "truth-value link" according to which the truth at t of "S will do A at $(t+1)$" entails the truth at $(t+1)$ of "S does A". There is a sense of "S will do A", where the (apparently) future-tensed statement merely expresses "present tendencies", in which this entailment does not hold. (See Dummett 1964, pp. 341–42; also Prior 1962, p. 34.) I set this sense aside as irrelevant here.

[5]For a discussion of the interpretation of Aristotle's views, see Sorabji 1980, ch. 5.

I have in mind theories that deny that it is appropriate to speak of anything's being true or false "at a time", and hence regard the claim that it *was* true yesterday that I would play tennis today as illegitimate, and perhaps even unintelligible.[6]

The second response: that although it *was* true yesterday that I would play tennis today, this fact exemplifies a class of exceptions to the general rule that we cannot affect the past, is associated with William of Ockham.[7] According to this "Ockhamist" response, although one cannot in general affect facts about the past—for example, I cannot now affect whether it was true yesterday that I had lunch that day—it is otherwise with facts about the past such as the fact that I would play tennis today. Contrary to what is implied by (3L), I now have the power to bring it about that it was true yesterday (or indeed 20 or 2,000 years ago) that I would play tennis today because I have the power to bring it about that I play tennis, and I now have the power to bring it about that it was false yesterday (or 20, or 2,000 years ago) that I would play tennis today because I have the power to bring it about that I do not play tennis.

This denial of (3L) would, however, be suspiciously ad hoc were it not combined with some account of why, in such a case, we have this exceptional power to affect the past. This may be provided by an appeal to a distinction between two types of proposition about times earlier than the present. There are propositions about times earlier than the present that are made true by events or states of affairs that occurred at (or before) those times. For example, the proposition that Charles I was executed in 1649 is "about" 1649—and hence about a time earlier than the present—in this sense. However, there are other propositions "about" times earlier than the present that are made true, not by past events or states of affairs, but by present or future ones. An example is the proposition that it was the case yesterday that I would play tennis later today. Since—in the absence of backwards causation—we have no causal power over past events or states of affairs, we have no power to affect the truth value of propositions that are made true or false by past events or states of affairs. But it is otherwise, according to the proponents of this view, with propositions "about the past" that are made true or false by future events or states of affairs.

[6]See Ayer 1963, pp. 235–37; van Inwagen 1983, ch. 2, §§ 3–5. It may be conceded by the proponents of the theory of timeless truth that the sentence "S will play tennis on day $(n+1)$" when indexed to some time (e.g., day n) expresses a proposition that is (timelessly) true. But these theorists deny that we can legitimately infer, from the fact that "S will play tennis on day $(n+1)$", indexed to day n, expresses a proposition that is timelessly true, that it *was* true, on day n, that S would play tennis on day $(n+1)$.
[7]See Prior 1967, p. 121, for references to Ockham's work and to other medieval versions of this view: a—restricted—denial of the principle *ad preteritum non est potentia*. Modern expressions of this view may be found in Horwich 1987, ch. 2, §4 and Sorabji 1980, pp. 101–03; it is also endorsed by Cargile (1996, pp. 5–6). The view is associated with a distinction between "hard" and "soft" facts about the past: see Zagzebski 1991 for references.

To the extent that we have some causal power over those future events and states of affairs, to that extent we can affect the truth values of those propositions. If we add to this the thesis that if the proposition that it was the case at some past time t that E would occur is true, then it *was true* at time t that E would occur, we get the conclusion that we can affect the past truth value of a proposition just in case its past truth value depends on future events and states of affairs that we have the power to affect.[8]

There are two points about the Ockhamist response (as I shall call it) to the fatalist argument that are important for the discussion that follows. First, the Ockhamist response involves the acceptance of the rule that *in general* one cannot affect the past: the denial of (3L) is presented as an exception to this rule. Secondly, the general rule that one cannot affect the past is justified by an appeal to the principle that we have no causal power over past events and states of affairs. For brevity, I shall describe the Ockhamist response to fatalism as involving the claim that the past truth of propositions about the future represents an exception to the general rule that one cannot affect the past.[9]

§2. THE INCOMPATIBILIST ARGUMENT

Consider, now, the following argument in support of the thesis that free will and causal determinism are incompatible. (As before, A is an action, for example, playing tennis, that I actually perform later today.)

Argument 2[10]

(1C) Where H is a true proposition specifying the intrinsic state of the world at some time in the remote past, and L is a true proposition specifying

---

[8]Cf. Horwich 1987, pp. 28–30. A version of this view may also be attributed to some proponents of the "timelessness of truth" response to fatalism. (See note 6 above.) For suppose one holds that the only legitimate interpretation that can be given to "It was true on day n that S would play tennis on day $(n+1)$" is: " 'S will play tennis on day $(n+1)$', indexed to day n, expresses a proposition that is timelessly true". Then one may also hold that what makes it the case that this sentence with this index expresses a proposition that is timelessly true is the event of S's playing tennis on day $(n+1)$: an event that occurs on day $(n+1)$. And this would mean that S's action on day $(n+1)$ could be seen as affecting whether (albeit in a loose and improper sense) it *was* true on day n that S would play tennis on day $(n+1)$. See van Inwagen 1983, ch. 2, §§3–5; cf. Smith and Oaklander 1995, p. 126. Perhaps Ryle's claim that "correct" is sometimes a "valedictory epithet" (1953, p. 20) may also be regarded as a version of this response to the fatalist argument.

[9]Of course, this must not be taken to involve the claim that one can affect the past truth value of *every* proposition about the future. For example, the Ockhamist is not committed to the claim that I can now affect whether it was true yesterday that the sun would rise two days later (i.e., tomorrow).

[10]Neither this version of Argument 2 nor the version presented in the following section is intended to reproduce the consequence argument as it is formulated by van Inwagen. However, in spite of significant differences, I think that it is reasonable to characterize Argument 2 as an instance of a type that may be called "the consequence argument". See also note 18.

what the laws of nature are, the conjunction of H and L entails that I do
A today.[11] (*Causal determinism*)

(2C) Necessarily, if the conjunction of H and L is true and entails that I do
A today, then I shall do A today.

(3C) I am, today, unable to affect whether the conjunction of H and L is true.
(One cannot affect a combination of facts about the past and facts about
what the laws of nature are)

Therefore:

(4C) I am (today) unable to avoid doing A today. (*No power to do otherwise*)

As it stands, Argument 2 is not an argument for incompatibilism as such, but,
rather, an argument from determinism to *hard determinism*: the combination of
determinism and incompatibilism. However, incompatibilists who are not hard
determinists, although they may reject premise (1C), will hold that Argument 2 is
valid, and will also accept premises (2C) and (3C). And such incompatibilists may
appeal to the argument in order to support their thesis that *if* causal determinism
were true, we would never have the ability to act otherwise than we actually do.

The similarity between Argument 2 and Argument 1 is obvious. However, it is
also obvious that neither of the standard moves employed by opponents of fatalism is available to the compatibilist about free will and causal determinism as a
response to Argument 2. First, whereas opponents of fatalism may respond to
Argument 1 by denying its first premise, compatibilism about free will and causal
determinism cannot be defended by denying premise (1C) of Argument 2. For the
question at issue between compatibilists and incompatibilists is not whether determinism is true, but whether, if it were true, we could act freely. As for the other
standard response to the fatalist argument, the (Ockhamist) rejection of its third
premise on the grounds that the past truth of propositions about the future represents an exception to the general rule that one cannot affect the past, it is clear that
this is not applicable to Argument 2. For no such propositions are involved in the
conjunction of H and L. If premise (3C) of Argument 2 is to be rejected, it must be
on quite different grounds.

A heroic strategy available to a compatibilist is to argue that while (setting aside
the possible falsity of premise (1C)) there is no fault to be found with Argument 2,
it is a mistake to suppose that its conclusion, if true, would undermine our freedom of action. This line may be taken by compatibilists who hold that freedom of
action ("free will") does not require the power to do other than what we actually
do. According to such compatibilists, all that is required is something weaker: for

[11]Cf. Lewis 1981, pp. 291–92; van Inwagen 1975, §1; van Inwagen 1983, p. 70.

example, that our actions come about as a result of our decisions, without external constraint or pathological psychological compulsion.[12] However, compatibilists who occupy this position should also be happy to embrace what I have called the "fatalist" conclusion (4L), while denying that the lack of power to do otherwise undermines our freedom of action.[13]

Nevertheless, in the remainder of this paper I propose to set aside this response. Many contemporary compatibilists hold that although free will *does* require a power to do otherwise than we actually do, our possession of this power (in the relevant sense) is compatible with the thesis that causal determinism governs all our actions. These compatibilist philosophers must respond to Argument 2 in one of two ways. Either they must contend that Argument 2 is invalid, or they must contend that its third premise is false. However, as I have already noted, the claim that (3C) is false must be independent of any special considerations concerning our ability to affect the past truth of propositions about the future.

I shall now argue that if either of these strategies succeeds in undermining Argument 2, it also succeeds in undermining Argument 1. But if either of these strategies succeeds in undermining Argument 1, the standard responses to fatalism are redundant.[14]

§3. REFORMULATIONS

It will be convenient to conduct the discussion in terms of revised formulations of Arguments 1 and 2. Using "Q" to denote the proposition that I shall play tennis today, and "P" to denote the proposition that it was true yesterday that I would play tennis today,[15] we may reformulate the fatalist Argument 1 as follows:

Argument 1
(1L) P is true.
(2L) P entails Q.
(3L) I cannot render P false.

---

[12]Frankfurt (1969) gives a sophisticated defense of the thesis that the power to do otherwise is not a necessary condition of free will. See also Dennett 1984, ch. 6.

[13]As far as I am aware, this response to fatalism has no advocates. This appears to exemplify another contrast between the treatment in the literature of the problem of fatalism and its treatment of the problem of free will and determinism.

[14]This is not to say that they are mistaken. It could be that the rejection of fatalism is overdetermined by the arguments against it.

[15]Is there such a thing as *the proposition that it was true yesterday that I would play tennis today?* Proponents of the "timelessness of truth" response to fatalism will presumably say that there is no such proposition, and will reject (1L) on these grounds. (See §1 above.) However, I do not think

Therefore:

(4L)   I cannot render Q false.

Additionally, where "H" and "L" have the same interpretations as in the original formulation of Argument 2, and—for convenience—allowing "(H & L)" as an abbreviation for "the proposition that is the conjunction of H and L", the incompatibilist's Argument 2 may be reformulated as:

Argument 2

(1C*)   (H & L) is true.

(2C*)   (H & L) entails Q.

  (3C)   I cannot render (H & L) false.

Therefore:

  (4C)   I cannot render Q false.

(Here "Q" again denotes the proposition that I shall play tennis today.)

There are two principal changes introduced by these revisions. First, in the reformulation of Argument 2, premises (1C) and (2C) have been replaced by two premises, (1C*) and (2C*), that are together equivalent to (1C) of the original argument. However, nothing is lost by this reformulation, since the original premise (2C) was, in fact, redundant, as the reader may verify. The second principal change is the use of the phrase "cannot render . . . false" in the third premise and the conclusion of each argument. (The interpretation of this phrase will be discussed in the following sections.) As a consequence, the conclusion of each argument now expresses the claim that I cannot *render false the proposition that I shall play tennis today*, rather than the claim that I am unable to avoid playing tennis today. However, this does not, I think, involve any substantial change to the import of either argument. For it is plausible to say that I can render false the proposition that I shall play tennis today if and only if I am able to avoid playing tennis today, and hence that the conclusions of the revised versions of the two arguments are equivalent to the conclusions of their old versions.[16]

---

this matters for my purposes, as long as the claim that there is such a proposition is acceptable to those who do not regard truth as timeless.

[16]In any case, in directing the discussion to these revised formulations, I cannot be accused of distorting the incompatibilist's argument. Van Inwagen himself formulates the consequence argument in terms of the "can(not) render false" locution: see his (1975) and ch. 3, §5 of his (1983).

With these reformulations of the arguments before us, we may now consider the two ways in which a compatibilist may reject Argument 2, and their implications for Argument 1.[17]

§4. INVALIDITY AND THE PRINCIPLE OF CLOSURE

Argument 2 relies on the following principle:

Closure: If S cannot render X false, and X entails Y, then S cannot render Y false.

According to *Closure*, "S cannot render X false" is closed under entailment.[18] Evidently, *Closure* is equivalent to the principle:

(C*)   If S can render Y false, and X entails Y, then S can render X false.

Hence if *Closure* is valid, I can avoid playing tennis today—and hence render it false that I shall play tennis today—only if I can render false any proposition that entails that I shall play tennis today. If determinism is true, then (given that I shall play tennis today) (H & L) is such a proposition. But if—as the incompatibilist maintains—I *cannot* render (H & L) false (premise (3C)), it follows that if determinism is true, and *Closure* is valid, then I cannot do other than I actually do.

Nevertheless, there are interpretations of "S cannot render X false" on which *Closure* appears to be unwarranted. The crucial point is this. It seems fair to say that, on *any* plausible interpretation of "S can render X false", the following form of argument is valid:

(i) S can render Y false.
(ii) X entails Y.

---

[17]According to the reformulation of Argument 1, premise (1L) no longer asserts simply that it *was* true yesterday that I would play tennis later today, but rather that it *is true* that it *was true* yesterday that I would play tennis later today. This requires me to represent the Ockhamist response to fatalism as involving not only the claim that we can affect the past truth of propositions about the future, but also the claim that we can affect the truth value of propositions whose truth *involves* the past truth of propositions about the future in the way that P does. I have not made this explicit in the following discussion.

[18]*Closure* is related to, but distinct from (and weaker than), the "Principle *Beta*" on which one version of van Inwagen's consequence argument relies (van Inwagen 1983, pp. 94 ff.). In terms of "cannot render false", van Inwagen's Principle *Beta* may be construed as the principle that if S cannot render X false, and S cannot render false the proposition that if X is true, Y is true, then S

Therefore:

(iii) S can do something such that, were S to do it, X would be false.

However, this is not enough to vindicate *Closure*. For "S can render X false" may be given an interpretation according to which (iii) does not entail:

(iv) S can render X false.

And if "S can render X false" is given such an interpretation, then *Closure* may fail.[19]

Consider, for example, a "conditional" interpretation of "S can render X false" that is consonant with the "conditional" analysis of "S can do A" favored by some compatibilists. On such a conditional analysis, the claim that I can render X false becomes the claim that, if I were to choose to render X false, I would render X false. In other words, on this conditional analysis, (iv) is equivalent to:

(iv*) If S were to choose to render X false, then S would render X false.

And (iii) does not appear to entail (iv*).[20]

The attempt to deny *Closure* by appeal to a conditional analysis of "S can render X false" may seem precarious. For one thing, the conditional analysis is extremely controversial, and is rejected even by many philosophers sympathetic to compatibilism.[21] However, the compatibilist who questions *Closure* may appeal to a perhaps less tendentious line of argument. Why, we may ask, does premise (3C) of the incompatibilist's argument seem compelling? It is plausible to suggest that this is because we regard facts about the intrinsic state of the world in the remote past and the laws of nature as beyond the reach of our current causal powers. We cannot do anything now that would have any *effect* on them. Yet if the contrast between what is and what is not within the scope of our causal powers is introduced into the definition of what we can and cannot render false, then *Closure* becomes questionable.

Suppose that we take it that the reason why I am unable to render (H & L) false is that (H & L) is true in virtue of events and states of affairs over which I have no

cannot render Y false. It is plausible to say that if X entails Y, then S cannot render false the proposition that if X is true, Y is true. But the converse does not appear to hold. The distinction between *Closure* and van Inwagen's Principle *Beta* is exploited by Finch and Warfield in their (1998).

[19]See Gallois 1977, Narveson 1977, Foley 1979, Slote 1982; also Kane 1996, pp. 47–48.

[20]See Kane 1996, p. 47.

[21]I think that the appeal to the conditional analysis suffers from a further limitation. For I do not see why we should accept that (iii) does not entail (iv*), unless a "causal" interpretation of "S can

causal influence. Extrapolating from this, we might suggest the following "Causal Influence Principle" (CIP):

(CIP) S can render X false only if X is true in virtue of events or states of affairs over which S has some causal influence.

If "S can render X false" is interpreted in accordance with (CIP), then *Closure* is questionable. For it does not appear to follow, from the assumption that I have some causal influence over the events and states of affairs in virtue of which it is true that I shall play tennis later today, that, in respect of every proposition that entails that I shall play tennis later today, I have some causal influence over the events and states of affairs in virtue of which that proposition is true.[22]

It may be questioned whether the interpretations of "S can render X false" according to which *Closure* fails are acceptable. I need not attempt to adjudicate this issue. For my purposes, the important point is the following.

Suppose that a compatibilist responds to Argument 2 by rejecting the principle of *Closure* on which the argument relies. Such a compatibilist will claim that Argument 2 is invalid. However, the compatibilist who takes this line should also claim that the fatalist's Argument 1 is invalid, for it is evident that it also relies on *Closure*. Such a compatibilist should therefore respond to the fatalist's argument as follows: "It may be the case that it was true yesterday that I would play tennis today. And it may be the case that I cannot now render it false that it was true yesterday that I would play tennis today. Nevertheless, even if the proposition that I shall play tennis today is entailed by a proposition that I cannot render false, it does not follow that I cannot render it false that I shall play tennis today. Hence it does not follow that I cannot avoid playing tennis." Evidently, this represents a response to fatalism that is distinct from either of the standard responses mentioned in §1 above. If this response is cogent, then, contrary to what appears to be standardly assumed, the rejection of fatalism requires neither the denial of "antecedent truth" nor the claim that one can

---

render X false" is being assumed. If so, one who wishes to reject *Closure* by appeal to a conditional interpretation of "S can render X false" will have to invoke some principle such as (CIP) (discussed below) in any case.

[22]This is similar to a point made by Narveson (1977, p. 84), although Narveson's point is about causally necessary conditions rather than logically sufficient (i.e., entailing) conditions. Michael Slote (1982, §4) introduces a sense of what is necessary for, or inevitable for, us that employs the notion of what is brought about by factors (and causal or explanatory chains) that do not involve our present abilities, desires, and so on. He argues that in this sense the past and the laws of nature are inevitable, but that in this sense *Closure* is questionable, at least given certain other assumptions (p. 21). For some difficulties for Slote's account, see Fischer 1994, pp. 40–44.

affect any truth about the past—even a truth about the past that consists in the past truth of a proposition about the future.[23]

§ 5. CHALLENGING PREMISE (3C)

The second strategy available to the compatibilist who wishes to challenge Argument 2 is to reject premise (3C). In other words, the compatibilist may contend that we *can* render false the conjunction of a historical proposition about the intrinsic state of the world in the remote past and a proposition specifying the laws of nature. If so, then even if Argument 2 is valid and determinism is true, we may yet have the power to do other than we actually do.[24]

But how can the compatibilist maintain, with any plausibility, that premise (3C) is false? The answer is: by exploiting the very fact to which the incompatibilist argument appeals; namely, that if determinism is true, then, were we to do otherwise than we actually do, it would have to be the case that either the past or the laws of nature were different from what they actually are.

Suppose that determinism is true, and hence that (H & L) is true and entails the proposition Q (that I play tennis later today). The following consequence obtains: *if* I can render Q false, then I can do something such that, were I to do it, (H & L) would be false. Suppose, now, that the compatibilist adopts the following interpretation of "S can render X false":

(CD) S can render X false iff S can do something such that, were S to do it, X would be false.

I shall call this "the counterfactual dependence sense" of "S can render X false". It is evident that, on this interpretation of "S can render X false", the principle of *Closure* must be accepted. For suppose that I can do something such that, were I to do it, Y would be false. It follows that, if X entails Y, I can do something such that, were I to do it, X would be false. But if nothing more is required for it to be the case that I have the ability to render X false, then *Closure* is vindicated.

---

[23]Of course, it remains the case that—given the entailment—if Q were false, then (necessarily) P would be false. However, the denial of *Closure* implies that although my ability to render Q false is (of course) an ability to do something such that, were I to do it, P would be false, it does not follow that I have the ability to render P false.

[24]The strategy of denying *Closure* and the strategy of challenging premise (3C) need not be regarded as mutually exclusive. The two strategies may be combined in a dilemma. The compatibilist may argue that there are two relevant interpretations of "can(not) render. . . false"; under one of these, premise (3C) is true, but Argument 2 is invalid; under the other, the argument is valid, but premise (3C) is false. See, for example, Narveson 1977 and Foley 1979.

However, the incompatibilist can draw little comfort from this. For while the counterfactual dependence sense of "S can render X false" vindicates *Closure*, it makes premise (3C) precarious. If nothing more is required for it to be the case that I can render false the conjunction (H & L) than that I should be able to do something (e.g., to refrain from playing tennis) such that, were I to do it, (H & L) would be false, why should it be denied that I can—in this sense—render (H & L) false? In particular, if the incompatibilist attempts to support the claim that I *cannot* render (H & L) false (premise (3C)) by appeal to the fact that I have no causal influence over the past or the laws of nature, the compatibilist may fairly reply that this is beside the point. For it is quite unwarranted to assume that my ability to render (H & L) false *in the counterfactual dependence sense* requires that I have any such causal influence. (If determinism is true, then propositions about the past and the laws of nature entail propositions about what we shall do in the future. The incompatibilist concludes that if determinism is true, then, since we cannot affect the truth values of propositions of the former kind, we cannot affect the truth values of propositions of the latter kind. The compatibilist who adopts the strategy discussed in the present section draws the opposite conclusion: since we *can* affect the truth values of propositions of the latter kind, we *can* affect the truth values of propositions of the former kind. The incompatibilist may retort that this begs the question, since what is at issue is precisely whether we can affect the truth values of propositions of the latter kind. The counter-retort by the compatibilist is that the incompatibilist has offered no argument against the claim that we can affect the truth values of propositions of the latter kind except an argument that rests on the assumption that we cannot affect the truth values of propositions of the former kind—an assumption that is equally question-begging.)

Once more, I need not assess the adequacy of this attempt to reject Argument 2. What I want to argue is that *if* this appeal to the counterfactual dependence sense of "S can render X false" vindicates the rejection of Argument 2, it also warrants a rejection of Argument 1 that is distinct from either of the standard responses to fatalism mentioned in §1 of this paper. According to this compatibilist response to Argument 2, I can render (H & L) false precisely because I can render false some proposition—the proposition Q that I shall play tennis today—whose falsity entails the falsity of (H & L). If this reasoning is cogent, then it seems that so should be the following: I can render P false, where P is the proposition that it was true yesterday that I would play tennis today, precisely because I can render false some proposition—the proposition Q that I shall play tennis today—whose falsity entails the falsity of P.

It is important to note that this argument for the rejection of premise (3L) of Argument 1 is entirely independent of any special considerations concerning our ability to affect the past truth of propositions about the future. Hence this response to the fatalist argument is distinct from the second standard response (the Ockhamist response) to fatalism mentioned in §1 above.[25] And in contrast to the Ockhamist response to fatalism, the argument for the falsity of (3C) and (3L) considered in the current section exploits the idea that I can have "power over"—in the counterfactual dependence sense—the truth value of some proposition (e.g., (H & L)) *even if the events and states of affairs that make that proposition true or false are ones over which I have no causal power.*

§ 6. FATALISM, INCOMPATIBILISM, AND THE PAST

The compatibilist who denies premise (3C) of Argument 2 says that I can render (H & L) false: that is, that I can render false the conjunction of a historical proposition H about intrinsic features of the remote past and a proposition L stating what the laws of nature are. However, the compatibilist is not thereby committed to the claim that I can render false the historical proposition H. This is for two reasons.

First—and obviously—the compatibilist may claim that I can render (H & L) false not because I can render H false, but because I can render L false. This is the line that would be taken by a compatibilist who holds that, given determinism plus the fact that I actually play tennis, if I were to avoid playing tennis, then the laws of nature would be different in some respect, although the intrinsic features of the remote past would have been the same as they actually were. This is the view adopted by David Lewis (in Lewis 1981).

Secondly, and less obviously, the compatibilist may argue that I can render (H & L) false although I can render false *neither* of its conjuncts. This involves the denial of the thesis that the kind of impossibility represented by "S cannot render X false" is "agglomerative": that is, closed under conjunction introduction. In other words, it involves the rejection of the principle:

Agglomeration: If S cannot render X false, and S cannot render Y false, then S cannot render (X & Y) false.

Both of these moves are to be found in the literature.[26] And they may be combined: a compatibilist may argue (as does David Lewis) that there is one relevant sense of "S can(not) render X false" in which I can render (H & L) false even though I can render false neither of its conjuncts, and another relevant sense of "S can(not)

---

[25]See also note 17 above.

[26]For the suggestion that the compatibilist may deny Agglomeration (for some relevant sense of "cannot render false"), see Gallois 1977, Lewis 1981, Slote 1982. On the principle of Agglomeration, see also Finch and Warfield 1998 and McKay and Johnson 1996.

render X false" in which I can render false both (H & L) and one of its conjuncts, namely L, although I cannot in this sense render H false.[27]

The objection that I must now confront is this. It appears that a compatibilist who adopts either of these strategies for denying (3C) may hold that (at least in the absence of backwards causation) the truth value of a historical proposition such as H is *never* counterfactually dependent on my actions.[28] Hence it seems that the compatibilist who denies premise (3C) by appeal to the "counterfactual dependence" sense of "can render false" may do so without abandoning the general principle that we cannot render false a proposition about the past.[29] But if the compatibilist adheres to the principle that *in general* we cannot render false—even in the counterfactual dependence sense—a proposition about the past, then it seems that the compatibilist's rejection of premise (3C) cannot serve as a model for a rejection of premise (3L) that is distinct from the standard responses to fatalism. (It is, of course, undeniable that if I have the ability to render false the proposition Q that I shall play tennis today, then I also have the ability to render false, *in the counterfactual dependence sense*, the proposition P that it was true yesterday that I would play tennis today, if there is such a proposition.[30] But if it were maintained that I have this ability to render P false only because P involves the past truth of a proposition about the future, and hence represents an exception to the general rule that one cannot render false a proposition about the past, this would be to revert to one of the standard responses to fatalism mentioned in §1: the Ockhamist response.) Things would be different, of course, if the compatibilist who rejects (3C) were to hold that I can render (H & L) false because I can do something such that, were I to do it, *the historical proposition H would have been false* (and hence some intrinsic features of the remote past would

---

[27]See Lewis's distinction (1981, p. 297) between a "strong" and a "weak" sense of "can render false". According to Lewis, I cannot render H false in either his strong or his weak sense, although I can render (H & L) false in both the strong and the weak sense, and I can render L false in the weak sense (although not the strong sense). If I were able to render H false in Lewis's strong sense, I would be able to do something such that, were I to do it, H would be falsified either by my action or by an event caused by my action. If I were able to render H false in Lewis's weak sense, I would be able to do something such that, were I to do it, H would be falsified, but not necessarily by my action or by any event caused by my action. (In Lewis's terminology, an event would falsify a proposition iff "necessarily, if that event occurs then that proposition is false". (ibid.))

[28]Lewis's own position is complicated by the fact that he does accept the possibility of backwards causation. See Lewis 1976. I shall set aside this complication here.

[29]Strictly speaking, this claim needs to be modified to accommodate the fact that if H is about the past, then presumably (H & L) is also (although not exclusively) about the past. For the theorist who adopts the strategy described above wants to say that the conjunction (H & L) may be counterfactually dependent on my actions, although its "historical" conjunct H is not.

[30]See note 15 above.

have been different from what they actually were). But there seems to be no obligation for the compatibilist who rejects premise (3C) to adopt this view.

This difficulty is, however, only apparent. We may distinguish three versions of the response to Argument 2 that denies premise (3C) by appealing to the counterfactual dependence sense of "can render false". I shall argue that none of these versions of the "counterfactual dependence response" (as I shall call it) provides a justification for the general principle that the past is not counterfactually dependent on our future actions. Hence none of them provides a justification for the claim that if I can render it false, in the counterfactual dependence sense, that it was true yesterday that I would play tennis today, this can only be because this involves the past truth of a proposition about the future.

First, although it is not obligatory, there is no evident reason why the compatibilist should not take the view that I can do something such that, were I to do it, the historical proposition H would have been false. For example, Terence Horgan distinguishes two versions of the "counterfactual dependence response" to arguments such as Argument 2. According to one version of the response, which he calls that of the "divergence-miracle compatibilist", if determinism is true, then, had I acted differently, the laws of nature would have been different, although the intrinsic features of the remote past would have been the same as they actually were. In other words, according to a divergence-miracle compatibilist, the truth value of L is counterfactually dependent on my actions, although the truth value of H is not. (This is the position adopted by David Lewis.) According to a second version of the response, which Horgan calls that of the "altered-past compatibilist", if determinism is true, then, had I acted differently, the intrinsic features of the remote past would have been different, although the laws of nature would have been the same as they actually were. In other words, according to the "altered-past compatibilist", it is the truth value of the historical proposition H, and not that of the "legal" proposition L, that is counterfactually dependent on my actions.[31]

This shows that there is at least one version of the "counterfactual dependence response" that requires the rejection of the general principle that one cannot render false a proposition about the past. Moreover, it is evident that the altered-past compatibilist is not thereby committed to the claim that we have any *causal* power over the past. As we have seen, a crucial component of the compatibilist strategy for rejecting premise (3C) by appeal to counterfactual dependence is the insistence that the counterfactual dependence of the truth value of a proposition on my actions

---

[31]Horgan 1985. Essentially the same distinction is made by Fischer in his (1994), ch. 4. The possibility of these two versions of what I am calling the "counterfactual dependence" response is recognized in earlier work by Fischer (e.g., his 1983) and in Foley 1979.

need not be construed as a form of causal dependence. It is significant that if the theorist holds (as does a "divergence-miracle" compatibilist such as Lewis) that I cannot render H false in the counterfactual dependence sense, this will not be on the grounds that I have no causal power over the past. Rather, it will be because—for independent reasons—the theorist adopts an analysis of counterfactuals according to which, under determinism, it is not the case that the closest possible world in which I act differently is one in which the intrinsic features of the remote past are different from what they actually are.

But this is not all. For although the divergence-miracle compatibilist denies that if I had acted differently, H would have been false, this theorist is not entitled to say that if I had acted differently, *none* of the intrinsic features of the past would have been different from what they actually were. According to the "divergence-miracle" account, if determinism is true, then, had I acted differently, there would have been a "small miracle" occurring shortly before the time at which I actually acted, as a result of which I would have acted differently. However, this small miracle would itself involve a divergence from the actual course of events shortly before the time of my action.[32] It follows that according to the divergence-miracle theorist, if determinism is true, then, had I acted differently, some intrinsic features of the *immediate* past would have been different from what they actually were, even if the intrinsic features of the remote past would have been exactly the same. Hence, far from being able to uphold the general principle that one cannot render false (in the counterfactual dependence sense) a proposition about the past, the divergence-miracle theorist is committed to its denial. (Could the divergence-miracle theorist escape this commitment by holding that, in the counterfactual situation in which I act differently, it is my action itself—rather than anything occurring before my action—that constitutes the divergence miracle? Not if the theorist is David Lewis. For Lewis is at pains to avoid the conclusion that I am able to perform an action that would itself constitute a violation of a law of nature, a conclusion that he regards as incredible (1981, pp. 292–95).)

It remains to consider the version of the "counterfactual dependence response" that relies on the denial of *Agglomeration*, and holds that, if determinism is true, I can render (H & L) false although I can render false neither of its conjuncts. On the face of it, the theorist who holds this view may consistently maintain the principle that in general I cannot, even in the counterfactual dependence sense, render false a proposition about the past.[33] However, the theorist's adherence to this principle would, I think, be unmotivated. Once it is conceded, as by this theorist it must be,

---

[32]Lewis 1981, p. 294. In an earlier paper, Lewis suggests that such a miracle might consist in the firing of a few extra neurons in a person's brain shortly before the time of action (1979, p. 44).
[33]Subject to the qualification mentioned in note 29 above.

that I may have the ability to render (H & L) false even if I have no causal power over the events and states of affairs in virtue of which (H & L) is true, what reason can the theorist have for insisting on the principle that in general one cannot render false a proposition about the past? The only possible reason that I can see is this. Suppose that the theorist were to hold that I have the ability to render a proposition false by performing an action A only if the falsity of that proposition is *entailed* by my doing A (as, under determinism, the falsity of (H & L) is entailed by the falsity of Q). Given the plausible assumption that no proposition about the past can, just by itself, *entail* a proposition specifying what I shall do in the future unless it is itself a future-tensed proposition (such as the proposition that it was the case yesterday that I would play tennis today), it would follow that, aside from such exceptional cases, I cannot render false any proposition about the past. However, this line of reasoning is unconvincing. For why should we accept the crucial assumption that it is only when the falsity of some proposition is *entailed* by my exercise of my ability to act differently that I am able to render that proposition false in the counterfactual dependence sense? Why should it not be enough that, *in the closest possible world* in which I exercise my ability to act differently, that proposition is false?

I conclude that whatever version of the counterfactual dependence response to Argument 2 we consider, one who rejects premise (3C) of the argument on these grounds should also conclude that I may have the ability to render false a proposition about the past, and, moreover, that I may have this ability even if I have no causal power over the events or states of affairs in virtue of which that proposition is true. If this is accepted, it provides a reason for rejecting premise (3L) of the fatalist argument that makes no appeal to the assumption, crucial to the Ockhamist response to fatalism, that my ability to render false the proposition that I would play tennis today is an exception to a general rule that we cannot affect the past.

§7. CONCLUSION

I am now in a position to establish the conclusion promised in the opening section of this paper. As I have shown, the compatibilist who takes issue with the "consequence argument" represented by Argument 2 may do so either by claiming that the argument is invalid or by claiming that its third premise is false. I have argued that if either of these strategies succeeds, it provides a model for a parallel strategy for rejecting the fatalist Argument 1. But if fatalism is to be rejected on either of these grounds, the standard strategies for responding to the fatalist argument are redundant. Whether this should be taken to show that, in the course of their attempts to respond to the consequence argument, compatibilists have unwittingly discovered two novel responses to the problem of logical fatalism, or whether it merely serves to cast doubt on these compatibilist attempts to evade the consequence argument, I leave to the reader to decide.[34]

REFERENCES

Ayer, A. J. (1963) "Fatalism." In Ayer, *The Concept of a Person and Other Essays*, pp. 235–304. London: Macmillan.

Cargile, J. (1996) "Some Comments on Fatalism," *The Philosophical Quarterly* 46, pp. 1–11.

Dennett, D. (1984) *Elbow Room: The Varieties of Free Will Worth Wanting.* Oxford: Clarendon Press.

Dummett, M. (1964) "Bringing About the Past," *The Philosophical Review* 73, pp. 333–59.

Finch, A., and Warfield, T. (1998) "The *Mind* Argument and Libertarianism," *Mind* 107, pp. 515–28.

Fischer, J. M. (1983) "Incompatibilism," *Philosophical Studies* 43, pp. 127–37.

Fischer, J. M. (1994) *The Metaphysics of Free Will.* Oxford: Blackwell.

Foley, R. (1979) "Compatibilism and Control over the Past," *Analysis* 39, pp. 70–74.

Frankfurt, H. (1969) "Alternate Possibilities and Moral Responsibility," *The Journal of Philosophy* 66, pp. 829–39.

Gallois, A. (1977) "Van Inwagen on Free Will and Determinism," *Philosophical Studies* 32, pp. 99–105.

Ginet, C. (1966) "Might We Have No Choice?" In *Freedom and Determinism*, ed. K. Lehrer, pp. 87–104. New York: Random House.

Horgan, T. (1985) "Compatibilism and the Consequence Argument," *Philosophical Studies* 47, pp. 339–56.

Horwich, P. (1987) *Asymmetries in Time.* Cambridge, Mass.: MIT Press.

Kane, R. (1996) *The Significance of Free Will.* Oxford: Oxford University Press.

Lamb, R. (1977) "On a Proof of Incompatibilism," *The Philosophical Review* 85, pp. 20–35.

Lewis, D. (1976) "The Paradoxes of Time Travel," *American Philosophical Quarterly* 13, pp. 145–52; reprinted in Lewis 1986.

Lewis, D. (1979) "Counterfactual Dependence and Time's Arrow," *Noûs* 13, pp. 455–76; reprinted in Lewis 1986. Page references are to the reprinted version.

Lewis, D. (1981) "Are We Free to Break the Laws?" *Theoria* 47, pp. 113–21; reprinted in Lewis 1986. Page references are to the reprinted version.

Lewis, D. (1986) *Philosophical Papers, Volume II.* Oxford: Oxford University Press.

McKay, T., and Johnson, D. (1996) "A Reconsideration of an Argument Against Compatibilism," *Philosophical Topics* 24, pp. 113–22.

Narveson, J. (1977) "Compatibilism Defended," *Philosophical Studies* 32, pp. 83–87.

Prior, A. N. (1962) "The Formalities of Omniscience," *Philosophy* 37, pp. 114–29; reprinted in Prior 1968. Page references are to the reprinted version.

Prior, A. N. (1967) *Past, Present and Future.* Oxford: Oxford University Press.

[34]Versions of this paper have been delivered to various audiences, including the Stapledon Society of the University of Liverpool Philosophy Department and a Philosophy staff seminar at the University of Birmingham. I thank all the participants in those discussions for helpful comments.

Prior, A. N. (1968) *Papers on Time and Tense.* Oxford: Oxford University Press.

Ryle, G. (1953) "It Was to Be," In Ryle, *Dilemmas*, pp. 15–35. Cambridge: Cambridge University Press.

Slote, M. (1982) "Selective Necessity and the Free-will Problem," *The Journal of Philosophy* 79, pp. 5–24.

Smith, Q., and Oaklander, L. N. (1995) *Time, Change and Freedom.* London: Routledge.

Sorabji, R. (1980) *Necessity, Cause, and Blame: Perspectives on Aristotle's Theory.* London: Duckworth.

Taylor, R. (1963–1992) *Metaphysics* (lst–4th editions). Englewood Cliffs, NJ: Prentice Hall.

van Inwagen, P. (1975) "The Incompatibility of Free Will and Determinism," *Philosophical Studies* 27, pp. 185–99; reprinted in Watson, ed. 1982.

van Inwagen, P. (1983) *An Essay on Free Will.* Oxford: Oxford University Press.

Watson, G., ed. (1982) *Free Will.* Oxford: Oxford University Press.

Wiggins, D. (1973) "Towards a Reasonable Libertarianism." In *Essays on Freedom of Action*, ed. T. Honderich, pp. 31–61. London: Routledge & Kegan Paul.

Zagzebski, L. T. (1991) *The Dilemma of Freedom and Foreknowledge.* Oxford: Oxford University Press.

6

PRESENTISM AND FATALISM

Michael C. Rea

Presentism is the view that it always has been and always will be the case that there are no actual but non-present objects. On this view, dinosaurs and other merely past objects did exist, but there is no sense in which they do exist. Likewise, merely future objects and events (your future grandchildren, for example) perhaps will exist; but, again, there is no sense in which they do exist. Yesterday's sins are quite literally gone; what tomorrow may bring is in no way actual.

It is widely believed that presentism is compatible with an unrestricted principle of bivalence. In particular, presentism is typically thought to be compatible with the view that bivalence holds for sentences of the form "S will do A". In fact, many of the most well-known defenders of presentism will insist on bivalence for such propositions because, as it happens, they are theists who believe that God knows in advance everything that will happen in the world. It is also widely believed that presentism is compatible with libertarianism—the view that we are free, and that freedom is incompatible with determinism. And many of the same people who insist on the compatibility of bivalence with presentism also insist on the truth of libertarianism. In what follows, however, I will argue that, in fact, presentists must *choose* between bivalence and libertarianism. This fact is yet another in a growing list of costs associated with presentism.[1]

The discussion that follows is divided into five sections. In Section I, I briefly explain the content of presentism. In Section II, I present one of the most common objections against it: the objection that presentists cannot supply grounds for past and future tense propositions. I also briefly sketch the sorts of things that presentists will have to say in order to respond adequately to the objection. In subsequent sections, I show how reflection on the grounding objection and the constraints on an adequate reply gives rise to a straightforward argument from presentism plus bivalence to the conclusion that no one is free. (I assume throughout that freedom

---

[1] For discussion of other costs associated with presentism, see Rea [2004 and references therein].

is to be understood as libertarians understand it.) In Section III, I discuss a fairly standard fatalist argument and I show that the standard responses to that argument are unavailable to a presentist. In Section IV, I present the main argument of this paper—the argument for the conclusion that, if presentism is true and bivalence holds, then no one is free. Finally, in Section V, I dismiss three responses to the argument of Section IV, thus reaching the conclusion that presentists must give up either bivalence or libertarianism.

I. PRESENTISM

One standard way of fleshing out the content of presentism is to compare the debate between presentists and their opponents with a parallel debate about possible worlds—the debate between *actualists* and *possibilists*. Actualists say that whatever exists exists in the actual world. Possibilists deny this. There are, they say, some things that do not actually exist. David Lewis is an example of a possibilist.[2] On his view, other possible worlds and their inhabitants exist; but they are not among the inhabitants of the actual world. There *are* flying horses, for example. They just don't exist here in the actual world. Actualists, on the other hand, deny the existence of mere possibilia. Other possible worlds might in fact exist. They might, for example, be abstract states of affairs. But if they do exist, they are among the inhabitants of the actual world. Moreover, talk of the inhabitants of other possible worlds isn't talk about some class of things that *exist* somewhere other than here in the actual world. Rather, it is simply talk about properties that would have been exemplified or states of affairs that would have obtained had things gone differently.

Presentism is analogous to actualism. Just as actualists say that there is nothing that exists outside the actual world, so presentists say that there is nothing in the actual world that exists outside the present time. Other times might in fact exist. They might, for example, be abstract states of affairs. But if they do exist, they are among the inhabitants of the present time. Moreover, talk of merely past (or merely future) objects isn't talk about some class of things that *exist* somewhere other than at the present time. Rather, it is simply talk about properties that were or will be

---

[2]Better: Lewis is an example of *one sort* of possibilist. Michael Bergmann [1999] distinguishes *anti-Meinongian actualism* (the view that, necessarily, everything exists) from *anti-Lewisian actualism* (the view that, necessarily, everything exists in the actual world). Lewis is an anti-Meinongian actualist: he agrees that, necessarily, there are no nonexistent objects. But, of course, he is not an anti-Lewisian actualist. For purposes here, *actualism* is being treated as equivalent to anti-Lewisian actualism.

exemplified, or states of affairs that did or will obtain, when other times were or will be present.

I said above that, on presentism, other times *might* exist—if, for example, they are thought of as abstract states of affairs. This is not the only way to think about times. For example, times might also be thought of as concrete events. For present purposes I will operate under the assumption that times are abstract. But nothing of substance depends on this assumption.[3]

As I shall think of them, then, times are analogous to abstract possible worlds. The present argument does not depend on any particular account of what abstract times are like; but if one is wanted, we might start by saying that a time is a *present-tense maximal* state of affairs. Intuitively, and very roughly, a present-tense maximal state of affairs is a total state of the world at an instant, *minus* all of the past- and future-tense truths. More rigorously: say that a state of affairs S *is future directed* just in case either S's obtaining entails that some contingent thing will exist or S's obtaining entails that no contingent thing will exist; and then define a *past-directed* state of affairs in the obviously parallel way.[4] Then a state of affairs S is present-tense maximal if and only if, for every atomic state of affairs S* that is neither future-directed nor past-directed, either S includes S* or S precludes S*.[5]

Given that times are abstract, talk of what is, was, or will be true when a time *t* is, was, or will be present just comes to talk about what *t* includes, with the added supposition that *t* in fact did, does, or will obtain. Thus, for example, to say that *it was true at t that* p is just to say that *t* includes p and that (on eternalism) *t* obtains at a region of spacetime earlier than now or (on presentism) *t* did obtain. Talk of what *will be true* at a time is to be understood in the obviously parallel way.

Note too that nothing in the definition of a present-tense maximal state of affairs rules out its including past- or future-directed states of affairs. As we shall see below, the grounding objection provides presentists with reason to suppose that times do include such states of affairs. It is to that issue that we now turn.

---

[3]One might worry that talk of times is unacceptable from the point of view of contemporary physics. The reason is that such talk might seem to presuppose that time as we know it is an absolute, observer-independent feature of reality, whereas the Special Theory of Relativity seems to imply that space and time are both mere appearances of a more fundamental reality—namely, spacetime. However, there are ways of understanding talk of times that get around this concern. For discussion, see, e.g., Rea [2004: sec.4].

[4]"Contingent things" might be objects or events; and I assume that an event exists when and only when it occurs.

[5]I assume that states of affairs that include laws of nature will not be atomic. One state of affairs includes another just in case the obtaining of the first state of affairs entails the obtaining of the second. One state of affairs precludes another just in case the obtaining of the first entails that the second does not obtain.

II. THE GROUNDING OBJECTION

Many philosophers are attracted to the idea that truth supervenes on being.[6] To say that truth supervenes on being is just to say that any world that duplicates ours with respect to what there is and how things are also duplicates ours with respect to what is true. The basic idea is that whatever is true—or at least whatever is contingently true—must somehow be grounded in what there actually is. Put this way, the principle that truth supervenes on being seems closely allied to the correspondence theory of truth (though the exact nature of the alliance is rather difficult to tease out). But, according to some philosophers, the principle that truth supervenes on being is incompatible with presentism. The argument proceeds as follows:

(i) Suppose presentism is true. Then (ii) our world doesn't include past or future objects or events. But (iii) if our world doesn't include past or future objects or events, then there is nothing in the world that could ground propositions about the past or future. Therefore, (iv) if truth supervenes on being, then propositions about the past and future are not true. But (v) truth does supervene on being, and (vi) at least some propositions about the past and future are true. Therefore, (vii) presentism must be false.[7]

If we grant that truth supervenes on being, the crucial premises in this argument are (iii) and (vi). The choice between the two is essentially a choice between supplying some "being" for truths about the past and future to supervene upon or somehow making plausible the claim that all of those propositions are false.

Of course, some presentists might not want to grant that truth supervenes on being.[8] Moreover, some might not even want to grant anything in the neighbourhood of that thesis—they might, for example, be happy to say that truths about the past are simply brute, not grounded in anything at all. For the moment, I will suppose that presentists in general will *not* want to go this route. In Section V, however, I will explicitly consider the question whether rejecting the demand for grounds provides the resources for a successful reply to my main argument; and I will conclude that it does not.

[6]For starters, see Armstrong [1997], Bigelow [1988: 122, 132–3], Lewis [2002], and Sider [2001, esp. chap. 2].

[7]This way of putting it generalizes a variety of more specific objections, some of which are discussed further later. For relevant discussion, see, e.g., Adams [1986], Bigelow [1996], Chisholm [1990], Crisp [2007], Fitch [1994], Keller [2004], Markosian [2004], Rea [2004], Sider [1999; 2001].

[8]Trenton Merricks is one such presentist. See his [2007] for extended arguments against the being-supervenience thesis and related principles.

I will also assume that presentists will not want to say that propositions about the past and the future are *all* false. Such a denial would make presentism unpalatable in the extreme. Thus, if presentists are to offer a response to the grounding objection, it seems that they must reject premise (iii).

Here is the standard way of rejecting premise (iii): Truths about the past and the future are grounded in irreducibly tensed properties of material objects or events.[9] What makes it true that there were dinosaurs is just some present object or some present event having the property of being such that there were dinosaurs. And what makes it true (if it is true) that there will be outposts on Mars is just some present object or event having the property of being such that there will be outposts on Mars. If an event is just the having of a property by some object or event, then, on this view, past and future tense truths are, one and all, grounded in present events.[10]

This response does not quite handle *all* of the truths about the past that we might want to handle. For example, it doesn't by itself tell us what grounds propositions that apparently refer to things that no longer exist. It also doesn't tell us what grounds truths apparently involving cross-temporal relations. So, for example, a presentist should want to affirm propositions like (1–3):

(1) Aristotle was a philosopher.
(2) Many contemporary philosophers admire Aristotle.
(3) Actions performed by Aristotle are among the causes of some of the mental states of contemporary philosophers.

But if presentism is true, then (assuming Aristotle is not currently enjoying some sort of post-mortem existence) Aristotle is not available to have properties, to be an object of admiration, or to be a cause of anything. Thus, it is hard to see how (1–3) could be true.

I will not take the trouble here, to spell out in detail the responses that presentists typically offer to this sort of problem. What I want to focus on is simply the general fact that *if* one accepts the demand for grounds for past and future tense propositions, the reply to questions about how to handle propositions like (1–3) will have to resemble what I called the standard reply to the initial grounding objection. To accommodate such propositions, all of the relevant grounds will have to

[9]See, especially, the works by Bigelow, Chisholm, Crisp, Keller, Markosian, and Rea cited in note 7.
[10]Or, what comes to the same thing: On this view, present tense propositions are grounded in *concrete states of affairs*, or in the *obtainings of abstract states of affairs*, or in *facts* (construed as identical to events, or concrete states of affairs, or obtainings of abstract states of affairs).

be somehow packed into the present time. So, in other words, presentists will have to posit a variety of things whose existence or occurrence *at the present time* will together entail the past and future tense truths that the presentist wants to be able to accommodate. Once this is clear, however, the argument for the conclusion that presentists must either reject bivalence or give up human freedom is straightforward, as the next two sections demonstrate.

III. FATALISM

Consider, for starters, the following fatalist argument. Suppose the present time is t, and Sally stands up at t; and let t^* be some time one thousand years prior to now. Then:

(F1)   It was true at t^* that Sally will stand up at t.[11]

(F2)   Necessarily, if it was true at t^* that Sally will stand up at t, then Sally stands up at t.

(F3)   Sally never had and never will have a choice about whether F1 is true.

(β3)   If p and if x never had and never will have a choice about p, and if p entails q, then x never had and never will have a choice about q.[12]

---

[11]Here and throughout I shall operate under the pretence that singular propositions containing Sally as subject exist and have truth values even at times when Sally does not exist. The pretence is harmless, however; for presentists who are bothered by it can simply adopt their favourite strategy for handling sentences like "Aristotle was a philosopher" in order to accommodate F1 and other sentences that appear to express propositions about Sally. And if it turns out that all such strategies fail, then presentists face even worse problems than I am here attributing to them.

[12]In his well-known Consequence Argument for incompatibilism, Peter van Inwagen [1983] relies on the following rule of inference (where "Np" abbreviates "p and no one has, had, or will have a choice about p"):

(β) $Np \mathbin{\&} N(p \supset q) \Rightarrow Nq$

As it turns out, Principle β has counterexamples. David Widerker [1987] has proposed an improvement that seems to be counterexample-free:

(β2) $Np \mathbin{\&} \square(p \supset q) \Rightarrow Nq$

(For discussion of this and other strengthened transfer principles, see Finch and Warfield [1998 and references therein].) Principle β3 which appears in my argument above is a version of β2 specified to an individual. The specification would be unneeded if I simply assumed (as seems plausible) that if x never had and never will have a choice about whether she stands at t, then no one has, had, or will have a choice about that. But the price of introducing this assumption is

(F4)   Therefore: Sally never had and never will have a choice about whether she stands at *t*.

F1 follows from the fact that Sally is now standing together with the assumption that bivalence holds for sentences of the form "S will do A". F2 is uncontroversial; and, for purposes here, I'll assume that β3 is as well. F3 is supposed to be true because facts about the past and facts about logical entailment aren't up to us.

For those who want to preserve bivalence, the standard response to this sort of argument is to give up F3, and to do so by saying that we have power over the truth of propositions like F1. But how could we have such power? How could Sally have power over what was true one thousand years ago? To this question we find two answers in the literature—answers that are superficially different, but, as I see it, identical at root:

Answer 1: The predicate "true at *t*" is like the predicate "true in Indiana". One might *say* things like:

(4)   "An earthquake is happening out west" is true in Indiana.

But presumably what one would mean by saying such a thing is that it is true *simpliciter* that an earthquake is happening, and that, from the point of view of Indiana, the occurrence of the earthquake is to the west. Likewise, then, with claims like F1: To say that it was true at *t** that Sally will stand up at *t* is just to say that, when *t** was present, "Sally stands at *t*" was true *simpliciter* and the occurrence of that event was, from the point of view of *t**, in the future. Thus, F1 is equivalent to something like F5:

(F5)   It is true at *t* that Sally stands up, and *t** is earlier than *t*.[13]

But once this is clear, the fatalist argument is defanged. For the fatalist has given us no reason for thinking that Sally never had and never will have a choice about the

added complexity later on. (For example, I would have to address questions about why we should think that no one existing *prior* to *t** could have acted freely in ways that would have made it false that *t** has the property *being such that Sally will stand at t*.)

[13]Peter van Inwagen [1983: 37ff] offers an understanding of the "true at *t* locution that implies that F1 would be equivalent not to F5 but to something like "If someone were to refer at *t** to the proposition that Sally stands up at *t*, she would refer to something true". But this understanding of "true at *t*" is problematic. To see why, let P be the proposition that no one is referring to any proposition at *t*. Now, P might be true at *t*; but it is clearly false that if someone were to refer to P at *t* they would refer to something true. Thus, the proposed understanding of true at *t* fails.

truth of F5. Indeed, there is good reason to think that Sally *does* have a choice about F5—namely, the fact that she seemingly has a choice about the occurrence of the event that explains, or grounds the truth of "Sally stands up at t". But if she has a choice about F5, and if F5 is equivalent to F1, then she has a choice about F1. Thus, F3 may safely be rejected.

This reply makes perfect sense on eternalism. According to the eternalist, when t^* is present, both t and the event of Sally's standing at t *exist*; they just exist *at a distance* from t^*. So there is no problem in affirming F5. But matters are different for a presentist. On presentism, F5 is either necessarily false or such that Sally could not possibly have a choice about its truth.

Taken at face value, F5 implies that there is an x and there is a y such that x is earlier than y. But this is unacceptable on presentism. For presentism implies that earlier events do not co-exist with later ones; and if they cannot co-exist, they cannot stand in relations to one another, and they cannot both be in the range of the existential quantifier. So, taken at face value, F5, on presentism, is necessarily false.

Of course, a presentist might insist that the right way to read F5 is as follows: "Sally stands up at t" is true; and when t^* was present, "t will be present" was true. But if this is how we are to read F5, then we have no reason to think that Sally could possibly have a choice about its truth. After all, when t^* obtained, Sally did not exist. How, then, could it have been up to her whether "t will be present" was true? This, of course, is precisely the question to which the fatalist demands an answer. Thus, any answer the presentist gives must be distinct from the one we are presently considering.

Answer 2: Rather than focus on the predicate "true at t", one might resist the fatalist by attempting to draw a principled distinction between facts about the past that we have a choice about and facts about the past that we have no choice about. The standard move here is to distinguish "hard facts" about the past, which do not depend on the present actions of free agents, from "soft facts", which do depend on the present actions of free agents. One then goes on to argue for the conclusion that facts like F1 are soft. This is what is often referred to as "Ockham's Way Out" [cf. Plantinga 1986]. If facts like F1 are soft, then there is no reason to doubt that we have a choice about whether they obtain. Thus, the road is clear to say that Sally has a choice about F1.

As with the previous response, this one, as well as the hard fact/soft fact distinction it depends on, makes perfectly good sense on eternalism. According to the eternalist, both t^* and the event of Sally's standing at t exist. Thus, there is no obstacle to saying that the event of Sally's standing explains, or is the ground of, the truth of

F1. Thus, there is no difficulty understanding how the truth of F1 might depend on Sally's free act.

On presentism, however, the Ockhamist response is untenable. When t^* was present, the event of Sally's standing at t did not exist. It was not within the range of the existential quantifier. There simply *was no such thing*. Thus, the truth of F1 could not have depended upon or been explained by it.[14]

So far I have simply been explaining why the standard response to the fatalist argument is not available to a presentist. I have not yet argued that presentists fall prey to the argument. For all I have said so far, there might yet be some other (perhaps even closely analogous) response to the fatalist argument that the presentist could endorse. But I will now argue that this is not so.

IV. THE MAIN ARGUMENT

As before, let t be the present time and let t^* be a time that obtained exactly one thousand years ago. Let P_S be the tensed proposition *that Sally will stand exactly one thousand years hence*; and let us suppose that P_S was true at t^*.

If presentism is true, then what grounds the truth of P_S at t^* is (something relevantly like) the occurrence at t^* of an event involving the irreducibly tensed property *being such that Sally will stand exactly one thousand years hence*. Let E_S be an event that grounds the truth of P_S (perhaps there is just one such event, or perhaps there is more than one), and let G_S be whatever tensed property is involved in E_S. Note that, on presentism (unlike eternalism), since Sally did not exist at t^*, G_S will not be a property that involves any relation to Sally or to contingent events involving Sally.[15] Thus, it looks as if G_S will be a property that is intrinsic to whatever has it.[16]

The argument, then, proceeds as follows:

Main Argument

(M1) Presentism is true. (Assumption)

(M2) P_S was true at t^*. (Assumption)

---

[14]For a fuller defence of this claim, see Finch and Rea in this volume.

[15]A *description* of G_S—like the description *being such that Sally will stand exactly one thousand years hence*—might make reference to Sally. But presentists must see that as only pretence—at least if, as we are assuming, G_S is a property that is exemplified at a time when Sally does not exist. Cf. n. 11.

[16]At any rate, it will be a property that is *independent of accompaniment by other contingent beings* [cf. Langton and Lewis 1998]. Whether that means it is a property that *cannot differ among duplicates*, however, is hard to say.

(M3) If presentism is true and if P_s was true at t^*, then the truth of P_s at t^* was not even partly grounded in the occurrence of any event involving Sally or in any exercising of her agent-causal power.[17] (Premise)

(M4) Therefore: The truth of P_s at t^* was not even partly grounded in the occurrence of any event involving Sally, or in any exercising of her agent-causal power. (From M1, M2, M3)

(M5) If the truth of a proposition p at a past time t_n was not even partly grounded in the occurrence of any event involving S, or in the agent causal activity of S, then S has never had and will never have a choice about whether p was true at t_n. (Premise)

(M6) Therefore: Sally has never had and will never have a choice about whether M2 is true. (From M2, M4, M5)

(M7) M2 entails that Sally stands now (at t, one thousand years later than t^*). (Trivial)

(β3) if p and if x never had and never will have a choice about p, and if p entails q, then x never had and never will have a choice about q. (Premise)

(M8) Therefore: Sally has never had and will never have a choice about whether Sally stands at t. (From M2, M6, M7, β3.)

If this argument is sound, and if (as seems obvious) one acts freely at a time only if one has, had, or will have a choice about what one does at that time, it follows that, given presentism and bivalence, Sally is not free. Moreover, the argument generalizes. Thus, if the Main Argument is sound, then, given presentism and bivalence, no one is free.

The unsupported premises in the argument are M2, M3, M5, and β3. To give up M2 is to give up bivalence. As I made clear at the outset of this paper, I am happy to concede that this is one way of resisting the argument. I have no argument to offer in support of β3; but I do not expect it to be a serious target for resistance as it seems, even upon close inspection, to be counterexample-free. M3 and M5, however, deserve some further comment.

M5 says, in short, that a person S has (or had, or will have) a choice about the truth of a proposition p only if the truth of p is at least partly grounded in what

---

[17] I include the second disjunct to avoid assuming that exercisings of agent-causal power are events. I do assume, however, that there are events like *Sally's not agent-causing anything at t* and *Sally's not refraining from standing up*. Thus, if one were to say that the truth of P_s at t^* depends in part on Sally's not refraining from standing up, one would (by this assumption) still be committed to saying that the truth of P_s at t depends on the *occurrence* of an event involving Sally. This assumption could be done away with, but at the cost of adding some complexity to the discussion.

S does. It is notoriously hard to say exactly what grounding amounts to; but it seems to me that, at a minimum, to say that the truth of p is grounded in some event e is to say that e explains the truth of p. Thus, if M5 is true, then if the truth of a proposition p is not even partly explained by what S does, then S has never had a choice about p. Here, two examples might be helpful.

First, laws of nature: Intuitively, nobody has a choice about the laws. But suppose that what laws obtain were partly explained by what acts you perform. (Perhaps a law is just a certain sort of exceptionless generalization; and perhaps your free acts at least partly explain what exceptionless generalizations of the relevant sort obtain.) If this were the case, it *might* be plausible to say that we have a choice about the laws. But, under the (more natural) assumption that our choices do not even partly explain what the laws of nature are, it is hard to see how we could possibly have a choice about the laws.

Second, divine decrees: Suppose that God has decreed that Sally will stand up at t. Does Sally have a choice about whether she stands up? That depends. Suppose that one of Sally's free acts partly explains God's decree. Perhaps God has eternally decreed that she will stand in (foreknowing) response to a prayer of Sally's that God will cause her to stand at t. In that case, it seems that Sally does have some choice about whether she stands at t. But, on the assumption that nothing that Sally does even partly explains God's decree, it seems wholly implausible to suppose that Sally has a choice about whether she stands. Of course, two examples hardly constitute an ironclad argument; but the principle seems sound nonetheless. If the truth of a proposition is not even partly explained by what you do, it is hard to see how you could possibly have a choice about its truth.

If that is right, however, then the crucial premise really is M3. In support of M3, I offer the following sub-argument: If P_S was true at t^*, then when t^* obtained, either P_S was true and grounded or it was true and ungrounded. Suppose its truth was ungrounded. Then, a fortiori, it was not grounded in any event involving Sally or in any exercising of her agent-causal power. On the other hand, suppose its truth was grounded. Necessarily, no truth is grounded in or explained by something that does not exist and has never existed. How could something possibly be explained by what has never been? Thus, if P_S was true and grounded when t^* obtained, then the truth of P_S was grounded in something (like E_S) that existed or occurred when or before t^* obtained. But if presentism is true, no event involving Sally, and no exercising of her agent causal power, had ever existed when or before t^* obtained. Therefore, if presentism is true, and if P_S was true and grounded when t^* obtained, then the truth of P_S at t^* was not grounded in any event involving Sally, or in any exercising of her agent-causal power. Thus, M3 is true.

I have now said all that I have to say in defence of the premises of the Main Argument. I want to close this section with a brief observation about backward causation. Note that attention to facts about grounding (which play a more important role in my Main Argument than is normal in the literature on fatalism) helps to highlight the reason why there is dispute about whether one would have to endorse backward causation in order to resist the fatalist. As I have already indicated, on eternalism, the property G_s involved in the grounding event E_s will be a relational property like *standing in the earlier-than relation to the event of Sally's standing at t*. Thus, by standing, *Sally* makes it the case that G_s is exemplified, and so she makes it the case that E_s occurs. It is her act, therefore, that explains the truth at t^* of P_s. And to say that Sally *could have* made it the case that P_s was false isn't to ascribe some mysterious backward causal power to Sally. Rather, it's just to say that Sally could have refrained from standing at t, and *if she did*, objects existing at t^* would have had some different relational properties. On presentism, however, if Sally were to refrain from standing at t, she would bring it about that some past object or event had a different intrinsic character than it in fact did. As we'll see in the next section, it is hard to see how, on presentism, Sally could do this, even if backward causation is in principle possible. But my point here is simply that if she were to do this, she would be exercising causal power over the past.

V. RESPONSES

How shall a presentist respond to the Main Argument? My own view, obviously enough, is that the right response for presentists is to accept one of the disjuncts I have offered. To drive that recommendation home, however, I must explain why several alternative responses ought to be set aside. The three that I will consider are these: (i) endorse backward causation; (ii) reject the demand for grounds; and (iii) endorse the claim that Sally does indeed have a choice about what was true in her distant past despite the fact that she has no causal power over the past. I'll take each in turn.

Response 1: Backward Causation. Suppose the presentist endorses the possibility of backward causation. One might think this to be a promising line of reply because, so it initially appears, if backward causation is possible, then it might be open to the presentist to say that Sally's standing is a cause of E_s, the event that grounds the truth of P_s. And if this were so, then (*contra* M3), Sally's standing could itself be a partial ground for the truth of P_s.

In fact, however, backward causation is of no use to a presentist. After all, the presentist believes that, when t^* was present, neither Sally nor her standing existed; so, for the presentist, neither Sally nor her standing could have been among the causes of E_s. Likewise, now that t is present, E_s does not exist and so is not available to stand in causal relations. Thus, no event at t^* can be among the effects of Sally's standing and no event involving Sally can be among the causes of E_s. Indeed, we can say more generally that, on presentism, no event *outside of t^** can, strictly speaking, be among the causes of any event that occurs at t^*. The reason, quite simply, is that to posit such relations is to suppose that existing things stand in relations with non-existing things—which, in turn, is to suppose, nonsensically, that there *are* some non-existing things.[18] So even if the presentist asserts that backward causation is possible, she will have to accommodate backward causation in the same way that she accommodates forward causation—namely, without positing cross-temporal dependence relations. But then she still lacks the resources for making strict and literal sense of the claim that the event of Sally's standing at t is causally responsible for E_s.

Response 2: Rejecting the Demand for Grounds. What about rejecting the demand for grounds altogether? Consider the debate about whether there are true coun-terfactuals of freedom (propositions of the form "If (non-actual) circumstances C were to obtain, S would freely do A"). Opponents of true counterfactuals of free-dom often say that there are no such truths because there is nothing in the world to ground them [cf., e.g., Adams 1977]. In response to this objection, Alvin Plantinga has made the following remark:

> It seems to me much clearer that some counterfactuals of freedom are at least pos-sibly true than that the truth of propositions must, in general, be grounded.
>
> —Plantinga 1985: 378

William Lane Craig offers even stronger words:

> I think it is evident that [those who reject the claim that there are true counter-factuals of freedom] have not even begun to do the necessary homework in order for their grounding objection to fly. They have yet to articulate their ontology of truth, including the nature of truth-bearers and truth-makers. Nor have they yet presented a systematic account of which truth-bearers require truth-makers.
>
> —Craig 2001: 348

[18]At any rate, *I* say that it is nonsense to suppose that there are nonexistent objects. Neo-Meinongians, of course, disagree; but I am happy to concede that presentists can avoid my argument if they embrace neo-Meinongianism. But the only alternative, it would seem, is to suppose that causal relations obtain not between events or objects existing at different times but rather between simultaneously exemplified properties or simultaneously occurring events [cf. Zimmerman 1997].

On their view, the demand for grounds for counterfactuals of freedom is unmotivated. Or, at any rate, it has not been *sufficiently* motivated to overthrow the antecedent conviction that there are true counterfactuals of freedom. (Indeed, on Craig's view, it has not even been adequately *articulated*.) And likewise, one might say, for the corresponding claim about future tense propositions about human free acts. Perhaps they simply do not require grounds. If so, then the account of grounding that drives the argument in Section IV may be rejected, and the demand to replace it with an alternative account of grounding may be rejected as well.

Whether the demand for grounds can sensibly be rejected is an interesting and difficult question, but it would take us too far afield to pursue that question here. For now, let us simply concede that the demand can sensibly be rejected. The question for our purposes is whether rejecting that demand is of any *use* to the presentist. Unfortunately, it is hard to see how it would be. Importantly, the response poses no direct threat to any premise of the argument. The hope would have to be that giving up the demand for grounds would somehow force a reformulation of the argument that would expose a flaw. But that hope is in vain. For the Sub-argument for M3 explicitly considers the possibility that P_s might be ungrounded, and it points out that, if P_s was true but ungrounded when t^* obtained, then its truth did not depend on any event involving Sally or on any exercise of her agent-causal power, and so M3 is true. Indeed, if the demand for grounds is given up, it looks as if the presentist must say that P_s was simply a *brute fact* at t^*. To see why, it will help to make a comparison with present tense truths.

Suppose it is true now that Sally stands up. A deflationist about truth can say that the state of affairs *it's being true that Sally stands up* is "ungrounded" because that state of affairs is nothing more than—indeed, is identical with—the state of affairs *Sally's standing up*. On this view, the notion of truth isn't to be cashed out in terms of correspondence; so, one might argue, talk of grounding makes no sense. But even if that is right, the present truth of "Sally stands up" is clearly not *brute*. Insofar as the *event* has an explanation, the truth of the sentence reporting its occurrence has an explanation. But a presentist deflationist cannot say this about P_s. That proposition's being true cannot be identified with any event involving Sally; for again, on presentism, Sally isn't around at t^* to be involved in events. Moreover, the only event that the proposition's truth can be identified with—E_s—has no apparent cause and, apparently, no other sort of explanation. But then the truth of P_s seems just to be a brute fact; and, if it is, then it is not the sort of thing that anybody could possibly have a choice about.

Response 3: Having a Choice about the Past. Suppose a presentist says something like this: Sally's choices are among the causal explanations of her behaviour at t;

there are worlds in which her choices do not cause her to stand at t; and in those worlds, E_s does not occur at t^*. Therefore, Sally has a choice about whether E_s occurs and thus about whether P_s was true when t^* obtained. Therefore, M6 is false.

This response is tempting, I think, because it parallels a response that compatibilists can give to a familiar argument for the conclusion that freedom is incompatible with causal determinism. According to the incompatibilist, we have no choice about the laws or about the (present tense) facts about times in our distant past; but, according to determinism, the laws together with the present tense facts about some time in our distant past entail our present behaviour. Thus, concludes the incompatibilist, we have no choice about our present behaviour. "But," the compatibilist replies, "our present behaviour is caused by our choices; there are worlds in which our choices do not cause us to behave as we are presently behaving; in those worlds either the laws or the facts about the relevant time in the distant past are different; therefore, we have a choice either about the laws or about the facts about times in our distant past."

Though I have some sympathy with this response (as wielded by the compatibilist), I think that incompatibilists should not be impressed by it. The reason is that, though the compatibilist hereby demonstrates that determinism is compatible with our having a choice *in some sense* about our present behaviour, it is not at all clear that her response shows that determinism is compatible with our having a choice *in the sense relevant to freedom* about our present behaviour. If this latter is conceded, then the compatibilist has scored a victory. But this is precisely what *must* be conceded if the parallel response to the argument of Section IV is to be successful. Incompatibilists, I think, will be reluctant to concede this. And since the Main Argument is given under the supposition of incompatibilism, that tells against the usefulness of this sort of response.

But even leaving this issue aside, there is a deeper and more compelling reason why the present response (unlike its compatibilist parallel) is useless against the Main Argument. At the heart of the present response (and its compatibilist parallel) is the idea that certain past-tense facts depend upon present events, such that had the present been different, certain features of the past would have been different as well. The trouble, however, is that the response makes sense only on the assumption that, not only the relevant *past-tense* facts, but also the corresponding *past present-tense facts* depend(ed) upon present events; and this latter assumption is unacceptable.

Let me illustrate: Consider the following two facts, the first of which obtained at t^* and the second of which obtains now:

F_1: P_s is true.
F_2: P_s was true at t^*.

Suppose one tries to say that F_2 depends on the event (E_1) *Sally's standing at t*. This makes sense only if, when t^* was present, F_1 depended on E_1. For, intuitively, F_2 and F_1 ought to have, apart from the passage of time, *precisely the same ground*. If they do not, then, it seems, the facts about the past are bizarrely disconnected from the events that occurred in the past. But, of course, F_1 cannot depend on E_1 unless it is possible for existing things to stand in relations with non-existing things.[19] If that *is* possible, then the Main Argument is indeed unsound (and the flaw lies in the explicit appeal in the Sub-Argument for M3 to the claim that only existing things have properties and stand in relations). But I take it that if it turns out that presentists are forced to abandon the principle that only existing things have properties and stand in relations, then presentism has been reduced to absurdity.

This concludes my survey of possible responses to the Main Argument. Again, the strength of that argument depends on the plausibility of M3, M5, and β3, all of which seem to me to be unassailable. But if those premises are true, then the ultimate conclusion of this paper is unavoidable. If presentism is true, then we must give up either libertarianism or the unrestricted principle of bivalence.[20]

REFERENCES

Adams, Robert 1977. Middle Knowledge and the Problem of Evil, *American Philosophical Quarterly* 14: 109–17.

Adams, Robert 1986. Time and Thisness, *Midwest Studies in Philosophy* 11: 315–30.

Armstrong, D. M. 1997. *A World of States of Affairs*, Cambridge: Cambridge University Press.

Bergmann, Michael 1999. (Serious) Actualism and (Serious) Presentism, *Noûs* 33: 118–32.

Bigelow, John 1988. *The Reality of Numbers*, Oxford: Clarendon Press.

Bigelow, John 1996. Presentism and Properties, *Philosophical Perspectives* 10: 35–52.

Chisholm, Roderick 1990. Referring to Things that No Longer Exist, *Philosophical Perspectives* 4: 545–56.

Craig, William Lane 2001. Middle Knowledge, Truth-Makers, and the Grounding Objection, *Faith and Philosophy* 18: 337–52.

Crisp, Thomas 2007. Presentism and the Grounding Objection. *Noûs* 41: 90–109.

---

[19]Note the consequence of this line of reasoning: If presentism is true, and if it really is true that facts like F1 and F2 in general ought to have the same ground, then it looks as if all tensed facts will have to be grounded in *eternal time-indexed events*—events like *it's being the case that Sally stands at t*, which might be said to occur at every time.

[20]I am grateful to Michael Bergmann, Jeff Brower, J. Brian Pitts, Tom Crisp, Isaac Choi, Trenton Merricks, Alvin Plantinga, and the referees for the *Australasian Journal of Philosophy* for helpful comments on an earlier draft of this paper. Thanks are also due to William Lane Craig, William Hasker, and Ted Warfield for helpful conversations and correspondence about various issues in the paper. I am especially grateful to Michael Bergmann for extended correspondence that resulted in substantial clarification of the main argument. Work on this paper was supported in part by an NEH Summer Stipend (2004).

Finch, Alicia and Michael Rea 2008. Presentism and Ockham's Way Out, *Oxford Studies in the Philosophy of Religion 1*, ed. Jonathan Kvanvig, Oxford: Clarendon Press: 1–17.

Finch, Alicia and Ted Warfield 1998. The *Mind* Argument and Libertarianism, *Mind* 107: 515–28.

Fitch, Greg 1994. Singular Propositions in Time, *Philosophical Studies* 73: 181–7.

Flint, Thomas 1998. *Divine Providence: The Molinist Account*, Ithaca NY: Cornell University Press.

Keller, Simon 2004. Presentism and Truthmaking, in *Oxford Studies in Metaphysics 1*, ed. Dean Zimmerman, Oxford: Clarendon Press: 83–104.

Langton, Rae and David Lewis 1998. Defining Intrinsic, *Philosophy and Phenomenological Research* 333–45.

Lewis, David 2002. Truthmaking and Difference-Making, *Noûs* 35: 602–15.

Markosian, Ned 2004. A Defense of Presentism, in *Oxford Studies in Metaphysics 1*, ed. Dean Zimmerman, Oxford: Clarendon Press: 47–82.

Merricks, Trenton 2007. *Truth and Ontology*, Oxford: Clarendon Press.

Plantinga, Alvin 1974. *The Nature of Necessity*, Oxford: Clarendon Press.

Plantinga, Alvin 1985. Replies, in *Alvin Plantinga*, ed. J. Tomberlin and P. van Inwagen, Dordrecht: D. Reidel: 372–82.

Plantinga, Alvin 1986. On Ockham's Way Out, *Faith and Philosophy* 3: 235–69.

Rea, Michael 2004. Four-Dimensionalism, in *Oxford Handbook of Metaphysics*, ed. Michael J. Loux and Dean Zimmerman, New York: Oxford University Press: 246–80.

Sider, Theodore 1999. Presentism and Ontological Commitment, *Journal of Philosophy* 96: 325–47.

Sider, Theodore 2001. *Four-Dimensionalism*, Oxford: Clarendon Press.

Van Inwagen, Peter 1983. *An Essay on Free Will*, Oxford: Clarendon Press.

Widerker, David 1987. On an Argument for Incompatibilism, *Analysis* 47: 37–41.

Zimmerman, Dean 1997. Chisholm on the Essences of Events, in *The Philosophy of Roderick M. Chisholm*, ed. L. E. Hahn, Chicago: Open Court: 73–100.

7

COMPATIBILIST OPTIONS

John Perry

... those who accept that responsibility for a situation implies an ability to bring it about and, perhaps, an ability to prevent it, must explain how agents are *able to do* other than they are caused to do. Without it, they can give no defense of their counterexamples. With it, they can be confident that the Consequence Argument, by itself, is no refutation of their position.
Tomis Kapitan (2002, 154)

1. INTRODUCTION

Compatibilism is the thesis that an act may be both free and determined by previous events and the laws of nature. I assume that in normal cases a condition of a person's performing an act freely is that the person is able to refrain from performing the act. Thus, I accept that if determinism entails that agents do not have this ability, we must give up compatibilism. In this paper I try to contribute to the rethinking of compatibilism by distinguishing between strong and weak accounts of laws and strong and weak accounts of ability. I argue that compatibilism is a tenable position when combined with either a weak account of laws, or a weak account of ability, or both. I shall concentrate on influential arguments for incompatibilism due to Peter van Inwagen, often called, collectively, the "consequence argument."

Some versions of the consequence argument seem to rely only on inescapable modal principles. In his excellent review and discussion of these arguments, Tomis Kapitan concludes that these principles are not so logically inescapable as to completely trap the compatibilist (Kapitan 2002). This is not to say van Inwagen's arguments are fallacious, but simply that they rely on certain principles about causation and ability that have not yet been fully articulated and defended. Kapitan says, just before making the remarks quoted above, that his assessment provides the compatibilist with "momentary breathing room at best" (2002, 154). I am trying to take advantage of the momentary breathing room afforded by Kapitan to explore and to a certain extent defend options available to the compatibilist. Using terms I explain below, my position is that van Inwagen's arguments do show that the combination of compatibilism with a strong account of laws and a strong account ability (as I define these terms) is not tenable. The options, then, are a weak account of laws, a weak account of ability, or both.

2. BASIC ARGUMENT

As a preliminary to considering a simple argument against compatibilism, let's look at an even simpler argument.

(1) $\forall t \, \forall x \, (\phi(x, t) \rightarrow \varphi(x, t+1))$

(2) $\phi\,(\text{Elwood}, t)$

(3) Elwood eats cookies at $t+1 \rightarrow \sim \varphi(\text{Elwood}, t+1)$

(4) So, $\sim (\text{Elwood eats cookies at } t+1)$

Here ϕ is a complex state a person together with a suitably large surrounding region the person can be in at a time. If Elwood is in ϕ at t, then at t states of Elwood and the things around him make it the case that he *really really* does not want a cookie at t, that no one is about to persuade him to change his mind, that there are no forces about to impinge on him that will change his mind about cookies, or force him to eat one whether he wants to or not, and so forth. For simplicity we suppose that time is discrete, and $t+1$ is the next instant after t. φ is a state of Elwood and a suitably large region that will succeed ϕ according to the laws of nature. It makes it the case that Elwood does not have any cookies in his mouth.

(1)–(4) constitute a valid argument. If Elwood is in a state that invariably leads to a state that precludes eating cookies, he will not eat cookies. However, it seems quite clear that we are not warranted in going further. To add to our argument:

(5) What's more, Elwood *cannot* eat a cookie at $t+1$

would turn it from a valid to an invalid argument.

Prior to being given some quite persuasive argument, we do not take *doing* something as a necessary condition of *being able* to do it, or *being able* to do something as a sufficient condition for *doing it*. We do not take a person's *not* doing something as a sufficient condition for their being *unable* to do it. We accept the inference from "cannot" to "does not" and from "does" to "can". But we do not accept the inference from "does not" to "cannot" or from "can" to "does".

If Elwood *did* eat a cookie at $t+1$, that would prove that one of the premises 1, 2, or 3 is false. But the fact that he *can* eat a cookie does not show that one of the premises is false. It merely shows that *if* he did do that thing that he is capable of doing, one of the premises *would* be false. Hence, the truth of the premises rules out his eating a cookie, but not his having the ability to eat a cookie.

Now suppose we add another premise, to the effect that (1) is not merely a true universal generalization, but something that follows from the laws of nature. We derive (1) from premise (0):

(0) According to the laws of nature, $\forall t \forall x (\phi(x, t) \rightarrow \phi(x, t+1))$

Now we have the basic argument underlying those used by many incompatibilists, although there are many variations on the basic theme.

The intuitive idea is that premise (0) provides enough extra strength to the premises to get not only to establish (4), that Elwood *does* not eat a cookie, but to establish (5), that he *cannot* eat a cookie. Van Inwagen often taps our intuitions that we cannot change the past or change the laws of nature. The idea is that if Elwood can eat a cookie, then he can falsify one of the premises. He cannot falsify any true statements about the past, so he cannot do anything at $t+1$ that changes the fact that he was in state ϕ at t. And he cannot falsify laws. So Elwood not only will not, but cannot, eat a cookie at $t+1$ if determinism is true.

Given this way of looking at the argument for incompatibilism, there is one basic strategy for the compatibilist. This is to deny that the replacement of (1) with (0) adds enough strength to the premises to validate the step from (4) to (5). There are two basic (and compatible) ways to implement this strategy: (i) adopt a weak theory of laws, and (ii) adopt a weak theory of ability, of *can*, and hence a strong theory of *cannot*. The compatibilist must maintain that it takes more extra power to rule out Elwood's being able to eat the cookie than supplementing (1) with (0) provides, by adopting one or both of these positions.

3. SOME PRELIMINARIES

Discussions of compatibilism usually employ at least implicitly two different concepts having to do with propositions and truth. Propositions *are* true or false. And propositions *are made* true and false by actions and other events. It will be helpful to be clear about these concepts, and how they are related, before plunging into the main items of business.

Intuitively, many propositions are *made* true, or *rendered* true, by events that occur at some time, or through some interval of time. For example, the proposition *that Nixon won the 1972 election* was not made true or rendered true until the events of election day, 1972, or perhaps not even until inauguration day, 1973. What was the status of this proposition before then?

One intuitive option is that propositions are not true or false until they are *made* true or false by events. On this view, many of our statements about the future express propositions that are neither true nor false when they are made, but become true or false when events make them so in the future. This option, though intuitive, does not mesh easily with the two-valued logic that most of us are taught and find easy and convenient to work with.

If we want our familiar logic to mesh smoothly with the concept of events making propositions true, the simplest way is to think of truth and falsity themselves as timeless properties of propositions, while the properties of being rendered or made true or false are properties that occur at times, or through intervals. "Timeless" here simply means "not relative to times". So it doesn't follow from the fact that a proposition is timelessly true that it is *true at every time* in any interesting sense. We can say that I am six feet tall because if I stand erect, one part of my body—the top of my head—is six feet above the floor. It's my whole body that is six feet tall. But I'm not six feet tall at every point on my body, if that means anything more than that I'm six feet tall.

So we have *two* properties having to do with truth of propositions: being true or false, and being made true or false. The first is not relative to times, the second is. This is the track I shall follow in this essay. All of the points I make, however, could be made in the more complicated system, in which some propositions have no truth value until they are made true by events.

How are the properties of being true and being made true related? The obvious way is that:

- if a proposition is ever *made* true, it *is* true.

It might be better to say it *be* true, using a tenseless form, and in fact I shall do so from now on, and say things like

- If a proposition is ever made true (or made false), then it *be* true (or be false).
- The fact that a proposition has not yet been made true (or made false) by events, does not imply that it *be* not true (or be not false).

Compare:

> The fact that Gore has not yet been chosen as our next president does not imply that he is not our next president.

If Gore ends up being nominated and elected in 2004, then he is our next president. If I call him "our next president" now, I'm correct if the future goes one way, incorrect if it goes the other. It is possible to become rather puzzled by this. How can Gore be our next president now, if it hasn't been decided yet? So he must not be our next president. By parity of reasoning, no one is our next president. That will be a constitutional crisis. But we can avoid the crisis. Being our next president is a property Gore has if at some point between now (summer 2002) and January 2005 he is elected and inaugurated and Bush hasn't been replaced in the meantime. It all works out, as long as we are careful about the difference between being our next president, a property Gore may have, and being elected and inaugurated as our next president, one that he does not yet have as I write this, in 2002. The fact that lots of propositions be true that have not yet been made true is sort of like that. It can be confusing. It may well be that from a metaphysical point of view our two-valued logic of propositions may not be optimal. Still, if we are careful, things will work out.

It will be useful to have the following locution available:

- Events *establish whether P* if they make *P* true or make it false (make ~*P* true).

Perhaps we should simply say "make whether *P*", but that sounds even worse.

It seems like there are lots of important propositions whose truth value is established not by being made true by events, but in some other way. For example, consider Pythagoras's theorem, the proposition *that the square of the hypotenuse of a right triangle is equal to the sum of the squares of the other two sides*. No event has ever *made* this proposition true, and none ever will. It's not at all like the proposition *that Nixon won the 1972 election*. There is no sequence of events, ending at a certain time, the occurrence of which makes Pythagoras's theorem true. So the converse of the principle above isn't right; it is not true that if a proposition is true, then some events either have made, are making, or will make it true.

It would not be correct to say that the truth of the proposition that Pythagoras's theorem is *independent* of events; events do *conform* to it. But they don't *make* it true. They *reflect* its truth.

For propositions that report ordinary facts, such as the proposition *that Eisenhower was president in 1954*, or *that Gore will be president in 2006*, it is natural to use the term "because":

- The proposition *that Eisenhower was president in June 1953* be true *because* of events that occurred prior to 1954, including his election in 1952 and inauguration in 1953.
- The proposition *that Gore will be president in 2006* be true, if it be, partly because of events that have yet to occur.

With propositions such as that of Pythagoras's theorem, a quite different kind of explanation of their truth seems appropriate, and of course there is a lot of philosophical controversy about what the correct explanation might be. I'll simply say that such propositions are *not* made true by events, and leave it at that for now.

Finally, and importantly, suppose that a true proposition, that is not made true by events, together with some other propositions, that have already been made true by events, entail a proposition that has yet to be made true. What should we say about that proposition? To return to our example, *suppose* that the laws of nature are not made true by events, and that these laws, together with propositions made true by events that have already happened, entail that Elwood will not eat cookies at future time *t*. I will say that although the proposition that Elwood will not eat the cookie at *t* has not yet been *made* true, its truth value has been *settled*. The proposition won't be made true until the events that the laws of nature and the past determine have actually occurred: the time *t* has arrived, and Elwood says "no" to the proffered cookie, keeps his arms at his sides, and walks away. But these events were *already* entailed by a combination of propositions, some of which were already made true and the rest of which aren't made true by events at all. So the truth value of the proposition that he would not eat was, in that sense, *already settled*, before he refrained from eating.

The two issues on which I believe the tenability of compatibilism turns are:

- Is the truth of laws *established* by the events that confirm them and fail to disconfirm them, so that laws are laws because events conform to them? Or is the truth of laws established, by something else, so that events *conform* to them because they are laws? The first view is a *weak* theory of laws, the second a *strong* theory of laws.
- Can one have the ability to perform or refrain from an action *A* at time *t*, even though the issue of whether one will perform *A* at *t* or refrain from doing so has been *settled* before *t*? A weak account of ability will allow us to answer *yes* to this question; a strong account will force us to answer *no*.

4. STRONG AND WEAK LAWS

One option for the compatibilist is to adopt a weak conception of laws. On a weak conception of laws, (0) does not add much, if anything, to the argument of section 2. Laws are basically true generalizations, and true generalizations are made true at least in part by the events that, as we say, confirm them. The laws that determine that Elwood won't eat a cookie may be true, but, nevertheless, not be made true until the last human or the last cookie has passed out of existence. Elwood's not eating cookies was part of the sequence that established the law, not something the law settled. The law and the facts leading up to Elwood's choice may have *determined* that Elwood would pass up the cookie, but they did not *settle* it, for the law itself wasn't made true until long after Elwood made his decision, and in fact his decision was part of what made it true.

A person can make true generalizations false in the following sense: the generalization be true, but there is something the person could have done, or can do, such that if they had done it, or were to do it, the generalization would not be true. Suppose there were two soccer teams, Manchester United and Nottingham Sherwood. Suppose that Nottingham Sherwood existed from 1960 to 2000 and then was disbanded. During that time it played Manchester United eighty times and never won or tied. So it is a true empirical generalization that

(G) For all soccer games g, if g is a game between Manchester United and Nottingham Sherwood, Nottingham Sherwood loses g.

While by 1975 or so this may have seemed like a decree of God to the Nottingham fans, we'll assume for now that it was really just a sad but true generalization. Suppose that in the second game between these two teams in 1978 they were in a 0 to 0 tie at the end of the game, and then Manchester won in overtime. In the last second of regulation play, Nottingham had a clear and easy shot on Manchester's goal, that their best player missed. Nottingham's worst player was watching a plane overhead skywriting advertisements for Guinness, and ran into their best player just as he kicked. I think the Nottingham fans at least would think that the Nottingham team could have won that game, even though they did not. And that means they could have made the true generalization G false.

I think it is common sense to suppose that laws are not simply true generalizations. Suppose that one Nottingham fan says "We could have won that game in 1978 . . ." Another particularly bitter Nottingham fan says,

No, you are wrong. You have not grasped that it is an *unshakable law of nature* that Manchester United beats Nottingham Sherwood. It's a law of nature because God decreed that Nottingham would always lose. Laws of nature are universal generalizations that God issued as fiats during creation week, and other things that follow from them. For reasons finite mortals can't be expected to fathom, he often punishes the virtuous and rewards the wicked. And in this spirit he decreed that Manchester United would always beat Nottingham Sherwood. It seemed like Nottingham could win, but in fact it could not.

This fan's remark embodies the intuition behind the argument of section 2. Intuitively, laws are *more* than true generalizations, and (0) adds something substantial to the argument. You can make a mere generalization false; even if no one gets around to doing so, it remains true that someone could have. But laws are laws. You cannot make a generalization false, if it follows from the laws of nature. This is the strong conception of laws. But of course, one can have a strong conception of laws without believing in an unfathomable God or any god at all.

Let's remind ourselves of (1):

(1) $\forall t\,\forall x\,(\phi(x, t) \to \varphi(x, t+1))$

If (1) is true then there have not been, and will not be, times t and individuals x such that $\phi(x, t)$ and $\sim \varphi(x, t+1)$. And (0) says that (1) is not simply true, but true according to the laws of nature.

The question is, does (1) make (0) true, or does (0) make (1) true? Is (0) true *because* (1) has no disconfirming instances? Or does (1) not have disconfirming instances *because* of the truth of (0)—because (1) follows from the laws of nature? Is the truth of (0) one of those things, like the truth of Pythagoras's theorem, that is established by something other than what happens? Is it the sort of things to which events conform, but do not make true? Or is it just a sort of fancy way of saying (1)?

To return to our soccer fans. A third soccer fan, also a fan of Hume's, may say:

> I don't think (G) is a decree of God. But I agree with you that it is a law of nature. A law of nature simply is an exceptionless generalization that we have grown used to so that it shapes our expectations. And (G) certainly is that.

This remark would express a *weak* conception of laws. It isn't *quite* enough for (G) to be a law that it is true. More is required: that we use it to form our expectations. But that's all. There is no big metaphysical condition, like a command from God, which is also required. Being a law is just being a true generalization that we have internalized so that our expectations about the future are shaped by it. On this conception, it is (1) being true that explains, or partly explains, that it is a law. (1) Explains (0), not the other way around.

On either conception of laws, laws will have no disconfirming instances. On the strong conception, the fact that L is a law *explains* why events conform to it; the truth of the law is due to something *other than* the lack of disconfirming instances. If determinism is also true, laws and propositions about the past not only entail propositions about the future, but also settle them.

On the weak conception of laws, however, the incompatibilist argument does not work. (0) adds nothing to the argument that might push the conclusion from (4) to (5). A Humean conception might add something to the requirement for being a law. (1) not only has to be true, but accepted and used to guide our expectations. But this doesn't push us from (4) to (5).

One option for the compatibilist, then, is to insist on this very weak, Humean conception of laws. What we do is up to us; laws are merely those descriptions of what we do that will end up being true once human actions are complete. Laws determine, but do not settle. I'll call this view "existentialist compatibilism".

I find existentialist compatibilism very appealing, but not wholly convincing. Consider the law that for every action there is an opposite and equal reaction. On the weak conception, this is a law because there never have been and never will be any exceptions to it, and we are attuned to it: when we see a reaction, we expect an opposite and equal reaction. There is nothing about things that *make* this law true, except that everything conforms to it. It seems to me much more plausible that this law *gets* at something (or some things) about the universe that explains why things conform to the law and it has no disconfirming instances. I find it hard to stick with the Humean conception of laws.

One nontheistic but strong conception of laws holds that they are true generalizations that derive from the nature of things, and so describe constraints that form the structure of the world. These constraints are relations between types of things and types of situations.

We can look on (1) as telling us that a certain relation holds between two types of events: coinstantiation. Whenever there is $\phi(x, t)$ type of event, there is a $\phi(x, t+1)$ type of event. On the constraints view, there are other relations between types, such as *causing, making happen,* and *forcing.* These are the relations Hume wanted to reduce to, or eliminate in favor of, coinstantiation plus psychology. He called them "necessary connections." I think that "necessary" is rather confusing, given the uses of the term that are familiar in current philosophy. Causal relations are not necessary in the sense of being analytic, or in the sense of being true in all logically possible worlds, or even all metaphysically possible worlds. Still, causal relations between types of events are basic to the structure of the actual world. So (0) explains (1), not the other way around. I'll call them *structural* connections. Structural connections are not necessary, like Pythagoras's theorem, but they are not made true by events, either. Events conform to them because they capture factors about the world that shape events, not because they report events.

On this conception, if a generalization is true according to the laws of nature, it reflects a constraint that holds among types of things or situations in virtue of their nature, or a necessary consequence of such constraints. Laws are rooted in the nature of matter, space, and time, or the nature of whatever else it is that makes up the universe. When one billiard ball hits another the direction and velocity of the second is determined by the direction, and velocity of the first in a certain way. What makes this so? Not some decree, sentence, statement, or proposition that truly describes it. Nor the facts about what has happened in similar situations in the past and will hold in the future. There are real connections between types of things and situations. This seems to be what Hume denied, or at least denied we could ever understand. Disagreeing with Hume makes me nervous, and I find it hard to say what else there is about the universe, other than the flow of events, that constitutes such constraints. Nevertheless, I can't bring myself to accept any *weaker* conception of laws.

On this conception, the states of Elwood that are involved in his being in ϕ cause him to not eat cookies. These states include such things as really not wanting to eat cookies, and seeing no reason to eat cookies. It seems to me that in this sort of case we are in touch with properties that cause us to take or not take certain actions in a pretty direct way. It seems in the nature of things that someone in such states would not take a cookie. It would be nicest, from a compatibilist point of view, to have a completely weak conception of laws. Nevertheless, this conception seems to hold some promise of fitting into a compatibilist picture when combined with a suitably weak conception of ability.

5. ABILITY AND ACTION

Consider this principle:

(S) If x can perform A at t, then at no time earlier than t is it *settled* whether x performs A at t

A strong theory of can supports (S), while a weak theory does not. I'll argue for a weak theory, and explain why it undercuts van Inwagen's arguments. First an analogy.

It's 1956 and Elwood *doesn't* buy a new Edsel. He thinks they are ugly, ungainly, and overpriced. He doesn't want one. So he doesn't buy one. Now does it follow that he can't afford one? Of course not. He may have all the money he needs, and simply not want one. One question has to do with what he wants in a car and what he thinks about the Edsel. These facts, what he thinks about Edsels and what he wants in the way of a car, are pretty much located in Elwood's head. At any rate, they are not located down the street at the bank. But that's where the facts about how much money he has in his account, and how much credit the bankers will give him, reside.

It may be that Elwood would rather be drawn and quartered or have rats gnaw out his eyes than buy an Edsel. But those facts about his mind don't tell us anything about his bank account. He may be loaded, so he can easily afford a fleet of Edsels. He can't buy the car without money or credit, but he can *not* buy the car even though he has plenty of money and plenty of credit.

We could put forward a little argument that Elwood won't buy an Edsel:

(1) Reasonable people don't buy cars that they think are ugly, ungainly, and overpriced and that they simply don't want and have no other reasons to buy (law of nature).

(2) Elwood thinks Edsels are all of those things, and has no other reason to buy one (fact about Elwood's mind).

(3) So he won't buy one (fact about Elwood's action).

No conclusions about Elwood's bank account can be validly drawn from this argument. It would be silly to draw the further conclusion

(4) So he can't afford one (fact about Elwood's bank account).

The premises don't say anything about Elwood's bank account or his credit. So no conclusions about his bank account or credit can be validly drawn.

That's the model for a weak account of ability. Whether Elwood performs A is one question, having to do with what he wants and believes. What he can do is something else, having to do with what abilities he has. If Elwood can't perform A then he won't. But it doesn't follow from the fact that he won't that he can't.

Of course, people's basic abilities aren't kept down the street in the bank. Elwood's ability to pay for an Edsel may depend in part on his bank account. But his ability to write a check, or say, "Please, sell me an Edsel," depend on facts about him. Still, facts about abilities are quite different than facts about desires and beliefs. Let us suppose—completely fancifully—in order to keep this important point vividly in mind, that one part of the brain has to do with what people actually do, and another has to do with what they can do. Let's say the left side contains the desires and beliefs and the other stuff that actually motivates actions. The right side contains all the basic abilities, the repertoire of actions.[1] The repertoire is tapped when one decides to do something that requires a certain ability.

---

[1] Let me emphasize that the right and left sides are chosen completely arbitrarily, simply as a way of easily visualizing the point. This is not an attempt to fit agency into what is known, or thought, or imagined, or claimed, about the differences between the right and left side of the brain.

When I learn how to do something, to walk or pick up a glass of water or ride a bicycle or write a check or balance a checkbook or prove a theorem, things change on the right side of my brain. My repertoire of abilities increases. As I learn to do these things, the left side of my brain may change, too. I may develop aversions to proving theorems and balancing checkbooks, while learning to like riding bicycles, walking, writing checks, and drinking. Then we can predict that I'll do a lot more riding bikes, walking, and drinking than theorem proving and checkbook balancing. What I want to do, and so what I will intentionally try to spend my time doing, depends on the left side. What I can do, depends on the right side.

Given a weak account of ability, the fact that someone did not do something in the way that we would describe as "intentionally and of his own free will" if we were not worried about determinism, and that his not doing that thing fell under a strong law of nature linking what one thinks and wants with what one does, could hardly have the implication that he *could* not do it. That he does not do it has to do with the lack of reasons he has for doing it, a fact about the left side of the brain. That he can do it depends on what is going on in the right side of the brain, a quite different question.

If we put an account of abilities in the context of a theory of intentional action, the weak conception of ability makes a lot of sense. Here is a sketch of what is involved in an intentional action; the sketch is no doubt simpleminded and controversial, but I do not think adding sophistication and resolving disputes should affect the points I make (see Israel, Perry, and Tutiya 1993 and Goldman 1970).

First, there is a *motivating complex of cognitions.* Such a motivating complex for an action A includes beliefs (broadly construed so beliefs include fleeting perceptual beliefs, implicit beliefs, and so forth) and desires (broadly construed to include wants, urges, whims, and so forth) that rationalize A-ing. A set of cognitions C *rationalizes* an action A if A-ing will promote the satisfaction of the desires in C given the truth of the beliefs in C. In other words, when a person does something intentionally, there are a bunch of beliefs, perceptions, wants, desires, preferences, and the like, which for convenience I'm just calling "desires and beliefs", relative to which it is reasonable for him to do it. For example, if I intentionally order a vanilla ice cream cone, the motivating complex might include the desire for a vanilla ice cream cone; the perception of a counter, a server, cones, and vanilla ice cream; knowledge of English; a belief that I can afford it; a belief that it won't do me any harm; a belief that I can get one by ordering it; a belief that I order one by asking for it; and so on.

The motivating complexes cause volitions to perform basic actions, which will cause the basic action, if it is in the repertoire of actions—that is, if the person has the ability to do it. I think of the basic actions as bodily movements, and so use the term "execute" for the special case of performing one of these basic actions: we execute movements, and thereby do lots of other things. I'll try to order a vanilla ice cream cone, by trying to execute coordinated movements of voice box, throat, lips, tongue, and the like that produce the sounds that will be recognized as the English sentence, "May I please have a vanilla ice cream cone?" *If* that is one of the things I *can* do, I'll say it.

These basic actions in turn cause various results, depending on the circumstances. And these results cause further results, depending on wider and wider circumstances. My words will cause events in the air between me and the ice cream server, in his ear, in his brain, and so on, until with a little luck I get my ice cream cone.

Here's another example. I am on an airplane and desire a drink of water, and a steward comes by and holds out a tray full of water glasses. I believe that there is a glass of water on the tray in front of me, due to perception and trust in airlines to fill glasses with water rather than gin or hydrochloric acid when they intend to offer them to passengers as water. I know that in these circumstances taking a glass from the tray and drinking from it is a way of quenching my thirst. I can't think of any reason not to take a drink of water. My beliefs and desires rationalize the action of taking a glass from the tray and drinking it, for this will satisfy my desire for a drink of water, without leading to any untoward consequences, given the truth of my beliefs.

This complex will then cause a volition to move in a certain way. Picking up a glass from a tray is a rather delicate movement, but even a klutz like myself can usually do it right. I can suit the movement to the situation based on perception, so that my hand moves to the glass and then brings it to my lips. An important piece of evidence that I can do this is that when I intend to get a glass of water, and see the glass in such and such a relative position, I usually move my hand in a way that succeeds in grabbing it and getting it to my lips. This is due to the ability to execute various movements, and know-how on my part that allows me to execute the right movements in the right situation based on perception. This is something I've gotten reasonably good at, thanks to years of picking up some things and dropping others.

If there is a glass of water there, and it is reachable in the ordinary ways, and I have the ability to execute the needed movements in the circumstances, then I *can* take a drink of water. If there is an invisible shield between me and the glass, or if the steward is a smart aleck who will move the tray when I get close to it, or if he is an evil airline demon who has brought around glasses full of hydrochloric acid, then I cannot get a drink of water. So, part of the question of whether I can do it is a matter of the circumstances I am in. The other part has to do with what actions are in my repertoire. If I cannot reach as far as I need to, or grab the glass as firmly as required, then I cannot get a drink.

A person has the ability to *bring it about that R in circumstance K* if (i) the person's repertoire of basic actions includes some movement M such that (ii) executing M *in K* will have the result that R. These conditions for being able to bring it about that R can be met when a person does not in fact bring it about that R or even try to. Neither of the conditions depends on the person actually bringing it about that A. Neither of them require that he *want* to do so, or *have a reason* to do so. They do not preclude the person *really really wanting not to A.* The person may be willing to die rather than perform A. Conditions (i) and (ii) clearly can be satisfied even if the person's not executing M falls under a law of nature to the effect that a person with his motivating complexes will not execute M.

This weak account of ability does not support (S). On this account of ability, it does *not* follow from the fact that the (strong) laws of nature plus Elwood's beliefs and desires *settle* that he will not raise his hand at t, that he does not have the *ability* to raise it at t. That this does not follow can be seen by considering our argument (0)–(5). With a weak theory of ability, it clearly does not work, even if we assume a strong theory of laws. Go down the steps. From (0) to (4) *nothing* is said about abilities. Then, in step (5), abilities are ruled out. It is a left-brain argument, with an invalid right-brain conclusion tacked on. It sounds sort of intuitive, but it just doesn't follow.

6. VAN INWAGEN'S ARGUMENTS

Changing the Past

Now let's turn to one version of van Inwagen's argument (1975, 23). The issue at hand is whether or not J could have raised his hand. Q is a proposition that rules out J having raised his hand at t. I'll just take Q to be the proposition that J did not raise his hand at t. Call the laws of nature L and call the facts up until t that are relevant PF. Assume that we cannot change the past. Then,

(1) If determinism is true, then the conjunction of PF and L entails that Q.

(2) If J had raised his hand at t, then Q would be false.

(3) If (2) is true, then if J could have raised his hand at t, J could have rendered Q false.

(4) If J could have rendered Q false, and if the conjunction of PF and L entails Q, then J could have rendered the conjunction of PF and L false.

(5) If J could have rendered the conjunction of PF and L false, then J could have rendered L false (since J cannot change PF).

(6) *J* could not have rendered *L* false.

(7) So *J* could not have raised his hand.

This argument, if valid, clearly generalizes to any action whatever, and so rules out compatibilism.

Premise (4) is false. The appearance of truth is due to ambiguity in "renders a proposition false". We have to resolve the ambiguity in favor of the sense of "renders false" in which step (3) follows from (2). In this sense (4) is false.

One sense of "render a proposition false" is to do something, which *changes* a proposition from being true, to being false. This seems quite impossible. Of course one can do something that makes a proposition that had *looked like* it was going to turn out to be true turn out to be false instead. It might seem virtually certain that one team is going to win a baseball game, but then the other team scores twelve runs with two outs in the ninth inning to win 12-11. They snatch victory from the jaws of defeat. But they do not really manage to change a proposition from true to false.[2]

It is crystal clear that in this sense of "render false", (3) does not follow from (2). In this sense, (3) says that if *J* could have raised his hand at *t*, then *J* could have changed the truth value of *that J does not raise his hand at t* from true to false. But this does not follow from (2).

The second sense of "render a proposition false" is to do something which *makes* the negation of the proposition true, at a point in time at which nothing has yet *made* the proposition true or made it false. This concept of "render a proposition false" makes perfectly good sense. By eating a cookie at *t*, I render the proposition *that I do not eat a cookie at t* false. So, the proposition *that I do not eat a cookie at t* be false, and it be false because at *t* I (will refrain/refrain/did refrain) from eating a cookie.

In this sense of "render a proposition false", (3) does follow from (2), as van Inwagen's argument requires. But (4) is false. It does *not* follow from the fact that one renders a proposition *Q* false, in this sense, and that some other proposition *R* entails *Q*, that one also renders *R* false.

Let *R* be the following proposition. Recall that *Q* is the proposition *that J does not raise his hand at t*. Let *t* be some day after 1950:

---

[2]Note that even if we adopted the more complicated account of the issues discussed in section 3, so that propositions were neither true nor false until events made them so, making a proposition false would not mean changing its truth value from true to false. If we did things this way, we would have to say that when a set of premises entail a proposition about the future, the truth of the premises requires that the proposition *will be true*, not that it *is* true.

(R)   Q & J's mother ate a carrot in 1944.

This proposition entails that J does not raise his hand at t. J can render the proposition Q false by raising his hand at t. If he renders Q false, R be false, too. But R may have already been rendered false by the time J renders Q false. This will be the case if J's mother did not eat a carrot in 1944. In this case, J will not render R false, even though R entails Q and he renders Q false. It simply does not follow from the fact that J will render Q false that he renders false every proposition that entails Q. What does follow is that there is no true proposition that entails Q.

Principles (i) and (ii) are clearly true, given the coherent concept of "render true" and "render false".

(i) Suppose one does something that renders P true. Then no proposition that entails the falsity of P be true.

(ii) Suppose one does something that renders P false. Then no proposition that entails P be true.

Principles (iii)* and (iv)* do not follow, however:

(iii)* Suppose one *can* do something that would render P true. Then no proposition that entails the falsity of P be true.

(iv)* Suppose one *can* do something that would render P false. Then no proposition that entails P be true.

Principles (iii)* and (iv)* simply amount to the principle that there is no difference between being able to do something and doing it—that *can* collapses into *does*, and *does not* into *cannot*.

If I can drink a beer, I can render *that I drink a beer* true. So, given (iii)*, if I can drink a beer, no proposition that entails *that I don't drink a beer* is true. So if I can drink a beer, *that I don't drink a beer* isn't true (since it entails itself), so it's false, so I drink a beer. If I can do it, I do it. Can implies does.

Suppose I don't drink the beer. Then, *that I don't drink the beer* is true. Then something is true that entails the falsity of *that I drink the beer*. Then, by (iv)*, I can't render it true that I drink the beer. So I can't drink the beer. Doesn't implies can't.

Such a collapse of "can" into "does" and "doesn't" into "can't" is, of course, just what the incompatibilist wants and the compatibilist needs to avoid. If we accept (iii)* and (iv)*, the collapse would be completed *without any appeal to determinism at all*. But of course there is no reason to accept (iii)* and (iv)*. On the contrary, it seems quite clear that on the weak conception of ability, (iii) and (iv) are true instead:

(iii) Suppose one *can* do something that would render *P* true. This does *not* imply that no proposition that entails the falsity of *P* is true.

(iv) Suppose one *can* do something that would render *P* false. This does *not* imply that no proposition that entails *P* is true.

Suppose *J* can raise his arm at *t*, but decides not to. Then *that J does not raise his arm at t is* true. This proposition entails itself. So *J* can raise his arm at *t*, even though a proposition that entails that he does not raise his arm at *t* is true. So (iii) is correct.

Suppose *J* can refrain from raising his arm at *t*, but in fact he raises it. Then *that J raises his arm at t* is true. This proposition entails itself. So *J* can refrain from raising his arm at *t*, even though a proposition that entails that he does raise his arm at *t* is true. So (iv) is true.

Now let's return to the crucial part of van Inwagen's argument:

(1) If determinism is true, then the conjunction of *PF* and *L* entails that *Q*.

(2) If *J* had raised his hand at *t*, then *Q* would be false.

(3) If (2) is true, then if *J* could have raised his hand at t, *J* could have rendered *Q* false.

(4) If *J* could have rendered *Q* false, and if the conjunction of *PF* and *L* entails *Q*, then *J* could have rendered the conjunction of *PF* and *L* false.

Since van Inwagen's argument proceeds by very general principles, it should work for any more concrete example we choose. So let:

PF = that at *t*−1 *J* really really does not want to raise his hand in the next instant.

L = that no one who at *t*−1 really really does not want to raise his hand in the next instant, raises his hand at *t*.

Q = that *J* does not raise his hand at *t*

This example meets the conditions of van Inwagen's argument. That is, *PF* & *L* entails *Q*.

We can certainly accept steps (2) and (3), given our understanding of "render *Q* false". But step (4) does not follow.

PF is the proposition that at *t*−1 *J* really really wants to not raise his hand in the next instant. So (4) says that if *J* could render *Q* false (i.e., if he could raise his hand at *t*), then he could render false the proposition:

that L & at $t-1$ J really really wants to not raise his hand in the next instant

But there is nothing that J can do at t, the doing of which would *make it the case* that it was not true at $t-1$ that he really really wanted not to raise his arm at t.

If J does raise his hand at t, that will *show*, given L, that *PF* is not true. However, that will not *make PF* untrue; it will not *render PF* untrue. If he raises his hand at t, that will be because he is in some state at $t-1$ than really really wanting not to raise his arm, perhaps in the state of wanting to raise it. In this case, *PF be* untrue, but it be untrue because the events at $t-1$ made it false, not because of what J does at t.

If we go back to our simple picture of what it is to be able to raise your hand at t, this should be reasonably clear. There are two facts about J and raising his hand, with these possible combinations:

	Does raise his hand	Does not raise his hand
Can raise his hand	1. *Possible*	2. *Possible*
Cannot raise his hand	3. *Not possible*	4. *Possible*

The argument starts with the premises that J *does not* raise his hand, that is, he is in cell 2 or cell 4. It then hypothesizes that he *can* raise his hand, putting him in cell 2. From this it is supposed to follow that he changes the past, since the past determines that he will not raise his hand. But it clearly does not follow, for in cell 2 he does not raise his hand, just as the past determines will happen.

I conclude, then, that as long as we have a weak but realistic and commonsense concept of ability, we can be determinists and compatibilists, even if we accept a reasonably strong conception of laws.

Van Inwagen's β Principle

Van Inwagen has produced several arguments for incompatibilism. The one I have discussed is the one that seemed most intuitive and convincing to me. Recently more attention has been paid to another argument from his book *An Essay on Free Will* (van Inwagen 1983, 93–104; see also van Inwagen 2002). The key principles are:

(α) $\Box p \rightarrow Np$

(β) From Np and $N(p \rightarrow q)$ deduce Nq,

where "Np" means "p and no one has, or ever had, any choice about whether p".

We are thinking of p and q as propositions, and entailment as a relation between propositions. It seems we should accept

if p entails q then $\Box(p \rightarrow q)$

Then if we also accept (α) and (β), we'll have to accept the rule,

(χ) From Np and p *entails* q deduce Nq.

Principle (χ) is fatal to compatibilism. If determinism is true, and p is the conjunction of the laws of nature and the facts up until life evolved on earth, and q is any proposition entailed by them describing an act, no one will have any choice whether q.

A holder of a weak theory of action will reject (β) and so be spared from (χ). The premises of the rule of inference (β) imply nothing about the ability to bring it about that q, while the conclusion does. On a weak theory of action, (β) is not valid.

Recall the criterion for a strong theory of ability:

> (S) If x *can* perform A at t, then at no time earlier than t is it *settled* whether x performs A at t.

To be settled at t is to follow from some set of propositions, each of which is either established or made true by time t. A strong theory of laws says that laws are either established or were made true a long time before humans began doing things. So, given a strong theory of laws and (S) and determinism, no one will be able to perform any act A at any time. A weak theory of ability denies (S). The weak theory holds that, since the question of whether a person has an ability at a given time need not be affected by his desires and beliefs, and yet it is his desires and beliefs that, together with the laws of nature, determine what he does, the fact that he will or will not do something does not preclude his having the ability to refrain or not refrain from doing it. The weak theorist thinks that a person can have a choice about something, in the sense that they have the ability to do it or refrain from doing it, even if that thing is determined by laws of nature that are established and facts that are already made true. The weak theorist, then, having rejected (S), need have no qualms about rejecting (β).

7. LEWIS'S ANALYSIS

In "Are We Free to Break the Laws?" David Lewis distinguishes between the following claims: "I am able to do something such that, if I did it, a law would be broken" and "I am able to break a law" (Lewis 2001, 31ff). Suppose the laws of nature and the history of the world up until time $t-2$ entail that I will not take the glass of water at *t*, but I do. Suppose, as Lewis does, I cannot change the past. There seem two possibilities:

(a) Something happened at *t* −1 that was contrary to the laws of nature, that is, a "divergence miracle".

(b) Everything up to and including *t* −1 was in accord with the laws of nature, but my action was not.

Lewis thinks the fact that I can take the glass of water implies that I am able to do something such that, if I did it, a law would have been broken at some earlier time, but this requires only (a). He does not think I am able to break a law, which would require (b).

I do not think the compatibilist need suppose that if I were to take the drink, any laws of nature would ever need to have been broken. There are auxiliary premises from Lewis's metaphysics and analyses of causation, counterfactuals, and the like that lead him to this defense of compatibilism. But compatibilism by itself does not force us to the divergent miracles defense, and it does not seem to me the most plausible thing to say about cases in which one has the ability to do differently than one does.

If I had taken the drink, freely and voluntarily, then surely my beliefs and preferences would have been different than they actually were. The most likely difference would be that I was thirsty. Assuming determinism, if I had been thirsty when the drink was offered, then something earlier also would have been different; perhaps I wouldn't have taken a drink at the fountain before stepping on the plane, as I did, because the fountain was broken. And that would mean some earlier state of the fountain and its surroundings had been different. And so on. Tracing the changes back to the big bang, perhaps it might be a slight difference in the direction in which one particle began its travels through time. Or perhaps it goes back to a deistic god creating the initial state of the universe a very little bit differently. Or perhaps it just goes back, infinitely. Who knows? It's certainly amazing and weird and in my opinion somewhat depressing that the trail of differences that would have led to my being thirsty rather than not being thirsty should lead back even a couple of thousand years, much less to the beginning of time, or forever. Still, I can't see why either (a) or (b) is required for me to take the glass. Assuming determinism, it follows from the fact that I can accept the drink and don't, that I can do something such that if I did it either the laws of nature or the events up until that time would have been different than they in fact are. It does not follow that if I did what I can do any law would thereby be broken, or any divergence miracle would ever have occurred, or I would have changed the past in any way. I wouldn't have had to change the past, because, according to determinism and the laws of nature, if I had been thirsty, the past would have been different.

8. CONCLUSION

A compatibilist can evade incompatibilist arguments by adopting a weak theory of laws, or a weak theory of ability, or both. My own inclination is in favor of a strong theory of laws and a weak theory of ability.

Although I believe in compatibilism, I am somewhat skeptical about the truth of determinism. I would be happy if it were not true, for I think that determinism is a doctrine that is not very accommodating to important human hopes and aspirations. I don't think the problem is that it rules out freedom, however. I hope I can address these issues in a helpful way on a future occasion. I'm sure I want to, but I'm not at all sure I have the ability to do so.

ACKNOWLEDGMENTS

Early versions of this paper were presented at the 2001 Inland Northwest Philosophy Conference and the Philosophy Department Colloquium at the University of Nottingham. I received helpful criticisms and suggestions, from members of both audiences. I received helpful comments from Michael Bratman, Joseph Keim Campbell, Eros Corazza, and Michael O'Rourke on later versions. Campbell commented on several versions; he saved me from bad mistakes, and suggested helpful repairs. I am very grateful. Much of what I understand about these topics is due to John Martin Fischer, through many conversations and his works, especially Fischer (1994) and Fischer (1996). None of these folks is responsible for the mistakes that remain, although of course if the whole paper is mistaken, and I'm wrong about everything, and both determinism and incompatibilism are true, I'm not either.

REFERENCES

Ekstrom, L. W., ed. 2001. *Agency and Responsibility: Essays on the Metaphysics of Freedom.* Boulder, Colo.: Westview Press.

Fischer, J. M. 1994. *The Metaphysics of Free Will: An Essay on Control.* Cambridge, Mass.: Blackwell.

——. 1996. A New Compatibilism. *Philosophical Topics* 24: 49–66. Reprinted in Ekstrom (2001): 38–56.

Goldman, A. 1970. A *Theory of Human Action.* Englewood Cliffs, N.J.: Prentice-Hall.

Israel, D., J. Perry and S. Tutiya. 1993. "Executions, Motivations and Accomplishments." *Philosophical Review* (October 1993): 515–40.

Kane, R., ed. 2002. *The Oxford Handbook of Free Will*. New York: Oxford University Press.

Kapitan, T. 2002. "A Master Argument for Incompatibilism." In Kane (2002): 127–57.

Lewis, D. 1981. "Are We Free to Break the Laws?" *Theoria* 47: 113–21. Reprinted in Ekstrom (2001): 30–37. (Page numbers refer to this latter work.)

Van Inwagen, P. 1975. "The Incompatibility of Free Will and Determinism." *Philosophical Studies* 27: 185–99. Reprinted in Ekstrom "(2001): 17–29. (Page numbers refer to this latter work.)

———. 1983. *An Essay on Free Will*. Oxford: Oxford University Press.

———. 2002. "Free Will Remains a Mystery." In Kane (2002): 158–77.

PART II

The Problem
of Foreknowledge

8

OMNISCIENCE AND THE ARROW OF TIME

Linda Zagzebski

This paper argues that the enduring dilemma of divine foreknowledge and human free will is an instance of a much deeper dilemma in the arrow of time. The assumption that the past has a kind of necessity that the future lacks is inconsistent with the principle that temporal necessity is transferred over entailment and the possibility that a proposition about the past entails a proposition about the future. A closer look at temporal modality leads to the proposal that the causal arrow of time is the underpinning of the modal arrow of time. The idea that propositions about the past and their negations are not causable, whereas propositions about the future (and perhaps some of their negations) are causable, is inconsistent with the transfer of causability principle and a variety of metaphysical postulates that imply that a proposition about the future entails or is entailed by a proposition about the past. This dilemma is independent of determinism. No particular way to resolve the dilemma is compelling, but is a matter of metaphysical judgment. Positions on free will, determinism, and omniscience are irrelevant to solving the dilemma in its most general form.

I. THE MODAL ARROW OF TIME

One of the ways in which the past and the future are allegedly asymmetrical is that the past has a kind of necessity the future lacks. Events in the past are purportedly necessary simply because they are past, not because of any metaphysical properties other than pastness. So it is said that we can do nothing about spilled milk, and that is meant to contrast with the idea that potentially we can do something about milk that is not yet spilled. This modal asymmetry is sometimes associated with an ontological asymmetry—the past is real, the future is not. The ontological asymmetry can clearly be questioned, but I mention it to call attention to the fact that all of the temporal asymmetries define a property of the past by contrast with the future. The nature of an asymmetry is to be two-sided. So the idea that the past is closed (fixed, necessary) is one side of a single intuition the other side of which is the intuition that the future is open (unfixed, contingent). The Principle of the Necessity of the Past therefore has a correlate: the Principle of the Contingency of the Future.

Perhaps the intuition of the necessity of the past is stronger than the intuition of the contingency of the future. That is possible, but then it is important to see that the rejection of either side of the asymmetry threatens the other and suggests that the idea of modal temporal asymmetry is confused. If the kind of necessity possessed by the past is possessed by the future, or even if it is possible that it is possessed by the future, the necessity of the past cannot be something it has simply in virtue of its pastness.

Sometimes when people say that an event in the past is now necessary what they mean is that nobody has any causal power over it. We can lack causal power over an event because it is causally necessary or because it is in the past, and these are not the same thing. Causal necessity and contingency are not temporally asymmetrical. Roughly, a causally necessary event E is one that is such that the conjunction of causal laws and events prior to E are sufficient for E to occur, whereas a causally contingent event E is one that is such that the conjunction of causal laws and events prior to E are not sufficient for E to occur. The causal necessity or contingency of an event has nothing to do with whether it is in our past or our future. An event possesses causal necessity or contingency in virtue of its enduring relations to other events. Assuming the metaphysical law that a cause must precede its effect, an event's causal necessity or contingency is determined by its enduring relations to events previous to it. But whether or not causes must precede effects, the causal modality of an event is not temporally asymmetrical. Even if it is possible for an event to be causally necessary because it is determined by an event later in time, its status as causally necessary never changes. There are causally contingent events in the past as well as in the future, and there are causally necessary events in the future as well as in the past.[1] When an event has the necessity of the past, its temporal status is sufficient to make it beyond the power of anybody to do anything about it. But it can still be causally contingent. Similarly, if an event has the contingency of the future, there is nothing about its temporal status that prevents it from being such that we can do something about it. But it can still be causally necessary. Therefore, it does not follow from the fact that an event is *temporally* contingent that we can do something about it since the event might be beyond our power for some other reason, say, because it is causally necessary. Similarly, it does not follow from the fact that an event is causally contingent that we can do something about

---

[1] I am assuming that both causally contingent and causally necessary events exist. If all events are causally necessary, it is obvious that causal necessity is not the same thing as the necessity of the past.

it since the event might be beyond our power for some other reason, say, because it is in the past.

So we lack power over causally necessary events and we also lack power over the past. The reason why we lack power over the past is presumably the metaphysical law that causes must precede effects, but the necessity of the past need not depend upon any explanation for our lack of power over the past. We will return to the causal arrow in section II. For this section I will not assume any laws of causality. What I will assume is that the modalities of necessity and contingency apply to the past and the future respectively and are related in standard ways. Let temporal modality be expressed by "now-necessary", "now-possible", "now-impossible", and "now-contingent". I will assume the following relations among the temporal modalities: P is now-necessary if and only if not p is now-impossible. If p is now-necessary, p is now-possible. If p, p is now-possible. To say that p is now-contingent is to say that it is now-possible that p and it is now-possible that not p.

The Principle of the Necessity of the Past can be formulated as follows:

Principle of the Necessity of the Past
If B is a proposition about the past and B is true, then nec$_t$ B.

Given the relation defined above between the now-necessary and the now-possible, when B is a true proposition about the past, it follows that not poss$_t$ not B.

Systems of modal logic always include a transfer of necessity principle for logical necessity. As applied to temporal necessity, the principle is the following:

Transfer of Necessity Principle (TNP)

$Nec_t p, Nec(p \rightarrow q) > Nec_t q,$

which is logically equivalent to

Transfer of Possibility Principle (TPP)

$Pos_t p, Nec(p \rightarrow q) > Pos_t q.$

TNP has the consequence that logically necessary propositions have the necessity of the past since a logically necessary truth is entailed by every proposition. I find this peculiar, but since nothing in what follows turns on it, I will not modify the principle here in the interests of simplicity.[2]

---

[2]I will not distinguish logical and metaphysical necessity in this paper. I assume that a logically or metaphysically necessary proposition is one that is true in all possible worlds.

Let us say that an essentially omniscient foreknower (EOF) is any being x who satisfies the following condition: Necessarily, for any proposition p and time t at which x exists, x believes p at t if and only if p. Essential omniscience can be shown to be inconsistent with modal temporal asymmetry as described above by the following argument:

1st Dilemma of Foreknowledge and Modal Temporal Asymmetry

Let B = the proposition that I will pour tea at noon tomorrow.

(1) There is (and was before now) an essentially omniscient foreknower (EOF) [Assumption for dilemma]

The Principle of the Contingency of the Future tells us that

(2) It is now-possible that B and it is now-possible that not B.

From (1) and the definition of an EOF it follows that

(3) Necessarily (B → The EOF believed before now that B), and necessarily (not B → The EOF believed before now that not B).

By the Transfer of Possibility Principle (TPP), (2) and (3) entail

(4) It is now-possible that the EOF believed before now that B and it is now-possible that the EOF believed before now that not B.

From (1) and the definition of an EOF we get

(5) Either the EOF believed before now that B or the EOF believed before now that not B.

From the Principle of the Necessity of the Past we get

(6) If he did, it is not now-possible that he did not and if he did not, it is not now-possible that he did.

(5) and (6) entail

(7) Either it is not now-possible that he did not or it is not now-possible that he did.

But (7) contradicts (4).[3]

We can formulate a parallel argument using TNP instead of TPP:

2nd Dilemma of Foreknowledge and Modal Temporal Asymmetry

(1) There is (and was before now) an essentially omniscient foreknower (EOF) [Assumption for dilemma]

(1) and the Principle of the Necessity of the Past tells us that

(2′) Either it is now-necessary that the EOF believed B before now or it is now-necessary that the EOF believed not B before now.

From (1) and the definition of an EOF it follows that

(3′) Necessarily (The EOF believed before now that $B \rightarrow B$), and necessarily (The EOF believed before now that not $B \rightarrow$ not B)

By the Transfer of Necessity Principle (TNP), (2′) and (3′) entail

(4′) Either it is now-necessary that B or it is now-necessary that not B.

(4′) is logically equivalent to

(5′) Either it is not now-possible that B or it is not now-possible that not B.

From the Principle of the Contingency of the Future we get

(6′) It is now-possible that B and it is now-possible that not B.

But (6′) contradicts (5′).

---

[3] I first presented a form of this argument in the Appendix to *The Dilemma of Freedom and Foreknowledge* (Oxford University Press, 1991). A version close to the one here appears in "Omniscience, Time, and Freedom," *Guide to Philosophy of Religion*, edited by William Mann, Blackwell, 2004. In that paper I did not notice that TPP is used in the inference to (4). I thank Ray Elugardo for pointing this out to me.

These arguments have nothing to do with free will. They show that the conflict between an essentially omniscient foreknower and free will rests upon a deeper conflict between essential omniscience and the modal asymmetry of past and future. In short, the following form an inconsistent triad:

(a) The existence of modal temporal asymmetry expressed in the contingency of the future and the necessity of the past [premises (2) and (6), and (2') and (6')].

(b) The possibility that there is an essentially omniscient foreknower. [Premise (1)]

(c) The Transfer of Possibility Principle or equivalently, the Transfer of Necessity Principle.

The problem of fatalism is not really about freedom or fate; it is about a type of modality that is temporally asymmetrical and that is transferred over logical entailment. If this type of modality is coherent, it rules out the possibility of essential omniscience. It follows that God could not have "given up" infallible foreknowledge in order to save human freedom since fundamentally the problem is not about free will at all.[4]

But the problem is even more general than this triad illustrates. The reason essential omniscience conflicts with temporal modality and the transfer principles is that the existence of an EOF requires that a proposition about the past entails a proposition about the future. But it straightforwardly follows from TNP that a proposition that is now-necessary cannot entail a proposition that is not now-necessary. So if the past is now-necessary and the future is not, a proposition about the past cannot entail a proposition about the future. Further, it follows from TPP that a proposition that is now-possible cannot entail a proposition that is not now-possible. But false propositions about the past are not now-possible. If the future is contingent, and p is about the future, both p and not p are now-possible. But if p is logically equivalent to a proposition about the past, one of either p or not p entails a false proposition about the past. Hence a proposition that is now-possible entails a proposition that is

---

[4]The view called the Open God view or Free Will theism has the position that God takes the risk of not having infallible foreknowledge in order to give humans free will. But if my argument here is right, there is nothing to give up because infallible foreknowledge is metaphysically impossible if time is modally asymmetrical and TNP holds. If time is not modally asymmetrical or TNP is false, giving up infallible foreknowledge is not necessary. For an early defense of the open God view, see Clark Pinnock, Richard Rice, John Sanders, William Hasker, and David Basinger. *The Openness of God: A Biblical Challenge to the Traditional Understanding of God* (Downers Grove, III: InterVarsity Press, 1994).

not now-possible, contrary to TPP. The conclusion is that if asymmetrical temporal modality is coherent, it can obey TNP and TPP, or it can permit a proposition about the past to entail or be logically equivalent to a proposition about the future, but not both.

The root of the problem, then, is that it is impossible for there to be a type of modality that has the following features:

(a) The past and future are asymmetrical in that the past is necessary with respect to this type of modality, whereas the future is contingent with respect to this type of modality.
(b') There are propositions about the past that entail (or are logically equivalent to) propositions about the future.
(c) TNP (or equivalently, TPP) obtains.

For most forms of modality M, we simply accept the transfer principles for M. But if there is a type of modality that is temporally asymmetrical, that pressures us to resist any principle of temporal modality that results in the past having the contingency of the future or the future having the necessity of the past under pain of reducing temporal modality to incoherence. It might be thought that a way out of this dilemma is to say that the transfer principles need not transfer the same type of necessity or possibility to q as is possessed by p. We could formulate a principle that transfers a type of necessity to q from the type of necessity possessed by p, whether or not it is the same type of necessity in both cases. This approach would avoid the incoherence of maintaining that TNP forces us to conclude that the future has the necessity of the past, but it does mean that the future has whatever type of necessity is transferred from the necessity of the past. This approach faces the same dilemma as the one addressed in this section, only it is more subtle. If the intuitions that undergird the necessity of the past require modal temporal asymmetry, the idea that the future inherits a type of necessity from the past undermines those intuitions. Modal temporal asymmetry is in tension with (b') and (c) whether or not the necessity the future inherits from the past is exactly the same kind of necessity as the necessity of the past.

We have seen that the problem of foreknowledge and free will is not about free will. Now we see that it is not even about foreknowledge. It is about the logic of a modality that expresses a common view of time. Either (a), (b'), or (c) is false. Either the transfer principles are false, it is not possible for a proposition about the past to entail a proposition about the future, or the modal asymmetry of time is confused.[5]

---

[5] I suggest that the modal asymmetry of time is incoherent in "Omniscience, Time, and Freedom."

Since the transfer principles are a part of every system of modal logic, the price of denying them is to adopt a non-standard system of temporal modality. But there is also a high metaphysical cost for taking the second option. If it is impossible that a proposition about the past can entail a proposition about the future, much more is ruled out than the possibility of infallible foreknowledge. It is impossible that there is a perfect rememberer, a being who infallibly remembers every one of her past conscious states. It is impossible that there is a perfectly constant lover, someone who necessarily continues to love once he begins to love. It is impossible that matter is indestructible. In fact, it is impossible that anything is indestructible. Each of these metaphysical hypotheses requires that it is metaphysically necessary that if some proposition about the past is true (e.g., matter existed), some proposition about the future is true (e.g., matter will exist next year). I do not find this option very appealing either.[6]

The final option is to reject modal temporal asymmetry as described in this section. Some form of temporal asymmetry is so firmly ingrained in ordinary thinking that it is virtually impossible to give it up, but that does not mean that the temporal arrow has been accurately described using standard modal notions. In order to choose among rejecting (a), (b'), or (c), I propose that we take a closer look at the temporal arrow.

II. THE CAUSAL ARROW OF TIME

In describing temporal asymmetry in section I, I made it artificially simple. I also followed common practice in subsuming temporal asymmetry under the standard modalities of necessity and possibility, which are assumed to be related in standard ways. This approach may make it seem obvious that the modalities of past and future are describable by the axioms of modal logic, including TNP. But I find it interesting that ordinary people rarely refer to the past as "necessary", and it is even less clear that they assume the standard relations among the modalities in their thinking about time. If a proposition is necessary, it is possible, but do we normally think of

---

[6]Notice that the option of rejecting (b') also rules out the possibility that the following propositions are both logically equivalent and have different temporal modalities:

(1) It was true yesterday that X would happen tomorrow.
(2) X will happen tomorrow.

Either (1) and (2) are not logically equivalent or it is not the case that (1) has the necessity of the past whereas (2) does not. Propositions like (1) and (2) are, of course, the ones typically used in arguments for logical fatalism. This shows that the deeper problem of logical fatalism is not a problem about fatalism either.

the past as possible? The negation of a necessary truth is impossible, but it seems to me that instead of treating propositions about the past and their negations as having contrary modalities, both the actual past and all alternate pasts are typically put in the category of *what we cannot do anything about*. Perhaps the logical relations among the necessary, the possible, and the impossible are more precise renderings of vague and untutored (and untrustworthy) ordinary intuitions about time. But it is also possible that the relations assumed in the previous section express to some extent a false precision. The idea that we cannot do anything about the past whereas we can in principle do something about (a portion of) the future is part of a network of ideas about time and causality. If there is an inconsistency within the network, the resolution of the conflict ought to do as little damage as possible to the network as a whole.

I will not attempt to identify all the key components of the network of beliefs about time and causation that underlie the intuition of modal temporal asymmetry, but I want to call attention to a few features that I think are relevant to resolving the inconsistency identified in the last section. First of all, I suspect that the intuitive basis for modal temporal asymmetry would be badly shaken if certain laws of causality turned out to be false, in particular, the law that causes must precede their effects. If I am right in this conjecture, what leads us to think there is a modal temporal arrow is our beliefs about what accompanies past and future, not pastness and futurity *per se*. The reason why we think we can do nothing about spilled milk may not be pastness of the spilled milk in itself, but pastness conjoined with the metaphysical principle that the cause must be prior to the effect. If this is the deeper intuition behind the modal asymmetry of time, it would explain the fact that we do not think our power over the future is on a par with our lack of power over the past The entire past is outside the realm of causal power, but that does not mean that the entire future is within the realm of causal power. We have no causal power over the past because it is too late to either cause it or to prevent it whether or not any of it is causally contingent, but we also have no power to prevent what is causally necessary in the future, although we can cause it. In fact, somebody or something *must* cause it if it is causally necessary. The most interesting category is that which we have both the power to cause and the power to prevent. If there is anything in this category, it has to be in the future. Temporal asymmetry, then, is fundamentally an asymmetry in what is causable. Anything that is either past or causally impossible is not causable. What is neither past nor causally impossible is causable. We can define the causally closed and causally open in terms of what is causable: Proposition p is causally closed just in case neither p nor not p is causable. Proposition p is causally open just in case both p and not p are causable. The entire past is causally closed; some of the future (it is hoped) is causally open.

The modes of causable and not causable as just described do not correspond very well to the standard modes of necessary, possible, impossible, and contingent. The actual past is not causable, but alternative pasts are not causable either. If it is too late to make something have happened, it is too late to make something else have happened instead. So if a proposition p is about the past, neither p nor not p is causable; p and not p are causally closed. This is one disanalogy with the standard modalities since if p is necessary, its negation is impossible. The realm of standard modality is divided into the possible and the impossible. The necessary is a subset of the possible and the contingent is the possible that is not necessary. In contrast, the modes I am suggesting divide events into the causable and the not causable. There is a set of propositions p which are such that both p and not p are not causable. And there is a set of propositions p which are such that both p and not p are causable. And there is a set of propositions p which are such that p is causable and not p is not causable. I am not assuming that none of these sets is empty. The three categories are meant only to describe the logical possibilities of causability.

I propose that the intuition of temporal asymmetry is related to causability in the following way:

(i)   If a proposition p is about the past, p is not causable and not p is not causable. Propositions about the past are causally closed. [Principle of the Causal Closure of the Past]

(ii) If a proposition p is about the future and p is true, p is causable. [Principle of the Causability of the Future][7]

(iii) There are propositions p about the future which are such that both p and not p are causable. Such propositions are causally open.

(iv) There are propositions p about the future which are such that p is causable and not p is not causable. The former are causally necessary and the latter are causally impossible.

These features seem to me to express the intuitive idea that a cause must precede its effect and that some of the future is causally determined, but some of it is not.

---

[7] Principle (ii) will need a qualification if there are events that are literally uncaused, such as the decay of an atom of plutonium. I assume that such events do not affect the causability of the ordinary events that are the topic of this paper. I thank Bill Hasker for pointing out this problem with the principle of the causability of the future.

Even if it turns out that all of the future is causally determined—and that needs to be decided on metaphysical and empirical grounds, not by the logic of cause—the causal arrow as just described recognizes a difference between our causal relation to the past and our causal relation to the future.

A more complicated part of the network of intuitions about time involves the metaphysically necessary conditions for events of certain kinds to occur. There is a time-honored metaphysical principle of causation that nothing can come from nothing. According to that principle, the proposition that something will exist in the future entails the proposition that something existed in the past. If it is metaphysically necessary that no object can come into existence uncaused, then the proposition that some x will exist in the future entails that some y existed in the past that is in the causal chain leading to the existence of x. If it is not metaphysically necessary that an object be caused by its actual causes, then the objects in the causal chain leading to x in one world will not be identical to the objects in the causal chain leading to x in another world. Nonetheless, there is no possible world containing a future x that does not have something existing in the past that is causally necessary for x's existence in that world.

Let us now consider the transfer principles for causability parallel to those for necessity and possibility:

> *Transfer of Causability Principle* (TCP)
> Causable p, Nec$(p \rightarrow q)$ > Causable q
>
> *Transfer of Noncausability Principle* (TNCP)
> Not causable p, Nec$(p \rightarrow q)$ > Not causable q

These principles are false as stated and must be modified. Since a logically necessary truth is entailed by every proposition, TCP has the consequence that if q is logically necessary, q is causable. But surely nobody has the causal power to bring about the truth of a logically necessary proposition. To avoid this problem TCP must be amended:

> *Transfer of Causability Principle 2* (TCP2)
> Causable p, Nec$(p \rightarrow q)$, & q is not logically necessary > Causable q

Similarly, since an impossible proposition entails every proposition, TNCP has the consequence that if p is logically impossible, q is not causable no matter what q is. It also needs to be amended:

Transfer of Noncausability Principle 2 (TNCP2)

Not causable p, Nec$(p \to q)$, & p is not logically impossible > Not causable q.[8]

The causal arrow, the assumption that a proposition about the past entails a proposition about the future, and TNCP2 can be shown to be inconsistent. The argument is similar to the second dilemma of section I except that since neither of the propositions *The EOF believed B before now* and *The EOF believed not B before now* are causable, two contradictions follow. A more interesting comparison is the form of the dilemma using TCP2, which is revealingly different from the first dilemma of section I. The causal arrow and TCP2 is inconsistent with the assumption that a proposition about the future entails a proposition about the past. The principle that nothing can come from nothing will suffice to generate the inconsistency. Let us consider the proposition that some human female will exist in the future. If there is more than one future human female, pick one for the sake of the argument and call her Eve. It is not necessary to assume that Eve's existence is open, that is, that both the proposition that Eve will exist and its negation are causable. It is sufficient that either Eve's existence or her non-existence is causable. The dilemma therefore does not assume the falsehood of determinism.

Dilemma of Causal Asymmetry

(10) Necessarily [[(Eve will exist in the future $\to$ The causally necessary conditions for Eve's existence obtained in the past, & (Eve will not exist in the future $\to$ the causally necessary conditions for Eve's non-existence obtained in the past)]

The Principle of the Causability of the Future tells us that

(11) Either it is causable that Eve will exist or it is causable that Eve will not exist.

From TCP2 we get

(12) Either it is causable that the causally necessary conditions for Eve's existence obtained in the past or it is causable that the causally necessary conditions for Eve's non-existence obtained in the past.

---

[8] These principles are forms of what William Hasker calls "Power Entailment Principles," which he defends in a number of places. See *God, Time, and Knowledge* (Ithaca: Cornell University Press, 1989) and "Zagzebski on Power Entailment," *Faith and Philosophy* 10, #2 (April 1993), 2250–55, and my rejoinder in the same issue.

From the Principle of the Causal Closure of the Past it follows that

(13) It is neither causable that the causally necessary conditions for Eve's existence obtained in the past nor causable that the causally necessary conditions for Eve's non-existence obtained in the past.

But (13) contradicts (12).

If Eve's existence is causally open, (11) will be a conjunction instead of a disjunction, permitting the derivation of two contradictions by the above pattern. The conclusion is that whether or not the future is causally open, the following forms an inconsistent triad:

(a′) The past and future are causally asymmetrical in that the past is not causable whereas the future is causable.

(b″) There are propositions about the future that entail propositions about the past

(c′) TCP2 obtains.

I find this a particularly intriguing dilemma because there is an inconsistency in the causal arrow not only when a proposition about the past entails or is equivalent to a proposition about the future, but even when a proposition about the future entails a proposition about the past. Furthermore, the dilemma does not depend upon the openness of the future in the sense that for some propositions p about the future, both p and not p are causable. The only assumption needed to generate the dilemma is that propositions about the future are causable, whether or not their negations are causable as well.

III. THE OPTIONS

What are the options for avoiding inconsistency in the causal arrow of time? How do they compare with those for escaping the inconsistency in the modal arrow? The options for escaping the two dilemmas are as follows:

Modal Arrow dilemma

1. The modal arrow is an illusion.
2. A proposition about the past cannot entail (nor be logically equivalent to) a proposition about the future.
3. TNP and TPP are false.

Causal Arrow dilemma

1. The causal arrow is an illusion.
2. A proposition about the future cannot entail or be entailed by a proposition about the past.
3. TCP2 and TNCP2 are false.

There is a difference in the plausibility of the first option in the two dilemmas if I am right that the causal arrow as described in section II is more plausible than the modal temporal arrow described in section I. The two arrows are obviously related, but they are not identical and I suggest that the intuitions about causality described in the last section are the underpinnings of the modal arrow of time. If the law that causes must precede effects turned out to be false, the modal arrow would collapse. Furthermore, the belief that there are causally necessary events in the future puts an important limitation on the intuition of temporal asymmetry that explains why the principle of the contingency of the future is weaker than the principle of the necessity of the past. The causal arrow reveals that; the modal temporal arrow does not. Of course, further investigation may reveal that both arrows are illusory, but I think the causal arrow is much less likely to be mistaken. I suggest, then, that whereas the modal arrow may be confused, the first option to escape the causal arrow dilemma is not very appealing and should be taken only as a last resort. In any case, almost all writers on both sides of the debate over theological fatalism assume the causal arrow.

That reduces our options for the causal dilemma to the second and third. Consider next the second option. As we saw in the discussion of the modal dilemma, there is a metaphysical price for taking the second option since it rules out the possibility that a proposition about the past entails a proposition about the future, and hence it is impossible that matter is indestructible, that there is a perfect rememberer, and many others. The second option in the causal dilemma is even more restrictive since it also rules out the possibility that a proposition about the future entails a proposition about the past. So it makes the traditional metaphysical principle that nothing can come from nothing metaphysically impossible. Furthermore, it is likely that there are particular metaphysically necessary conditions that must obtain prior to any given event. If so, the proposition that the event occurs entails a proposition about conditions obtaining previously. A simple way this can occur is when an event is part of a more complex event extended in time, say a baseball game. A necessary condition for the ninth inning to begin is that eight innings have been previously played. So the proposition expressed by "The ninth inning is about to begin" entails "Eight innings were played already". More complex conditions are those required for the exercise of human agency. I am not interested in identifying any particular conditions for human agency here. I merely want to point out that there probably are some. For example, propositions about future human choices probably entail propositions about the past existence of rational beings. More subtle examples involve responses to past events. It is arguably necessary that nobody can forgive someone for a past wrong unless something previously happened that is the object of the forgiveness.[9] But according to the option we are considering, the transfer principles are permitted to trump all of the metaphysical postulates we have considered: that matter is indestructible, that nothing can come from nothing, that essential omniscience or a perfect rememberer is possible, that the beginning of the ninth inning entails that eight innings have been previously played, and so on. Of course, some of these postulates may be quirky or have no basis in a plausible metaphysical theory. The issue, however, is whether their rejection should be decided on metaphysical grounds or whether they should be automatically eliminated because TCP2 and TNCP2 take precedence.

The final option is to reject the transfer principles. TNP and TPP are considered to be indisputable by some writers on fatalism because TNP is an axiom of modal logic, but the same defense cannot be made of TCP2 and TNCP2. Neither is an instance of a standard transfer of modality principle and causability is not a standard modality. TCP2 and TNCP2 need defense. It seems to me that TCP2 and TNCP2 are probably false, but my purpose in this paper is not to argue for their falsehood, but to argue that there are metaphysical costs in adopting TCP2 and TNCP2 that are much more far-reaching than merely denying the possibility of essential omniscience.

Rejecting TCP2 and TNCP2 leaves open the possibility that a proposition about the future entails a proposition about the past and that a proposition about the past entails a proposition about the future. Such possibilities in particular cases would be decided by features of logic and metaphysics that do not automatically give precedence to the transfer principles. This option has the advantage of not ruling out in advance the hypothesis that nothing comes from nothing, that matter is indestructible, that there is an essentially omniscient being, and many others. Whether TNP and TPP are false also is somewhat more problematic because I have already given reasons for thinking that the modal temporal arrow is confused, or at least incompletely described. Since it is not clear to me that the standard modalities apply to time at all, I have no position on rejecting TNP and TPP.[10]

---

[9] I thank Dan Speak for this example.

[10] Note that TNP and TPP would fail if sentences of the form "It is now-possible that p" and "It is now-necessary that p" are hyper-intensional. A context U is hyper-intensional when logically equivalent propositions are not inter-substitutable in U. For example, belief contexts are hyper-intensional since we cannot substitute "The even prime number is greater than 1" for "2 is greater than 1" in the sentence "Sally believes that 2 is greater than 1". Sally may be a young child

I conclude that the logic of modality does not force us to accept the transfer of causability and non-causability principles. It does not even force us to accept the transfer of necessity and the transfer of possibility principles for temporal modality. The way we escape the inconsistency in the causal and modal arrows of time is the result of metaphysical choice.

IV. THE TOOLEY DEFENSE OF TNP

Michael Tooley argues in his critique of my book on foreknowledge that TNP is true for temporally asymmetrical necessity as he defines it.[11] He uses the convention of calling the necessity of the past accidental necessity, which he defines as follows:

It is accidentally necessary that p at time t if and only if p is not preventable at t.

After a few attempts at interpreting preventability, Tooley settles on the following definition of accidental necessity:

(AN) It is accidentally necessary that p at time t if and only if no being, either actual or possible, acting at time t, could causally bring it about that p is false. (220).

By this definition accidental necessity is not the same as the necessity of the past, the modality I addressed in section I. Instead, accidental necessity is close to what I have called causability:

Why might one think that this connection [between accidental necessity and preventability] obtains? The basic reason is that, in the world as it is, we can perform actions that determine, at least in part, how the future is, but we cannot perform actions that determine how the past is, and it seems plausible that it is this fact about the world that leads many people to feel that there is a deep asymmetry between the past and the future, and, in particular, that the past is fixed, or accidentally necessary, while the future is not. For suppose, by contrast, that we *were* able to perform actions now that would determine how the

who knows that 2 is greater than 1, but has never heard of prime numbers. If contexts of temporally relative modality are hyper-intensional, the proposition *The essentially omniscient foreknower believed B before now* is not inter-substitutable with the logically equivalent proposition *B* in (2) and (2′). Unlike belief contexts, however, I doubt that we can appeal to our intuitions to settle the issue of whether temporally modal contexts are hyper-intensional.

[11]Michael Tooley, "Freedom and Foreknowledge," *Faith and Philosophy* 17.2 (April 2000), 212–24.

past is. Surely we would no longer view past events as accidentally necessary (p. 219).

So Tooley thinks of accidental necessity as temporally asymmetrical in that the past has it and some part of the future does not. Further, it is a type of necessity that depends upon the view that we have no causal power over the past. Given that intuition, we can no more bring about the past than prevent it, but it is preventability that Tooley thinks is particularly salient for the foreknowledge dilemma. Tooley says (AN) is very plausible (220).

Notice first that (AN) cannot capture what Tooley intends by accidental necessity since it immediately follows from (AN) that logically impossible propositions are accidentally necessary. (AN) therefore must be modified:

(AN2) It is accidentally necessary that p at time t if and only if p is not logically impossible and no being, either actual or possible, acting at time t, could causally bring it about that p is false.

Tooley says that given (AN), it can be shown that the transfer of necessity is true for accidental necessity. His demonstration consists of (AN) and one premise which he asserts is an analytic truth, and which is logically equivalent to the conclusion he wants to prove. His argument is as follows:

(1) It is accidentally necessary that p at time t if and only if no being, actual or possible, acting at time t, could causally bring it about that p is false. (AN)

Tooley follows this with the premise he takes to be analytic:

(2) If p entails q, then causally to bring it about that q is false is also causally to bring it about that p is false.

From (2) it follows that

(3) If p entails q, and some actual or possible being, acting at time t could causally bring it about that q is false, then that being, acting at t, could also bring it about that p is false.

By contraposition he gets

(4) If p entails q, and no actual or possible being, acting at time t, could causally bring it about that p is false, then no actual or possible being, acting at time t, could causally bring it about that q is false.

By (AN) he concludes

(5) If p entails q, and it is accidentally necessary that p at t, then it is accidentally necessary that q at t. (Transfer of Accidental Necessity Principle)

Notice first that (2), which Tooley takes to be an analytic truth, is false. If p is logically impossible, p entails q no matter what q is. Hence, according to (2), to causally bring about that some q is false is to causally bring it about that a logically impossible proposition is false. But surely we do not get causal credit for bringing about the falsehood of every logically impossible proposition whenever we bring about the falsehood of some other proposition. So we must add the qualification that p is not impossible to (2):

(2a) If p entails q and p is not logically impossible, then causally to bring it about that q is false is also causally to bring it about that p is false.[12]

But whether or not (2) is modified as (2a), it is just another form of the transfer of necessity principle that Tooley wants to prove. The conclusion is logically equivalent to the premise, as his own argument shows. And if (4) is not analytic, neither is (2), so the argument above is hardly a proof of it.

So Tooley does not have a proof of his transfer principle. Notice also that his transfer principle (5) is not a standard transfer of necessity principle, but is equivalent to the transfer of causability principle (TCP):

causable p, nec$(p \rightarrow q)$ > causable q.

The equivalence follows from the fact that to cause p to be true is to cause not p to be false. Hence, TCP is equivalent to

Nec $(p \rightarrow q)$, causable not p is false > causable not q is false.

By contraposition and exportation we get

Nec (not q $\rightarrow$ not p), causable not p is false > causable not q is false,

---

[12]Bill Hasker has observed to me that Tooley's (2) is false for another reason. It may be that p is false for some reason that is independent of the truth of q. For example, p might be the proposition *Hasker is short of money and Al Gore is US President*, and q is the proposition *Hasker is short of money*. I can cause the falsehood of q by giving Hasker money, but I do not thereby cause the falsehood of p, which is already false.

which by substitution is equivalent to

Nec $(p \rightarrow q)$, causable q is false > causable p is false.

By exportation we get

Nec $(p \rightarrow q)$ > (causable q is false > causable p is false).

And contraposition yields

Nec $(p \rightarrow q)$ > (not causable p is false > not causable q is false),

which is the same as Tooley's (4). His (5) is a substitution in (4) of his definition of accidental necessity (AN).

So Tooley accepts TCP. That means he is faced with the dilemma of the causal arrow. Given his acceptance of TCP (suitably modified to TCP2), if he is serious about the assumption of temporal causal asymmetry to which he appeals in explaining accidental necessity, he must reject the possibility of entailments between propositions about the past and propositions about the future, not just the possibility of infallible foreknowledge of the contingent future, as shown in section II.

In explaining his own position, Tooley says, "If, as I have argued in detail elsewhere, the future is not real, then I think it can be shown that it is logically impossible for anyone to have knowledge of future states of affairs unless those states of affairs are causally determined." (223). But if the futurity of the future makes it unreal, then the causally determined future is unreal also. And if unreality is sufficient to make something unknowable, the determined future should be unknowable as well. In any case, the problem is not knowability; it is a problem about logical relations between past and future propositions.

V. CONCLUSION

In this paper I have argued that the perennial dilemma of infallible foreknowledge and free will is not unique to either foreknowledge or free will. The problem arises for a multitude of metaphysical hypotheses in addition to the hypothesis of essential omniscience, and it reveals an inconsistency between any of these hypotheses and a common view of the asymmetry of time. No particular solution to the problem is forced. We are neither forced to give up temporal asymmetry nor the possibility that there are entailments between propositions about the past and the future, nor are we forced to give up the principle that the relevant type of temporally asymmetrical modality is closed under entailment. But we are forced to give up one of the three. The choice ought to be made on metaphysical grounds, retaining as much as possible our firmest intuitions about time and causality.

Notice that any approach to the classic dilemma of theological fatalism that is specifically designed to handle essential omniscience, such as the timelessness move or the Ockhamist move, will not help with the dilemmas of this paper. It is, of course, possible, perhaps likely, that there is more than one solution to the fore-knowledge/free will dilemma, but whatever solves the dilemmas of this paper will solve the foreknowledge dilemma as well.

Notice also that the problem of this paper is independent of determinism. It is sometimes argued that if determinism is true, there is no problem of theological fatalism because determinism has the consequence that whatever kind of freedom we have is compatible with the inability to do otherwise. But the problem of this paper arises whether or not freedom requires the ability to do otherwise since freedom is not the problem. There is a conflict within a common view of time whether or not the universe is causally determined.

9

TROUBLES WITH OCKHAMISM

David Widerker

Suppose that Jack signs his work contract on January 3, 1985. According to many traditional theologians, there is no contradiction between Jack's *freely* performing this act on January 3 and God's foreknowing this fact, say, on January 1.[1] What follows logically from the assumption that

(K) God foreknows on January 1, 1985, that Jack will sign his contract on January 3, 1985.

is only that Jack, in fact, will do so, but not that he has to or must do so. On this account, God not only knows that Jack will sign the contract on the said date, but he also knows that Jack will do so freely, i.e., that it is in his power to do otherwise. In the mid-1960s, Nelson Pike launched a vigorous attack on this common view in his well-known article, "Divine Omniscience and Voluntary Action,"[2] presenting an argument purporting to show that divine foreknowledge and human freedom are inconsistent. Here is a version of Pike's argument.

(TF)   (a) "God" is a proper name. "t_1", "t_2", etc., refer respectively to January 1, 1985; January 2, 1985; etc. (Premise)

      (b) God exists at every moment of time, and is essentially omniscient in the sense that it is logically impossible for him to believe a false proposition, or to fail to believe any true proposition. (Premise)

      (c) Jack signs his contract at t_3, and it is within Jack's power at t_2 to bring it about that he does not sign his contract at t_3. (Premise)

  (G) God believes at t_1 that Jack signs his contract at t_3. [By (b) and (c)]

(PRW) If q is a logically necessary condition for p, and q does not obtain, then an agent has it within his power at t to bring it about that p only

---

[1] The term "freely performing" I understand here in the libertarian sense.
[2] *The Philosophical Review*, LXXIV(1965): 31–35.

if he has it within his power at t to bring it about that q. (Here p and q range over dated states of affairs like the sun is shining at t_3, Jack eats lunch at t_4, etc.) (Premise)[3]

(d) That it is not the case that God believes at t_1 that Jack signs his contract at t_3, is a logically necessary condition for Jack's not signing his contract at t_3. [By (b)][4]

(e) It is within Jack's power at t_2 to bring it about that God does not believe at t_1 that Jack signs his contract at t_3. [By (c), (d), (G), and (PRW)][5]

But, (e) contradicts the intuitive principle that we do not have power over the past. We may refer to this principle as *the principle of the fixity of the past* or PFP.

One way of responding to this argument is Ockhamism. The Ockhamist distinguishes between two sorts of facts about the past; genuine or *hard facts* about the past which are subject to the principle of the fixity of the past; and *soft facts* about the past which, since being somehow also about the future, do not intuitively fall under this principle. For example, facts such as

---

[3]This principle is an improved version of a principle employed by Richard Taylor in "Fatalism," *The Philosophical Review*, LXXI (1962), p. 58. Cf. William L. Rowe, "Fatalism and Truth," *The Southern Journal of Philosophy*, XVIII (1980), p. 217. Note that (PRW) ought to be distinguished from the following fallacious principle:

(PR) If q is a logically necessary condition for p, then an agent has it within his power at t to bring it about that p only if he has it within his power at t to bring it about that q.

The fact that q is a necessary condition for p does not imply that my having the power to bring about p is contingent upon my having the power to bring it about that q. I may have the power to bring about p, even if I lack the power to bring about q in situations where q is already in existence or will be in existence anyway. E.g., provided I did not smoke a cigarette until t_5, I may have the power at t_4 to smoke a cigarette for the first time at t_5, and this even though I do not have at t_4 the power to bring it about that I did not smoke a cigarette in the past. Or given that the sun will be shining at t_5, I may have the power at t_2 to bring it about that I raise my arm at t_5 while the sun is shining. But surely, I do not have the power at t_2 to bring it about that the sun will be shining at t_3. For similar counterexamples to (PR), see Joshua Hoffman and Gary Rosenkrantz, "On Divine Foreknowledge and Human Freedom," *Philosophical Studies*, XXXVII (1980), pp. 292–93. I discuss the relation between (PR) and (PRW) also in my "Two Forms of Fatalism," in John Fischer, ed., *God, Foreknowledge, and Freedom* (Stanford: University Press, 1989).

[4]Here, as well as in what follows, I shall use terms such as "necessarily" and "logically necessary" to signify broadly logical necessity.

[5]This version of Pike's argument differs somewhat from Pike's original formulation of it (see pp. 33–35). It has the advantage of spelling out precisely the transition from (i) Jack's having it within his power at t_2 to bring it about that it is not the case that Qt_3, to (ii) his having the power at t_2 to bring it about that God did not believe at t_1 that Qt_3. (Qt_3 abbreviates "Jack signs his contract on January 3, 1985.")

(1) Hitler attacked Russia in 1941.

(2) Smith uttered on January 1, 1985, the sentence "Jack will sign his contract on January 3, 1985".

(3) Smith believed on January 1, 1985, that Jack will sign his contract on January 3, 1985.

are considered hard facts about the past, relative to January 2, 1985, whereas

(4) Hitler attacked Russia in 1941, 44 years before Jack's signing his contract on January 3, 1985.

(5) Smith uttered on January 1, 1985, the *true* sentence "Jack will sign his contract on January 3, 1985."

(6) Smith correctly believed on January 1, 1985, that Jack will sign his contract on January 3, 1985.

are paradigm examples of soft facts about the past, relative to January 2, 1985. Furthermore, the Ockhamist claims that facts about God's foreknowledge of future events, and more specifically a fact such as

(G) God believes at t_1 that Jack will sign his contract at t_3.[6]

may be treated as soft facts about the past on a par with (4)–(6). Consequently, since the power attributed to Jack in (e) is the power to bring about the nonobtaining of a soft fact about the past, the principle of the fixity of the past is not violated.[7]

In this paper, I wish to question the adequacy of the Ockhamistic approach to reconciling divine foreknowledge with human freedom.[8] I argue that there is an important asymmetry between (G) and the likes of (4)–(6) which bears importantly on the question of their fixity. The attempt to treat (G) as a soft fact about the past on a par with (4)–(6) is, in my view, misguided. The discussion to follow

---

[6]Note that, in view of the fact that God is essentially omniscient, (G) is logically equivalent with the fact (K) God foreknew at t_1 that Jack will sign his contract at t_3.

[7]This solution to the problem of divine foreknowledge and human freedom bears a close similarity to a solution to the problem suggested by the fourteenth-century philosopher William of Ockham. For an excellent presentation of Ockham's view, see Marilyn Adams and Norman Kretzmann's introduction to their translation of Ockham's *Predestination, God's Foreknowledge and Future Contingents* (New York: Appleton Century Crofts, 1969).

[8]Thus, the optimism that I expressed in an earlier article with regard to the prospects of working out an acceptable Ockhamistic position seems to me now to have been a bit premature. See Eddy M. Zemach and David Widerker, "Facts, Freedom and Foreknowledge," *Religious Studies*, XXIII (1987): 19–28.

is divided into four parts. In part I, I examine the reasons offered by some contemporary Ockhamists for treating (G) as a soft fact about the past, and argue that these reasons are either of doubtful relevance or rest on assumptions that are mistaken.[9] In parts II and III, I offer an account of the intuitive nonfixity of facts like (4)–(6), and argue that, on pain of leading to counterintuitive consequences, this account cannot be applied to facts about divine foreknowledge. Finally, in part IV, I examine a recent attempt by John Fischer which is also intended to bring out the asymmetry between (G) and standard cases of soft facts and contend that it is incomplete.

I

There are two requirements that must be met by the Ockhamist in order for him to be justified in treating (G) as a soft fact about the past on a par with (4)–(6).

R1. He must specify a property that (G) shares with (4)–(6).

R2. Most importantly, he must give us a good reason to think that it is *in virtue of* having this property or feature that facts like (4)–(6) are not subject to PFP.

The idea underlying this last requirement is clear. It is intended to rule out attempts to assimilate (G) to (4)–(6) based on similarities between these two sorts of facts which are irrelevant to the issue of past fixity. Let us examine now whether contemporary Ockhamistic accounts can be said to meet these requirements.

In describing the Ockhamistic position, William Rowe,[10] for example, claims that the softness of (4)–(6) is due to the fact that they entail a fact about the future. Indeed, this is the reason why, according to him, such facts are not subject to PFP. He refers to such facts as "facts which are *not simply* about the past," as opposed to those which are "*simply* about the past." Consequently, since (G) shares this feature with (4)–(6), it also is not subject to PFP. He says:

> ... our conviction that the past is beyond our power to affect is certainly true, so far as facts which are simply about the past are concerned. Facts which are about the past, but *not simply* about the past, may not, however be beyond our power to affect. And

---

[9]Contemporary Ockhamistic accounts have been also criticized by John Fischer in "Freedom and Foreknowledge," *The Philosophical Review*, XCII (1983): 69–79; "Ockhamism," *The Philosophical Review*, XCIV (1985): 81–100; and "Hard-Type Soft Facts," *The Philosophical Review*, XCV (1986): 591–601; and by William Hasker in "Hard Facts and Theological Fatalism," *Noûs*, XXII (1988): 419–36.

[10]*Philosophy of Religion* (Encino: Dickenson, 1978), pp. 162–65.

what Ockham saw is that facts about divine foreknowledge which are used as the basis for denying human freedom are facts about the past, but *not simply* about the past (*ibid.,* p. 164).

But what has a past fact's entailing a fact about the future got to do with its not being subject to PFP? What is the conceptual link between a past fact's entailing a fact about the future and its being immune to this principle? We may agree with Rowe that (4)–(6) do not seem subject to PFP and that they entail a fact about the future. But is it *because* of having this feature that PFP does not apply to them? On this issue, Rowe leaves us completely in the dark. Also, the mere fact that a past fact entails a fact about the future does not render it immune to PFP. For example, the fact that Jack raises his arm at t_1, entails the future fact that it is not the case that he raises his arm for the first time at t_3. But despite this entailment, once having raised his arm at t_1, Jack no longer has it within his power not to raise his arm at t_1.[11]

Consider next the Ockhamistic position as expounded by Marilyn Adams[12] and refined later by Joshua Hoffman and Gary Rosenkrantz.[13] Adams's idea is that a hard fact about a past time t, i.e., the kind of past fact to which PFP does apply, is a fact which is at least in part about t, but is not about any time that is future relative to t. (Or stating it more precisely, it is a fact that may be expressed by a statement that is at least in part about t, but is not about any time that is future relative to t.) She then provides a definition of "hard fact about t," one central component of which is that such a fact (or the statement expressing it) must not entail the obtaining of a state of affairs at a time later than t.[14] On this account, (4)–(6) as well as (G) turn out to be a soft facts about t_1, since they entail that the state of affairs that Jack signs the contract obtains at t_3. As in the case of Rowe, we may ask: What bearing does a past fact's entailing the obtaining of a state of affairs in the future have upon its not being

---

[11]See Fischer, "Hard-Type Soft Facts," p. 593.
[12]"Is the Existence of God a 'Hard Fact'?" *The Philosophical Review,* LXXVI (1967), pp. 493–94.
[13]"Hard and Soft Facts," *The Philosophical Review,* XCIII (1984): 419–34.
[14]According to Adams,

   (B) "Statement p is at least in part about time T" = df "The happening or not happening, actuality or non-actuality of something at T, is a necessary condition of the truth of p"
   (C) "Statement p expresses a hard fact about a time T" = df "p is not at least in part about any time future to T" (pp. 492–93).

Hoffman and Rosenkrantz give a much more elaborate account of the notion of a hard fact about a time t. What is relevant for our purpose here, however, is that they, too, require that a hard fact about t must not entail the obtaining of an "immediate" state of affairs or what they call an "URP" state of affairs at a time later than t. By the latter they understand such simple state of affairs, such as Socrates is walking, Socrates is wise, Jack mows his lawn, etc. (pp. 425–26). My criticism of Adams's position is not affected by this refinement.

subject to PFP? To be sure, (G) differs from a hard fact such as (1) in that it entails the obtaining of a state of affairs at t_3. But why should this difference be a relevant one? We may gain a better understanding of Adams's position by inquiring what led her to try to capture the notion of a hard fact about a past time t the way she did in the first place. She says:

> It is useful before proceeding ... to examine the distinction between "hard" and "soft" facts. Pike makes the distinction between "hard" and "soft" facts about the past by contrasting facts which were "fully accomplished" or "over-and-done with" at a given past time with those which were not. I think that the distinction Pike has in mind can also be drawn in terms of a statement's being about a given time (*op. cit.*, p. 493).

Adams, as we can see, takes the notion of a hard fact about a time t to be equivalent in meaning or closely related to the notion of a fact's being fully accomplished or over-and-done-with at times after t. This by itself is perfectly acceptable, since we can agree that a fact that has this feature is fixed at times after t. But by requiring that a hard fact about t should not entail the obtaining of a certain state of affairs at a time later than t, Adams makes the further assumption that

(HD)   A fact about t that entails the obtaining of a state of affairs at a time t' later than t cannot be deemed over-and-done-with before t'.[15]

Notice that Adams's account is not vulnerable to the objection that since

(s1) Jack raises his arm t_1.

entails

(s2) It is not the case that Jack raises his arm for the first time at t_3.

(s1) is in part about t_3, and hence the fact expressed by it cannot be deemed a hard fact about t_1. (See Fischer, "Hard-Type Soft Facts," p. 593, and "Freedom and Foreknowledge," p. 75.) Rebuttal: Although (s1) entails (s2), (s1) does not entail, as is required by Adams's account, that

(i) Some state of affairs obtains *at t_3*.

nor, more specifically, that

(j) The state of affairs that it is not the case that Jack raises his arm for the first time at t_3, obtains *at t_3*.

For instance, (i) are (j) are both false in a possible world in which John raises his arm at t_1, but in which there are no times later than t_1. But in such a world, (s1) and (s2) would still be true. On this point, see also my "Two Fallacious Objections to Adams's Soft/Hard Fact Distinction," *Philosophical Studies* LVII (1989): 103-107.

[15]Or stating this assumption alternatively as follows:

(HD) A fact about the past, relative to a time t' which entails the obtaining of a state of affairs at a time later than t' cannot be deemed over-and-done-with at t'.

This assumption is problematic. To see this, let us suppose that God promises Smith at t_1 that Jack will sign the contract at t_3. Suppose further that it is impossible for God to break his promises, i.e.,

    (I) Necessarily, if God promises to Smith at t_1 that Qt_3, then Qt_3.

(Qt_3 abbreviates "Jack signs his contract on January 3, 1985".) It seems intuitive to assume that the fact that God promised Smith at t_1 that Jack will sign the contract at t_3 is fully accomplished and over-and-done-with at t_2. But, on (HD), this fact would not have this feature, since it entails a fact about t_3. To take another example, suppose that God decrees at t that of those (over twenty years old) who rebelled against Moses after the return of the spies, only Caleb and Joshua will enter the land of Canaan at t' ($t' > t$). Abbreviate the statement expressing the decree to Rt'. Suppose further that God's will cannot be thwarted, i.e.,

    (J) Necessarily, if God decrees at t that P, then P.

Again, the fact that God decreed at t that Rt' seems intuitively to be over-and-done-with immediately after t, although it entails the obtaining of a state of affairs at a time later than t. The moral to be drawn from these examples is that an assumption such as (HD) is justified as long as we do not allow for the possibility of there being logically (or metaphysically) necessary connections between temporally distinct events.[16] Once we deviate from this policy, however, and allow for such necessary connections between events as those which obtain between divine forebeliefs and human free actions, we can easily conceive of situations in which (HD) does not hold.

    Another philosopher to take the Ockhamistic line is Alvin Plantinga.[17] His justification for treating (G) as a soft fact about the past is the following: Plantinga starts from the assumption that

    (PL1) A hard fact about the past must be one that is *strictly* about the past.[18]

---

[16]Here, as well as in what follows, I take "event" to refer to concrete, dated, nonrepeatable events. Also, I include under the rubric "event" states of substances and processes. In addition to events, I countenance also such entities as states of affairs and facts.

[17]"On Ockham's Way Out," *Faith and Philosophy*, III (1986), pp. 247–48. See, especially, the passage starting with: "We may not be able to give a criterion for being strictly about the past . . ." (p. 248).

[18]Plantinga also says that a hard fact about the past must be a *genuine* fact about the past (*ibid.*, p. 247). Aside from making only some cursory remarks about what it is for a fact to be a genuine fact about the past, however, he does not explain this notion.

Although Plantinga does not offer us an account of strictness in this sense, he gives us a sufficient condition for nonstrictness, which is that

(PL2) No conjunctive proposition that contains as a conjunct a simple proposition about the future, like Paul will mow his lawn in 1999, can be deemed strictly about the past.

So, for example, the conjunctive proposition

(7) Smith believed at t_1 that Jack will sign the contract at t_3, and Jack will sign the contract at t_3

would not be strictly about the past, relative to t_2, since it contains as a conjunct the proposition

(8) Jack will sign the contract at t_3.

Plantinga's third assumption is that

(PL3) Hard facthood is closed under logical equivalence.

Consequently, since (G) is logically equivalent to the conjunction of (G) and (8), (G) is not a hard fact about the past, according to Plantinga. This argument for the soft facthood of (G) is again unconvincing. The problematic assumption is (PL3). As in the case of (HD), once we allow for the possibility of logically (or metaphysically) necessary connections between temporally distinct events, there seems to be no reason to accept (PL3). The divine promise example mentioned earlier is revealing here as well. The proposition

(9) God promises to Smith at t_1 that Jack will sign the contract at t_3.

surely expresses a hard fact about the past (relative to t_2), in the sense of that fact's being over-and-done-with at t_2. It expresses a fact that at t_2 can be remembered by Smith, can be empirically detected by him, e.g., by hearing the promise, and may have traces at t_2 just like regular hard facts about the past (relative to t_2) do. According to Plantinga, however, (9) would not express a hard fact about the past; for it is logically equivalent to the conjunction

(10) God promises to Smith at t_1 that Jack will sign the contract at t_3, and Jack will sign the contract at t_3.[19]

---

[19] To be sure, Plantinga might argue that he is operating with a notion of a hard fact about the past according to which the fact expressed by (9) would not count as a hard fact about t_1. But then he

What the above discussion suggests is that the reasons offered by contemporary Ockhamists for treating (G) as a soft fact about the past on a par with (4)–(6) are either of doubtful relevance to the freedom and foreknowledge debate, or else are based upon assumptions that are very problematic. In effect, these philosophers have failed to give us a plausible explanation why soft facts such as (4)–(6) do not seem to be subject to PFP. The question that arises now is whether someone who is attracted to the Ockhamistic strategy of reconciling divine foreknowledge with human freedom can do better?

II

What is it that accounts for the intuitive nonfixity of facts like (4)–(6)? To answer this question, let us consider more closely the following version of the principle of the fixity of the past:

(PFP1) If a given event occurs at a time t, then no one has it within his power at a time later than t to bring it about that that event did not occur at t.

or more formally put:

$$O(e, t) \supset \sim(\exists x)(\exists t')[t' > t \cdot P^*_{x, t'}(\sim O(e, t))]$$

(where e, t, and X range respectively over events, times, and agents, and O and $P^*_{x, t'}$ are short for "occurred" and "it is within X's power at t' to bring it about that").

Notice that, although we do not have the power to bring about the nonoccurrence of a given past event E, we sometimes have the power to bring it about that that event does, or does not, exemplify certain future-contingent properties, namely, those properties it exemplifies *in virtue* of standing in certain relations to events or states of affairs occurring in the future. So, for example, Jack does not have it within his power, on January 2, 1985, to bring about the nonoccurrence of events such as

E1: Smith's uttering on January 1 the sentence "Jack will sign the contract on January 3"
E2: Smith's believing on January 1 that Jack will sign the contract on January 3.

still owes us an explanation why this fact, despite its being intuitively over-and-done-with at t_2, and despite its having all the other features mentioned in the text, is not subject to PFP.

Given that Jack is free with respect to signing the contract, however, it is within his power on January 2 to bring it about that E1 and E2 do or do not exemplify properties like

P1: occurring two days before Jack's signing the contract on January 3

P2: being such that Jack signs the contract on January 3

P3: being an uttering of the true (false) sentence "Jack will sign the contract on January 3"

Once having drawn the distinction between

(i) having the power to bring about the nonoccurrence of a certain past event
and

(ii) having the power to bring it about that a past event does or does not exemplify a certain future contingent property

we are in a position to provide an adequate answer to the question why soft facts like (4)–(6) are intuitively not fixed. The answer is this. Each of these facts may be viewed as an exemplification of a future-contingent property P by some past event E. Hence, to the extent that an agent has the power to bring about the nonoccurrence of the future event or fact in virtue of which E exemplifies P, that agent also has the power to bring about the nonobtaining of the relevant soft fact. By crediting him with that power, we do not credit him with the power to bring about the nonoccurrence of a past event, but merely with the innocuous power to make it the case that a past event does not exemplify a certain future-contingent property. To be sure, an agent does not always have the power to bring about the nonoccurrence of the future event that figures in a soft fact. Sometimes this may be due to the fact that the agent does not have the knowledge or the means to prevent the occurrence of the event. In other cases, he may lack that power because the future event is causally determined, as, e.g., in the case of the sun's shining at t_3. Thus, the following facts, though being exemplifications of some future-contingent property by an event occurring at t_1 (and hence soft facts about t_1) would still be fixed for Smith, relative to t_2.

(11) Smith saw Jack at t_1, two days before the event of his mother's getting cancer at t_3.

(12) Smith correctly believed at t_1 that the sun will be shining at t_3.

But their fixity (relative to t_2), as opposed to the fixity of a hard fact about t_1 like

(13) Smith saw Jack at t_1.

does not derive from their being fully accomplished and over-and-done-with at t_2, i.e., it does not derive from PFP.[20]

It may be useful at this point to state the idea of a future-contingent property of an event schematically as follows:

(FCP) P is a future-contingent property of an event E_t occurring at a time t, iff

1 E_t exemplifies P

2 The state of affairs of E_t exemplifying P can be analyzed either

(i) as a relation of some sort obtaining between E_t and some event $F_{t'}$, which occurs at a time t' later than t, i.e., $R(Et, Ft')$, $t' > t$,

or it can be analyzed

(ii) as a relation of some sort obtaining between Et and some fact Cf that is future-based, relative to t, i.e., $R(Et, Cf)$. A future-based fact, relative to t, will typically be a fact expressible by a true proposition Pt' to the effect that an object exemplifies a certain property at a time t' later than t. Or it will be a fact expressible by a proposition R that is 1-entailed by some such proposition Pt' (The term "1-entails" applies here only to first-order logic entailments.)[21]

So, for example, $P1$ is a future-contingent property of $E1$, since the state of affairs of $E1$'s exemplifying $P1$ can be analyzed as a relation obtaining between the event of Smith's uttering at t_1 the sentence "Jack will sign his contract on January 3, 1985," and the event of Jack's signing the contract on January 3. Similarly, $P2$ is a future-contingent property of $E2$, since the state of affairs of $E2$ exemplifying $P2$, can be analyzed as a relation holding between $E2$ and the fact that Jack signs the contract at t_3, which is future-based, relative to t_1, i.e., $E2$'s being such that Jack signs the contract at t_3.

---

[20]Cf. Rowe, *op. cit.*, p. 165; and Fischer, "Hard-Type Soft Facts," p. 595.

[21]These are only some informal, explicatory remarks on the notion of a state of affairs which is future-based, relative to t. I do not attempt in this paper to give a precise account of this notion. The discussion to follow is not affected by this limitation. Another way of informally explicating the notion of a future-based fact is to characterize it as a fact expressible by a true proposition R *made true* by the occurrence of some future event.

This schematic account of the notion of a future-contingent property of an *event* occurring at t can be easily generalized to yield a similar account of the notion of a future-contingent property of an *object* existing at t.

III

Given the above account of the intuitive nonfixity of soft facts such as (4)–(6), let us ask now whether the Ockhamist can use this account to justify his claim regarding the alleged nonfixity of (G). In other words, can the Ockhamist offer a relational analysis of (G) on the pattern of $R(Et, Ft')$ or $R(Et, Cf)$, and then claim that the assumption as to Jack's power at t_2 to bring about the nonobtaining of (G) does not imply that Jack has the power to bring about the nonoccurrence of a past event, but merely implies that he has the power to bring it about that some past event does not stand in some relation to some future event or fact? To answer this question, let us first ask: What would be the elements figuring in such a relation R? One possibility that immediately suggests itself is to identify these elements with the event

> EG: God's believing at t_1 that Qt_3

and the fact

> Qt_3: Jack signs the contract at t_3.

That is, the suggestion here is to view (G) as some sort of relational fact

> (G*) $R(EG, Qt_3)$

This suggestion, however, would be of no help to the Ockhamist. The Ockhamist wants to claim that it is within Jack's power to bring about the nonobtaining of (G), i.e., (G*). Note, however, that, in order to be credited with the power to bring about the nonobtaining of (G*), Jack must have the power to bring about the nonobtaining of Qt_3. But since the nonobtaining of Qt_3 entails the nonoccurrence of EG, it follows [given (PRW) and given the fact that EG occurred] that Jack can be said to have that latter power only if he has the power to bring about the nonoccurrence of EG, i.e., only at the expense of violating PFP1. It is instructive to note that this objection would not apply in the case of a typical soft fact, such as

> (6) Smith correctly believed at t_1 that Qt_3.

Although (6), too, can be analyzed as $R(E2, Qt_3)$ the nonobtaining of Qt_3 does not entail the nonoccurrence of $E2$. If Jack had not signed the contract, the event $E2$ of Smith's believing at t_1 that Qt_3 would still have occurred, but would have merely lacked the property of being a believing of a true proposition.

At this point, the Ockhamist might try to construe (G) as a relation that obtains between some mental state M of God *other than EG*, and Jack's future action of signing the contract at t_3, i.e., $R(M, Et_3)$. Of course, the question that immediately arises is what would be the nature of this relation R? In the absence of an answer to this question, the proposal in question appears to be empty.[22] To help the Ockhamist, let us, for the sake of discussion, consider a different account of divine foreknowledge. Instead of viewing the latter on the model of belief, let us conceive of it on the model of immediate or direct awareness. That is, let us suppose that, just as humans are directly aware of their thoughts, sensations, and perhaps some abstract entities, God is directly aware of future-contingent events or facts.[23] On this account, $R(X, Et_3)$ would denote the relational property of being an awareness of Et_3, a property had by some appropriate mental state M of God. The logical form of "God knows at t_1 that Qt_3" would be then given by:

$$(\exists M) \ [M \text{ is a mental state of God \& } M \text{ occurs at } t_1 \text{ and } R(M, Et_3)]$$

This account seems to me the most promising proposal an Ockhamist can come up with in his attempt to treat facts about God's knowledge of future-contingent events as soft facts about the past on a par with (4)–(6). Because

(K) God knows at t_1 that Qt_3.

is construed as a relation obtaining between some mental state M of God and Jack's action of signing the contract, Jack, by having power over one of the relata of R, also has the power to bring about the nonobtaining of (K). Given the relational analysis of God's knowledge, this power does not imply a power to bring about the nonoccurrence of M, but merely implies a power to bring it about that M does not have the future-contingent property of being an awareness of Et_3.

Despite its initial attractiveness, however, this analysis of God's knowledge of future-contingent events turns out to be unsatisfactory. One problem with it is the intelligibility of the assumption that God can be directly aware *at t_1* of an event that occurs at t_3. It would appear that (i) if someone is directly aware at t_1 of a certain event, then that event also occurs at t_1 (in which case the assumption that God is directly aware at t_1 of Et_3 would be contradictory).[24] This seems to be clearly so in the case of our knowledge of our own mental states, where, e.g., the event of my

---

[22]For an attempt to work out an account of divine belief which deals with this question, see Zemach and Widerker, p. 26. But this account seems to me now unsatisfactory in view of the objection of future-contingent causal chains which I raise later.

[23]For a similar approach to God's knowledge, see William L. Alston, "Does God Have Beliefs?" *Religious Studies*, XXII (1986): 287–306.

[24]I am indebted to the editors of *The Journal of Philosophy* for the emphasis of this point. Note that one can at t_1 be aware of an event in the sense of having at t_1 an inner mental representation of it. But such an awareness would not be a direct awareness of the event *itself*.

feeling pain and that of my being aware of my feeling pain are simultaneous. In response to this objection, an Ockhamist might want to reject (i) and insist that God, unlike humans, *can* be directly aware of events before they occur. Although this reply seems to me to be unconvincing, I shall not discuss it here any further.[25] Instead, I shall develop a general objection to any sort of Ockhamist attempt to reconcile divine foreknowledge with human freedom by treating facts about God's foreknowledge of future contingent events as soft facts about the past over which an agent may have power. I shall try to show that power over such facts sometimes gives an agent power over clear hard facts about the past, and hence leads to a violation of PFP1. This point, I claim, holds independently of the specific analysis of divine foreknowledge one adopts: the belief analysis or the direct-awareness analysis. The

[25]Another objection one might raise against the account of divine foreknowledge under consideration is that (i) being an awareness of Et_3 is an essential property of a mental state that has it. Consequently, the Ockhamist's claim that it is within Jack's power at t_1 to bring it about that God does not know at t_1 that Qt_3 results not only in Jack's having at t_2 the power to bring it about that M lacks the said property, but it also results in Jack's having the power to bring about the nonoccurrence of M, and hence involves a violation of PFP1. An interesting way in which the Ockhamist might try to respond to the above objection, aside from squarely rejecting the claim that being an awareness of Et_3 is an essential property an event, is the following:

(a) The Ockhamist might first extend Jaegwon Kim's notion of event so as to apply also to events that have among their constitutive objects other events. E.g., events such as Jack's seeing the accident at t_1 or Jack's accepting Jim's offer at t_1, etc. [As remembered, according to Kim an event is conceived of as an n-tuple of objects exemplifying an n-adic property at a given time t, i.e.,

$$[(X1, X2,..., Xn), Pn, t]$$

where the elements of the n-tuple are called "the constitutive objects of the event", the said property is called "the constitutive property of the event", and t is called the "constitutive time of an event." See Kim, "Causation, Nomic Subsumption and the Concept of an Event," *The Journal of Philosophy*, LXX (1973): 217–36.]

(b) He might then restrict the application of PFP1 only to events that do *not* have among their constitutive objects events occurring after their constitutive time t. Genuine past events, an Ockhamist might insist, should not have such elements among their constitutive objects. On this account, PFP1 would apply to events such as Jack's mowing his lawn at t_1, or Jack's raising his arm at t_2, i.e.,

[(Jack, the lawn), 1 mows 2, t_1]
[(Jack, his arm), 1 raises 2, t_1]

But PFP1 would not apply to events such as God's being directly aware of Et_5, where Et_5 is the event of Jack's pulling the trigger at t_5 i.e.,

[(God, Et_5, 1 is aware of 2, t_1]

or to Peter's predicting the occurrence of Et_5, i.e.,

[(Peter, Et_5), 1 predicts 2, t_1]

objection to follow will be formulated, for the sake of inclusiveness, in terms of God's knowledge. Depending upon the specific account of divine foreknowledge the Ockhamist adopts, however, it can be restated by replacing "God knows ..." with "God believes ..." or with "God is directly aware of ..."

IV. THE OBJECTION FROM FUTURE-CONTINGENT CAUSAL CHAINS

(S) Suppose that God knows at t_1 that Jack will freely pull the trigger at t_5, with the intention of killing Smith. Suppose further that, wanting to save Smith, God reveals this fact to Smith at t_3. As a result, Smith by taking appropriate precautions is able to save his life. Now, the Ockhamist concedes that, by having the power to refrain from attempting to kill Smith, Jack also has at t_4 the power to make it the case that God did not know at t_1 that Jack would attempt to kill Smith at t_5.[26] On the other hand, God's knowing that Jack will attempt to kill Smith is a condition that in the circumstances causally contributes to the occurrence of the event of God's warning Smith at t_3, in the sense of being (in the circumstances) a causally necessary condition for it. Surely, if God had not known at t_1 that Jack would try to kill Smith, he would not have told Smith that Jack will attempt to kill him. But then it follows that, by having the power to bring about the nonobtaining of that condition, Jack would have it within his power at t_4 to bring about the nonoccurrence of past events, such as:

> Wt_3: God's warning Smith at t_3
> Xt_3: Smith's hearing at t_3 a voice telling him that Jack will attempt to kill him
> Yt_3: Smith's coming to believe at t_3 that Jack will attempt to kill him, etc.[27]

This, of course, would be a violation of the principle of the fixity of the past in the sense of PFP1. The intuitive principle underlying the last inference is this:

> (i) If p, and q is a causally necessary condition (in the circumstances) for p, and $P^*_{x,t}$ (not-q), then $P^*_{x,t}$ (not-p)[28]

[26]Note that this point holds both in case the Ockhamist adopts the belief model of divine foreknowledge (see the conclusion of Pike's argument) and in case he adopts the direct-awareness model of it.

[27]Here I am assuming that the occurrence of Wt_3 is causally necessary (in the circumstances) for Xt_3 and that of Xt_3 is causally necessary (in the circumstances) for Yt_3.

[28]In my "A Problem for the Eternity Solution," *International Journal for Philosophy of Religion* XXIX (1991): 87–95, I employ a similar argument against the attempt to solve the conflict between divine foreknowledge and human freedom by conceiving of God as existing outside time.

There seem to be two ways in which an Ockhamist may try to respond to this objection.

(a) He may diagnose the moral to be drawn from the objection differently. Instead of viewing the objection as showing that power over God's foreknowledge of human free actions may give an agent power over hard facts about the past, he may take it as showing that the following assumption implicit in the objection is false:

(PV) God has it within his power to intervene in the course of events on the basis of his knowledge of future-contingent events.

This inability to intervene, he might say, is the price that an essentially omniscient God must pay if he wants to allow for human freedom.

(b) He may argue that, although God may sometimes intervene in the course of history, he never does so *because* of his knowledge of future-contingent events, but for some other reason that does not involve such knowledge.

Both these responses do not seem to me adequate. The first one is theologically implausible. God as portrayed in the Judeo-Christian tradition often intervenes in human history acting in the light of his knowledge of future-contingent events. For example, God appears to Abraham and reveals to him that his descendants will be enslaved and mistreated for four hundred years (Genesis 15:13). He tells Moses that Pharaoh will at first refuse to let the People of Israel go (Exodus 3:19). Knowing that Pharaoh will go in the morning to bathe in the Nile, God orders Moses to meet Pharaoh at the river and to tell him about the first plague (Exodus 7:15). He reveals to the prophet Ahijah that Jeroboam's wife will come to him to consult him about the health of her son, and that she will be coming in disguise (1 Kings 14:5), and so on. Thus, the first response seems inconsistent with the traditional account of God's providential activity. It is, of course, open for someone to argue that, on all the occasions on which God allegedly intervened in human history in the light of his knowledge of future-contingent events, those events were inevitable. But note that the objector can make this response only at the expense of violating the notion of divine justice, hence, only at the expense of further attenuating the Judeo-Christian concept of God. For in some of the cases described above (e.g., the one in Genesis 15:13 and that in Exodus 3:19), the agents involved were explicitly punished by God for their deed. Hence, this way out is inadequate.

The weakness of the second response consists in the fact that it renders God's knowledge of future-contingent events completely epiphenomenal. One wonders what role, if any, it plays in God's overall plan for the world. Secondly, if God's knowledge of the future does not play any causal role in his interventions in human affairs, there is the danger that we may end up with situations in which God may tell Smith that Jack will attempt to kill him, even though He knows that Jack does not intend to do so, in which case God would be telling a lie. Needless to say, it is not difficult to conceive of situations that are even more morally repugnant than the foregoing.

It is important to see that the objection from future-contingent causal chains fails when applied to standard-type soft facts, such as (6). If one were to state the objection by replacing "God knows" with "Peter correctly believes", it would break down at the point where it assumes that the fact that Peter correctly believed that Jack will pull the trigger at t_5 is a causally necessary condition for the event of his warning Smith. What is in those alternative circumstances a causally necessary condition for the occurrence of that event is not the fact that

(B1) Peter *correctly* believed at t_1 that Rt_5.
(Rt_5 abbreviates Jack pulls the trigger at t_5'.)

but rather the fact that

(B) Peter *believed* at t_1 that Rt_5.

And that is a fact about the past, over which contrary to a fact like

(K1) God foreknew at t_1 that Rt_5.

Jack has no power at t_4. [Unlike (K1), (B) is not a fact concerning which one can say that Jack has it within his power to bring about its nonobtaining, if he has the power to refrain from pulling the trigger at t_5.] Now, someone who adopts a belief model of divine foreknowledge might argue that, when applying the objection to God's case, it is also *not* the fact (K1) that forms a causally necessary condition for God's warning Smith, but rather the fact that

(G1) God believed at t_1 that Rt_5.

But this claim would not be correct, since (K1) is equivalent to (G1). The above remarks suggest a further important difference between God's beliefs and regular soft facts, which is that the causal power of the latter is somehow limited by time. Thus, soft facts such as (4)–(6) cannot, on pain of backward causation, be deemed causally efficacious prior to t_3. They become causally efficacious only after t_3, only after becoming hard facts. Facts like (G) or (G1), on the other hand, are not so limited. Like regular hard facts about t_1 they can be causally efficacious even before t_3.

V

In a recent article, Fischer has also argued that it is a mistake to assimilate a fact like

(G) God believed at t_1 that Qt_3.

to standard-type soft facts, such as

(6) Smith correctly believed at t_1 that Qt_3.

when it comes to the question of their fixity.[29] Fischer adopts the account of the soft/hard fact distinction provided by Hoffman and Rosenkrantz, according to which (G) is classified as a soft fact about t_1. But he maintains that (G) is a very special sort of soft fact about t_1, what he calls a "hard-type soft fact." By this he understands a soft fact whose constitutive property, that of believing that Qt_3, is a temporally genuine property or what he calls a "hard property," relative to t_1. Moreover, he assumes that no human has it within his power at a time later than t so to act that what is a bearer of a hard property relative to t would not have possessed that property at t. Consequently, hard-type soft facts about t are in his view fixed at times later than t. Fischer offers the following account of the notion of a hard property: a hard property, relative to a given time t, is one which is not soft, relative to t, where by a "soft property" he understands a property P such that, if *anything* were to have that property at t, it would necessarily follow that some immediate fact obtains after t, in any plausible sense of "immediate". So, for instance, temporally relational properties, such as correctly believing that Qt_3, waking up four hours prior to eating lunch, uttering the true sentence "Jack will sign the contract on January 3", and so on, would be examples of soft properties, relative to the pertinent times; whereas those like believing that Qt_3, waking up, eating lunch, and so on, would count as hard properties. The motivation underlying this distinction between the two sorts of property is to stress the resemblance between (G) and regular hard facts about t_1 such as that Jack wakes up at t_1, which also have as their constitutive property a hard

---

[29]Fischer, "Hard-Type Soft Facts," pp. 595–99. I discuss this claim of Fischer's more briefly also in "Two Forms of Fatalism," pp. 108–10.

property. While being sympathetic to this strategy by Fischer of characterizing the asymmetry between (G) and (6), I think that his account of the notion of a temporally genuine or hard property is problematic, and is, therefore, incomplete. To see this, let us assume that

(14) Smith correctly believes at t_1 that it is not the case that Jack will sign the contract at t_4.

Suppose further that Jack has it within his power at t_2 to sign the contract at t_4, but for some reason decides not to do so. Intuitively, (14) is a soft fact about the past (relative to t_2) of the rather soft sort. If Jack had decided to sign the contract at t_4, he could have brought about the nonobtaining of (14). But now let us examine the constitutive property of (14), the property of correctly believing that it is not the case that Jack signs the contract at t_4. On Fischer's account, this property is a hard property, relative to t_1. Clearly, it is not the case that, if anything were to have that property at t_1, it would necessarily follow that some immediate fact obtains at a time later than t_1. For example, we can conceive of a possible world in which the said property is exemplified by Smith at t_1, but in which there are no times later than t_1. In such a world, (14) would be true, although no immediate state of affairs would obtain in it at times later than t_1. Consequently, Fischer would have to treat (14) as a hard-type soft fact about t_1, which is counterintuitive. A further problem for Fischer's account is posed by properties, such as *being true* (as applied to sentences), correctly believing that all ravens are white, or Jack will sign the contract at t_3, and so on. These properties, too, would have to be treated by Fischer as hard properties, relative to t_1. (E.g., if Jack raises his arm at t_0, then "Jack raised his arm at t_0" has the property of *being true* at t_1. But this does not imply that some immediate fact obtains at some time after t_1.) But their exemplification by an object at t_1, may easily yield soft facts of the standard (soft) type, i.e.,

(15) The sentence "Jack will sign the contract at t_3" is true at t_1.
(16) Smith correctly believes at t_1 that all ravens are white or Jack will sign the contract at t_3.

A further indication that Fischer's account of a hard property is incomplete is provided by the property

P4: being immersed in water and being soluble in water.

This property, which consists of two hard properties—the property of being immersed in water, and the dispositional property of being soluble in water—seems intuitively a hard property, relative to the pertinent time. But on Fischer's account, it would count as a soft property.[30] Keeping in mind that by "hard property" Fischer understands a temporally genuine property, and assuming that he wants his account of the notion of a temporally genuine property to be more than merely a *stipulative* definition, Fischer owes us an explanation of how is it that by combining two temporally genuine properties we get a temporally nongenuine property. Note that, being a conjunction of two temporally genuine (hard) properties, P4 differs crucially from all of Fischer's paradigm examples of soft properties, each of which is either a simple soft property itself, or contains a soft property as a part. Also, unlike Fischer's examples of soft properties, P4, when exemplified by an object at a time t, yields a fact about t that can be analyzed as consisting of two *hard* facts about t.

VI. CONCLUSION

In this paper, I have considered the Ockhamistic response to the problem of divine foreknowledge and human freedom. Having examined various ways in which this response might be construed, the conclusion I have reached is that none of them seems satisfactory. This conclusion may be viewed as lending support to Pike's main claim that, given the truth of PFP, the existence of an everlasting, essentially omniscient God cannot be reconciled with human freedom.

ACKNOWLEDGMENTS

I am greatly indebted to John Fischer, Harry Friedman, Jerome Gellman, Dale Gottlieb, Charlotte Katzoff, Phillip Quinn, William Rowe, and the editors of *The Journal of Philosophy* for excellent comments on an earlier version of this chapter.

[30]Another example of such a property would be the property of P5: infallibly believing that Qt_3, which may be viewed as consisting of the property of believing that Qt_3 and the property of being infallible, each a hard property, relative to t_1.

10

PRESENTISM AND OCKHAM'S WAY OUT

Alicia Finch and Michael Rea

Presentism is, roughly, the thesis that only present objects exist; *eternalism* is, roughly, the thesis that past, present, and future objects exist. *Ockham's way out* purports to be a way out of fatalist arguments for the impossibility of free action. Fatalist arguments come in two varieties: logical and theological. Arguments for logical fatalism run something like this:[1]

Let t_{-1B} = a time that obtained exactly one billion years ago.

Let p_S abbreviate: one billion years after t_{-1B}, S will perform A.

Let q_S abbreviate: p_S was true at t_{-1B}.

Let r_S abbreviate: S performs A now.

Let t_S abbreviate: it is now exactly one billion years after t_{-1B}.

1. $(q_S \& t_S)$ is true, and S does not have, and never had, any choice about $(q_S \& t_S)$.

2. $\Box\left[(q_S \& t_S) \supset r_S\right]$.

3. Therefore, r_S is true and S does not have, and never had, any choice about r_S.

Arguments for theological fatalism are similar, but they replace q_S with something like:

k_S : God knew at t_{-1B} that p_S was true.

---

[1]Those familiar with the literature on fatalism will note that fatalist arguments more commonly open with a premise like this:

(1^*) It is true at t_{-1B} that S performs A at t and S does not have, and never had, any choice about the proposition that it is true at t_{-1B} that S performs A at t.

And, of course, subsequent premises would then have to be modified accordingly. For present purposes, however, we have chosen to work with a "presentist-friendly" version of the standard fatalist argument—that is, a version that takes tense seriously and that doesn't implicitly presuppose (as 1^* does—for example, by employing the locution "it is true at t_{-1B} ") that non-present times exist.

They then go on to derive the same conclusion: that for any agent S and act A, S does not have, and never had, any choice about the proposition that S performs A. Of course, it is trivially true that if an agent does not have and never had a choice about the proposition that she performs a particular act, then the agent does not perform the act freely. So, the fatalist's conclusion is that no agent acts freely.

Ockham's way out of the problem of fatalism is of interest to *libertarians* with respect to the metaphysics of free will. A libertarian is one who accepts the theses that: (a) agents perform free acts in the actual world and (b) agents cannot perform free acts if determinism is true.[2] Non-libertarians who accept (a) accept *compatibil-ism*, where compatibilism is the thesis that (c) even if determinism is true, agents might perform free acts. Fatalist arguments present no special problem for compatibilists. Whatever considerations can be marshalled in support of the position that:

> (C) An agent S might act freely even if the combination of the state of the world in the distant past and the laws of nature is inconsistent with S's acting other than she does.

can also be marshalled in support of the position that:

> (C*) An agent S might act freely even if the past truth of future contingents[3] is inconsistent with S's acting other than she does.

as well as the position that:

> (C**) An agent S might act freely even if divine foreknowledge[4] of S's act is inconsistent with S's acting other than she does.

So, the proponent of free will who needs a way out of fatalism is the libertarian.

What way out does Ockham offer? Ockham offers us a distinction between *hard facts* and *soft facts* about the past. While the distinction is somewhat difficult to characterize, the rough idea is that a hard fact about the past is *entirely* about the past whereas a soft fact is not: a hard fact about, say, t_{-1B} is a fact whose obtaining

---

[2]Determinism is the thesis that the proposition P0 that expresses the complete state of the world at some time in the distant past (at, say, t_{-1B}) and the proposition L that expresses the entirety of the laws of nature entails every true proposition whatever—including, of course, every proposition about which acts agents perform at various times.

[3]The relevant "future contingent" in our argument is p_S. The argument from logical fatalism is sometimes referred to as the argument from future contingents.

[4]k_S is a proposition about divine foreknowledge: God knows that S will perform A one billion years before she does so. The argument from theological fatalism is sometimes called the argument from, or problem of, divine foreknowledge.

is entirely independent of whatever might happen after t_{-1B} whereas a soft fact about t_{-1B} somehow depends on, involves, or includes events that take place at later times.[5] This distinction is supposed to help the libertarian respond to the fatalist by allowing her to insist that past facts about future contingents, as well as past facts about divine foreknowledge, are soft, and therefore dependent in some way upon events that lie in their future. Once this dependence is granted, there is no longer any clear obstacle to saying that present agents can have a choice about such facts.

Some will find Ockhamism incredible. And why not? At first blush, the view seems to imply that agents have the power to change the past. Ockhamists say that their view implies no such power. But even if they are right about this, their insistence that facts about the past can depend in some way upon the present acts of purportedly free agents might, all by itself, seem problematic enough. Our goal in this paper is to show that whether this claim is problematic depends crucially on whether presentism or eternalism is true.

We will proceed as follows. In the next section, we will lay out the fatalist's argument more clearly, making sure to clarify which dialectical moves are available to the libertarian. We will then offer a more robust presentation of Ockhamism, responding to obvious objections and teasing out the implications of the view. At this point, we will discuss presentism and eternalism in more detail. We will then present our argument for the claim that the libertarian cannot take Ockham's way out of the fatalism argument unless she rejects presentism. Finally, we will consider and dispense with objections to our argument. In the end, it ought to be clear that the libertarian must make a choice between Ockham's way out and presentism.

1. FATALISM

There is a great deal of debate about whether the two types of fatalist argument are logically equivalent: some say that they are, while others insist that the theological argument is stronger. Given that we are arguing that the presentist libertarian cannot use Ockham's way out of fatalism, and given that no one seems to think that the logical fatalist argument is more difficult to quash than its theological analogue, we will hereafter focus our attention on the logical fatalist version of the argument. Moreover, we will hereafter drop the "logical" qualifier and use the terms "fatalism" and "fatalist argument" to refer to the logical versions of each.

---

[5]For a good start into the literature on Ockhamism and the hard-fact/soft-fact distinction, see John Martin Fischer (ed.), *God, Foreknowledge, and Freedom* (Stanford: Stanford University Press, 1989).

The fatalist argument as we have presented it relies on two premises and a some-what controversial rule of inference. We will first consider the rule of inference, then the premises, in order to see which avenues of response are available for the libertar-ian confronted with the fatalist argument.

We can present the rule of inference more elegantly if we employ the following abbreviation:

> $N_s\,p$ abbreviates: p and S does not have, and never had, any choice about whether p is true.

With this, it becomes clear that the fatalist relies on the following inference prin-ciple (substituting $(q_s\,\&\,t_s)$ and r_s for p and q, respectively):

$$\big[N_s\,p\,\&\,\square(p\supset q)\big]\ \text{entails}\ N_s\,q.$$

This sort of principle will be familiar to participants in the debate over the com-patibility of causal determinism and free action. In his famed "Modal Version of the Consequence Argument" for the incompatibility of determinism and free action, Peter van Inwagen stipulates that:

> $N\,p$ abbreviates: p and no one has, or ever had, any choice about whether p is true.

He then introduces "Principle β", the rule of inference according to which:

$$(\beta)\big[Np\,\&\,N\big(p\supset q\big)\big]\ \text{entails}\ Nq.$$

Though van Inwagen's original β is demonstrably invalid, many "β-style" inference principles are on offer and, at the very least, the following principle has remained immune to counter-example:

$$(\beta_\square)\big[Np\,\&\,\square\big(p\supset q\big)\big]\ \text{entails}\ Nq.$$

Principle $\beta_\square$ is relevantly similar to the inference principle we employed in present-ing the fatalist's argument. Granted, our presentation of the fatalist's argument relies on a version of β that relativizes the N-operator to a particular agent S. However, the fatalist's rule of inference is clearly of the "β-style". We will christen it "$\beta_{S,\square}$":

$$(\beta_{S,\square})\big[Np\,\&\,\square\big(p\supset q\big)\big]\ \text{entails}\ N_s q$$

Given that $\beta_\square$ is valid only if $\beta_{s,\square}$ is, libertarians-qua-incompatibilists who are inclined to accept $\beta_\square$ ought to be inclined to accept $\beta_{s,\square}$ as well. But it is a vexed question whether the libertarian-qua-incompatibilist must endorse the modal version of the Consequence Argument, let alone $\beta_\square$. For this reason, it is fortunate that the issue is irrelevant in the present context. Our purpose in this chapter is to consider Ockham's way out of fatalism, and Ockham's way out does not depend on a denial of the validity of β-style inference principles. It is worth noting, though, that $\beta_{s,\square}$ certainly *seems* to be valid and that, given its association with arguments for the incompatibilist component of libertarianism, it would seem to be in the libertarian's best interest to find a way out of fatalism that does not require a rejection of that principle.

Since Ockham's way out does not involve a rejection of Principle $\beta_{s,\square}$'s validity, it obviously involves a rejection of one of the fatalist's premises. Moreover, the Ockhamist qua Ockhamist has no objection to either the first conjunct of the fatalist's first premise:

1a. $(q_s \& t_s)$ is true (i.e., the conjunction of the proposition that it was true at t_{-1B} that one billion years after t_{-1B}, S will perform A and the proposition that it is exactly one billion years after t_{-1B} is true).

or to the second premise of the fatalist's argument:

2. $\square \left[(q_s \& t_s) \supset r_s \right]$

While some libertarians reject both 1a and 2 on the grounds that the locution "true at t_{-1B}" is nonsensical, and other libertarians reject 1a on the grounds that q_s is false given that bivalence fails for future-tensed propositions, neither strategy is part of Ockham's way out. Ockham's way out of fatalism is to assert the falsity of the second conjunct of the fatalist's first premise:

1b. S does not have, and never had, any choice about $\left(q_s \& t_s \right)$.

Moreover, the Ockhamist thinks that S has, or had, a choice about the truth of the conjunction $\left(q_s \& t_s \right)$ in virtue of the fact that S has, or had, a choice about the truth of q_s: it is no part of the Ockhamist's position to assert that an agent has, had, or might have a choice about the passage of time.

In the next section, we will explain the Ockhamist's strategy in some detail, dispensing with the obvious objections along the way. But first we must offer a few words about the locution "S has a choice about whether p is true" or, what is the same thing, "S has a choice about whether it is true that p". We take it as trivially true that S has a choice about whether it is true that p if and only if:

    a. S is able to render p false.
    b. S can render p false.
    c. S has the power to render p false.

and:

    d. S has power over the truth value of p.

This assumption is standard both in the free-will literature generally and in the literature on fatalism in particular. Given this, and given that it will be far easier to explain the Ockhamist's position if we talk in terms of the ability to render a proposition false rather than in terms of having a choice about a proposition, we will employ the former terminology from here on out. Thus, for example, instead of focusing on the Ockhamist's denial of:

    1b. S does not have, and never had, any choice about $\left(q_S \,\&\, t_S \right)$.

we will instead focus our attention on the Ockhamist's denial of the equivalent proposition that:

    1b*. S does not have, and never had, the power to render $\left(q_S \,\&\, t_S \right)$ false.

II. OCKHAM'S WAY OUT

As we have just seen, Ockham's way out of the fatalist argument is to reconcile the affirmation of:

    1a. $\left(q_S \,\&\, t_S \right)$ is true.

with a denial of:

    1b*. S does not have, and never had, the power to render $\left(q_S \,\&\, t_S \right)$ false.

Given that the Ockhamist does not attribute to S any power over the passage of time, it might seem that 1a and the denial of 1b* are reconcilable only if agents have the power to change the past; however, the Ockhamist emphatically denies that this is so. Indeed, the very heart of Ockhamism is the insistence that there is an analysis of "power to render a proposition false" such that an agent might have this power over q_S without having the ability to change the past.

When Ockhamists give an account of the power to render a contingent proposition false, they include a condition similar to this:

(P) S has the power to render p false only if there is an action X such that

(i) S has the power to perform X and (ii) necessarily, if S performs X, then p is false.[6]

We can see how this partial account of "S has the power to render p false" aids the Ockhamist's response to the fatalist if we recall our terminological stipulations:

p_S = the proposition that, one billion years after t_{-1B}, S will perform A.

q_S = the proposition that p_S was true at t_{-1B}.

Given this, it obviously follows that the affirmation of the following proposition entails the denial of the fatalist's $(1b^*)$:

(O) S has the power to render q_S false.

Moreover, if the Ockhamist cashes out (O) by applying the condition on "power to render p false" given in (P), the Ockhamist denial of $(1b^*)$ implies:

$(O^{\cdot})$ There is an action X such that (i) S has the power to perform X and (ii) necessarily, if S performs X, then q_S is false.

Obviously enough, the relevant act X will be some act distinct from A—perhaps the very act of refraining from A—such that S's performance of X entails that S refrains from performing A one billion years after t_{-1B}. So, according to the Ockhamist, because S performs A now, it is and always has been the case that, at t_{-1B}, it was true that S will perform A exactly one billion years later. However, S has both the power to perform A and the power to refrain from performing A; and given the latter power, S therefore also has the power to render q_S false—*contra* $1b^*$. Thus, $1b^*$ is false.

---

[6]While there may be some Ockhamists who would prefer to tweak this condition a bit, a commitment to Ockhamism requires a commitment to an analysis of "power to render P false" that includes a condition relevantly similar to it. We will thus proceed on the assumption that (P) is part of the Ockhamist's response to the fatalist: nothing of importance will hinge on the details of any particular analysis of "power to render false".

And now the distinction between hard and soft facts becomes relevant. Recall that hard facts about the past are, roughly, facts that obtain wholly independently of whatever events lie in their future; soft facts are facts that are not so independent. According to the Ockhamist, q_S expresses a soft fact about the past; for the truth of q_S depends partly on the way in which S exercises her power now, one billion years after t_{-1B}. But if the truth of q_S depends partly on what S does now, then there is no clear obstacle to saying that S has the power to render q_S false. To be sure, this is no argument for the conclusion that S *does* have this power; but offering such an argument is not the Ockhamist's goal. Ockhamism is entirely a defensive maneuver.[7] And, at this juncture in the dialectic, if the fatalist wants to carry on with her insistence that S lacks that power, she owes the Ockhamist further argument.

What more can the fatalist offer? The only way forward is to try to defend 1b* — or, more to the point, to defend the truth of the claim that the Ockhamist denies:

1b*q_S S does not have, and never had, the power to render q_S false.

Toward doing so, the fatalist can begin by noting that all parties to the debate will admit that:

    i. q_S is a proposition that expresses a fact about the past—indeed, a fact about t_{-1B}, a time one billion years prior to the present time.

But (i) implies:

    ii. q_S was true before S came into existence.

Moreover, the Ockhamist herself will agree that:

    iii. q_S cannot change its truth value.

But, surely, the fatalist will say, nothing could be more obvious than that (ii) and (iii) imply:

---

[7] For this reason, there is nothing question-begging in the Ockhamist's strategy. She cannot be accused of assuming what she is trying to prove because she is not trying to prove anything. Rather, her strategy is simply to assume what the fatalist denies—that S has the power to perform some act other than A—and to expose the fact that the fatalist still has not offered any reason for thinking that S lacks precisely those powers that she must possess in order for that assumption to be true.

$1b^*q_S$ S does not have, and never had, the power to render q_S false.

This is the pith of the fatalist's support for $1b^*q_S$: S did not exist at t_{-1B} and q_S is (and has been, at least since t_{-1B}) unchangeably true.[8] But if an agent did not yet exist when a proposition was (already) unchangeably true, the agent cannot have (and can never have had) the power to render the proposition false. Thus, if q_S was true a billion years before S ever existed, and if q_S has been unchangeably true for as long as it has been true at all, then S does not have, and never has had, the power to render q_S false. Hence, $1b^*q_S$ is true.

Given that the Ockhamist assents to (ii) and (iii), the dialectical standoff is this: the Ockhamist rejects the inference from (ii) and (iii) to $(1b^*q_S)$; the fatalist takes the opposite view. So, the issue, then, is which of the following two claims is more plausible:

I.   (ii) and (iii) imply $(1b^*q_S)$

or

II.   S has the power to perform an act other than A.

In the next section, we will argue that the Ockhamist can *easily* reject (I) in favor of (II) provided that she is an eternalist. We will further argue that if the Ockhamist commits to presentism, her position is untenable. Thus, we will conclude that if libertarians want to employ Ockham's way out as a way of responding to fatalist arguments, they must abandon presentism.

III. PRESENTISM, ETERNALISM, AND OCKHAM'S WAY OUT

As we have said, presentism is (roughly) the thesis that only present objects exist, while eternalism is (again, roughly) the thesis that everything that ever did or ever will exist does exist. A more precise expression of presentism is: it has always been and always will be the case that there are no actual but non-present objects.[9]

---

[8] Whether q_S was true—and unchangeably so—prior to t_{-1B} depends on how seriously one wants to take the tense of the verb in q_S. Out of respect for the presentist position, we are throughout taking tense as seriously as possible.

[9] The "always" quantifier is added so that presentism does not turn out to be true at the beginning of time (if time had a beginning) and false thereafter. The actuality qualifier is added so that

Eternalism can be more precisely characterized as the thesis that past, present, and future objects (and, by extension, events) exist; the phrase "everything that exists" refers not only to things that occupy the present time, but also to objects that occupy past and future times. According to the eternalist, past, present, and future events bear relations of *earlier-than, simultaneous-with,* and *later-than* to one another, but each time has the same ontological status. So, on the presentist view, all of reality—all that exists *simpliciter*—is what exists now, whereas on the eternalist view, what exists *simpliciter* includes everything that exists at every time.

But what is a "time"? The literature on presentism and eternalism includes at least two different ways of answering this question. On the one hand, times may be thought of as abstract states of affairs; on the other hand, they may be thought of as concrete events. Abstract times are analogous to abstract possible worlds. Abstract times might fruitfully be thought of as *present-tense maximal* states of affairs. Intuitively, and very roughly, a present-tense maximal state of affairs is a total state of the world at an instant, *minus* all of the past- and future-tense truths. More rigorously: Say that a state of affairs S is *future directed* just in case either S's obtaining entails that some contingent thing will exist or S's obtaining entails that no contingent thing will exist; and then define a *past-directed* state of affairs in the obviously parallel way.[10] Then a state of affairs S is present-tense maximal if and only if, for every atomic state of affairs S^* that is neither future-directed nor past-directed, either S includes S^* or S precludes S^*.[11] A concrete time might then be thought of as the event of some particular abstract state of affairs obtaining.

For convenience, we will assume that times are concrete events. On this assumption, the presentist denies that there are past or future times whereas the eternalist says that there are. And now let us begin to consider how the eternalist and the presentist each fare when confronted with the fatalist's argument.

---

presentism does not imply the falsity of David Lewis's brand of possibilism, according to which there are objects that do not exist in the actual world and therefore do not exist in our present time by virtue of not existing in our space-time at all (David Lewis, *On the Plurality of Worlds,* Malden, Mass.: Blackwell, 1986). Given that we are assuming that every event involves an object, we take it that insofar as presentists and their rivals differ about the existence of past and future objects they also differ about the existence of past and future events. We also assume that every event with non-zero duration is composed of momentary events.

[10]"Contingent things" might be objects or events; and we assume that an event exists when and only when it occurs.

[11]We shall assume that states of affairs that include laws of nature will not be atomic. One state of affairs includes another just in case the obtaining of the first state of affairs entails the obtaining of the second. One state of affairs precludes another just in case the obtaining of the first entails that the second does not obtain.

239 Presentism and Ockham's Way Out

Recall that the Ockhamist must explain why:

ii. q_S was true before S came into existence

and

iii. q_S cannot change its truth value

fail to imply

1b*q_S S does not have, and never had, the power to render q_S false.

The eternalist Ockhamist blocks this inference by pointing out that it seems plausible only if one assumes the truth of the suppressed premise that:

ii.* q_S was true before S came into existence only if there was a time t^* such that (a) q_S was true at t^*, and (b) it was false at t^* and at every time prior to t^* that S exists.

The eternalist Ockhamist then points out that the truth of eternalism implies that, given that there is some time or other at which it is true that S exists, condition (b) in (ii*) cannot be satisfied.

Moreover, the eternalist Ockhamist can go on to point out that, just as it has always been true that S performs A one billion years later than t_{-1B}, so, too, it has always been true that S exists. To say that S did not exist at t_{-1B} is not to say that, at t_{-1B} it was false that S exists. Rather, it is just to say that none of the events of S's life are located at t_{-1B}. Thus, given that it was true at t_{-1B} that S exists, it is hard to see any obstacle to saying that the truth of q_S is ontologically dependent on S's actual performance of A at the present time. Indeed, from an eternalist point of view, q_S is quite plausibly viewed as just an alternative (if rather oblique) way of expressing the conjunction of r_S and t_S: i.e., S performs A now and it is now one billion years after than t_{-1B}. And since everyone will agree that it is plausible to say that the truth of this latter proposition depends on what S does (in particular, r_S clearly depends on S), rather than the other way around, so, too, everyone should agree that q_S depends on what S does.

Thus, the eternalist Ockhamist can tell the following story: since q_S depends for its truth value on what S actually does at the present time, it makes perfect sense to say that S performs A freely and that S has (or had) the power to render q_S false. S's performing A at t is, we might say, "ontologically prior", even if not temporally prior, to the truth (at t_{-1B}) of the proposition that S will perform A one billion years later than t_{-1B}. Thus, on this way of thinking about why the inference from (ii) and (iii) to ($1b^*q_S$) fails, the fatalist simply gets things the wrong way around: the fatalist assumes that since the truth (at t_{-1B}) of "S will perform A one billion years later than t_{-1B}" is temporally prior to S's performance of A, its truth is ontologically prior as well; but this is precisely what the eternalist Ockhamist denies.[12]

Of course, it would be nice if the eternalist Ockhamist could give a thorough explication of the notions of "ontological dependence" and "ontological priority" that figure in her response to the fatalist. As it is, it is simply not clear whether such dependence or priority is best thought of in terms of explanation, or supervenience, or causation, or what. But it seems that, in the present case, the eternalist Ockhamist need not work this out completely. Indeed, it seems that she can point out that, ordinarily, we do not think that the truth of the proposition that S performs A is ontologically prior to S's performance of A. Indeed, we are fully prepared, in the ordinary case, to think that the proposition that S performs A is ontologically dependent on S's performance of A and, moreover, that S's performance of A is ontologically prior to the truth of the proposition that S performs A. The eternalist Ockhamist's point is that, however we ordinarily understand the relationship between true propositions about agents' actions and the agents' actions themselves, this is how we should understand the relationship between true propositions like q_S and S's performance of A at t. The action comes first, in some ontologically significant sense of "first", and the truth of the proposition succeeds it.

Note, too, that the eternalist Ockhamist can make her points about the ontological dependence of past truths like q_S on present acts of free agents in any number of ways. If she relies on the distinction between hard and soft facts, she can say that a fact F is soft (simpliciter) just in case (i) F is contingent and (ii) F is not included in any present-tense maximal state of affairs; and F is a hard fact about the past (from the point of view of a time t) just in case F is included in some present-tense maximal state of affairs that obtains earlier than t. She can then add, as seems plausible, that soft facts about the past are ontologically posterior to and dependent on the hard facts about the past. Moreover, the eternalist Ockhamist might offer, as a heuristic device, the image of two "levels" of reality: first, there's the level of hard facts, which

---

[12]Of course, the eternalist Ockhamist need not deny that there are concrete events that are both temporally *and* ontologically prior to other events. For instance, the eternalist Ockhamist need not deny that there are causal events that are both temporally and ontologically prior to their effects. Indeed, the eternalist Ockhamist qua eternalist Ockhamist is not committed to any unusual claims about the relations between concrete events. What sets her apart is her conception of the relationship between the truth value of contingently true propositions and the concrete events on which their truth values depend.

includes the concrete events that bear relations of temporal simultaneity, priority, and posteriority to one another; then there is the level of reality that includes soft facts, the temporal relations among concrete events.

Alternatively, the eternalist Ockhamist might think in terms of two distinct "ontological moments": what's ontologically "first" is the moment that includes all the concrete events and the relations of temporal simultaneity, priority, and posteriority that they bear to one another; what's ontologically "second" is the moment at which all the contingent propositions about the course of concrete events are true. But we must not allow this notion of ontological moments to confuse us: on the eternalist scheme, every concrete event that ever takes place in the course of history exists *simpliciter* just as every true proposition that describes the concrete course of events has its truth value *simpliciter*. On this scheme, a principle of unrestricted bivalence holds at all times, and every time-contingent proposition is ontologically dependent on the course of concrete events that exists *simpliciter*.

At this point, we hope that it is obvious that the presentist Ockhamist cannot tell the same story as the eternalist about the failure of the inference from:

ii. q_S was true before S came into existence,

and

iii. q_S cannot change its truth value,

to

$1b^*q_S$ S does not have, and never had, the power to render q_S false.

The presentist, after all, insists that the only time that exists *simpliciter* is the present time. She believes that the only concrete events that exist *simpliciter* are the events that are currently taking place and the only concrete objects that exist *simpliciter* are those that exist now; she cannot abide an ontological distinction between what exists *simpliciter* and what exists at the present time. So, according to the presentist, S's performance of A exists only if S is performing A at the present time. Since the presentist denies that S's performing A exists when other times—times at which S is not performing A—are present, she obviously cannot say that the truth value of q_S depends on anything that S is doing or has done. For, again, q_S was true (and unchangeably so) nearly a billion years before S ever existed; so its truth value does not depend on S's existence. Moreover, it seems clear that if presentism is true, then temporal priority implies ontological priority. So, not only are earlier events ontologically prior to later events, but the truth of propositions true at earlier times is ontologically prior to later events.

The presentist, therefore, must affirm the suppressed premise that the eternalist denied:

ii.* q_S was true before S came into existence only if there was a time t^* such that (a) q_S was true at t^*, and (b) it was false at t^* and at every time prior to t^* that S exists.

But (ii), (ii*), and (iii) together seem to imply:

iv. The unchangeable truth of q_S is temporally prior to and therefore ontologically prior to S's existence.

Moreover, it obviously follows from (iv) that:

iv*. The unchangeable truth of q_S does not depend on S or any of S's actions.

And it is difficult to deny that:

v*. If the unchangeable truth value of q_S does not depend on S or anything that S does, S does not have the power to render q_S false.

But, of course, (iv*) and (v*) together imply $1b^*q_S$. Thus, in short, the truth of (iv) seems to lead ineluctably to the truth of $1b^*q_S$. Given that this is so, and given that Ockham's way out of fatalism depends crucially on S's having the power to render q_S false, the presentist Ockhamist must deny the truth of (iv).

But to deny the truth of (iv) is to affirm the truth of:

(M) Possibly: there is a time t, proposition p, and agent S such that at t, S has the power to render p false, and S does not exist at t.

Meinongians may not balk at M's clear implication that non-existent things can be quantified over and can have and even exercise powers; but the rest of us will. And if it turns out that presentists can ward off fatalist arguments only by becoming Meinongians, most of us will be inclined to say, "So much the worse for presentism." At any rate, so *we* say. Thus we conclude that presentists cannot, in the end, rely on the Ockhamist strategy as a way out of fatalism.

IV. AN OBJECTION

But is this really fair to the presentist? After all, presentists have developed various strategies for accommodating the truth of sentences that apparently make reference to merely past or merely future objects; and they have likewise developed strategies for making sense of apparent assertions of cross-time relations (such as causal relations). So a natural thought at this junction is that perhaps these same strategies might help presentists who are attracted to Ockhamism to avoid the sorts of objections that we have been lodging against the conjunction of those two positions.

Perhaps the most promising strategy for accommodating the sorts of sentences just mentioned is what might be called the "essence strategy". We will briefly consider what this strategy amounts to and how it might be adapted as a response to the fatalist. We will then argue that the essence strategy fails to provide the presentist Ockhamist with a satisfactory response to the fatalist's argument. Though we acknowledge that there are other strategies on offer for accommodating apparent reference to merely past and future objects and for making room for apparent assertions of cross-time relations, we omit consideration of these because they all strike us as being subject to the same sorts of objections that we will raise against the essence strategy.

The essence strategy is just an extension of a familiar strategy for handling apparently problematic modal claims like:

(L) Possibly, David Letterman does not exist.

On the standard semantics for modal claims, L implies:

(L*) There is a possible world in which it is true that David Letterman does not exist.

The trouble, however, is that it looks as if the proposition that Letterman does not exist *cannot* be true in any world because in worlds where Letterman does not exist, he is not available to be a subject of predication. In other words: the proposition that Letterman does not exist is true only if it is about Letterman; but if it is about Letterman, then it cannot be true; for only existing things can stand in relations (and "aboutness" is a relation). Thus, many philosophers are inclined to treat (L) as equivalent to not (L*) but to:

(L**) There is a possible world in which nothing exemplifies an essence of David Letterman.

An essence of David Letterman is a property that is essential to Letterman and that cannot be exemplified by anything distinct from Letterman. The attraction of understanding (L) as equivalent to (L**) should be obvious: properties are abstract objects, so they exist necessarily; thus, they are guaranteed to be available in every world to be subjects of predications. Whereas it is deeply problematic to suppose that "Letterman does not exist" is about Letterman himself in worlds in which that proposition is true, it is wholly unproblematic to suppose that it is instead a proposition about Letterman's essence—equivalent to something like "Letterman's essence is not exemplified".

So goes the essence strategy for modal claims. And, of course, the presentist can adopt it to accommodate both sentences that seem to be about merely past or future objects, as well as sentences that appear to imply that there are objects that stand in diachronic relations to one another. The trick is simple: treat the problematic sentences as equivalent to claims about (necessarily existing) essences rather than as claims about concrete objects. Thus, "Abraham Lincoln was tall" will get treated as equivalent to something like "The property of being identical to Abraham Lincoln was exemplified by a tall person". Likewise, "Many philosophers admire Aristotle" will get treated as a claim about an essence of Aristotle, the causal relations between the exemplifier of that essence, things that coexisted with him, later things that coexisted with them, and, ultimately, various feelings of admiration in contemporary philosophers. The details of this story do not much matter in the context at hand. What matters for our purposes is just the basic fact that, on the essence strategy, sentences that appear to refer overtly or covertly to non-existent "things" will get treated as expressing propositions about necessarily existing properties rather than propositions about concrete objects.

The question, however, is whether the essence strategy will be of any help to the presentist in rendering plausible the claim that:

(M) Possibly: there is a time t, proposition p, and agent S such that at t S has the power to render p false, and S does not exist at t.

Obviously the proponent of the essence strategy won't want to employ the strategy in so ham-fisted a way as to make (M) imply that S's *essence* has power over the truth value of p. For, after all, essences, being properties, can't have such powers. Rather, the most natural way of employing the strategy would be to begin by arguing that:

(R1) S has the power to render p false

is (in some contexts, anyway) equivalent to something like:

$(R1_E)$ S's essence will be exemplified by something that has the power to render p false.

Likewise, then,

(E1)   E does not exist

may be treated as equivalent to:

$(E1_E)$ S's essence is not currently exemplified.

So, then, (M) becomes:

(M_E) Possibly: there is a time t, proposition p, and essence S_E such that it is true at t that S_E will be exemplified by something that has the power to render p false, and S_E is not exemplified at t.

Unlike (M), (M_E) carries no commitment to the claim that non-existent 'things' can have or exercise powers, or stand in relations. Thus M_E has the virtue of avoiding what was the primary objection to M.

The trouble, however, is that even if we grant that M_E is on better footing than M, we still must acknowledge that the fatalist can offer against M_E almost the exact same argument (with only minor alternations) that she offers against $1b^*q_S$. Thus:

v. q_S was true at a time prior to S_E's being exemplified.
vi. q_S cannot change its truth value.

Therefore:

vii. S_E cannot be exemplified by something that has the power to render q_S false.

Eternalists could (if they wished) resist this argument in just the same way that they would resist the earlier argument from (ii) and (iii) to $1b^*q_S$. But the basic problem for the presentist remains: q_S is unchangeably true *before it is ever true that S exists*; thus, it is difficult to see how S could possibly have power over the truth value of q_S. Asserting M_E —presumably with an eye to saying that it was true one billion years ago that S's essence will be exemplified by someone who has the power to render q_S

false—does not demonstrate how S could have power over the truth value of q_s. Rather, it simply asserts that it can. This is not argument; it is merely contradicting the fatalist's conclusion.

So, the essence strategy seems unpromising. Again, there are other strategies upon which a presentist might try to draw; but, as we said earlier, all of those strategies are subject to similar objections. This is because every extant strategy for accommodating sentences that appear either to refer to merely past or merely future things or to posit cross-time relations between objects will share one thing in common with the essence strategy: they will imply that, for times at which S does not exist, a sentence like "at t, S has the power to render p false" is to be understood as expressing a proposition that is (a) false; (b) about a non-existent object; or (c) about something other than S. But—for exactly the reasons discussed in our treatment of the essence strategy—none of these alternatives will issue in a translation of M that will help us to see how S could have the power to render q_s false at those times prior to S's ever having existed.

And so we conclude that eternalists are able to adopt Ockham's way out of fatalism while presentists cannot. At this point, at least one of us wishes to leave open the possibility that the presentist can offer a successful response to the fatalist's argument. But we must conclude that the response that some consider the best response available—Ockham's way out—is unavailable to the presentist.

ACKNOWLEDGMENTS

We are grateful to Michael Bergmann, Alvin Plantinga, and Dean Zimmerman for helpful comments on earlier versions of this paper, and we are especially grateful to Michael Bergmann for many helpful conversations and extended correspondence about the issues discussed herein. Alicia Finch's work on this paper was supported by the Notre Dame Center for Philosophy of Religion; Michael Rea's work on this paper was supported by an NEH Summer Stipend.

11

GEACHIANISM

Patrick Todd

In his 1977 monograph, *Providence and Evil*, P. T. Geach articulated a position on divine omniscience, future contingents, and providence that has been widely interpreted as a version of (or precursor to) "open theism." Unfortunately, however, and despite Geach's philosophical eminence, the distinctive view that he proposed has had little impact on the massive literature on such topics.[1] Indeed, those philosophers—with one primary exception—who have read *Providence and Evil* have either failed to notice that Geach was arguing for a radically new view on the logic of future contingents or have not thought it worth commenting on. Admittedly, this is perhaps because Geach himself did not systematically develop the distinctive view he was proposing. I aim to do so here, albeit in a non-exhaustive, preliminary way. I call the resulting view "Geachianism".[2] Though Geach's view is certain to be controversial, I claim that it deserves the status of a theoretical contender in these debates. Moreover, a discussion of Geach's view illuminates various subtle and fascinating points about the dilemma of freedom and foreknowledge not previously noticed in the literature on these topics.

The plan of the paper is as follows. To set the stage, I first briefly present the most sophisticated characterization of "open-theism" on offer, one recently developed by Alan Rhoda.[3] Having other "open-theistic" views on the table will allow us better to understand and situate Geach's view. Second, I explain and motivate Geach's view of future contingents, and respond to some of the objections it faces,

---

[1]This is a deficiency my co-authors (John Martin Fischer and Neal Tognazzini) and I have recently tried to remedy. See Fischer et al. (2009). We give a brief sketch of the Geachian view that I here develop at length.

[2]However, just as there is sometimes a question as to whether Aristotle is an Aristotelian, there may likewise be a question whether Geach is a Geachian. As I remarked, Geach did not systematically develop his position on these matters. Thus, while the position I develop seems to me to be the plain consequence of what Geach suggests, in what follows I may go beyond what Geach himself would endorse.

[3]See Rhoda (2008).

notably those made by Jonathan Kvanvig, in what is (as far as I know) the only explicit discussion of Geach's view in the philosophical literature.[4] Next, I show how such a view enables a particular reply to the argument for the incompatibility of foreknowledge and freedom of Nelson Pike's seminal 1965 paper, "Divine Omniscience and Voluntary Action." Historically, however, open theism has not been a mere reaction to this argument, but has had distinctively theological motivations stemming from a (putative) "plain reading" of certain scriptural passages and the desire for a particular account of divine providence. An application of Geach's view to such topics will show that it has certain advantages over traditional "open" views.

I. RHODA ON "GENERIC OPEN THEISM"

First, Rhoda thinks all open theists must be committed to theism (rather than *process theism*) and indeterminism, or the "causal openness" of the future.[5] As Rhoda notes, the primary, historical motivation for the adoption of indeterminism amongst theists has been the (putative) existence of *libertarian freedom*, the exercise of which requires indeterminism. Now, on Rhoda's view, open theists depart from other indeterminist theists in maintaining that if it is causally open whether some state of affairs occurs at some time, then it is impossible for God to know beforehand that it will or will not occur. Ockhamists and Molinists, for instance, maintain that, of the causally possible futures, God knows that some *particular* future is the actual one. Open theists (says Rhoda) demur; on open theism, the future is "epistemically open" for God in the sense that there are some states of affairs such that God neither knows that they *will* obtain nor that they *will not* obtain. This is the central feature of Rhoda's characterization of "generic open theism".

In brief, the characterization is "generic" in the sense that it is neutral between the camps of the two most prominent open-theist positions. According to one camp, future contingents—propositions which say of some undetermined event that it will happen—are never true. On this view, if it is causally open whether X obtains at $t3$, then it cannot even be *true* at (some earlier time) $t1$ that X will obtain at $t3$. And if it is not *true at* $t1$ that X will obtain at $t3$, then God (given his essential omniscience) does not believe at $t1$ that X will (or will not) obtain at $t3$. The future is thus epistemically open for God in the sense at stake. We may call those

---

[4]See Kvanvig (1986: ch. 1).

[5]The relationship between process theism and open theism is historically complex, but I need not enter into the relevant details. In short, open theists have consistently wished to distinguish their views from those of process theists, who *inter alia* deny creation *ex nihilo* and God's ability to unilaterally intervene in the world in the ways imagined by traditional theists.

in this camp "open-future open theists". In this camp, there is yet another important division: those who maintain that the relevant future contingent propositions are neither true nor false (hence denying bivalence) and those who believe such propositions are uniformly false. This is an important (and often neglected) distinction, and interested readers would do well to consult Rhoda's work on these issues.[6] Prominent open-future open theists include (anachronistically, controversially, and somewhat tendentiously) Aristotle[7] and J. R. Lucas (who deny bivalence),[8] and Charles Hartshorne[9] and Rhoda himself (who do not).[10]

The other prominent open-theist camp does not maintain that future contingent propositions are not *true*, but that it is impossible for God to know them, despite their being true. This impossibility generates the relevant divine epistemic openness. According to this version of open theism, it is logically impossible for God to know how future indeterminacies (such as our free decisions) will unfold. Assuming indeterminism, then it follows that the future is epistemically open for God. Taking after Rhoda, we may call this version "limited foreknowledge open theism". Richard Swinburne and William Hasker have been the primary defenders of this version of open theism, though Peter van Inwagen has recently defended it as well.[11]

Rhoda's analysis of "generic open theism" helpfully shows what these versions of open theism have in common. Both maintain that the future is epistemically open for God. That is, both maintain that there are some possibly future states of affairs such that God knows neither that they will nor will not obtain. And it would seem that this thesis is essential to open theism; it apparently captures its defining

---

[6]See, e.g., Rhoda et al. (2006).

[7]Though Aristotle is widely interpreted as denying bivalence for future contingents in *On Interpretation* 9, some philosophers—notably Anscombe—have disputed this.

[8]See Lucas (1989).

[9]By including Hartshorne here, I do not mean to imply that Hartshorne is himself an open theist; he is, rather, a process theist whose views on future contingents are amenable both to process theism and open theism. Hartshorne was the first (of which I am aware) to defend the view that future contingents are uniformly false. According to Hartshorne (and later Rhoda), if at $t1$ it is not determined that X happens at $t3$ (or does not happen at $t3$), then at $t1$ it is false that X will happen at $t3$ and it is false that X will not happen at $t3$. "Will" and "will not" are *contraries* rather than *contradictories*. Even if the view in question entered contemporary discussion primarily through Prior (Rhoda's primary source for the view), as seems to be the case, it would be unseemly not to credit Hartshorne here. Even if he is not an open theist, his view can be (and has been) adopted by open theists. See Hartshorne (1965) for his development of the view.

[10]See Rhoda et al. (2006). See also Prior (2003). Prior seems to *formulate* the view in question (see especially p. 54's discussion of Peirce), but does not unambiguously endorse it, and in places would seem to deny bivalence. Prior's work on this matter is complicated, and for the purposes of this paper I set aside the question of his actual views.

[11]See Swinburne (1993); Hasker (1989); and Van Inwagen (2008).

feature—what puts the "open" in "open theism", as Rhoda says. Indeed, how could one be an open theist if one *denies* that there are some things about which God neither knows that they will nor will not happen? If for every state of affairs, God knows that it will happen or that it will not happen, the future would plainly be epistemically *settled* for God, as Rhoda puts it. Of the myriad causally possible futures, God would know that some one of them is *the actual one*. If we think of causal possibility in terms of branches off a single path, God would see that one such branch is "lit up" with what Nuel Belnap and Mitchell Green have called "the thin red line", indicating that *it* is the special branch—the one that uniquely *will* obtain, the one which is such that it is *going to happen*.[12] And this is just the traditional view of divine foreknowledge. Such considerations would appear to be decisive, but they are decisive only under the supposition that something that is going to happen cannot later be such that it is no longer going to happen—only under the supposition, that is, that *the future cannot change*. Geach denies this. To these issues I now turn.

II. GEACH AND THE MUTABILITY OF THE FUTURE

As I remarked at the outset, it would be an understatement to say that Geach's views about future contingents have not been widely influential. But what is the view?

To begin, what is distinctive of Geach's view is that it is possible for something to be such that, at *t*1, it will happen at *t*3, but at *t*2 such that it will not happen at *t*3. That is, at *t*1, it was true that X would happen at *t*3, but at *t*2, something intervened to make it the case that X would not happen at *t*3. The future thus *changes* in the sense that something was going to happen, but now no longer is going to happen, and does not happen. In support of his case, Geach points to the logic of *prevention*. According to Geach, those things are *prevented* from happening which were such that they were *going to happen* but nevertheless do not happen. Moreover, if something is *going to happen*, then it *will* happen; these expressions are logically equivalent.[13] The result is that what will occur as of one time may later be such that it will not occur. It seems best to let Geach (largely) speak for himself. In considering one example, Geach asks rhetorically:

> But what then is prevented? Not what did happen, but assuredly what was going
> to happen. The aeroplane was going to crash into the sea and 100 men were going

to be drowned; the pilot's prompt action prevented this. For not everything that does not happen is prevented: only what was going to happen.[14]

Geach says he takes it as a "truism" that "anything that is prevented is something that was going to happen but didn't happen." He then asks:

> But if something did happen, doesn't this show it was after all going to happen? Certainly; but not that it *always* was going to happen. Perhaps, before the preventative action was taken, not this but something else was going to happen; but then the preventative action was taken, and after that *this* was going to happen and did happen. Before the pilot's daring manoeuvre, the plane was going to crash; but after that the plane was going to land safely and did land safely.[15]

Geach goes on:

> So what was going to happen at an earlier time may not be going to happen at a later time, because of some action taken in the interim. This is the way we can change the future: we can and often do bring it about that it will not be the case that *p*; although before our action it was going to be the case that *p*; it was right to say, then, "It is going to be the case that *p*." Before the operation it was right to say "Johnny is going to bleed to death from the injury": after the operation this was no longer the case.[16]

So the view is that the future is *mutable* in a particular way. On open-future views, we often so act that we give the future a more determinate shape; we sometimes make it so that (previously) what only *might* or *will probably* happen becomes such that now it simply *will* happen. Geach's view is different. We change the future in a more radical way: we make it so that what will happen ends up not happening, or that what previously was such that it will not happen *does* happen. What will happen changes. No other view—"open" or otherwise—maintains this distinctive thesis.

I believe we can best understand Geach's position by contrasting it with the other possible views on whether a future contingent proposition can change its truth-value over time. For simplicity, I consider only other *tensed* views which take it that in saying "X will happen at *t*10", one expresses a proposition in which the

[14]Geach (1977: 47).
[15]Ibid. (48).
[16]Ibid. (50).

future tense is fundamental and irreducible; one does *not* express a proposition like "X happens at *t*10". Consider:

(P) X will happen at *t*10.

Suppose (P) is future contingent. Can (P) change its truth-value over time? There are three (somewhat arbitrarily named) options we must consider. Intuitively, the three options are no change, change in one direction only, and change in both directions. Consider first:

The standard tensed theory of time: (P) cannot go from being false to being true, and cannot go from being true to being false until *t*10 is present.

According to what I am calling the "standard" tensed view, (P) cannot go from being false to true, and can only go from true to false *once t10 is present or in the past*. On the tensed view, recall, a proposition like (P) is *not* reducible to a tenseless proposition; the tense is fundamental or basic. So while "X will happen at *t*10", if true, has always been true up until *t*10, it becomes false at and after *t*10. That is, if *t*10 is in the present or past, it is false that something *will* happen at *t*10.

The next option to consider is the one endorsed by those who believe there are no true future contingent propositions, such as open-future open theists. If future contingents are uniformly false, then we have:

The open-bivalentist tensed theory of time: (P) can go from being false to being true, but cannot go from being true to being false until *t*10 is present.

And if future contingents are neither true nor false:

The open-non-bivalentist tensed theory of time: (P) can go from being neither true nor false to being true, but cannot go from being true to being neither true nor false (or false), until *t*10 is present.

On the view in question, it is not true that X *will* happen at *t*10 unless it is causally necessary that X happens at *t*10. Such causal factors may not be in place at *t*1, but may come into place at *t*3. Thus, at *t*3 it becomes true (whereas it was previously false, or neither true nor false) that X will happen at *t*10. In this way, a proposition about the future can become true. Once X is determined to occur at *t*10, it cannot later become undetermined that it occurs at *t*10. Thus, (P) cannot go from being true to being false (or neither true nor false), at least until *t*10 is present or past, in which case (P) will be false for the reasons just given on the "standard" view.

The last view is Geach's:

Geachianism: (P) can go from being true to being false, and from being false to being true, but must remain false when *t*10 is present or past.

We have seen the reasons Geach cites for thinking that (P) can change its truth values in these ways. X could have been going to happen, but got prevented from happening. In that case, (P) goes from true to false. On the other hand, perhaps X was not going to happen, but something arose that prevented what was going to happen, with the result that now X *is* going to happen. In that case, (P) goes from being false to being true. In sum, then, we have three intuitive options concerning whether (P) can change in truth value (before *t*10): no change in truth value (the standard view), change in one direction only (open-future views), and change in both directions (Geachianism).

III. ON BEHALF OF GEACHIANISM

Well, what can be said on behalf of Geachianism? The first thing to say on its behalf is simply that we very often *say* that things were going to happen but were prevented from happening. The plane was going to crash, but it didn't. Johnny was going to bleed to death, but he didn't. And not only do we say these things, but they seem true. Once we recognize it as such, the mutability of the future actually turns out to be a presupposition of a wide range of our discourse. So the first thing to say on behalf of Geachianism is that it very often seems true to say that the future changed.

Of course, many will want to attempt to explain away the appearances here. The second thing to say on behalf of Geachianism is that explaining it all away turns out to be surprisingly difficult. Recall Geach's example of the plane crash; the plane was going to crash, but the pilot prevented this from happening. The most obvious way to try to explain away the appearance of a changing future here is to maintain that it was never true that the plane was going to crash *simpliciter*, but only that it was going to crash *unless some preventative action is taken*. In other words, one interprets "The plane is going to crash" as elliptical for a merely *conditional* claim. Geach anticipates this response. As he says:

> I am prepared for the objection that I have been systematically equivocating upon two senses of "going to happen": what actually will happen, and—well, what? What will happen if nothing prevents it, perhaps. My complaint now is not that this phrase just boils down to "What will happen unless it doesn't"; for I myself do not identify what does not happen with what is prevented. But I do say that the

explanation is useless. For what is prevented is always something that is going to happen, in the very sense of "going to happen" that we are supposed to be explaining; "prevent" has to be explained in terms of *this* "going to happen," so we cannot use "prevent" to explain it. As for the "actually" in "what will actually happen," it has no more logical force than a thump on the table has.[17]

In other words, Geach claims that some notion of something's "going to happen" is required for an analysis of prevention. The point is subtle, yet important. What is prevented is that which was *in some sense* going to happen. But in what sense? Here, one cannot say: what was going to happen unless something prevented it. For this sense of "going to happen" already *includes* the notion of prevention, and what we are looking for is the sense in which what is prevented was "going to happen". According to Geach, prevention cannot be properly analyzed without appeal to what is "going to happen". Thus, this way of explaining away the appearance of a changing future fails.

Of course, this strategy of responding to Geach would be back on the table if one could provide an alternative account of prevention—an account that does not identify the prevented with what was going to happen but did not. Again, the objector wishes to explain away the appearance of a changing future in Geach's examples; it was never really true that the plane was going to crash, only that it was going to crash unless prevented from crashing. But here Geach complains that what is prevented *just is* what was going to happen. Geach's (unspoken) challenge, then, is to provide an analysis of prevention that does not identify the prevented with what was going to happen but didn't. And, in the only critical discussion of Geach's view of which I am aware, Jonathan Kvanvig aims to do precisely that.[18] To Kvanvig's analysis I now turn.

IV. KVANVIG ON PREVENTION

As an analysis of prevention, Kvanvig offers us this:

> The truth of p is prevented by $S = df$ S's doing A is causally sufficient in the circumstances for the falsity of p, and the circumstances apart from S's doing A are such that p would have been true, were those circumstances to obtain.[19]

---

[17]Geach (1977: 51–52).

[18]There is a brief statement of Geach's view in Anthony Kenny (1987: 53–54). There is also a discussion of Geach's view of the future in the Introduction to Fischer (1989: 23–25). In short, Fischer—taking after Kvanvig—represents Geach as claiming that truths about the future are only *apparently* about the future, and are really about the present tendencies of things. But these issues are orthogonal to my purposes in this paper; I thus set them aside. Also, Alfred Freddoso (1983) has a brief mention of the view, as does Michael Dummett (1982: 87).

[19]Kvanvig (1986: 10).

Kvanvig analyzes what it is for an *action* to prevent the truth of a *proposition*. However, we might wish for a more general account of prevention; while the sort of prevention at issue concerns human actions, presumably non-agential causes can still be preventative. Moreover, I find it more natural to think in terms of one *event* preventing another. Hence, I propose to replace Kvanvig's analysis with the following (compatible) analysis, where X and Y are *events*:

> X is prevented by Y = df. Y is causally sufficient for X's failing to obtain, and had Y not obtained, X would have obtained.

Let us call the proposed analysis *the counterfactual analysis of prevention*. The idea here is simple enough. On this analysis, the pilot's action prevented the crash because, had the pilot not acted, the plane would have crashed, and the pilot's action was sufficient for the plane's not crashing. Isn't this a satisfactory analysis of prevention? Geach identifies the prevented as that which was going to happen but did not. Kvanvig's counterfactual account identifies it as what would have happened had something else not.[20]

But the counterfactual account of prevention faces problems. First, it appears to lead to an explosion of preventions. Consider the following case. Presumably nearly everyone in Los Angeles went to bed at roughly the normal hour last night. Now, what would have happened had they not? Well, it is hard to say, but we can imagine that there would have been some additional car crashes today (on account of drowsy drivers) and perhaps some additional fights (on account of irritability), and a great deal else. But everyone's going to bed at the normal hour was causally sufficient for these things not happening. Now, suppose some intrepid reporter at the *Los Angeles Times*, desperate for a story, and getting hold of the counterfactual account of prevention, pens the following:

> Actions of L.A. Residents Prevent Car Crashes and Fights
> In what would prove to be a fortunate turn of events, most L.A. residents went to bed at the normal hour last night, thereby preventing the great many car crashes and fights that would have resulted had they not.

---

[20]Other philosophers have sought to analyze prevention counterfactually. The literature on this topic has as its primary origin attempts to understand the nature of *causation*. That is, the central questions are, e.g., whether preventions can be causes, whether by catching a ball that was headed toward a window, I prevent the window's being broken, even if you would have caught the ball anyway, and so on. See, e.g., Dowe (2001). I believe Dowe's analysis, while slightly different than Kvanvig's, is subject to the same problems.

This is not an altogether comfortable result for the counterfactual account of prevention. One might think it more appropriate to deny that L.A. residents going to bed at the normal hour prevented all this from happening. But the counterfactual account of prevention would have it that this is precisely what they did. Examples such as this could be multiplied *ad nauseam*, but the point is clear. A great many things that would have happened had something else not are not generally thought to have been *prevented* from happening. Geach has a diagnosis of why not: they were never going to happen in the first place.

Of course, this problem for the counterfactual account of prevention does not (so it seems to me) *decisively refute* the account. It is open to one to simply maintain that everyone's going to sleep at the normal time did prevent these things. But there are other potential problems for the view. Consider this example suggested to me by Kenneth Boyce:

> Nuclear war is not going to happen because our adversaries have firmly decided that they will not launch their nuclear weapons (in such a way as to causally settle the matter), regardless of whether Obama chooses to sign the peace treaty or not. But Obama does sign the peace treaty, and his doing so is also causally sufficient for nuclear war's not happening. However, in all the nearest worlds in which Obama does not sign the peace treaty, it is because McCain won the election. And in all those worlds, McCain launches *our* nuclear weapons, thereby causing nuclear war. So we have it that Obama does something that is causally sufficient for nuclear war's failing to occur, and we have it that had Obama not signed the treaty, nuclear war would have occurred. Yet it is false that Obama prevented nuclear war, since our adversaries had already decided not to launch the nuclear weapons regardless of whether he signs the treaty.

Geach, however, is not susceptible to this problem: given the firm intentions of our adversaries, nuclear war is not going to happen, and thus Obama does not prevent it by signing the treaty. But there are several features of this counter-example that deserve brief comment. First, it relies on the Lewis-Stalnaker account of the truth of counterfactuals, namely that their truth is determined by so-called "nearness" to the actual world. Second, it exploits overdetermination: Obama's signing the treaty overdetermines that there is no nuclear war. Third, it relies on the truth of a *back-tracker*: had Obama not signed the treaty, then McCain would have been elected (and would have launched our nuclear weapons). This last feature of the case is, of course, especially controversial; many would balk at the notion that this counterfactual is true. However, certainly many accept that such backtrackers are sometimes true, and thus this counter-example would seem to have some degree of purchase.

At any rate, what is clear is that the counterfactual account of prevention faces problems, problems the diagnosis of which seem to point toward Geachianism. And whether *any* counterfactual analysis of prevention can be successful is far from clear—especially so clearly successful as to make its adoption mandatory in the face of Geach's. However, if indeed no counterfactual account of prevention can be successful, then what would seem the most promising way of explaining away the appearance of a changing future is lost. Reconsider Geach's plane crash case. The plane was going to crash, but the pilot prevented this from happening. Geach sees here a changing future. But if one is averse to a changing future, by far the most natural thing to say about this case is simply that the plane would have crashed had the pilot not acted. However, it turns out that this counterfactual *does not* capture the fact that the pilot prevented the plane from crashing; prevention cannot be analyzed counterfactually. How then to explain away the appearance of a changing future? It isn't clear.

V. A PROBLEM FOR GEACH'S TREATMENT OF PREVENTION?

Suppose prevention cannot be analyzed counterfactually. That would certainly make it more difficult to explain away the force of Geach's examples. However, the mere failure (if it is a failure) of the counterfactual account does not by itself vindicate Geach's account of prevention. Geach's account may have problems of its own. Consider this case.[21] Suppose Jones is working on the uppermost levels of a skyscraper when he loses his balance and falls. Thankfully, he is caught by a safety net, which had been in place all along, and thus does not fall to his death. In this case, it is natural to say that the safety net prevented his death. However, it does not seem appropriate in this case to say that Jones was going to fall to his death. He was never going to, precisely because the net was always there—the net was always going to prevent his fall. In this case, then, something prevented Jones from falling to his death, even though this was never going to happen. We thus seemingly have a counterexample to Geach's account of prevention.

What should the Geachian say in response to this example? I think the Geachian should argue that this case is not an instance of the phenomenon the analysis of which is currently at stake. The Geachian should say that what we are trying to analyze is what it is for one event to prevent another. But in this case, it is notable that it is the *net* that is said to have prevented Jones's fall to his death. And the net is not an event. Of course, one could attempt to translate this case into the parlance of

---

[21]Thanks to an anonymous referee for pressing this case.

events—perhaps the event of *the net's being there* prevented Jones's fall. But this is at best a gerrymandered event, and thus it is open to the Geachian to argue that the case is not an instance of the phenomenon in question.

But the Geachian can say more—much more. Suppose that workers on this particular building regularly fall and are caught by the net. Suppose, in fact, that they treat the net as just another feature of the building itself, which they perhaps jump on when they wish to quickly descend a few levels of the structure, and as it happens Jones merely slipped just prior to when he was about to jump in any case. It would then seem like the net prevents Jones's death in precisely the same manner in which the *floor* he is standing on prevents his death. For without the floor, of course, Jones would fall to his death. (Jumping on the net is, so the thought goes, just like stepping on the floor.) Of course, once we see prevention here, we'll see it *everywhere*. The couch I am sitting on prevents me from falling to the ground. The pillow supporting my laptop prevents it from falling onto my lap. And so on.

And if one claims that these cases are cases of the same sort of phenomenon Geach sought to analyze—that of one event preventing another—then the explosion problem not only returns, but returns with a vengeance. For it will turn out that (seemingly) an infinite number of events are now preventing my death. Which events? Well, for starters, *the oxygen in the room's being there*, since without that oxygen, I would asphyxiate and die. Or suppose we have yet another intrepid reporter, this time at *The New York Times*. And suppose he pens the following headline: "Events in New York today prevent the deaths of millions." What drama unfolded today in New York? Why, the braces of the skyscrapers in the city being there! Such a result is, of course, absurd. One could admit that the braces prevent the collapse of the buildings, but deny that any events do so. But I do not see how this result can be avoided if one allows *the net's being there* to be an event that prevented Jones's death. In sum, then, the Geachian may argue that an analysis of one event's preventing another is something worth having, and contend that cases of the sort in question pose no threat to Geach's analysis of this phenomenon.[22]

---

[22]More generally, of course, the Geachian should (I say) contend that in those cases in which it *is* correct to say that one (non-gerrymandered) event prevented another, it will also be the case that the prevented event was going to happen. However, I hesitate to tie the success of Geachianism too closely to Geach's claim that what is prevented is always what was going to happen. What would it mean for Geachianism if this case (or some other) were a counterexample to this claim? Recall the initial challenge: that all that was true prior to the pilot's action was that the plane was going to crash unless prevented from crashing. Again, here Geach says: but what is prevented just is what was going to happen. But this reply is not open to Geach if there are counterexamples to this thesis. And if so, then Geachianism certainly loses some strength; part of its strength comes from the availability of this Geachian reply and its forcing the objector to take up the seriously problematic counterfactual account of prevention. So I would recommend to any Geachian a

So let us recap. We began with a challenge to the Geachian: that all that was true, prior to the pilot's action, was *not* that the plane was going to crash, but that it was going to unless the pilot prevented it. Here, however, Geach complains that what is prevented *just is* what was going to happen, and thus that this way of explaining away the appearance of a changing future fails. Kvanvig objects that we can understand prevention counterfactually: we can understand the claim that the plane was going to crash but that the pilot prevented it (roughly) as the claim that it would have crashed had he not acted.[23] But I raised what I think are serious problems for the counterfactual account, problems the diagnosis of which point toward Geachianism. In sum, then, I do not think Kvanvig's objection decisively refutes Geach's view.

VI. KVANVIG ON PREDICTIONS

But Kvanvig has another criticism of Geach's view, which he nicely puts as follows:

> Before Johnny's operation, Geach correctly notes that it was right to say "Johnny is going to bleed to death." However, what is not clear is that the statement *Johnny is going to bleed to death* is true before the operation. From the perspective of the observers, it appeared true and hence it was proper to claim to be true; but something can be proper to claim even though untrue. In this case we can appreciate the difference by noting that it would be appropriate for the observers to note, after the operation, that their earlier claim was false.[24]

By way of response, we first ought to note that Geach's view need not have it that *every time* something appears to us as if it is going to happen, it is true that it *is* going to happen. Thus, it could very well be that (despite appearances) Johnny was not going to bleed to death all along, and thus it would be appropriate for the observers

---

stalwart defense of Geach's account of prevention. However, a Geachian *could* simply insist that even if one could maintain that only the mere conditional was true, there is no ultimately compelling reason to adopt this thesis. That is, perhaps someone will say that all that was true was that the plane was going to crash unless prevented from crashing. However, the Geachian may simply have the firm intuition that this *isn't* all that was true: it was also true that the plane was going to crash. If so, he needn't rely on the reply that what is prevented just is what was going to happen (though, again, this claim would certainly help his case). And thus he needn't defend this claim against (putative) counterexamples. In short, he simply needs the claim that prevention *sometimes* changes the future, not that it always does.

[23]Note: the Geachian's claim is not (or needn't be) the claim that this counterfactual is not *true*, but that it does not account for the case being one of prevention.

[24]Kvanvig (1986: 7).

to note after the operation that their earlier claim was false. Despite what Geach may intimate, his examples are best thought of as what is *in principle possible*, and not as examples of how things always are.

But suppose this is a case in which it is indeed taken to be true that Johnny was going to bleed to death.[25] Then the response to Kvanvig must be hard-line. In this case, it is not appropriate for the observers to note after the operation that their earlier claim was false. Rather, it is appropriate for them to be thankful that the future changed. Suppose Rob unexpectedly loses his job. Should he conclude that he was going to lose it all along—that it was true two weeks ago, when he was working on his crucial project, that he was going to lose it? Of course not, says the Geachian. Perhaps he *was* going to keep it, but disaster struck his project. In the present case, should we conclude from the fact that Johnny has not bled to death that he never was going to? Again, of course not.[26]

It is well known that views denying that future contingents are true face the problem of accounting for the practice of retroactively predicating truth to predictions. This is Kvanvig's criticism; since Johnny has not in fact bled to death, it follows that it would have been true to say before the operation that he would not, and consequently that it was false that he would.[27] It must be admitted, I think, that this practice does constitute some evidence against such views. Geach's view faces the same problem. Various strategies of explaining away such retroactive predications

---

[25]These points raise questions for the Geachian. Just when is it true—and what, if anything, makes it true—that something is "going to happen"? This is an extremely difficult question, and I do not have the space to adequately address it. I note only that all those philosophers who have commented on Geach's view have attributed to him—and for good textual reason—the view that X is going to happen iff there is some appropriate present tendency toward X's happening. While such a view is an option for the Geachian, it is not the only one: the Geachian can maintain that what is going to happen is simply brute—that what, if anything, makes it true that X is going to happen is the fact that it is going to. Ironically, it seems plain to me that the only theorists in this debate who can mount a principled objection to this claim are other open theists—open futurists who claim that such truths must be grounded in determinative causal tendencies. These points deserve further elaboration, like others in this paper, but I must set them aside.

[26]Perhaps some will complain that I am cheating here by framing the issue in terms of what was *going to* happen rather than in terms of what *would* happen. For some may say that it is more counterintuitive to suppose that something *would* happen but later does not than it is to suppose that something *was going to* happen but later does not. Well, perhaps I am indeed cheating here. However, at this stage of the dialectic, I believe the Geachian is entitled to the equivalence of *X is going to happen* with *X will happen*. Perhaps these expressions mean different things or have different truth conditions. If so, then perhaps this raises a problem for the Geachian, or makes the present problem more difficult. But I do not see that it is dialectically infelicitous to rely on this equivalence in the current defense of the view.

[27]For another (later) statement of this objection, see Freddoso (1988: 71–72).

of truth have been proposed, and here I simply note that such (or similar) strategies are likewise available to the Geachian.[28] In short, I do not believe this problem to be decisive against the Geachian. Thus, while Kvanvig's criticism of Geach's proposal does point out a legitimate problem for his approach, Geachianism still (I claim) emerges as a theoretical contender.

VII. SMART AND PLANTINGA ON THE IMPOSSIBILITY OF CHANGING THE FUTURE

Besides the logic of prevention, there is at least one other argumentative strategy one may use to reach Geach's conclusions, a strategy recently pursued by Mark Hinchliff.[29] According to Hinchliff, it is commonplace and intuitive that we cannot change the past, but that we can change the future. It is a virtue of a theory if it can preserve this asymmetry. But (arguably) only on Geach's view can we genuinely change the future.

But it is here that we encounter incredulous dismissals of a changing future by J. J. C. Smart and Alvin Plantinga.[30] Here is Smart:

> It makes no more sense to talk of changing the future than it does of changing the past. Suppose that I decide to change the future, by having coffee for breakfast tomorrow instead of my usual tea. Have I changed the future? No. For coffee for breakfast *was* the future. . . . [T]he fact that our present actions determine the future would be most misleadingly expressed or described by saying that we can change the future. A man can change his trousers, his club, or his job. . . . But one thing he cannot change is the future, since whatever he brings about *is* the future, and nothing else is, or ever was.[31]

---

[28]See, e.g., Rhoda (2006). Note: I am not claiming that the problem Kvanvig has raised for Geach is entirely isomorphic to the similar problem facing open-future open theists. For on Geach's view, from the fact that X has not happened, we cannot conclude that it was never going to—"X will happen" might have been true at some time in the past. Not so for open futurists. Still, *both* maintain that from the fact that X *has* happened, we cannot conclude that it was always going to. However, it is not clear that this difference makes the prediction problem any harder for the Geachian than it is for the open futurist; at any rate, I set this issue aside.

[29]As far as I know, Hinchliff is the only contemporary philosopher who defends Geach's position. Hinchliff defended the view in a talk given at the University of California, Riverside in the fall of 2007. Indeed, I owe it to Hinchliff for bringing Geach's view to my attention. A defense of the Geachian position has not yet appeared in Hinchliff's published work.

[30]To be clear, neither Smart nor Plantinga are explicitly addressing Geach in these passages.

[31]Geach (1977: 52).

Not surprisingly, Geach regards Smart's statements here as mere assertion. After giving us Smart's quote, Geach immediately says:

> "Or ever was," indeed! If A is bringing something about, no doubt that is what *is now* going to happen; but what has Smart done to show that it *always was* going to happen, even before A's action? Nothing; he has merely asserted it.[32]

Plantinga says even less than Smart. Can someone, say Paul, change the future? Says Plantinga:

> To alter the future, Paul must do something like this: he must perform some action *A* at a time *t* before 9:21 such that prior to *t* it is true that Paul will walk out at 9:21, but after *t* (after he performs *A*) false that he will.

This is, of course, precisely what Geach believes can happen. But Plantinga says, "neither Paul nor anyone—not even God—can do something like that. So the future is no more alterable than the past."[33] The Geachian diagnosis is again clear: this is mere assertion.

In Smart's case, the fundamental disagreement clearly arises from the fact that Smart is a *reductionist* about tense or a so-called *de-tenser*.[34] Such a view is plainly at odds with Geach's. According to the reductionist, all tensed statements are to be analyzed in purely *tenseless* terms; tense is not a fundamental feature of reality. On such a view, propositions have their truth values *eternally*, so it is impossible for a proposition to have one truth value at one time and a different one at another; in fact, propositions are not true at times at all, but simply *true*. Such a view is closely related to the so-called B-theory of time. According to the B-theory, there is no objective present or "now." Events are not objectively past, present, or future, but are merely earlier than, simultaneous with, and later than one's vantage point. And events have their B-series order *eternally*—if X is ever earlier than Y, then X is *always* earlier than Y.

Geach, however, is working with a rival conception of time and tense.[35] Unlike Smart's, Geach's is a *tensed* theory of time—he "takes tense seriously," as it is sometimes said. On this view, tensed features of our statements are not reducible to, and cannot be understood in terms of, tenseless statements. Propositions are true *at*

---

[32]Ibid. (52).

[33]Plantinga (1986), reprinted in Fischer (1989: 189). I thank Mark Hinchliff for bringing this passage to my attention.

[34]See Smart (1964).

[35]See, e.g., Geach's important and influential 1965 essay, "Some Problems about Time."

times and can change truth values over time. The tensed view is closely related to the A-theory of time. On the A-theory, there *is* an objective present, and events have irreducibly tensed properties of being past, present, or future. To be sure, a tensed theory of time does not straightforwardly *entail* Geach's position. But it is important to see whether objections to Geach's view are in fact objections to the tensed theory of time more generally, which has many able defenders, including, of course, Geach himself.[36]

So much for Smart and Plantinga on changing the future. But one last point. On Geach's view, even though something *will* happen—*actually* will happen—it can very well fail to happen. Perhaps you think this is a strange, counterintuitive result. If it really is true that something is going to happen, how could it fail to? If this has been your reaction to Geach's view, then I must warn you that you may be in danger of becoming an open futurist. For it is clearly the central thesis of open-future views—and logical fatalism—that if something will happen in the future, it *cannot* later fail to happen. If it will happen, then it is inevitable. Some of Geach's in-house rivals are welcome to feel incredulity at this feature of Geach's view. Those who do not wish to enter the fold are not.[37]

This is, I believe, an important issue. Indeed, commenting on an earlier draft of this paper, one friend (and a very good philosopher!), himself certainly no friend to open-future views, fell hard for the "trap" I had wanted to set up above. That is, he expressed wholehearted agreement that the relevant claim—that what will happen can fail to happen—is a "strange, counterintuitive result." But moments later he noticed where that had led him: away from Geach, but now into the arms—or the jaws—of the fatalist. Of course, this lone anecdote hardly *establishes* anything. But I believe it reveals something important. Geach presents us with a view on which what will happen might not. Open futurists (and fatalists) have an easy time criticizing this view. Others, however, must tread carefully. They must claim that what is objectionable about Geach's view is his claim that what will happen might—well, what? Not *might not*. Perhaps *might later be such that it won't*. But I think it is

---

[36]There are important related issues here regarding the *ontology* of time that deserve mention. Eternalism is the view that past, present, and future objects all equally exist. Geachianism would seem plainly to require non-eternalism; surely, that is, we are not to imagine that when the pilot prevents the crash, he brings it about that the concrete mangled ruins of a (future) plane pop out of existence. As Geach says (somewhat cryptically), "future-land is a region of fairytale" (1977: 53). A Geachian's non-eternalist options are *presentism*, which holds that only *present* objects exist, and the *growing-block theory*, which holds that both past and present (but no future) objects exist.
[37]At any rate, those who maintain that alternative possibilities (i.e. that we "can do otherwise") are required for freedom (and that we are indeed free) cannot balk at the notion that something that *will* happen *can* fail to happen, unless he or she is an open futurist, i.e. unless he or she denies that there *are* truths about what we will freely do.

implausible to suppose that intuition discriminates so finely between these claims; in the case of my friend, it clearly did not—at least initially. That is, I claim that if you find the idea of a changing future counterintuitive, it may very well be because (deep down, in the fatalist recesses within us all) you find the claim that what will happen nevertheless might not be counterintuitive as well.[38] If so, then we have some ironic results: in expressing what is wrong with one version of open theism, one expresses what is right about another. No doubt many would resist this claim, and maintain that we can perfectly well see that Geach's view is wrong, but not because we do not like his result that what will happen might not happen. I'm skeptical. But I here merely register my skepticism.[39]

This must end our discussion of Geach's view of the mutability of the future, which, needless to say, raises many fascinating questions that we cannot address here.[40] A new issue now arises. How does Geach's view bear on the compatibility of divine foreknowledge and human freedom? And how does the application of the view to this issue relate to other versions of open theism? To answer these questions, we first need to investigate the argument to which open theism has largely been a reaction. In the minds of most, especially those coming at this topic from a philosophical angle, open theism is primarily a particular sort of response to the argument for the incompatibility of divine foreknowledge and human freedom, an argument that was crystallized by Nelson Pike in his 1965 paper, "Divine Omniscience and Voluntary Action." I thus turn to a brief discussion of this argument, after which we will see how Geach's view opens up an interesting new response to it.

[38]Perhaps the Ockhamist would wish to claim that what is objectionable about Geach's view is that what will happen *can epistemically* still fail to happen, though not its claim that what will happen *can causally* still fail to happen. Again, however, while this may be the Ockhamist's official position, I am skeptical that intuition clearly distinguishes between these two senses of "can" at the level of an initial reaction to Geach's position. Is it really *just* the claim that what will happen can *epistemically* fail to happen that is (allegedly) counterintuitive about Geach's proposal? Again, I simply note that philosophers unsympathetic to Geach's view *and* to fatalism ought to tread carefully.

[39]Note: there is arguably no contradiction in saying, as would Plantinga and other Ockhamists, both that the future cannot change *and* that what will happen can fail to happen. For Ockhamists, while we cannot change the future, we *can so* act that the actual future *wouldn't have been* the future. In that sense what will happen *can* fail to happen. But the future cannot change: nothing that will happen can become such that it will not.

[40]Though *Providence and Evil* contains the most complete statement of his view, the view is also articulated in Geach (1973). Moreover, in an essay in his 1998 book *Truth and Hope*, Geach reiterated his view, saying he is "sharply opposed to a view widespread in our day: that . . . 'changing the future' is a self-contradictory concept: 'It was going to happen but didn't happen' is on this view a violently improper use of language and in no circumstances can be literally true." See p. 88 of ch. 6, "Prophecy."

VIII. GEACH AND THE (IN?)COMPATIBILITY OF FOREKNOWLEDGE AND FREEDOM

Pike's 1965 paper provoked a veritable avalanche of work on the problem of divine foreknowledge and human freedom. According to Pike, one can argue from certain plausible premises together with the thesis that God exists to the conclusion that no human action is free (in the sense requiring the ability to do otherwise). Here, it is worth simply replicating Pike's argument in full:

1. "God existed at $t1$" entails "If Jones did X at $t2$, God believed at $t1$ that Jones would do X at $t2$".
2. "God believes X" entails "X is true".
3. It is not within one's power at a given time to do something having a description that is logically contradictory.
4. It is not within one's power at a given time to do something that would bring it about that someone who held a certain belief at a time prior to the time in question did not hold that belief at the time prior to the time in question.
5. It is not within one's power at a given time to do something that would bring it about that a person who existed at an earlier time did not exist at that earlier time.
6. If God existed at $t1$ and if God believed at $t1$ that Jones would do X at $t2$, then if it was within Jones's power at $t2$ to refrain from doing X, then (1) it was within Jones's power at $t2$ to do something that would have brought it about that God held a false belief at $t1$, or (2) it was within Jones's power at $t2$ to do something which would have brought it about that God did not hold the belief He held at $t1$, or (3) it was within Jones's power at $t2$ to do something that would have brought it about that any person who believed at $t1$ that Jones would do X at $t2$ (one of whom was, by hypothesis, God) held a false belief and thus was not God—that is, that God (who by hypothesis existed at $t1$) did not exist at $t1$.
7. Alternative 1 in the consequent of item 6 is false. (from 2 and 3)
8. Alternative 2 in the consequent of item 6 is false. (from 4)
9. Alternative 3 in the consequent of item 6 is false. (from 5)
10. Therefore, if God existed at $t1$ and if God believed at $t1$ that Jones would do X at $t2$, then it was not within Jones's power at $t2$ to refrain from doing X. (from 6 through 9)
11. Therefore, if God existed at $t1$, and if Jones did X at $t2$, it was not within Jones's power at $t2$ to refrain from doing A. (from 1 and 10)[41]

---

[41] Pike, reprinted in Fischer (1989: 63).

It is beyond the scope of this paper to detail all the objections philosophers have had with Pike's argument and all the sorts of replies it has provoked. Notably, however, perhaps the most common reply has been the so-called "Ockhamist solution" advocated by (amongst others) Marilyn Adams and Alvin Plantinga.[42] The Ockhamist denies premise (4) of Pike's argument on grounds that God's beliefs are "temporally relational" or "soft" facts, and thus not subject to the (tacit) principle of the fixity of the past underlying (4).[43] That is, by the Ockhamist's lights, we can sometimes so act that God would not have believed what he actually did believe.

The open theist does not take this route. The open theist's response to Pike's argument is to deny (1), the thesis that it follows from Jones's doing X at $t2$ that God believed (and hence knew) at $t1$ that Jones would do X at $t2$. Both versions of open theism discussed in Rhoda's analysis make this reply salient. On one version, it was not *true* at $t1$ that Jones would freely do X at $t2$, and on the other, it was logically impossible (for reasons Pike's argument—setting aside certain niceties—itself brings out) for God to believe at $t1$ that Jones would freely do X at $t2$. But now we can see how Geach's view also makes possible a denial of (1). Recall Geach's rhetorical question:

> But if something did happen, doesn't this show it was after all going to happen? Certainly; but not that it *always* was going to happen.

In other words, Geach denies the inference from X's happening at $t2$ to its being true at all earlier times that X would happen at $t2$. Thus, it does not *follow* from Jones's doing X at $t2$ that it was true at $t1$ that Jones would do X at $t2$. At $t1$, it may have been true that Jones was going to do ~X at $t2$ rather than X, and in the time between $t1$ and $t2$ prevented what was going to happen (his refraining from X-ing at $t2$) and did X at $t2$ instead. Moreover, the Geachian may plainly maintain that if it was not true at $t1$ that Jones would do X at $t2$, then God did not believe at $t1$ that he would do X at $t2$, contrary to Pike's first premise.[44]

On Geach's analysis, it could very well be that at $t1$ God believes of Jones that he will do X at $t10$, but at $t7$ something happens (perhaps a decision of Jones himself) so as to prevent Jones from doing X at $t10$, with the result that Jones does not

---

[42]See Adams and Plantinga in Fischer (1989).

[43]Note: the Ockhamist does not claim that *all* soft facts fail to be fixed; just those involving our free decisions.

[44]Geach nowhere says this explicitly, which is somewhat disconcerting, since this is the plain consequence of the account of the mutability of the future he offers. And Geach emphasizes that God must believe all and only what is true.

do X at *t*10, contrary to what at *t*1 God believed he would do. Someone in the grips of a view opposed to Geach's would immediately infer from this result that God was *mistaken* at *t*1 in his belief about Jones doing X at *t*10. But such an inference would be the real mistake, according to the Geachian. Rather, if God believes at *t*1 that Jones is going to do X at *t*10, then at *t*1 it of course really is the case that Jones is going to do X at *t*10; God is making no mistake. Nevertheless, it is consistent with its being true at *t*1 that Jones will do X at *t*10 that at *t*7 it becomes false that Jones will do X at *t*10. In this case, while God begins believing at *t*7 that Jones will not do X at *t*10, he has not always believed this; previously, he believed (correctly) that Jones would do X at *t*10, but adjusted his beliefs about what would happen to accommodate the fact that what was going to happen has been prevented from happening, and a new thing now will happen. Whether this picture of God's beliefs is plausible is an open question, but there is clearly no basis for a charge that God would be making mistakes.

But Geach's view opens up another way of replying to Pike's argument that is somewhat more complicated than a simple denial of (1). Geach may deny that the trichotomy in (6) is exhaustive.[45] On Geach's view, Jones's power to refrain from doing X at *t*2 (despite God's belief at *t*1 that he would do X at *t*2) need not be the power so to act that God either would have held a different belief at *t*1, a false belief at *t*1, or would not have existed at *t*1. Rather, Jones's power could simply be the power so to act that though God believed at *t*1 that Jones would do X at *t*2, what God believed would happen fails to happen. In other words, by preventing what was going to be (as of *t*1) from coming to pass, Jones brings it about that what God believed would happen was prevented from happening. Again, it is tempting here to insist that this power of Jones's is the power to bring it about that God was mistaken, but the Geachian denies this. Moreover, Jones's power is *not* the counterfactual control over the past invoked by Ockhamists that open theists have traditionally found problematic. Jones *does not* have the power so to act that God's beliefs would have been different, as the Ockhamist claims. Rather, he has the power so to act that God's (present) beliefs *become* different.

IX. GEACHIANISM AND OPEN THEISM

As we just saw, given Geach's view, one may maintain that Jones has the power to refrain from doing X at *t*2 (despite God's belief at *t*1) without invoking any problematic power over the past. Given this result, it is worth briefly pausing to consider how this result squares with open theism commonly conceived. Suppose we are at *t*20,

---

[45]I owe this point to Neal Tognazzini.

a time later than *t*10. Using the past-tense construction to avoid certain difficulties about a tenseless "happens" or "does", notice that Geach's view maintains that:

(A) God believed at *t*1 that Jones would do X at *t*10

does not entail that:

(B) Jones did X at *t*10.[46]

Now, if it does not follow from God's belief at *t*1 that Jones would do X at *t*10 that (looking backwards) Jones *did* X at *t*10, it will be hard to see how it could follow from God's belief that Jones would do X at *t*10 that Jones *could not have done otherwise* than X at *t*10. Given Geach's views about future contingents, it will be impossible to generate an argument for the incompatibility of mere divine foreknowledge and human freedom.[47] Even if God knew that Jones would do X at *t*10, Jones could have (*ceteris paribus*) acted so as to prevent its being the case that he did X at *t*10—again, even if he did X at *t*10 and God knew he would.

Given this result, we can notice that Geachianism is in an important respect significantly different than other versions of open theism. After all, while all open theists deny (1) of Pike's argument, the claim that it follows from Jones's doing X at *t*2 that God believed at *t*1 that Jones would do X at *t*2, open theists are typically taken to maintain that if God *really did* believe of Jones that he would do X at *t*2, then of course it would follow that Jones cannot refrain from doing X at *t*2. In other words, the traditional motivation for open theism has been the thought that divine foreknowledge and human freedom are incompatible, with the consequence that we must deny that God has foreknowledge of future free actions. Though Geach's view entails a denial of (1), it also has the consequence that mere divine foreknowledge is consistent with human freedom.

Some might take this fact to call into question the claim that Geachianism is a version of open theism. Of course, I have no decisive argument against the view that

---

[46]The reason for the past-tensed construction is the following. The Geachian need not—and should not—maintain that "Jones will do X at *t*10" does not entail "Jones (tenselessly) does X at *t*10". Rather, the Geachian should maintain that such an entailment holds, but that the tenseless "does" must itself be analyzed in terms of tensed propositions, i.e. that "Jones does X at *t*10" is true if "Jones has done X at *t*10, is doing X at *t*10, or will do X at *t*10" is true. Clearly, then, if "Jones will do X at *t*10" is true, so is "Jones does X at *t*10", since the third disjunct of the analysis will be true. More generally, the Geachian plainly ought to deny that there is some immutable, tenseless fact about what "happens" at times.

[47]Of course, this is hardly a cost of the view, and many would find such a result to speak in its favor.

the incompatibility thesis is essential to open theism. And anyway, so long as we are clear about how we use our terms, what we call the relevant views is not of ultimate concern. However, it strikes me that Geachianism *is* a version of the view, and that what makes it so is its denial of premise (1) of Pike's argument: from Jones's doing X at *t*2, it follows that at *t*1 God believed he would. I submit that open theists must deny this claim. More generally, I submit that you are an open theist if and only if you maintain Rhoda's first two criteria (theism and indeterminism), together with the following:

(OT) Some things happen and have happened which God has not always known would happen.

Notice that this thesis is directed toward the *present* and the *past*, and not the future. This makes sense, since the disagreements that mark different versions of open theism are disagreements about the nature of the *future*.

So let us come full circle and reconsider Rhoda's characterization of "generic open theism". Recall that Rhoda maintained that open theists must endorse the claim that there are some states of affairs such that God knows neither that they *will* nor *will not* happen. But we can see that the Geachian need not admit this. It is not essential to Geachianism that there are some things about which God must say, "I do not believe that that is going to happen, and nor do I believe that it is not." Admittedly, this would imply that God has in mind some unique, maximal blueprint of how the world will be. But how the world will be changes. The result is a denial of premise (1) of Pike's argument, and thus, I suggest, a version of open theism. So I suggest replacing Rhoda's analysis of "generic open theism" with the one suggested above.[48]

X. GEACHIANISM AND DIVINE REPENTANCE TEXTS

In the final two sections of this paper, I consider how Geachianism bears on two distinctively theological considerations historically relevant to open theism: so-called

---

[48]Of course, if the reader will permit me a sociological remark, I am not confident that the usage of the term "open theism" in popular discourse will be sensitive to the variety of views that open theists actually (or could possibly) hold. In popular discourse, open theism is often simply the view that God lacks "comprehensive" or "exhaustive" foreknowledge. As Rhoda notes, such a characterization may be appropriate for views like Hasker's, but it is not appropriate for those views denying that future contingents are true. On that view, God *does* have comprehensive or exhaustive knowledge of everything that will be the case. Likewise on Geachianism.

"divine repentance texts" and the doctrine of providence. Consider this passage from Isaiah, which, along with others like it, is often cited by open-theist theologians:

> In those days Hezekiah became ill and was at the point of death. The prophet Isaiah son of Amoz went to him and said, "This is what the LORD says: Put your house in order, because you are going to die; you will not recover."
>
> Hezekiah turned his face to the wall and prayed to the LORD, "Remember, O LORD, how I have walked before you faithfully and with wholehearted devotion and have done what is good in your eyes." And Hezekiah wept bitterly.
>
> Then the word of the LORD came to Isaiah: "Go and tell Hezekiah, 'This is what the LORD, the God of your father David, says: I have heard your prayer and seen your tears; I will add fifteen years to your life'." (38:1–5, New International Version)

According to open theologians, a straightforward reading of this and similar passages puts pressure on the traditional model of divine foreknowledge. After all, so the thought goes, if God eternally and infallibly knew that Hezekiah was not going to die, it would seem that God was being disingenuous when he told Hezekiah that he would.

Perhaps open theologians are right in seeing a problem for the traditional model here. What is remarkable, however, is that a straightforward reading of the passage—and that is what the theologians in question claim to be interested in—supports *Geachianism* rather than familiar models of open theism. For only on Geachianism can God's statements to Hezekiah come out *true*. Hezekiah really *was* going to die, and God was *correct* in saying that he would not recover. But Hezekiah's earnest prayer *prevented* what was going to happen, so that what was once true (that he would die) now becomes false. Indeed, a Geachian of a certain sort might say that just as such texts pose a stark problem for the traditional model (on account of putting a known falsehood in God's mouth), they pose the very same problem for traditional open views. Traditional openness theologians must explain how God could have said that Hezekiah would die, even though this was (by their lights) not true. At any rate, a Geachian approach to such passages seems required if we really are to take them at face value and preserve the notion that God is no deceiver. I think it is remarkable that this fact has not been widely noticed. Perhaps I have just provided theologians of a certain inclination good reason to become Geachians.

Moreover, even if there is no good reason to want (let alone *require*) "straightforward" readings of such texts (or even if one accords no even *prima facie* authority to such texts in the first place), the text in question still seems to help the Geachian.

For what would be so problematic about reading the text in the straightforward way? It is not clearly *incoherent* or in any obvious sense *impossible* that the text could be representing things as they really are. Indeed, the text seems to be a perfect illustration of Geachianism in action. Of course, those in the grip of the traditional view would have to insist that God was merely teaching Hezekiah a lesson (or some such), and that he knew all along that his (God's) message to Hezekiah would lead to Hezekiah's earnest prayer and his "adding" fifteen years to Hezekiah's life. But why is an explanation along these lines *required*? Why not rather say that Hezekiah (or God) changed the future?

XI. GEACHIANISM AND PROVIDENCE

Perhaps the easiest way to consider how Geachianism might affect one's theory of providence is to consider one at least *prima facie* difficulty a Geachian model of providence faces. It may seem as if Geachianism would imply that God cannot count on hardly *anything's* happening in the future, and if so, this fact would seem to call into question God's ability to providentially govern the world as required. After all, Geachianism has the result that God could know that X will happen, but that it (causally) could still fail to happen. Moreover, God would not have access to some immutable fact about whether X "happens" at the relevant time. Knowing that something will happen by itself provides no guarantees that it later will not.

Is this a severe problem for Geachianism? Not obviously. Geachianism would seem to call for a distinction between those things that *must* happen and those things that are merely *going to* happen. If God were wise, he would know to build his plans—at any rate, the really important ones—only on the foundation of those things that *must* happen. Whereas open-future open theists identify what *will* happen with what *must* happen, Geach would deny this. Nonetheless, a Geachian could agree that there are some things that are now determined, and could maintain that these are those things that must happen. Just as on open-future open views God would be unwise to base some crucial plan on what merely will *probably* be, so the Geachian could insist that God would be unwise to base some crucial plan on merely what will be. For that could always change. At any rate, what is clear is that Geach's God will be in the exact same providential situation as traditional open views suggest. So if traditional open views have an adequate account of providence, so does Geachianism.

Moreover, it is at this point that I believe Geachianism is able to shine considerable light on controversial issues concerning the providential usefulness (or lack thereof) of so-called "simple foreknowledge". As I remarked above, the Geachian

God could know that X will happen, but it also be true that X could (causally) still fail to happen. Of course, Ockhamists, too, must accept this thesis, but the distinctions here are obvious: the Ockhamist God would still know that X *does unchangeably* happen, even if it causally might not. This knowledge might seem to give the Ockhamist God a providential advantage over the Geachian God (or any God lacking such knowledge). But William Hasker has vigorously—and, in my judgment, correctly—argued that this knowledge is in fact providentially *useless* to God.[49] For on the Ockhamist view, facts about what unchangeably happens at times are facts logically and explanatorily *posterior* to God's deliberations (or other providential activities). Thus, God cannot *use* knowledge of what (unchangeably) happens as data in deciding what the future is to be like; by that (logical) time, the future is already unchangeably fixed.

Suppose, as I believe to be the case, that Hasker is right in holding that (given Ockhamist suppositions) knowledge of what will be is providentially useless to God. This would seem to be a cost for Ockhamism. For it is counterintuitive to suppose that knowledge of what will be would be useless in controlling the world as one sees fit. Plausibly, however, only Geachianism can properly accommodate this intuition. That is, on Geachianism, knowledge of what will be is *clearly* providentially advantageous: by knowing what will happen, one is thereby in much better position to prevent it should one wish to do so. Or, if something one *does* want to happen (at the moment) *will not* happen, then one can then act (or try to act) so as to bring it about that it will. Common sense has it that total knowledge of what is going to happen would be a great help to someone wishing to control the future. Traditional models of foreknowledge cannot accommodate this result. Geachianism can. Though these points clearly deserve further elaboration, I believe they constitute an independent argument for Geachianism.[50]

---

[49]See Hasker (1989).

[50]Other open theists—both of the open-future and limited-foreknowledge variety— might complain that their views can also properly accommodate the providential usefulness of knowing what will be. On such views, God will know that something will be as a result of seeing that it is causally determined. Thus, so long as the future is to some extent causally open, God would be able to use his knowledge of these facts to casually affect other (undetermined) aspects of the future, thereby giving it a more determinate shape. But it is unclear whether this account can truly capture the relevant intuitions. For it seems as if (on this account) what is useful to God is not knowledge of what will be *qua* knowledge of what will be, but knowledge of the causal structure of the world and what it makes inevitable. In other words, that what is causally determined also *will be* is *epiphenomenal* in the relevant sense. For the Geachian, knowing what will be *qua* knowing what will be is by itself useful. At any rate, if other open theists *can* properly accommodate the providential usefulness of such knowledge, then the above claims support merely the *disjunction* of Geachianism and other open views.

XII. CONCLUSION: ADVANTAGE
TO THE GEACHIAN?

Here ends my application of Geach's view to the issues of divine foreknowledge and providence. The view that emerges is unique, and it is worth pausing to consider whether it has distinctive advantages over its more familiar rivals. It does. First, consider open-future versions of open theism. One such version denies bivalence. This has been seen to be a severe cost for the view. Geachianism requires no rejection of bivalence. The other such version maintains that *will* and *will not* are not contradictories, so that "Jones will swim tomorrow, or Jones will not swim tomorrow" is not an instance of $p v \sim p$. This has struck many as dubious, and at any rate is not the view of the overwhelming majority. Geachianism does not deny that *will* and *will not* are contradictories. Next, consider Hasker's limited-foreknowledge version of open theism, the version maintaining that there are truths about the future that God does not know. Hasker and company must explain how it is that God can still be omniscient, despite not knowing these truths. The Geachian faces no such problem. These are the most familiar problems for these versions of open theism. Geachianism avoids them all.

Moreover, looking beyond its advantages over other open views, many have thought the Ockhamist's counterfactual control over the past to be problematic. Not a problem for the Geachian. Nor does the Geachian have any problems arising from God's supposed atemporality. There are no counterfactuals of freedom in need of grounds. One has a straightforward account of the providential usefulness of knowing what will happen. All this can be bought by maintaining that the future is mutable. But what is the cost? As Kvanvig's critique showed, one has the problem of accounting for retroactive predications of truth to predictions. But this cost does not strike me as decisive against open views of the future. Perhaps there are other problems for the Geachian, but they must fall outside the scope of this paper.

In this paper, I have tried to develop Geach's view on future contingents and apply it to the problems of divine foreknowledge, providence, and human freedom. Geach's work is provocative, but he did not systematically explain how his views are related to and are different from rival views about time, tense, foreknowledge, and freedom. I have sought to do so here, albeit in a preliminary way. I do not claim to have considered—let alone explored—all the various problems that might face the Geachian. However, I do claim that philosophers should be aware of Geach's view as a theoretical possibility in these debates. Geach's case from the logic of prevention is stronger than the arguments of *Providence and Evil* might make it seem. Kvanvig's criticisms are not decisive. The quick dismissals of Smart and Plantinga are too quick. And Geachianism has certain attractive advantages over its rivals.

The dialectical terrain about such matters very rarely sees a genuinely new position emerge. Perhaps the dialectic was going to proceed as it has been for some time to come. If so, then in a bold Geachian spirit, I hope to have changed the future.[51]

REFERENCES

Belnap, Nuel and Green, Mitchell (1994), "Indeterminism and the Thin Red Line," *Philosophical Perspectives*, vol. 8, in *Logic and Language*, James Tomberlin (ed.) (Atascadero, CA: Ridgeview Publishing Co.), 365–88.

Dowe, Phil. (2006), "A Counterfactual Theory of Prevention and 'Causation by Omission," *Australasian Journal of Philosophy* 79: 216–26.

Dummett, Michael (1982), "Realism," *Synthese* 52: 1.

Fischer, John Martin (ed.) (1989), *God, Foreknowledge, and Freedom* (Stanford, CA: Stanford University Press).

—— Todd, Patrick, and Tognazzini, Neal (2009), "Engaging with Pike: God, Freedom, and Time,"*Philosophical Papers* 38: 2 (July 2009): 247–70.

Freddoso, Alfred (1983), "Accidental Necessity and Logical Determinism," *Journal of Philosophy* 80: 257–78, reprinted in Fischer (1989: 136–58).

—— (1988), "Introduction" to Luis de Molina, *On Divine Foreknowledge: Part IV of the Concordia*, tr. Alfred J. Freddoso (Ithaca, NY: Cornell University Press).

Geach, Peter (1965), "Some Problems about Time," *Proceedings of the British Academy* 11.

—— (1973), "The Future," *New Blackfriars* 54, 208–18.

—— (1977), *Providence and Evil* (Cambridge: Cambridge University Press).

—— (1998), *Truth and Hope* (Notre Dame, IN: University of Notre Dame Press).

Hartshorne, Charles (1965), "The Meaning of 'Is Going to Be'," *Mind* 74: 293: 46–58.

Hasker, William (1989), *God, Time, and Knowledge* (Ithaca, NY: Cornell University Press).

Kenny, Anthony (1987), *The God of the Philosophers* (Oxford: Oxford University Press).

Kvanvig, Jonathan (1986), *The Possibility of an All-Knowing God* (New York: Macmillan).

Lucas, John Randolph (1989), *The Future: An Essay on God, Temporality, and Truth* (Oxford: Basil Blackwell, 1989).

Pike, Nelson (1965), "Divine Omniscience and Voluntary Action," *The Philosophical Review* 74: 27–46, reprinted in Fischer (1989: 57–73).

Plantinga, Alvin (1986), "On Ockham's Way Out," *Faith and Philosophy* 3: 235–69, reprinted in Fischer (1989: 178–215).

[51]For helpful comments on earlier versions of this paper, I wish to thank William Hasker, Eleonore Stump, Alan Rhoda, Kevin Timpe, Michael Nelson, Justin McBrayer, Andrew Moon, Kenneth Boyce, and my colleagues and fellow members of the agency reading group at the University of California, Riverside—Justin Coates, Garrett Pendergraft, Chris Franklin, and especially Philip Swenson and Neal Tognazzini, both of whom were invaluable discussion partners while writing this paper. I am indebted to Mark Hinchliff both for bringing the view to my attention and for several helpful conversations about these topics. Most of all, I owe deep thanks to John Martin Fischer for his constant support and encouragement of this project and for valuable comments on numerous drafts of the paper.

Prior, A. N. (2003), "The Formalities of Omniscience," *Papers on Time and Tense* (Oxford: Oxford University Press).

Rhoda, Alan (2008), "Generic Open Theism and Some Varieties Thereof," *Religious Studies* 44: 225–34.

—— Boyd, Gregory, and Belt, Thomas (2006), "Open Theism, Omniscience, and the Nature of the Future," *Faith and Philosophy* 23: 432–59.

Smart, J. J. C. (1964), "Introduction," in his *Problems of Space and Time* (New York: Macmillan).

Swinburne, Richard (1993), *The Coherence of Theism* (Oxford: Oxford University Press).

Van Inwagen, Peter (2008), "What Does an Omniscient Being Know About the Future?" *Oxford Studies in Philosophy of Religion* vol. 1, Jonathan Kvanvig (ed.) (Oxford: Oxford University Press).

12

ON AUGUSTINE'S WAY OUT

David P. Hunt

On the traditional understanding of divine omniscience, God is both infallible and also cognizant of future contingents. But a prediction is infallible only if, once made, it cannot turn out false. Since nothing escapes divine foresight, no part of the future can happen in any way other than it will actually happen. But if no alternative to the actual future is so much as possible, a standard condition for free and morally responsible agency can never be satisfied. It follows that divine omniscience and free agency, as traditionally understood, are not compossible.

This is the ancient problem of "theological fatalism", which received its first clear expression in St. Augustine's *On Free Choice of the Will*. Renewed interest in this problem during the last thirty years has pushed the ideas of William Ockham to the center of discussion, with "Ockham's way out" (the title of a notable defense of this approach by Alvin Plantinga) attracting more defenders than any rival solution to the problem.[1]

---

[1] Alvin Plantinga, "On Ockham's Way Out," *Faith and Philosophy* 3 (July 1986), pp. 235–69. The contemporary debate was initiated by Nelson Pike in his "Divine Foreknowledge and Voluntary Action," *Philosophical Review* 74 (January 1965), pp. 27–46. The first published response to Pike, John Turk Saunders's "Of God and Freedom," *Philosophical Review* 75 (April 1966), pp. 219–25, challenged the idea that all past-tense propositions are temporally necessary, thus anticipating the explicitly Ockhamist strategy of Marilyn McCord Adams in "Is the Existence of God a 'Hard' Fact?" *Philosophical Review* 76 (October 1967), pp. 492–503. Others who have defended a more or less Ockhamist line on the problem include Alfred J. Freddoso, "Accidental Necessity and Logical Determinism," *Journal of Philosophy* 80 (1983), pp. 257–78; Joshua Hoffman & Gary Rosenkrantz, "Hard and Soft Facts," *Philosophical Review* 93 (July 1984), pp. 419–34; Jonathan Kvanvig, *The Possibility of an All-Knowing God*, Library of Philosophy and Religion (Houndmills, UK: Macmillan Press, 1986); Eddy M. Zemach & David Widerker, "Facts, Freedom and Foreknowledge," *Religious Studies* 23 (March 1987), pp. 19–28; Bruce Reichenbach, "Fatalism and Freedom," *International Philosophical Quarterly* 28 (September 1988), pp. 271–85; Edward Wierenga, *The Nature of God: An Inquiry into Divine Attributes*, Cornell Studies in the Philosophy of Religion (Ithaca: Cornell U. Press, 1989); William Lane Craig, *Divine Foreknowledge and Human Freedom*, Brill's Studies in Intellectual History, vol. 19 (Leiden: E. J. Brill, 1991); and Thomas Talbott, "Theological Fatalism and Modal Confusion," *International Journal for Philosophy of Religion* 33 (April 1993), pp. 65–88.

But while Ockham's star has risen, Augustine's own solution to the problem has suffered from relative neglect. The purpose of this paper is to redress the imbalance.

My primary objective in rehabilitating Augustine is to make a contribution toward the current debate over theological fatalism, not to advance the frontiers of Augustine scholarship. At the same time, an important reason that Augustine's analysis has not been taken more seriously is that it has been widely misunderstood. This makes it necessary to provide a corrected account of Augustine's position before arguing its rightful place in contemporary discussions of theological fatalism. The plan of the paper, then, is this: section I warns against mistaken approaches to Augustine's position, while section II presents Augustine's actual solution; section III then compares Augustine's way out with Ockham's, and section IV sums up the case for Augustine's relevance to the current debate. While it is always profitable for Christian philosophers to spend time in Augustine's company, readers uncorrupted by the standard interpretation of his position or endowed with little interest in Augustinian exegesis might wish to skip the bulk of section I.[2]

I

The most widely cited sources for Augustine's treatment of theological fatalism are *On Free Choice of the Will* and *The City of God*. Neither is transparent in its teaching; but the latter is especially untidy, owing in large measure to Augustine's polemical engagement with Roman history, which leads him in Book V to introduce the topic of fatalism as a problem in Roman Stoicism, an approach which results in his importing into the argument various Stoic concerns (such as an "order of causes" mediating between divine knowledge and human actions) which play no essential role in recent formulations of the problem. For this reason, the search for a single strategy to put forward under the rubric of "Augustine's Way Out" will be better served by a focus on the more direct form that the argument takes in *On Free Choice of the Will*.

The problem of theological fatalism is raised in this dialogue at the beginning of Book III, in response to Evodius's worry that the doctrine of divine foreknowledge may thwart Augustine's attempt to trace the origin of evil to free choice of the will. Augustine summarizes the problem as follows:

> Surely this is the question that troubles and perplexes you: how can the following two propositions, that God has foreknowledge of all future events, and that we

---

[2]Readers who are uncommonly corrupted or endowed with even more exegetical curiosity than section I can satisfy might wish to consult my "Augustine on Theological Fatalism: The Argument of *De Libero Arbitrio* III.1–4," *Medieval Philosophy and Theology* 6 (Spring 1996), pp. 1–30.

do not sin by necessity but by free will, be made consistent with each other? "If God foreknows that man will sin," you say, "it is necessary that man sin." If man must sin, his sin is not a result of the will's choice, but is instead a fixed and inevitable necessity. You fear now that this reasoning results either in the blasphemous denial of God's foreknowledge or, if we deny this, the admission that we sin by necessity, not by will. (III.3)

If we let "W" stand for any sinful movement of the will, the argument Augustine is called upon to counter can be formulated as follows:

(1) W is foreknown (by God) → W is necessary
(2) W is necessary →~(W is free)
∴ W is foreknown (by God) →~(W is free)

This conclusion, if accepted, leaves the theist with the unpalatable option of affirming the antecedent (and losing free will) or denying the consequent (and losing divine foreknowledge). Since the argument is clearly valid, its conclusion can be resisted only if one of its premises is false.

The argument above, though highly schematic, is nevertheless congruent with modern formulations. (The latter tend to pay more attention to the derivation of step (1).) So Augustine is at least addressing the same problem as modern commentators. It is his solution to the problem that has been thought to be of questionable relevance to the contemporary debate. In coming to a just appreciation of Augustine's position, however, there are at least two red herrings that must be avoided.

The first of these is a mistaken assimilation of the problem of theological fatalism, addressed in chs. 2–4, to a related problem taken up in ch. 1. In that chapter Evodius is concerned with the threat to free will posed by what might be called "natural necessity": "if free will has been given in such a way that this movement [of the will] is natural to it, then it is turned to lesser goods by necessity. There is no blame to be found where nature and necessity rule." Augustine concurs: "If this movement exists naturally and necessarily, it cannot be blameworthy at all." It can thus appear that Augustine is endorsing the following conditional:

(2′) W is necessary →~(W is blameworthy).

But since he also avers that "this movement by which the will is turned from immutable to transitory goods . . . is voluntary and therefore blameworthy," the following conditional also comes into play:

(2*) W is free → W is blameworthy.

And (2′) together with (2*) entails (2). This suggests that Augustine has already granted (2) when he comes to formulate the argument for theological fatalism in chs. 2 and 3, so that his response to this argument (whatever it turns out to be) must involve a denial of (1).

This suggestion, however, is in error. Augustine in fact never asserts in ch. 1 that necessity *simpliciter* is incompatible with moral blame or free agency; instead, he resolutely restricts his claims to the narrower notion of *natural* necessity (whatever that might be). But there is no reason to think that the freedom-annihilating necessity which governs the movement of a falling stone (Augustine's example of natural necessity from ch. 1) is relevantly similar to the kind of necessity with which divine foreknowledge threatens future actions. Nor does Augustine do anything to encourage a conflation between the two cases: the word *natura* and its cognates, which bulk so large in ch. 1, are nowhere to be found in chs. 2–4, where the problem posed by divine foreknowledge is being raised and addressed. The discussion of natural necessity in ch. 1 therefore leaves it an open question whether the (possibly quite different) kind of necessity supposedly implied by divine foreknowledge is also incompatible with free agency. This means that the truth-value of premise (2), contrary appearances notwithstanding, remains to be settled as Augustine undertakes the assessment of theological fatalism in chs. 2–4.

The other red herring consists of various indications in ch. 3 that this is where Augustine provides his principal response to the argument for theological fatalism. This herring is a bit slipperier than the first, but it is nevertheless worth pinning down. It certainly seems, on a first reading (and perhaps even a second and a third), that Augustine raises the problem of theological fatalism in ch. 2, then restates and solves it (to his satisfaction) in ch.3. There is enough evidence for this reading that most commentators have accepted some version of it.[3] The evidence that Augustine's solution is to be found in ch. 3 is threefold. First, Augustine brings various conditions for free will into play in ch. 3, and endeavors to show that these conditions are unaffected by divine foreknowledge—just the sort of move one would expect him to make when presenting a solution to

[3]See, e.g., William Rowe, "Augustine on Foreknowledge and Free Will," *Review of Metaphysics* 18 (December 1964), pp. 356–63; William Lane Craig, "Augustine on Foreknowledge and Free Will," *Augustinian Studies* 15 (1984), pp. 41–63; and Christopher Kirwan, *Augustine*, The Arguments of the Philosophers (London & New Work: Routledge, 1989), ch. 5. This scholarly neglect is then reflected in anthologies like Louis Pojman's widely used *Philosophy of Religion*, 3d ed. (Belmont, CA: Wadsworth, 1998), where the excerpt from *On Free Choice of the Will* stops short at the end of Bk. III, ch. 3. A juster appreciation of Augustine's argument and the critical role of ch. 4 may be found in David De Celles, "Divine Prescience and Human Freedom in Augustine," *Augustinian Studies* 8 (1977), pp. 151–60.

the problem. Second, Augustine concludes his examination of these conditions with what sounds like a declaration of victory over theological fatalism: "So it follows that we do not deny that God has foreknowledge of all things to be, and yet that we will what we will." Finally, the chapter ends with Evodius's apparent capitulation: "I no longer deny that whatever God foreknows must come to be, and that he foreknows our sins in such a way that our will still remains free in us and lies in our power."

A strong indication that something must be wrong with this interpretation, despite the evidence in its favor, comes at the beginning of the next chapter, where we find Evodius's doubts still unresolved:

> Of course I do not dare deny any of these points. Yet I still cannot see how God's foreknowledge of our sins can be reconciled with our free choice in sinning. God must, we admit, be just and have foreknowledge. But I would like to know by what justice God punishes sins which must be; or how it is that they do not have to be, when He foreknows that they will be; or why anything which is necessarily done in His creation is not to be attributed to the Creator. (III.4)

Either Evodius has already forgotten what was just accomplished in ch. 3, or the accomplishments of that chapter (despite initial appearances) leave the problem of theological fatalism still in place. There can be little doubt that the latter possibility is the correct one, given the reply Augustine makes to Evodius's renewed query in ch. 4 (to which we will soon turn). Rereading Evodius's apparent capitulation at the end of ch. 3 in light of the continuing discussion in ch. 4 makes it clear that Evodius is not thereby declaring the problem solved, but simply admitting its "aporetic" nature: the two poles of the dilemma (divine foreknowledge and free will) *are* compatible with each other after all, but *how* they can be compatible is another matter altogether. This latter is the problem remaining for ch. 4, as Evodius explicitly announces at its outset.

It's a good thing that Augustine cannot have regarded the discussion in ch. 3 as complete, since it is clearly inadequate as it stands. The three conditions for free will that he deploys in this chapter are: (i) that W be possessed by the subject in the right way ("God's foreknowledge ... does not take from you the will to be happy when you begin to be happy"); (ii) that W be approved by the subject ("When we will, if the will itself is lacking in us, we surely do not will"); and (iii) that W lie within the subject's power ("Nor can it be a will if it is not in our power"). While these three conditions are plausibly thought to be *necessary* for free will, they are clearly not *sufficient* in any robustly incompatibilist sense. This can be brought out by noting how all three tests could be satisfied even when W is causally determined by events or states obtaining prior to the subject's birth. Nothing about causal determinism is incompatible with the first two tests: there are no grounds for denying that W belongs to the subject, so long as the causal chain eventuating in W passes through the subject for a sufficient length of time and in a sufficiently intimate manner; nor are there any grounds for doubting that the subject genuinely approves of W (and approves his approval, etc.), since any level of approval may itself be causally determined. The same is true of the third test, since Augustine offers a "conditional" analysis of power very much like that of 20th-century philosophers whose goal is to render human freedom compatible with causal determinism: "we cannot deny that we have the power, unless we cannot obtain what we will through an act of will or unless the will is absent." But of course the incompatibilist will maintain that there is yet another ground for ascribing powerlessness to someone, beyond the inability to obtain what one wills, namely, the inability to control one's will, i.e., to will otherwise than one actually wills. Even taken jointly, then, the three conditions from ch. 3 are insufficient to show that W can remain free in the incompatibilist sense that is at issue in the argument for theological fatalism.

Of course, the fact that a 20th-century incompatibilist would be disappointed by the analysis of free will in ch. 3 does not by itself show that Augustine would find it similarly inadequate. This is, after all, a man who could say at the end of his life, "I tried hard to maintain the free decision of the human will, but the grace of God was victorious."[4] Even in *On Free Choice of the Will*, written while he was still struggling to maintain freedom of the will, it is no easy matter to locate Augustine with any precision along the compatibilist-incompatibilist continuum.[5] But all this is beside the point: the evidence for Augustine's attitude toward the three conditions of ch. 3 is to be found, not in speculation on how he *would* have responded to those conditions had he been an incompatibilist, but in the place those conditions actually occupy in the text. It is the text which reveals how unlikely it is that Augustine could have regarded the three conditions of ch. 3 as jointly sufficient for free will, and in revealing this, incidentally preserves the incompatibilist credentials of Augustine's solution, whether or not he was himself an incompatibilist. The suspicion that this second herring (like the first) is indeed red finds confirmation once we turn to the solution Augustine actually puts forward.

---

[4]*Retractationes* 2.1.

[5]For a recent study of Augustine's evolution during this critical period, see Gregory E. Ganssle, "The Development of Augustine's View of the Freedom of the Will (386–97)," *The Modern Schoolman* 74 (November 1996), pp. 1–18.

II

We have seen that Augustine's analysis in ch. 3 is incomplete and that he recognizes it as such. How then does it fit into his larger solution to the problem of theological fatalism?

An important clue to Augustine's understanding of the three conditions from ch. 3 is the fact that the discussion of natural necessity in ch. 1 makes use of the same three conditions: (i) the "possession" condition ("it belongs to the spirit alone"); (ii) the "approval" condition ("we accuse a spirit of sin when we prove that it has preferred to enjoy lower goods"); and (iii) the "power" condition ("the stone does not have it in its power to check its downward motion"). But another condition is also mooted in ch. 1, alongside these three, when Augustine reminds Evodius of the conclusion, reached in Bk. I, that "the mind . . . cannot be forced (cogi) to serve lust by something superior, or by an equal, . . . [or] by something inferior." This "compulsion" condition is not brought into play at all in the analysis of ch. 3; indeed, the word cogo and its cognates are completely absent from chs. 2–3. This is itself good reason to think that the resources Augustine was at pains to develop in ch. 1 are not yet fully deployed by the end of ch. 3; the problem's persistence into ch. 4 should not then be surprising.

Cogo does, however, reappear with a vengeance in ch. 4, which begins with Augustine asking, "Will you deny that we sin by will and not under compulsion (cogente) from anyone, either higher, lower, or equal?" The key passage in ch. 4 is saturated with compulsion-talk:

> unless I am mistaken, your foreknowledge that a man will sin does not of itself necessitate (cogeres) the sin. Your foreknowledge did not force (cogeret) him to sin even though he was, without doubt, going to sin; otherwise you would not foreknow that which was to be. Thus these two things are not contradictories. As you, by your foreknowledge, know what someone else is going to do of his own will, so God forces (cogens) no one to sin; yet He foreknows those who will sin by their own will.
>
> Why cannot He justly punish what He does not force (cogit) to be done, even though He foreknows it? Your recollection of events in the past does not compel (cogis) them to occur. In the same way God's foreknowledge of future events does not compel (cogit) them to take place. As you remember certain things that you have done and yet have not done all the things that you remember, so God foreknows all the things of which He Himself is the Cause, and yet He is not the Cause of all that He foreknows.

Augustine admits elsewhere in ch. 4 that foreknowledge entails necessity in the sense that what is foreknown *must* happen and is *certain* to happen; but in the quoted passage he denies that it entails necessity by *compelling* or *causing* what is foreknown, and claims that this is enough to defuse the conflict between divine foreknowledge and voluntary agency. Lack of causal compulsion provides the final necessary condition for free will, one which in conjunction with the other three conditions is finally sufficient as well.

What becomes clear in ch. 4, once the red herrings discussed in the preceding section of this paper have been identified and the proper significance of this chapter has been appreciated, is that Augustine's real objection to the argument for theological fatalism is directed against premise (2). He is perfectly willing, on the other hand, to grant the fatalistic case for premise (1). To understand what is distinctive about Augustine's position, it is necessary to elaborate on this adjudication of the argument's two premises.

In one sense, at least, practically everyone would acknowledge that (1) can be true while (2) is false. For suppose, in saying that W is necessary when foreknown (by God), (1) is asserting only that W *follows necessarily* from its being foreknown (by God); that is,

(1′) Necessarily [W is foreknown (by God) → W].

Then (1) is clearly true, because (1′) is true; but (2) would then be just as clearly false. If W were necessary only in the sense that it follows necessarily from something or other (e.g., from divine knowledge of W, or—why not eliminate the middleman?—from W itself), this would go no distance at all toward showing that W is unfree.

For (2) to stand a chance of being true, it is W itself that must be necessary, and this requires that the first premise be parsable in the form

(1*) W is foreknown (by God) → necessarily (W).

Call this "absolute necessity", as opposed to the "hypothetical necessity" displayed by (1′). But is (1*) remotely plausible as a non-question-begging premise in an argument designed to *demonstrate* (and not just assert) theological fatalism? Sure it is, and anyone at all familiar with debates over fatalism (particularly as they have developed during the last thirty years) knows how the moves go at this point. Since God has *always* foreknown W, He foreknew W prior to any time (before the occurrence of W) that one cares to specify. Let "t" designate such a time. Relative to t, God already possesses foreknowledge of W. But what is already the case cannot be made *not* to be the case. The fact that God foreknew W is therefore *necessary* in the sense that it is no longer possible (relative to t) for God not to have foreknown W. This is a very strong form of necessity, much stronger than natural necessity. (Presumably God can countermand natural necessity, but not even God, Augustine notes in *Against Faustus* 25.5, can undo the past.) Since such necessity is relative to time (what is unavoidably necessary when past might not have been unavoidably necessary when future), let us call it "temporal necessity". Because W was foreknown (by God) prior to t, its being foreknown (by God) is temporally necessary at t. But God's cognizing W entails W (since He can't be mistaken in anything He believes). It therefore follows that W is also temporally necessary at t (on the grounds that, if something is unavoidably necessary, whatever it entails is also unavoidably necessary). Thus there is a defensible (1*)-like reading of premise (1). And this reading, unlike the hypothetically necessary (1'), is at least relevant to the claim being made in premise (2). Since t can be set as early as one pleases, let it be a time prior to the birth of our erring agent. Then W is necessary in virtue of the fact that, before the agent even comes into existence, it is already too late for W to be avoided. This is just the sense of necessity in which it might plausibly be thought that (2) is true.

This is theological fatalism in its most credible form. Is this the form in which Augustine is engaging it? That's hard to say. Augustine nowhere distinguishes between hypothetical and absolute necessity, as Boethius would later do.[6] This ambiguity in Augustine's analysis cuts two ways: on the one hand, it's doubtful that his endorsement of (1) reflects a full appreciation of the case that can be made on behalf of absolute necessity (as formulated in the preceding paragraph); on the other hand, there is little reason to suppose that his acceptance of (1) is based on nothing more than hypothetical necessity, and that he simply overlooks the fallacy of equivocation that arises when (1') is combined with (2).[7] In the absence of a clear Augustinian account of the necessity at work in the fatalist's argument, the best one can do when looking to Augustine for insight into the current debate is to examine his denial of (2) and see whether it addresses the argument in its strongest (1*)-like form.

Given his suspect credentials on the free will issue, it is noteworthy that Augustine does *not* deny premise (2) because he's a soft determinist who believes free agency to be compatible with causal determinism. *On Free Choice of the Will* admittedly

---

[6]See *The Consolation of Philosophy*, Bk. V, Prose 6.

[7]This is the way Plantinga understands him in "On Ockham's Way Out," pp. 235–37. But this interpretation fails to motivate the solution Augustine actually offers, and is in any case the least charitable of the available readings. Textual reasons favoring (1*) are reviewed by Jasper Hopkins in "Augustine on Foreknowledge and Free Will," *International Journal for Philosophy of Religion* 8 (1977), pp. 116–17.

presents a compromised picture of creaturely freedom, and the "ignorance and difficulty" which Augustine ascribes to the post-lapsarian human condition undoubtedly leaves us vulnerable to causal forces; but none of the threats to human agency canvassed in this work derives from God's foreknowledge of our deeds. Far from presupposing soft determinism, Augustine insists that the reason divine foreknowledge does not jeopardize free agency is precisely that it does *not* cause our actions. Augustine can happily grant the fatalist everything he wants in premise (1) because temporal necessity (as implied by divine foreknowledge) does not entail causal necessity, and only the latter conflicts with free will. Temporal necessity is determined by the temporal order; but what is relevant to free agency, Augustine maintains, is the *causal/explanatory* order. The two orders normally coincide: what is prior in the one order is prior in the other. In cases of divine foreknowledge, however, the two orders diverge, and what is temporally closed (because infallibly foreknown) may remain causally/explanatorily open; as Augustine notes in *The City of God*, "a man does not therefore sin *because* God foreknew that he would sin" (V.10). This is enough for Augustine to regard W as free despite the fact that God's foreknowledge of W renders it unavoidably necessary.[8]

I will say more about this view of free will at the end of section III. What I want to pursue in the remainder of this section is the conception of foreknowledge which makes such freedom possible. Augustine's account in chapter 4 begins with a comparison between divine and *human* foreknowledge. In cases where one human being knows what another is going to do, the foreknowledge of the first person does not stand in a cause-effect relationship with the future action of the second person. If the second person's action is in fact causally compelled, it isn't the foreknowledge of the first person that accounts for the compulsion; nor is there any special reason to think that divine foreknowledge *per se* has a coercive force lacked by human

---

[8] An anonymous referee wondered whether the independence of temporal and causal orders I am imputing to Augustine isn't incompatible with the best contemporary theories of time and inconsistent with Augustine's own account of time in the *Confessions* Bk. XI. I'm inclined to answer in the negative to both questions. Even if the direction of "time's arrow" is determined by the order of causation, there are at least a couple of possibilities which are consistent with my account of Augustine. One is that an overall order of causation may be set by the *preponderance* of causal relations, or the most *important* causal relations, even if there are local exceptions (e.g., divine foreknowledge). The other is that the order of causation determines the direction of *physical* time, implying nothing about the relationship between the temporal and causal orders within the Divine Mind. The latter suggests a way to handle the question about *Confessions* XI. The worry here is that Augustine's account of time appears to make it parasitical on such causal processes as memory and perception. But Augustine's psychological analysis of temporal experience may make empirical time thoroughly causal without this having any implications for the way *God* experiences time and relations of causal/explanatory dependence.

foreknowledge. Unfortunately, foreknowledge might still entail compulsion, despite its causal inefficacy, if the causal unavoidability of future events is a *condition* for their being known with certainty. Augustine indeed holds that this is the only condition under which *human beings* can know the future: "when we speak of seeing the future, obviously what is seen is not the things which are not yet because they are still to come, but their causes and signs do exist here and now."[9] But *God* is not similarly limited to knowing the future only insofar as it is determined by present causes. It is for this reason that the comparison with human foreknowledge cannot take Augustine as far as he needs to go, and we find him switching in mid-argument to human *memory* as his model for divine foreknowledge.

Memory is more favorable to Augustine's purposes than is ordinary human foreknowledge. Not only is memory (like foreknowledge) not the cause of its object, but it is also (*unlike* human foreknowledge) independent of present causes determining its object. Indeed, the relationship between memory and remembered event goes in the other direction: it is the past event that causes, explains, or accounts for the remembrance of that event. Likewise, Augustine wants to understand God's foreknowledge in such a way that it is the foreknown event that causes, explains, or accounts for His knowledge, not the other way around. In this respect, at least, divine foreknowledge is more like human memory than it is like human foreknowledge.[10]

---

[9]*Confessions* XI. 18.

[10]This may appear to conflict with things that Augustine says elsewhere, e.g., at *De Trinitate* XV.13.22:

> God is not acquainted with any of his creatures, whether spiritual or corporeal, because they are, but they are because he is acquainted with them. For he did not lack knowledge of the things he was to create; he created, therefore, because he knew, not knew because he created.

This is the passage cited by Thomas Aquinas in the *sed contra* of *Summa Theologiae* Ia. q14. a8, where he is defending the thesis that God's knowledge is the cause of things. But we cannot read Thomas's elaborate theory of divine omniscience back into the passage from Augustine, which is concerned solely with the *existence* of creatures, not the particular facts about what they freely do. (It should be noted that Eleonore Stump and Norman Kretzmann, in a recent paper on Aquinas—"God's Knowledge and Its Causal Efficacy," in Thomas D. Senor, ed., *The Rationality of Belief and the Plurality of Faith* (Ithaca: Cornell University Press, 1995), pp. 94–124—argue that even St. Thomas is concerned primarily with creatures' existence rather than states when he maintains the causal efficacy of divine knowledge.) In any case, we know that for Augustine God cannot be causative for *everything* He knows if only because some of what He knows is evil: "he can foreknow even those things which he himself does not do, such as whatever sins there may be" (*De Praedestinatione Sanctorum* 10.19). All in all, there is no reason to doubt Augustine's seriousness in proposing that future acts of will escape freedom-annihilating compulsion because divine foreknowledge operates like "reverse memory."

This position is perfectly compatible with God's creative and providential endeavors requiring a complex interplay between foreknowledge and agency in which much of the future is also available to Him through knowledge of His own intentions. Against the common objection that

One puzzle regarding Augustine's use of the "reverse memory" model in *On Free Choice of the Will* is why he fails to invoke the doctrine of "timeless eternity" which he endorses elsewhere[11] and which Boethius later draws on in developing his own solution to the problem of theological fatalism in Book V of *The Consolation of Philosophy*. The "reverse memory" model is thoroughly temporal. God's anticipation of future events, like our remembrance of past events, involves two temporal relata, so that even though the explanatory arrow moves *with* the temporal arrow in cases of human memory and *against* it in cases of divine foreknowledge, God's knowledge (so understood) is nevertheless situated in the temporal order. Augustine's failure to correct the temporalist presuppositions underlying the argument for theological fatalism, along with his adoption of a model which reinforces those presuppositions, does admittedly look initially puzzling.

It is nevertheless arguable that the account in *On Free Choice of the Will* fits quite well with the "timeless eternity" theory, and may even be essential to it. Though the ascription to God of an eternal existence outside time blocks any straightforward appeal to temporal necessity, this is insufficient by itself to dispel the fatalistic threat posed by divine omniscience. If God's knowing 100 years ago what I will do tomorrow is enough to make tomorrow's actions unavoidable, it's far from obvious that those actions are less inevitable just because God knows them "from eternity".

The most common brief on behalf of the "Boethian" solution goes something like this. God's atemporal perspective on events is like (timelessly) observing things *while* they are happening; but simultaneous observation of someone else's actions does not render them unavoidably necessary (the fact that I happen to be watching while you roll down a hill has no implications for the contingency or evitability of your behavior); by analogy, then, God's timeless observation of events should have no effect on *their* contingency.[12]

One problem with the analogy is that, strictly speaking, the observation (e.g., of your hillside antics) occurs *later* than the observed event (information from the event can't reach the observer faster than the speed of light), so that there is no ground for any inference regarding the benignancy of truly simultaneous

complete foreknowledge stultifies rather than abets providential agency, see my "Omniprescient Agency," *Religious Studies* 28 (September 1992), pp. 351–69; "Divine Providence and Simple Foreknowledge," *Faith and Philosophy* 10 (July 1993), pp. 394–414; "Prescience and Providence: A Reply to My Critics," *Faith and Philosophy* 10 (July 1993), pp. 430–40; and "The Compatibility of Omniscience and Intentional Action: A Reply to Tomis Kapitan," *Religious Studies* 32 (March 1996), pp. 49–60.

[11]E.g., *Confessions* Bk. XI, *De Trinitate* Bk. XV, *Ad Simplicianum de Diversis Quaestionibus* Bk. II.2.2.

[12]Boethius himself employs this reasoning in Prose 6 of Bk. V.

observation. But suppose we ignore this nicety and prescind from the scientific details ("it's only a thought-experiment, after all"), imagining that observation and observed event are strictly simultaneous; and let us grant that the observation, in this counterfactual scenario, would have no more effect on the agency of the observed than would observations which obeyed the laws of physics. How would this suggest, even by analogy, that the assumption of a Boethian relationship between God and history is a condition (either necessary or sufficient) for the defeat of fatalism? Consider another analogy, that of a driver's hands on the steering wheel of a car. Hands and wheel move together, though strictly speaking the hands move first and their motion is then communicated to the wheel (as the flesh stretches and tautens in the direction of the hands' motion). Disregard this slight temporal lapse, as we did in the first case, and imagine that the two motions are strictly simultaneous. The assumption of simultaneity does nothing to save the wheel from control by the driver or salvage for it any vestige of "freedom." What make the difference between the observation and steering cases, when both are assumed to operate under conditions of fictional simultaneity, are the different relations of causal/explanatory dependence which tie observer to observed in the first case and manipulator to manipulated in the second. The temporal status of the relata in the two cases is irrelevant.

The same is true in the divine case. Augustine's fundamental insight in chapter 4 is that free choice must be uncompelled, and that it is the explanatory/causal order which is therefore relevant in determining whether foreknowledge implies fatalism. This insight, inasmuch as it makes the temporal order (and temporal necessity with it) irrelevant, applies equally well to *atemporal* knowledge of the future. Augustine can't be bothered with correcting the temporalist bias which underlies the fatalist's argument for the simple reason that his solution to the problem is indifferent to the question whether God's knowledge of W can be located in time.[13] It is "reverse memory" rather than "simultaneous observation" which best models the relevant relations. More exactly, while "observation" models the relevant relations just fine, "simultaneity" has nothing to do with it. Since "simultaneity" appears to be the whole point of appealing to divine eternity in response to the problem of

---

[13]This is equally the reason why Boethius *does* feel it essential to correct this bias in *The Consolation of Philosophy*. In Prose 3 of Book V, while setting up the problem of theological fatalism for Lady Philosophy to solve, Boethius urges the *irrelevance* of causal/explanatory relations when W is temporally necessary on other grounds: "I cannot agree with the argument by which some people believe that they can solve this problem. They say that things do not happen because Providence foresees that they will happen, but, on the contrary, that Providence foresees what is to come because it will happen . . ." His elaboration in the passage that follows certainly looks like an explicit rejection of Augustine's way out.

theological fatalism, Augustine would regard the appeal as irrelevant.[14] Because Augustine sees the threat to free will as arising from (narrowly) causal necessity rather than (broadly) temporal necessity, the Boethian move, which arguably succeeds against temporal necessity, cannot defuse the threat. This makes any Augustinian anticipation of Boethius's solution otiose, despite Augustine's adherence to a "Boethian" conception of God on other (largely Neoplatonic) grounds.[15]

Augustine's way out, then, comes to this. Divine foreknowledge does indeed imply a kind of necessity; it even implies a kind of *absolute* necessity, namely, "temporal necessity". W is temporally necessary inasmuch as the future (given what God has already believed about it) is unavoidable. So premise (1) is true, and it is true in just as strong a form as the fatalist claims. But premise (2) is not true. Not every form of unavoidability is incompatible with free will. This premise would be true only if W's necessity derived from its being causally determined, or if W were in some other way explanatorily dependent on those factors that make it unavoidable. But divine foreknowledge makes the future unavoidable without causing or explaining it; whether or not God exists in time, the causal/explanatory arrow runs in the wrong direction for omniscience to undermine agency.[16]

III

Is Augustine's real solution from ch. 4 any better than the supposed solution commentators have claimed to discover in ch. 3? In assessing the merits of Augustine's position, it is helpful to compare it with its leading challenger, the solution first proposed by William Ockham. There are many points of agreement between the two. Consider the following assumptions which bear on the fatalist's argument: (a) that divine omniscience encompasses the future as well as the past and present; (b) that

---

[14]Among recent accounts of eternal-temporal "simultaneity," the most prominent is that of Eleonore Stump and Norman Kretzmann in "Eternity," *Journal of Philosophy* 78 (August 1981), pp. 429–58.

[15]Augustine's solution may, however, favor a Boethian move *indirectly*. If God's knowledge of W precedes W in time, the causal/explanatory dependence of the former on the latter raises the specter of retrocausation. Insofar as this is metaphysically abhorrent, it provides some reason for holding that God's knowledge of W does *not* precede W in time (because it is instead "ET-simultaneous" with it.)

[16]If the Augustinian line is correct, the implications may extend beyond theological fatalism to another problem foreknowledge is alleged to generate for agency, based on the principle that one cannot deliberate (or even engage in the most minimal decision-making required by intentional agency) with respect to what one already knows is going to happen. For previously unnoticed connections between these two foreknowledge problems, see my "Two Problems with Knowing the Future," *American Philosophical Quarterly* 34 (April 1997), pp. 273–85.

God may be said to know future contingents *before* they take place; (c) that God knows something at a time only if He believes it at that time; (d) that God's beliefs are not just inerrant but infallible; (e) that what is genuinely past is temporally necessary (i.e., no longer avoidable); and (f) that temporal necessity is closed under entailment (i.e., that if P is temporally necessary and P entails Q, then Q is temporally necessary as well). On each of these points Augustine and Ockham either accept the assumption (if only for the sake of argument) or fail to challenge it (perhaps by overlooking it altogether).

The difference between Augustine and Ockham concerns two further premises. Ockham's approach is to deny (g) that God's past beliefs about future contingents are genuinely past. Ockham noted that, in the case of "propositions [which] are about the present as regards both their wording and their subject matter . . . it is universally true that every true proposition about the present has [corresponding to it] a necessary one about the past."[17] In the year 428 A.D., for example, the true proposition

(1) Augustine writes *De haeresibus ad Quodvultdeum* in 428 A.D.

is about the present in subject matter as well as wording; consequently the corresponding proposition about the past,

(2) Augustine wrote *De haeresibus ad Quodvultdeum* in 428 A.D.,

is necessary at all later times, in the sense that its truth is then a *fait accompli* which cannot be altered. Past-tense versions of propositions like (1), in virtue of their temporal necessity, have come to be called "hard" facts about the past. But Ockham denied that what is true for (1) and propositions like it is true for all propositions: "that proposition that is about the present in such a way that it is nevertheless equivalent to one about the future does not have [corresponding to it] a necessary proposition about the past." Taking 428 A.D. once again as the present, consider

(3) Augustine writes *De haeresibus ad Quodvultdeum* in 428 A.D., nine hundred years before Ockham will flee Avignon.

This is equivalent to the future-tense proposition

---

[17]William Ockham, *Predestination, God's Foreknowledge, and Future Contingents*, trans. with intro., notes, and appendices by Marilyn McCord Adams & Norman Kretzmann (New York: Appleton-Century-Crofts, 1969), p. 46.

(4) Ockham will flee Avignon nine hundred years after Augustine writes *De haeresibus ad Quodvultdeum* in 428 A.D.

Because (3) is not simply about the present but is equally about the future, the past-tense proposition corresponding to it, namely,

(5) Augustine wrote *De haeresibus ad Quodvultdeum* in 428 A.D., nine hundred years before Ockham would flee Avignon,

need not set forth a fact that is necessary or unavoidable simply in virtue of its being past. Relative to the year 1000 A.D., for example, (5) is only a "soft" fact about the past: its truth is not yet a *fait accompli*. It is only when there is no longer an equivalent proposition about the future, i.e., after 1328, that (5) becomes a "hard" fact about the past.

Given the notion of a soft fact about the past, Ockham further claimed that "[a]ll propositions having to do with predestination and reprobation are of this sort . . ., since they all are equivalently about the future even when they are verbally about the present or about the past."[18] In the contemporary discussion this position has been extended to God's past beliefs about future events. Just as (5) is a soft fact relative to 1000 A.D., so

(6) God believed in 428 A.D. that Ockham would flee Avignon in 1328 A.D.

is also a soft fact relative to 1000 A.D., since both refer to and depend upon events subsequent to the year 1000. Only when Ockham actually flees does it become a hard fact that God believed that he would do so. In general, until X actually A's at t, God's prior belief that X will A at t is not available as a hard fact about the past which can then mandate that the future unfold in line with it. Thus divine foreknowledge provides no basis for inferring that future events are temporally necessary, and acts of will like W emerge with their freedom intact.

This is a sufficient characterization of Ockham's solution for present purposes. An important question is whether Ockham's denial of (g) is supposed to be *demonstrable*, or whether it is simply proposed as a plausible "for-all-we-know" defense against the argument for theological fatalism. The former is not, I think, very promising. For it even to get off the ground, there would have to be some agreed-upon account of what it is for a fact to be soft rather than hard. Attempts to provide such an account have yielded increasingly baroque results whose complexities bear little evident

---

[18]*Ibid.*, p. 38.

relation to the simple idea they are meant to capture.[19] Most accounts friendly to Ockhamism are elaborations on an "entailment criterion" according to which the past-tense statement, *God believed in 428 that Ockham would flee in 1328*, comes out as soft (relative, say, to 1000 A.D.) in virtue of the fact that it entails the future-tense statement, *Ockham will flee in 1328*. But this is not a neutral account of soft facthood, in that it takes the very entailment by which temporal necessity is transferred from God's past belief to the future event and cites it as grounds for denying that God's belief is temporally necessary in the first place. For the anti-Ockhamist, the fact that God's antecedent beliefs metaphysically entail subsequent events shows, not that the antecedent beliefs are soft facts about the past, but that metaphysical entailment can link hard features of the past with distinct facts about the future.[20]

If the basic problem with Ockhamistic proofs is that their accounts of the hard/soft distinction beg the question, it is worth considering an argument presented by Alvin Plantinga and recently revived by Ted A. Warfield which is formulable without any reference to this problematic distinction.[21] The argument assumes that *logical* fatalism rests on a fallacy, and then goes on to show that theological fatalism is in the same boat. "Logical fatalism" is the position that fatalistic consequences can be derived directly from future-tense truths, whether or not there is a God who infallibly believes those truths. A logical fatalist would hold, for example, that the argument Augustine considers in *On Free Choice of the Will* would be sound even if premise (1) were replaced by

(1#)   W will occur → W is necessary.

Now Plantinga and Warfield are surely right about logical fatalism: there is absolutely no reason to think that (1#), if true, involves anything stronger than hypothetical necessity, and this poses no threat at all to free will.[22] The Plantinga-Warfield argument then proceeds as follows. *W is foreknown (by God)* both entails and is

[19]Linda Zagzebski does a fine job of explaining why the complexity of these results is worrisome in her excellent *The Dilemma of Freedom and Foreknowledge* (New York: Oxford University Press, 1991), pp. 74–76.

[20]William Hasker distinguishes between metaphysical and conceptual entailment, and argues that only the latter is relevant to "entailment criteria" for soft facthood, in his "Hard Facts and Theological Fatalism," *Noûs* 22 (September 1988), pp. 419–36.

[21]Plantinga's version of the argument is contained in "On Ockham's Way Out," pp. 247–51; while the hard/soft fact distinction permeates this article, there are two sentences at the top of p. 250 which contain the entire argument in a nutshell without invoking the distinction either explicitly or implicitly. Warfield's argument may be found in "Divine Foreknowledge and Human Freedom Are Compatible," *Noûs* 31 (March 1997), pp. 80–86.

[22]One way to explain this, though it's not essential to the argument, is in terms of the hard/soft distinction. While it's true that, for any time t prior to the occurrence of W, it *was* the case

entailed by *W will occur*; given that God is necessarily existent and essentially omniscient, the two are logically equivalent. But if *W will occur* is consistent with W's freedom (as it must be if logical fatalism is rejected), then *W is foreknown (by God)* must also be consistent with W's freedom. (Warfield cites the principle, "If *p* and *q* are logically consistent, then *p* is consistent with any proposition that is logically equivalent to *q*."[23]) So theological fatalism must suffer the same fate as logical fatalism, and Ockhamism is triumphant.[24]

The main problem with this approach is that there is no obvious notion of consistency under which the argument is as apodeictic as its supporters take it to be. Warfield, for example, understands the consistency of *p* and *q* as simply the logical possibility that the conjunction of *p* and *q* is true.[25] But even if this qualifies as *a* sense of "consistency", it is not the sense that is relevant to the argument. In rejecting the case for logical fatalism, we grant that there is nothing in the mere fact that W *will* occur which entails that W *must* occur; it is in this sense that the former is consistent with the negation of the latter. But in granting this we are not thereby committing ourselves to the proposition that there is a possible world in which W occurs without having to occur, for there may be *other* facts which rule out this possibility. So in asserting the consistency of *p* and *q*, we can't be asserting the logical possibility of (*p*&*q*), as Warfield supposes. Furthermore, something which is consistent with the fact of W's occurrence may be inconsistent with some other fact *even when the second fact is logically equivalent to the first*. This can be shown through the following story. A puckish paper appears in a philosophy journal purporting to demonstrate that, on the assumption that $3 + 4 = 7$, it follows that existence is a good overall. The most brilliant minds of the profession dissect the argument and discover the inevitable flaw. A notorious atheologian named Waringa then takes advantage of the situation to formulate his own argument, the gist of which is this: "The idea that $3 + 4 = 7$ entails the

---

(relative to t) that W will occur, this fact about the past is a paradigmatically soft fact about the past, on anyone's account of soft facthood. So logical fatalism cannot secure for premise (1) a temporally necessary antecedent, and therefore lacks anything inimical to free agency which it can then transfer to (1)'s consequent.

[23]"Divine Foreknowledge and Human Freedom are Compatible," p. 81.

[24]It might be wondered why Warfield's version of the argument is Ockhamistic, despite his eschewing any appeal to the hard fact/soft fact distinction. The answer to this question is quite simple. The heart of Warfield's defense against fatalism is the logical equivalence of *W is foreknown (by God)* with *W will occur*. But *W is foreknown (by God)*, since it is equivalent to *W will occur,* is "equivalently about the future." This is the essential Ockhamist move. The fact that Warfield finesses the hard-soft distinction is irrelevant, since Ockham did so as well—it was Nelson Pike who introduced the terms "hard fact" and "soft fact" in his "Of God and Freedom: A Rejoinder," *Philosophical Review* 75 (July 1966), pp. 369–79, in order to address a counterexample proposed by John Turk Saunders.

[25]"Divine Foreknowledge and Human Freedom are Compatible," p. 81.

overall goodness of existence has been demolished, as everyone will agree. The fact that 3 added to 4 equals 7, just by itself, is quite *consistent* with existence not being a good overall. But $3+4=7$ is logically equivalent to *God exists*, since both propositions are true in all possible worlds. Given that the overall badness of existence is consistent with the fact that $3+4=7$, it must also be consistent with the existence of God, since these are logically equivalent. So God isn't the paragon of virtue theists take Him to be." I trust that no one is swept away by this argument, and that the moral of the story is clear. For the consistency of divine foreknowledge with human freedom to follow from the consistency of future-tense truth with human freedom, it is not enough that divine foreknowledge of W entails and is entailed by W; the conclusion requires that there be *nothing more* to God's foreknowledge of W than there is to W itself. But this can't be right. Theism surely adds *something* to the data-set for fatalism, even if what it adds (assuming theism to be true) goes hand-in-hand with the non-theistic data across all possible worlds. At the very least, if W and God's knowing W were just the same fact, this would be an astonishing property of divine omniscience requiring considerable independent justification—hardly the sort of thing one could blithely presuppose in a proof of the Ockhamist position.[26]

In the absence of a convincing demonstration, we are left to judge Ockhamism on grounds of general plausibility. Unfortunately, Ockham's solution is highly counterintuitive. I have nothing new to add here to the many critiques of Ockhamism that have already been offered in the literature, so let me simply sum up what I take the fundamental difficulty to be. It is very hard to see how the beliefs God holds at a time could be soft at a later time just because the content of those beliefs concerns an even later time. Consider the following propositions, treating them as factual:

[26]This critique of Warfield arrives at much the same destination as Dale Eric Brant's critique of Plantinga in his "On Plantinga's Way Out," *Faith and Philosophy* 14 (July 1997), pp. 334–52. Brant formulates the key assumption in Plantinga's argument as

The Equivalence Principle
 If two propositions are equivalent, then one of them is strictly about a given time period *just in case* the other is also strictly about that time period. (p. 339)

Brant raises some questions for this principle and argues that it should be replaced by

The Reassertion Principle
 If asserting one proposition is a roundabout way of asserting another, then the one is strictly about a given time period just in case the other is also. (p. 349)

Brant's article was not yet in print when I was writing this paper, but my requirement that divine foreknowledge of W be the same fact as W (and not just logically equivalent to W) if Warfield's consistency argument is to succeed is virtually identical to Brant's requirement that the one be a roundabout way of asserting the other if Plantinga's earlier argument is to go through.

(α) God believed in 1895 that Hunt would attend the Pacific Division Meeting of the American Philosophical Association in 1995.

(β) Mahler's Second Symphony premiered in Berlin 100 years before Hunt would attend the 1995 Pacific APA.

(γ) Mahler's Second Symphony premiered in Berlin in 1895.

(δ) Mahler hoped Richard Strauss would attend the premiere.

(ε) Mahler believed his Second Symphony would ensure his fame.

(ζ) Zeldon Prime [a time-traveler from 43rd-century Greenland] attended the premiere of Mahler's Second in 1895.

The problem is that (α) seems more like (γ) than like (β), in that something already in place at, e.g., 1900 settles the question whether (α) and (γ) are true but does not settle the question whether (β) is true. (α) seems even more like (δ)–(ζ): like (δ) and (ε), it reports a propositional attitude held by the subject at an earlier time; and like (ζ), the state of affairs it sets forth depends on a later state of affairs (my attending the Pacific APA in 1995, Zeldon Prime's entering a time machine in the 43rd century). But (δ)–(ζ) are no less hard facts relative to 1900 than is (γ): given that they are true, nothing can happen in, e.g., 1900, to bring it about that Mahler did not so hope and believe, or that Zeldon Prime did not so act, any more than one could bring it about in 1900 that the premiere did not take place. And it's just not clear how (α) is relevantly different from these hard facts about the past.

Of course the difference, according to Ockhamism, is that (α), like (β), entails a future event. (Perhaps (ζ) also qualifies by this criterion.) But it's unclear why this difference should make a difference; it does nothing to shake one's intuition that a complete cosmic record of everything that has transpired up to 1000 A.D. will include the fact that *God believed in 428 that Ockham would flee in 1328* but will not include the fact that *Ockham will flee in 1328*, though it can be *inferred* that the record *will* include the latter fact in 1328. It is very hard to see what a divine belief could *be* if it is to behave in the ways required by Ockham's solution.[27]

---

[27]Perhaps it could behave this way if it were understood as *dispositional* rather than occurrent belief. I explore this question and give it a qualifiedly favorable answer in my "Does Theological Fatalism Rest on an Equivocation?" *American Philosophical Quarterly* 32 (April 1995), pp. 153–65; I also develop and motivate the requisite concept of divine knowledge in my "Dispositional Omniscience," *Philosophical Studies* 80 (December 1995), pp. 243–78. But this is at best a *theological* solution to the problem. (See section IV for the distinction between a theological, an anthropological, and a metaphysical solution to the problem, and reasons why we should aim for the latter.)

Much more could be (and has been) said about the counterintuitive baggage accompanying Ockham's rejection of (g), but this is enough for present purposes, which call for nothing more than a comparison with Augustine. In lieu of a proof that God's forebeliefs are soft (requiring that the baggage be borne *faute de mieux*) or some way of reconceiving the problematic scenarios or correcting the contrary intuitions (making the baggage disappear), these difficulties must count against Ockhamism in any cost-benefit analysis.[28]

Let us return, then, to Augustine's way out, which is to deny (h) that temporal necessity is incompatible with free will. This premise may seem hardly less negotiable than (g). If the actual past leaves no accessible futures in which the agent refrains from performing W, how can the agent be regarded as genuinely free and morally responsible in performing W? Harry Frankfurt, discussing the related "principle of alternate possibilities," or

> PAP: A person is morally responsible for what he has done only if he could have done otherwise,

noted that it "has generally seemed so overwhelmingly plausible that some philosophers have even characterized it as an *a priori* truth."[29] As most readers are doubtless aware, however, Frankfurt went on to challenge this "overwhelmingly plausible" principle. In denying (h), Augustine can be said to anticipate Frankfurt and others who reject PAP as a requirement for morally responsible agency.

An important advantage of looking to (h) rather than (g) for a response to theological fatalism is that there are good reasons to question this assumption, quite apart from any theistic motive to reconcile human freedom with divine foreknowledge. What Frankfurt et al. have tried to show is that conditions rendering an action unavoidable negate the agent's moral responsibility only if these same conditions also enter into the "actual sequence" leading up to the action; otherwise they are irrelevant. For example, if I murder someone, and in so doing satisfy the most exacting conditions for free will, except that an irresistible power (a demon, crazed

---

[28] The following are especially good at bringing out what is mind-boggling about Ockhamism while also treating the position with great care: John Martin Fischer, "Freedom and Foreknowledge," *Philosophical Review* 92 (January 1983), pp. 67–79; William Hasker, "Foreknowledge and Necessity," *Faith and Philosophy* 2 (April 1985), pp. 121–57; David Widerker, "Troubles with Ockhamism," *Journal of Philosophy* (1990), pp. 462–80; Linda Zagzebski, *The Dilemma of Freedom and Foreknowledge, op. cit.,* ch. 3, §3; and Nelson Pike, "A Latter-Day Look at the Foreknowledge Problem," *International Journal for Philosophy of Religion* 33 (June 1993), pp. 129–64.

[29] Harry Frankfurt, "Alternate Possibilities and Moral Responsibility," *Journal of Philosophy* 46 (1969), p. 829.

neurophysiologist, etc.) *would have* forced me to murder the person if I hadn't done so on my own, this last factor does not appear to mitigate my responsibility in the least. Here no alternative to murder is available to me (so PAP is unsatisfied), but I am nevertheless free and responsible in what I do, since the factor excluding alternatives makes no causal contribution to my actions, and indeed makes no difference at all to what actually happens. The same can be said in cases involving divine foreknowledge. God's foreknowing the murder may make it unavoidable, but it does so without making any causal contribution to the murder, which would have occurred just as it did in the absence of divine foreknowledge. We appear to have the same reasons in this case for affirming my freedom and responsibility, despite the unavoidability of my action, as we have in the first (nontheological) case. Indeed, divine foreknowledge provides *superior* counterexamples to PAP, since it induces unavoidability without invoking the counterfactual intervener whose presence in the typical Frankfurt-style counterexample is at the root of most objections to the anti-PAP argument.[30]

It would be a serious liability for the Augustinian denial of (h) if this move were unavailable to a libertarian. Fortunately this is not the case. One can consistently maintain that W's freedom is compatible with temporal necessity while denying that it is compatible with causal necessity. John Martin Fischer has dubbed this position "hyper-incompatibilism", presumably because the hyper-incompatibilist is *so excessively* committed to the incompatibility of free agency and causal determinism that she is willing to persist in this commitment regardless of PAP's fate.[31] (In this respect, at least, it is the hyper-incompatibilist rather than the PAPist who might lay claim to the title of "more-incompatibilist-than-thou"!)

Of course, the fact that the position is consistent doesn't mean that it is also attractive or even plausible. If one regards PAP (combined with a robust understanding of "could have done otherwise") as the main *reason* for endorsing the incompatibility of causal determinism and moral agency, there may seem little point to insisting on incompatibilism once PAP is withdrawn. The principal critics of PAP, like Frankfurt and Fischer, are compatibilists, while its main defenders, like William Rowe and Peter Van Inwagen, are incompatibilists.[32] Nevertheless, "hyper-incompatibilism"

---

[30]Or so I argue in my "Frankfurt Counterexamples: Some Comments on the Widerker-Fischer Debate," *Faith and Philosophy* 13 (July 1996), pp. 395–401.

[31]Fischer introduces the term on p. 180 of *The Metaphysics of Free Will* (Oxford, UK, and Cambridge, Mass.: Blackwell, 1994).

[32]Frankfurt discusses implications for compatibilism at the end of "Alternate Possibilities and Moral Responsibility," and Fischer in ch. 7 of *The Metaphysics of Free Will, op. cit.* For Rowe and Van Inwagen, see (respectively) their "Two Concepts of Freedom," *Proceedings and Addresses of the American Philosophical Association* 61 (1987), pp. 43–64, and "Ability and Responsibility," *Philosophical Review* 87 (April 1978), pp. 201–24.

is not without worthy proponents, such as Eleonore Stump and Linda Zagzebski.[33] There *are* reasons other than PAP that one could appeal to in making causal indeterminism a requirement of free agency. Consider, for example, Augustine's paradigm case of a causally undetermined will from *The City of God*:

> The bad will is the cause of the bad action, but nothing is the efficient cause of the bad will. . . . For if two men, alike in physical and moral constitution, see the same corporal beauty, and one of them is excited by the sight to desire an illicit enjoyment while the other steadfastly maintains a modest restraint of his will, what do we suppose brings it about, that there is an evil will in the one and not in the other? . . . The same beauty was equally obvious to the eyes of both; the same secret temptation pressed on both with equal violence. However minutely we examine the case, therefore, we can discern nothing which caused the will of the one to be evil. (XII.6)

One thing we can say about this agent, which we might not be able to say if his will were causally determined, is that he is the autonomous initiator of his actions, a little "first cause", so that in tracking moral responsibility we can point to him and say with a fair degree of truth, "the buck stops here". If this is what is important to the libertarian about causal indeterminism, she should not be concerned about any form of determinism which leaves these features of agency intact. If Augustine's analysis of theological fatalism is correct, the unavoidability which characterizes actions in virtue of their being foreknown by God is just such a form of determinism.

Whether divine beliefs can be soft features of the past, and whether anyone can be free in the libertarian sense despite an absence of alternative possibilities, are complex issues which the brief discussion in this section leaves far from resolved. Nothing said here *shows* Ockhamism to be false or Augustinism to be true; I have simply engaged in an intuitive eyeballing of the two accounts for purposes of handicapping the race. In so doing, it is fair to say that I have given Augustine an easier time than Ockham. My assessment of the latter is, I believe, reasonably objective, in the sense that the defender of Ockham's solution would probably allow that it is counterintuitive in the ways I have suggested (while presumably insisting that the overall case for Ockhamism is nevertheless strong and that intuitions sometimes mislead). But the brief glance at Augustine's rejection of (h) has emphasized the

---

[33]For Stump, see "Intellect, Will, and the Principle of Alternate Possibilities," *Christian Theism and the Problems of Philosophy*, ed. Michael Beaty (Notre Dame, Ind.: Notre Dame University Press, 1990), pp. 254–85; and for Zagzebski, see *The Dilemma of Freedom and Foreknowledge*, ch. 6, §2.1. I weigh in on the hyper-incompatibilist side in my "Moral Responsibility and Unavoidable Action," *Philosophical Studies* 97 (2000), pp. 195—227.

positive without drawing attention to potential difficulties, like the proper analysis of the *because*-relation and the best way to formulate libertarian freedom in terms of causal/explanatory openness rather than temporal openness. Certainly much about Augustine's position requires further development and defense; but this would be out of place in the present paper, whose aim is simply to make Augustine a "player" in a game currently dominated by Ockham. While my own judgment is that Augustine's approach shows high promise while Ockham's is a virtual non-starter, it is enough for the purposes of this essay if the reader is persuaded by the considerations set forth in this section that Augustine's way out is at least *no less plausible* than Ockham's.

IV

This minimalist conclusion could amount to damning with faint praise, depending on how one assesses the Ockhamist position. Some readers may be tempted to pronounce a pox on both houses, demoting Ockham's solution rather than promoting Augustine's. To avoid this outcome, I want now to persuade the reader of a further conclusion: that Augustine and Ockham represent the main options for anyone seeking a solution to the problem of theological fatalism.

In response to an argument purporting to show that divine foreknowledge is incompatible with libertarian agency, there are only two strategies available: accept the argument and deny one of the allegedly incompatible terms, or assert their compatibility and reject the argument. The main rivals to Ockham and Augustine follow the first strategy, most by denying divine foreknowledge of future contingents. Some of these (e.g., Richard Swinburne, William Hasker, and Peter Geach) place future contingents off-limits to God's knowledge, either by excluding them from the stock of truths or by frankly denying divine omniscience; others (e.g., Boethius and Aquinas) include them in divine knowledge but deny that God knows them as future. Call this a *theological* response to the problem, since it alleges an error in the fatalist's assumptions about God. Fewer theists deny libertarian agency, at least on grounds of divine omniscience (as opposed to, e.g., considerations of divine sovereignty). Jonathan Edwards, for example, denies it on both grounds. Call this an *anthropological* response to the problem, inasmuch as it addresses the human side of the alleged incompatibility. In contrast to those who accept the argument but deny its application to reality on theological or anthropological grounds, Ockham and Augustine pursue the second strategy, rejecting the argument and affirming the compatibility of freedom and foreknowledge.

They are right to do so. If the argument is indeed sound, an action which is in every other respect an ideal candidate for free agency can be deprived of this status merely by adding infallible foreknowledge to the mix. But this is preposterous on its face. How could a third-party's knowledge of my future action, just by itself (and without special assumptions about the conditions under which such knowledge is possible), have any effect at all on the action, let alone transform it to such an extent that it no longer qualifies as free? List everything that could possibly be relevant to whether an action A is an instance of free agency: that A is done willingly; that the will to do A doesn't flout any of the agent's second-order desires; that the agent can abstain from A should he choose to do so; that the agent is not acting under coercion or duress; that A is not causally determined by events prior to the agent's birth; that the agent is not acting in ignorance of relevant circumstances; and so on. Now assume that God has infallible foreknowledge of A. This assumption should leave A completely unchanged with respect to every item on the list. As Augustine rightly observes in *On Free Choice of the Will*, "his foreknowledge does not take away my power; in fact, it is all the more certain that I will have that power, since he whose foreknowledge never errs foreknows that I will have it" (III.3). The "aporetic" character of the problem in this text reflects not only Augustine's theological commitments—his policy of believing first and understanding later (I.2)—but the inherent implausibility of what the argument for theological fatalism is trying to demonstrate.

The appropriate response to such an argument is aptly stated by William Lane Craig: "Fatalism posits a constraint on human freedom which is entirely unintelligible. Therefore, it must be false. Somewhere there is a fallacy in the argument, and we need only examine it carefully to find the error."[34] Fatalism presents us with a conceptual puzzle, not a serious proposal for how the world is arranged; its seductiveness reflects our uncertain grip on the underlying concepts rather than testifying to the truth about reality. The value of the fatalist's argument, like that of most philosophical puzzles, is that it invites us to reexamine basic assumptions and put our conceptual house in order. What mistakes in our thinking on such topics as knowledge, time, agency, modality, and so on, need to be rectified if we are not to be taken in by the argument? Theological and anthropological revisionism avoid this question rather than engaging it. There may, of course, be good independent reasons for rejecting divine foreknowledge or libertarian freedom; Augustine himself, to one degree or another, was a revisionist on both scores. But the argument for theological fatalism is too dubious to serve as a reason in its own right, while those who embrace revisionism on other grounds can (and should) still treat the fatalist's argument as a thought-experiment whose philosophical interest lies in the *aporia* it raises. In either case, complaining that God is not in fact omniprescient

[34]*The Only Wise God* (Grand Rapids: Baker Book House, 1987), p. 69.

or that humans are not in fact libertarianly free is as little to the point as dismissing Zeno's "Achilles" paradox with the observation that Achilles was perhaps not as fast as legend makes him out to be. Should anyone so misconstrue this problem as to imagine that a challenge to Achilles' credentials would undermine the force of the paradox, it may be necessary simply to *stipulate* Achilles' celerity and leave the "facts" (such as they are) to one side. The same is true for theological fatalism, if one agrees with Craig (and me) that the supposed incompatibility of divine foreknowledge and human freedom lacks all prima facie credibility. In response to the revisionist who imagines that denying one of these puzzle conditions does anything to undermine the force of the problem, one should simply *stipulate* God's infallible omniprescience and man's libertarian freedom and leave the truth on these matters (whatever it might be) to one side.[35]

If we approach the problem aporetically, there are basically two tacks that can be taken, corresponding to the two premises in Augustine's formulation of the argument. The list of two paragraphs back rather obviously omits the very condition for free agency to which the fatalist's argument is supposed to make a difference: that the action be avoidable, i.e., that the agent have access to alternative futures (given the actual past). Unlike the other conditions on the list, which concern (in whole or in part) what is or is not the case in the actual world, this one prescribes how things must be in *other* possible worlds. Omitting it from the list was not entirely disingenuous, if one suspects that any modal requirement for free agency must supervene on properties that the action and agent possess in the actual world; for then the difference infallible foreknowledge is supposed to make to free agency should register as a difference in one or more of these other properties. But ignore this possibility. Avoidability is the only feature of free agency which fatalism directly contests. So there are just two aporetic responses to the fatalist's argument: show how infallible foreknowledge is in fact compatible with avoidability; or explain why even a libertarian can deny that avoidability is a condition of free agency. Ockham and his modern followers have provided by far the most thorough and interesting case for the former, while Augustine and the anti-PAPists have made the most powerful case for the latter. These are the main options for anyone who eschews the easy out provided by theological and anthropological revisionism.[36]

[35]In "What Is the Problem of Theological Fatalism?," *International Philosophical Quarterly* 38 (March 1998), pp. 17–30, I develop in considerably more detail the idea that the problem of theological fatalism should be regarded less as a theological challenge than as a metaphysical puzzle which is best approached aporetically.
[36]Of course there are other options as well. *Scotism* and *Molinism*, for example, both deny the transfer of necessity from God's past forebeliefs to the future objects of those beliefs, as required by premise (1) of the fatalist's argument. But neither of these alternatives comes close to

Of the two, Augustine's has been widely dismissed out of hand, leaving Ockham's as the only viable option. I hope that my explication and defense of Augustine's position in *On Free Choice of the Will* have gone some way toward correcting the bad press that he has received over the years. Augustine's is not a solution that will satisfy only a compatibilist, as those who fail to read past ch. 3 might suppose; nor is its "reverse memory" model of divine foreknowledge more problematic in any obvious way than Ockham's counterintuitive claims regarding the soft facthood of God's past forebeliefs; nor does his "Frankfurtian" line on free will disqualify his solution from serious consideration. Given the quantities of ink that have been spilled on Ockham's way out, there is little doubt that Augustine's is deserving of more attention than it has received.[37]

challenging Ockhamism's front-runner status. For the Scotist approach, see Anthony Kenny, *The God of the Philosophers* (Oxford: Clarendon Press, 1979), pp. 55–58; for a critique of this approach, see John Martin Fischer, "Scotism," *Mind* 94 (April 1985), pp. 231–43. For Molinism, see Alfred J. Freddoso, "Introduction," Luis de Molina's *On Divine Foreknowledge: Part IV of the Concordia* (Ithaca, NY: Cornell University Press, 1988), pp. 53–62. Linda Zagzebski devotes an entire chapter of *The Dilemma of Freedom and Foreknowledge* to the Molinist "solution," but admits that "It is not perfectly clear to me from Freddoso's account just how middle knowledge is connected with the denial of the TNPs [Transfer of Necessity Principles]" (p. 132).

[37]For useful responses to the paper, I would like to thank Bob Kane, Bill Wainwright, Linda Zagzebski, and an anonymous referee for this journal.

PART III

The Logic of Future Contingents

13

THE MEANING OF "IS GOING TO BE"

Charles Hartshorne

R. Montague[1] and R. D. Bradley[2] have defended the view that the untruth of "A will occur" is equivalent to the truth of "A will not occur". They are aware that this equivalence has sometimes been denied, but they argue that the reasons given for the denial are unsound, and that no alternative position is tenable. What, however, is the most reasonable form of alternative, and what are the strongest arguments in its favour? As Popper has so well insisted, unless the most promising opposing theories and the best arguments for them have been considered, one's own view has not been rationally justified. Anyone can refute the more foolish forms of theory competitive with his own, no matter how foolish his own may be. I do not find in either of the authors mentioned a realization of what an intelligent opponent could urge against the equivalence referred to above.

I shall first state what I think to be the most reasonable contrasting position, with some of the arguments for it (to give all would be to expound an entire philosophy). Then I shall indicate a few of the ways in which the two authors fail to meet their opponent on anything like his strongest ground.

The notion of "X doing act A at time t" may turn out to fit the facts when t becomes the present; but a prediction is not a timeless utterance like "X performing A at t". It is rather an assertion that at a certain time, future to the time when the assertion is made, events *will* exhibit such and such a character. What is the sense of "will" in this non-volitional use? Many writers appear to find nothing problematic here: "will" simply turns a verb into the future tense, enabling it to refer to later events. Yes, but in what sense are there events which have not yet happened?

Suppose a blind guess "comes true" (as we say); the question remains, was the guess true when made? X has done A, but it need not follow that he "was going to do it all along" (from the time of utterance). Note that "is going" (to do it) is the

[1]"Mr. Bradley on the future," *Mind*, October 1960, pp. 550–554.
[2]"Must the future be what it is going to be?" *Mind*, April 1959, pp. 193–208.

present progressive tense of the verb "to go", just as "I *will* do it" in the volitional sense means, I am even now resolved upon the deed. These linguistic hints can, I believe, be taken seriously. "*X* will do *A*" in the strict meaning (as will be seen presently, we often speak more loosely) implies, "*X*'s doing of *A* is already determined or settled upon", or "there is no longer another possibility for *X* at time *t* than doing *A*" or "all the real possibilities allowed by the present causal conditions include *X*'s doing of *A*". Thus there is a formal analogy to volition, provided a present decision is taken as irrevocable, invincible. "*X* will not do *A*" means, if intended in the strictest sense, "none of the now causally open possibilities include his doing the deed; it has been ruled out by the 'march of events'". If this is the meaning, no law of excluded middle as between true and false can restrict us to the two cases, will and will not; for some of the real possibilities may include *A* while others do not. The march of events may neither have ruled it out nor ruled it in. (To reject this indeterminate case *a priori* is to assert complete determinism, a topic to which we shall return presently.) We may then say, "It is false that *A* will, also false that *A* will not, but true that *A* may-or-may-not occur, since the real possibilities are divided between those including and those excluding *A*". Whatever happens later will neither prove nor disprove this statement. The only way decisively to refute or establish a "may-or-may-not" assertion is to know all the relevant current conditions and causal laws and to see that they do, or do not, determine the choice between *A* and not-*A*. To accomplish this perhaps exceeds human powers; but it is not meaningless. A thing is not unknowable simply because knowing it with certainty is a humanly unattainable ideal.

"Will" and "will not", like "may-or-may-not", statements are unprovable in any simple decisive way by subsequent events. That *A* happened cannot show that there was no other real possibility (unless determinism is an *a priori* truth); similarly, if *A* fails to happen, its happening may yet have been really possible. If anyone finds it paradoxical that a prediction can be "fulfilled" or "verified" and yet have been untrue, I ask him to recall that we use similarly paradoxical language when we say that a scientific law may be verified, that is, found to fit known cases, and still not be a valid law. For this reason, Popper rejects the term "verify" and prefers the weaker "corroborate". And just as he rightly insists that the decisive operation is the falsification of laws, so we may say that the decisive operation as to predictions is similarly the negative one. "*A* will occur" is decisively falsified if *A* does not occur; for the "will" here means that no causally open possibility fails to include *A*, and the subsequent non-occurrence of *A* shows that at least one possibility did fail to include it. By contrast, the prediction is only indecisively corroborated if *A* does occur; for we thus learn only that some possibility included the *A* feature, not that all did. We have then a genuine analogy to the corroboration of laws.

In the foregoing, we have shown how the causal conception of predictive truth may be embraced in the general theory of scientific reasoning, without assuming strict determinism. To suppose determinism absolutely true is to imply that the "may-or-may-not" form is always vacuous, or a mere profession of ignorance. Certainly if there is but a single real possibility in each case, this possibility either does or does not involve *A*, and hence either *A* will, or *A* will not happen. Accordingly, the semantic analysis of truth with reference to future events should not be so formulated as to make "will" and "will not" the sole possibilities. For to accept this dichotomy is to decide by definition, or from semantic considerations alone, that there cannot be a plurality of real possibilities for a given future date. It is to make determinism in the maximal sense logically true. (I shall mention later a supposed escape from this consequence of the dichotomous view.) One of the rules of philosophizing should be, first seek the completely general or necessary principle, then define special or contingent forms by restriction. But we should also bear in mind that certain forms may, in some sorts of problem, be mere limiting conceptions which could not be actualized but, at most, approximated to. Determinism is, I believe, precisely such a limiting conception, the infinitely special case in which indeterminacy or creativity would shrink universally to zero. Absolute zeros are hard to establish, and in some contexts may be nonsensical. If indeterminateness were always zero, what would "determinate" express? There are even objections to thinking it could be ever zero. How can an absolute prescription for a later event be in its conditioning predecessors? Everything of the future event would thus become present except a featureless, diaphanous "reality". And if the principle is generalized, the whole of becoming is in effect being viewed as though mapped, with infinite exactitude, in each of its states. If people had more imagination, I question if there would be so many determinists.

Our analysis leaves the principle of excluded middle intact as to propositions. Any will, will-not, or may-or-may-not statement, if not true, is definitely false; it can only be right or wrong to say that all, or that only some, or that no possibilities at a specified present or past time for a later time include *A*. But whichever of the three statements is true, the others are both false. We have here simply one more instance of the familiar exclusive and exhaustive triad: all, some only, or none. The third "value" is thus in the statement forms, not in their truth status. And since, by hypothesis, we are not dealing with an empty class (there are possibilities for the future), and "all" and "none" are contraries, they can both be false, but cannot both be true.

It is worth noting that the volitional meaning of "will" behaves in the same way, formally regarded. "It is untrue that he wills or intends to do it" fails to imply "he wills not to do it", for he may be irresolute or neutral as to the deed. If we abstract from the volitional tinge, we have in this third case simply that he may or may not do it. The outcome has yet to be "decided". The all, some, or none pattern is involved here too; for there are possible actions one is opposed to taking, those one wills to take, and those about which one is indifferent or irresolute. To translate these subjective meanings into objective characteristics of the future one must abstract from the fallibility of human decision, which may be overruled either by the subject himself or by factors beyond his control. But the triadic structure remains in spite of this abstraction. There might be an irrevocable decision for or against, or no decision. All this has nothing to do with the law of excluded middle as to propositional truth values, but much to do with how the propositions whose truth is in question are to be interpreted or formulated.

Concerning "changes in truth value", a basic principle for interpreting this ambiguous phrase is the irreversibly increasing definiteness of truth. What today, Monday, is settled for the day after tomorrow, Wednesday, will still be settled on Tuesday, and ever after, for that Wednesday; but some of what are now open possibilities for Wednesday will become closed, one way or the other, on Tuesday. Thus a will or will not statement changes status only from false to true; and may or may nots change only from true to false. In either case, however, what changes is not really the truth value of a certain proposition, but the status of some quasi-proposition; a "statement schema", rather than a well-defined statement. Thus consider "X doing A at t"; if we do not know what actual world state is held to exhibit this act, we do not know what evidence is relevant to its truth and how, and hence we do not know what the statement commits us to. If t is understood to be in the past of the assertion, then indeed it does not matter at all when, more particularly, the assertion was made. But if it is a prediction, then it does matter. For the closer the time of utterance approaches t, the more numerous must the true will (and will not) statements become, and the less numerous the true may-or-may-nots. If, however, the time of utterance is fixed, then one of the three forms of futuristic statements must have been and must ever after remain true, since the possibilities for t must at that earlier time have been: all positive as to A, all negative, or divided. If the last, no subsequent happening can alter this retrospectively dated modal feature of reality: it can never in future be false that A was among the things which might or might not have followed the utterance after the specified interval. I am assuming that, as Peirce said, "time is a form of objective modality". Or rather, I am challenging anyone to refute this assumption without begging the question. "Truth changes", then, in the sense in which it does change, not in random fashion, but according to a necessary general rule. The vague and highly indefinite real possibilities for the remote future become step by step replaced, or rather supplemented, by more and more definite possibilities, as that future becomes imminent. Predictive truths, properly specified as to time of utterance, are never subsequently falsified; the only change is the addition of new truths for new times of utterance, new real states of nature, as these come into being. The very propositions themselves are new, for the "now" to which they refer is no mere date, but an actual situation, which as such could not be referred to beforehand, still less timelessly, or "in eternity".

Should any persistent reader argue that it must be true in advance or timelessly that a certain statement is to become true at a certain time, the answer of course is that, on the contrary, from a timeless, or remotely past, point of view, we should have at most "the statement may-or-may-not become true". This statement itself will suffer from indefiniteness. For it cannot identify anything concrete or particular, such as John's intentions at such and such a time. A semantic theory which contradicts this doctrine is trying to settle ontological questions by fiat, or, at best, according to logical convenience. I believe convenience at this level has little if any weight. The possible truth of blind guesses has value for science or common sense only if there is some connection, known or unknown, with causal laws; and so far as such laws obtain there is, according to our theory, definite truth about the future. What more do we need? Scientific corroboration can be achieved in the usual way, by eliminating the falsified claims to predictive understanding, and trying thus to narrow down the predictive and law-like assertions among which the true ones must be found.

A year ago it may have been settled that today roughly so and so many suicides would occur; a week ago, the inevitable number of suicides for today must have been considerably more precisely defined; a half minute ago nearly every suicide occurring during the past ten seconds may have become already inevitable, a settled fact. All these degrees of determinateness will remain valid for all the future, with respect to their dates of assertion and the events of today or the last ten seconds. Such, on the theory we are explaining, is the modal structure of time, or if you prefer, of happenings. Definiteness is progressively made; it is never unmade. There is becoming, but no unbecoming or de-becoming, of facts.

If "it will happen" means, it is now already settled that "it" cannot fail to happen, then that a statement schema of this sort should change its truth is no more odd than that "it is now raining" should do so. In both cases the assertion is incomplete until the time reference is fixed. Moreover, the notion that dates can be assigned from eternity is one of the fairy tales—or controversial assumptions—which haunt this subject. Dating requires actual events and experiences somewhere. So far from "now" being dispensable, in favour of mere values on a time coordinate, it is the other way; all dating derives from "token-reflexive" demonstratives whose meaning varies with the contexts of their utterance. Besides, it is no mere date which makes an "it is now and henceforth settled that" determinately true or false, but an actual event or event sequence, which cannot be referred to except retrospectively, as the process which has just been going on, or which went on in the less immediate past.

Prior and others have tried to formalize the modal theory of factual truth, and have been severely criticized by Quine, Martin, and others for the way they have done this.[3] The criticisms have not, I learn, convinced Prior. Since both he and his critics know more logic than I do, I hesitate to take sides in this controversy. But there is perhaps a third possibility. The crux of the matter is the theory of denotation. If this is a simple relation between language and things, then it is difficult to avoid the timeless theory of truth.[4] But if, as seems evident to me, denotation is a triadic affair, which for some purposes may be collapsed into a dyadic one, between language, experience, and things experienced, then it is another matter. For experiences occur, they have no status in eternity, hence neither do denotations. But without denotation, there is no factual truth. Actual experiences are either now, or they are past; the future of experience, like all things future, is merely the limited real potentiality whose indeterminacy must be resolved somehow, but need not be resolved this way instead of that, rather than that way instead of this. Since the more concrete or definite the denotation, the more we must know about the experiences which embody it, the utterly abstract standpoint which surveys all time from the vantage point of no time can contain only completely abstract truths such as those of arithmetic, or metaphysics. That all factual truth is time-dependent is itself a timeless truth; for it is utterly abstract and affirms no fact, but only a universal necessity of any and every fact, wholly neutral to factual alternatives.

Suppose W_1 means that at time t_1 all the possibilities for time t_3 include A, so that, as of t_1 A "will" happen; and W_2 means that at time t_2 all the possibilities for t_3 include A; then there is no contradiction in $W_2 . \sim W_1$. For the possibilities not including A may have been ruled out by the further becoming of the world's definiteness between t_1 and t_2. There would, however, be contradiction if the conjunction held timelessly, for then the said possibilities would *always* be excluded for t_3, and W_1 would never be false. (I owe this symbolism and some other suggestions utilized in this essay to my former colleague John Wilcox.) Nor can $W_2 . \sim W_1$ have obtained at t_1, for then both statements in the conjunction could only refer to the same possibilities. Possibilities already ruled out at t_1 for t_3 cannot be reinstated at t_2: process is always a narrowing of the "openness" of a given moment of the future, never its widening. On the other hand, if M_1 means, possibilities for A at t_3 are at t_1 divided, and M_2 that they are divided at t_2, then $M_1 . \sim M_2$ may obtain, even at t_1, for it may then be already settled that the indeterminacy concerning A at t_3 cannot last beyond t_2. The status of other combinations can readily be worked out.

---

[3]A. N. Prior, *Time and Modality* (Oxford, 1957). See the review by Martin, *Mind*, lxviii (1959), 271–275; also by K. J. J. Hintikka, *Philos. Rev.*, lxvii (1958), 401–404.
[4]See R. M. Martin, *Truth and Denotation* (Chicago, 1958), chap. iv.

Besides attacks from formal logicians we have to expect objections in the name of ordinary uses of words. Do people always and consistently mean by "A will be" that nothing else is any longer really possible, and by "A will not be" that A has become really impossible? Or by "may or may not", a division of real possibilities? Hardly, and if ordinary speech had this degree and kind of clarity and consistency, the history of philosophy must have run very differently. People commonly hesitate, in this and many other matters, between two or more meanings, and only if the requirements of their situation are very exacting with respect to the distinction do they attempt to resolve the ambiguity. How exacting are the requirements with respect to our issue? We deal with the future largely in terms of probabilities, scarcely in terms of absolute inevitabilities and impossibilities. Yet only the latter can be distinguished from situations of divided possibilities. Thus our ordinary practical predictions are, strictly speaking, qualified may or may nots, whose correlates are divided possibilities, but so strongly weighted toward one side or another of the division in terms of probability as to be not worth distinguishing from the strict will or will not forms. Also we cannot ordinarily undertake to contrast possibility and impossibility in the subjective sense, the possible, for instance, being taken as what is not known to be false, with objective possibility and impossibility. After we have summoned available knowledge, "possible" and "probable" as bases for our decisions have to mean what that knowledge seems to exhibit as possible or probable. The question what perfect knowledge would make of these categories is a highly theoretical one, and it is not surprising that common sense and common speech avoid it so far as possible.

We have philosophy in order to encourage more careful consideration of just such neglected subtleties. The notion that only science is concerned with them is a position which may have its plausibility, but is not self-evident. Even ordinary speech does get into situations in which distinctions between probable and inevitable, and improbable and impossible, become relevant. Thus if it be argued that "what will be will be", and hence the future is fixed in advance and our choices must have been fixed in advance, the reply is that "what will be" and "the future" need not be identical; we must consider the may or may not be, the unsettled. Again, it is an easy step from ordinary ways of speaking to the at least verbal notion of a divine or perfect knower for whom everything is simply thus and thus, or not thus and thus, and nothing is merely possible or probable. This gives us a familiar theological idea, whose familiarity does nothing to mitigate the extreme and only less familiar paradoxes which it entails. Centuries ago another idea was proposed in Socinian theology, the idea that perfect knowledge would exhibit all things as they are, the definite or settled as settled, and the indeterminate, unsettled, but open to further decisions, as precisely that. Many superior minds have elaborated the consequences of this view, which are, in important respects, much less painful or intellectually frustrating than those of the other view. Is ordinary language supposed to adjudicate this issue? I think it is, on the whole, on the side of real indeterminacy, but clearly, consistently, and obviously on this side? . . . Why should it or must it be? It is merely usual language for usual purposes.

There is one apparently serious difficulty. If we say, "it is possible that it will, but also possible that it will not occur", "will" cannot in this use be interpreted as I have recommended that it be. But this difficulty is like that posed by the various meanings of "or", and many another term which logicians have found cannot be simply adopted from ordinary use, but must be limited somewhat artificially. One could simply say, "A at t possible or probable now, at time t^1"; there is no necessity to say, "possibly or probably A will happen at t". But since ordinarily we are not trying to make explicit the distinction between reality as relative to our knowledge and as absolute, or as relative to complete knowledge, there is no particular harm, or philosophical significance, in the usage, "probably it will occur". It is merely a verbal way of doing a certain job well enough for the usual purpose. Philosophical purposes are not very usual. It is somewhat exasperating to have to emphasize this point so often nowadays.

An analysis which in part duplicates the one I have given is offered by Colin Strang, who, if he does not enter the promised land, is just outside the gate.[5] The sense of "will be" which implies something about the present state of reality Strang terms the "loaded" sense, and he shows as I have done that there are three cases—will, will not, and may or may not—one of which is in any given case true and the other two false. He also admits that ordinarily when we refer to the future the loaded sense is what we have in mind. But in rare cases, he thinks, we do mean "will" or "will not" in a "straight" or unloaded sense to which the present state of affairs is irrelevant. The only case he suggests, however, is that of a wager. One can wager only that something will, or that it will not, take place, and one of these is bound to win and so be proved true. My proposition here is, timeless or "straight", "truth" is irrelevant to a wager. The wager when made is more or less likely, or not likely, to win, and hence reasonable or unreasonable, according to the causal probabilities; eventually, it has won or not won; suppose it has won, this does not show it to have been true when made, any more than a successful prediction from a law establishes the law, still less, that it is timelessly true. Truth is some sort of correspondence, and the temporal status of the truth is the same as that of the correspondence. There can be no timeless relation to something whose mode of being is temporal, for relation to X includes X, and if X comes into being, so does the relation.

[5]"Aristotle and the Sea Battle," *Mind* (October 1960), pp. 447–465.

Thus my difference from Strang is simply that I reject his "straight sense" of altogether, so far as factual propositions are concerned. He makes no effort to s. how from the ultimate success of a wager one passes either to its antecedent or its timeless correctness. Note also that the reason we do not treat "may or may not" as subject to wagering is that we lack the resources to ascertain with certainty that the non-occurrence of an event which has, or the occurrence of an event which has not, in due time, occurred was nevertheless causally possible. Hence, if we were unable to agree about the scope of the causal conditioning at the time the wager was made, we shall probably not agree even when the event has taken place. Betting on the point is thus impracticable. Yet the causal conditioning at any given time does go as far as it goes and no farther; and if two men differ about this, one of them is correct and the other in error.

How clear Aristotle was about these things I am not prepared to say. I do think that in some passages, particularly in the discussion *(Metaphysics E*3) of what will be as also necessary, and the illustration of the inevitable, contrasted to the fortuitous, aspects of a man's death, he was closer to the truth than many a contemporary philosopher.

The rejection of determinism which our doctrine requires will of course trouble many. Thus some will ask, If the antecedent conditions of an event do not uniquely determine the event, for instance, a human choice, what does determine it? The answer is simple: precisely that freedom which the whole argument is about. The chooser, in the present, selects or makes his act; the antecedent conditions, including the chooser's previous "character", do not select or make it. They select or settle the range of possibilities any one of which he can choose; but only he, then and there, determines the precise action itself. This is the creative element in life, the actual making of definiteness where before was the indefinite, the possible. An explication of "truth" which rules this out is employing an ontological argument to settle a metaphysical issue. Predictions are made true or false by the real world they describe; "future events", as fully determinate already, are not a part of this or any world. How there can be an objective distinction between past and future which is compatible with the principles of relativity physics is one of the really hard questions, now being avoided by most writers partly because of its difficulty, and partly because it is unfashionable for physicists and philosophers to try to connect their two subjects.

A theory of "freedom" which denies the objective openness of the future can of course easily be reconciled with the law of excluded middle taken as restricting the possible cases to will and will-not. But some of us think Bergson, Whitehead, Berdyaev, James, Peirce, and many others have been right in holding that "freedom", in its normal moral meaning, and in some measure even all "process", implies creative power to add to the world's definiteness. The alternative is that events merely enact a plan or requirement laid down "at the beginning", or else not laid down at all but just always there. Yet since other worlds remain conceivable, in effect a selection has been made somehow. Determinism thus makes the mystery of definiteness impenetrable. It denies us the dignity of participating, however minutely and humbly, in the creative process, belief in which is the only consistent positive view of how the decision among logical possibilities gets itself made.

So far I have avoided comparison of my views with those of Bradley or Montague. Any reader who wishes can make the comparison; and for me to attempt it would greatly increase the length of this essay. But I should like to make a few remarks directed chiefly to Bradley's analysis. I have not argued or implied that "logical determinism", the view that the future is determinate, implies fatalism, the contention that our choices and efforts "make no difference", or are futile.

Mr. Bradley objects to "true now" because if not redundant (or worse) it implies "not true at some other time", and this the "logical determinist" regards as absurd. However, what is true timelessly is not false at any time, and the indeterminist contends that unless it is now false that X will do A and false that X will not do A, it cannot now be true that X may-or-may-not do A, this present indeterminacy being part of the very meaning of "decision not yet made but pending". The real possibilities either are or are not now divided with respect to A.

Mr. Bradley rejects, but without careful argument, the view that the future is definite only to the extent that present causal conditions imply some of its features, or restrict its range of real possibilities. He does not see perhaps how this view explicates the structure of time. Because future events are incompletely defined particulars, they are not past events; because nevertheless they are to some extent defined, this advance definiteness including the necessity that the residual indefiniteness be resolved *somehow* as the events become present, the events in question are not mere logical possibilities, but characterize the future. This is what it is to be future, on our theory. One may reject the theory; but have sufficient grounds for the rejection been given? Precognition is cited as at least a logical possibility, and hence an objection to the theory. This, however, is the question at issue. One must presuppose that "future" in "awareness of the future" has some other meaning than the one proposed. Since I see no other meaning that will stand analysis, I regard precognition of wholly definite particulars as logically impossible.

We are told (Waismann had said it before) that if will, or will not, statements about events "become true", we can have no idea when. But of course, in principle we can: they become true when the real possibilities have been causally narrowed down to the point required by the statements. Naturally having once been closed for a specified feature and date, they can never afterwards be reopened. "The moving finger writes . . . ." One knows the quotation. But it is a *non sequitur*, and an example of the "prejudice of symmetry" that the future events must be written down beforehand in similar detail. It is also a *non sequitur* to suppose that the "open future" theory must mean that no *will*, or *will not*, statement is ever true or false. So far as causal conditioning is definitely determinative, many such statements are true, and all the rest are false. But the appropriate meaning of "conditioning" is not to be ascertained casually. Newtonian views of causal laws are, in my opinion, no longer adequate, and some astute scientists and philosophers rather long ago began to challenge their literal validity.

Mr. Montague suggests that the crucial question is, what must eventually be the case for a prediction to be true? He can see nothing else than the occurrence of the predicted event. This is, I have argued, a form of the verificatory fallacy which Popper never wearies of attacking. Just as for a law to obtain it is not enough for there to be an instance in conformity with the law, but in addition contrary instances must be universally excluded; so with a prediction, contrary real possibilities must all be excluded. With this substitution, the analogy is exact. Indeed, is it a mere substitution? Recall that laws tell us not only what does and what does not occur, but also what would and would not occur under counterfactual conditions, and does this not involve the idea of real potentialities? On this point, Peirce seems to me to have seen more clearly than most students since his day. The only way to render single verifications of predictions decisive is to reject the concept of real possibilities, that is, to make determinism logically true.

One may indeed deny that the determinateness of the future need be one of law, of repetitive pattern, or of any kind of necessity. Thus Mr. Bradley seems to think that there might be a random sequence of unconnected yet determinate events, and that propositions might be timelessly true of members of this sequence. This implies two time series: the actual one which we experience, with a settled past and a future which we take, pragmatically at least, as partly settled and partly unsettled but open to settlement, beginning now; and another one, laid up in heaven, so to speak, and complete once for all, thanks to which propositions have their timeless truth. For propositions are not true simply in themselves, unless perhaps when they are analytic, but only thanks to some reality other than the propositions. If either of our authors is acquainted with this second series of mutually independent events, or anything remotely like it, he has the advantage of me. I have no access to it and fail to see how he has. I find no serious attempt to explain how the trick is done. Access is always to the present or past, and the causally-conditioned but not fully-determined future. Should we not leave the second series, complete once for all, and whether casual or not, to the timeless vision of the Schoolmen's God, of which it is a sort of ghost, and content ourselves with the only time we can genu-inely deal with, the ever-unfinished series whose prospective members are merely advance outlines drawn by causality, members which, when more than outlined, when fully detailed or actual, will be past and not future? This actual series is a partly new series each moment, a totality enriched by new members. "All reality", "all truth", are then token-reflexive terms, like "this", "I", and "now", changing their referents from use to use, though only by addition, by inclusion of the old reality or truth in the new. Events, on this view, are not mere constituents of the universe, but steps in its very making, a making which cannot ever be complete and properly final, since ultimate or logical possibilities are "absolutely infinite", or infinite in infinitely many respects—or a continuum of respects—hence inexhaustible by any actuality, however great or infinite in some respects. An actuality infinite in all respects, in the sense in which possibility is so, is nonsense or contradiction. This world-view is not in its bare outlines very complicated, and it has so many advantages that the near unanimity with which writers are failing even to mention it with any definiteness seems almost hypnotic to me. Am I dreaming, or are a great many others doing so? Someone, it seems, must be thinking rather oddly.

14

IT WAS TO BE

A. N. Prior

One feature of the ordinary unreflective view of free will is that it presupposes an enormous difference between the future and the past. Over what has already happened, the ordinary view would be, we have no further control; but we do have some control over what is going to happen. Whatever is past, we might say, is now *unpreventable*; we cannot now stop its having happened; but what is still as it were on the way to happening, we *can* sometimes stop happening, and whether it actually happens or not may depend on what we decide and do.

Some philosophers, however, have argued against this view as follows: Whatever is *logically equivalent* to something unpreventable must itself be unpreventable; but every fact about the future can be shown to have corresponding to it a logically equivalent fact about the past, so whatever unpreventableness is admitted to attach to the past must attach to the future also. The proof that to every fact about the future there corresponds a logically equivalent fact about the past, is roughly as follows: We need only concern ourselves, for the purposes of this argument, with what we might call elementary facts about the future, i.e. facts to the effect that something or other will take place at some definite future time, say n time-units hence. Now corresponding to any fact-about-the-future to the effect that X *will* take place n time-units *hence* there is always a logically equivalent fact-about-the-past, in fact a whole infinite *range* of logically equivalent facts-about-the-past, to the effect that m time-units *ago* the statement "X will take place $m+n$ time-units hence" *was* true. To take a simple example: if and only if it is a fact-about-the-future that I *shall* have a smoke *tomorrow* then it is a fact-about-the-past that *yesterday* the statement "Prior will have a smoke the day after tomorrow" *was* true, and for that matter the statement "Prior will have a smoke a million years and a day hereafter" *was* true a million years ago. But these, being facts about the past, are about what's over and done with now; they're things, therefore, that it's now too late for us to stop; *ergo* it's equally too late now for us to stop myself smoking tomorrow, since I could only do this by undoing the million-year-old truth that I've mentioned, which is absurd.

There are, of course, a variety of ways of breaking this chain, if one doesn't like what one finds oneself with at the end. One way of sliding out, on which I don't think it's necessary to waste much time, is to make nonsense of most of the argument by denying that you can attach a time to a truth-value. But in fact we all use phrases like "was true yesterday" perfectly happily when we are not philosophising, and we even *have to* use them if we are talking about the truth-values of statements with words like "was" and "will" in them. Not that I think we can settle all philosophical questions by considering what we do when we are not philosophising; but the consideration is relevant in the present case. For the argument that I stated professes to demonstrate an incoherence in our ordinary unreflective notions; it puts together a few premises that men are ordinarily disposed to assent to, and draws from these a conclusion which they are ordinarily disposed to deny; and it won't do as a defence of the ordinary unreflective point of view to deny that there is an intelligible use of phrases like "true yesterday", for this is simply *abandoning* the ordinary unreflective point of view at another point. In any case, the whole argument can pretty obviously be rephrased without using the words "true" and "false" at all; for example we can say that if and only if I *am* going to have a smoke tomorrow then yesterday I *was* going to have a smoke the day after the following day.

For my own part, I would say that the argument I stated not only claims to show but *does* show that our ordinary unreflective view of these matters is a little bit incoherent, and how we ought to straighten it out is partly a matter of what is true and partly a matter of how it's most convenient to talk. Whether or not we ought to accept the conclusion that we have no control over what will be, seems to me a matter of what is true; but assuming that in fact we *have* some control over what will be, which premises of the argument we reject or how we modify them seems to me to be a linguistic matter, and this is what I want now to talk about in some detail.

The argument has two principal premises—the unpreventableness of the past, and the logical equivalence of every statement whose principal verb is in the future tense to a set of statements with the principal verb in the past tense. So ways of avoiding the conclusion will divide into ones which deny the logical equivalence just mentioned, and ones which deny the unpreventableness of the past. Denials of the logical equivalence just mentioned—denials for example, of the equivalence between "There will be a sea-battle tomorrow" and "It was true yesterday that there would be a sea-battle the day after the following day"—are often associated with denials of the law of excluded middle. That is, it may be said that statements to the effect that X *will* take place at a certain time are only true if it is already settled and determined that they will take place, and are false only if it is already settled and determined that they will *not* take place, and are some third thing, say neuter or undecided, if it is still an open question whether X will take place or not. If, let us say, a sea-battle tomorrow is now past stopping but might have been stopped yesterday, then on this three-valued view we would say that the statement "There will be a sea-battle tomorrow" is now true while yesterday the statement "There will be a sea-battle the day after tomorrow" was not true but neuter; and this of course suffices to destroy the logical equivalence between future-tense and past-tense statements on which the argument we are considering depends.

But we can also destroy this equivalence, as I tried to show in the tenth chapter of my *Time and Modality, without* denying the law of excluded middle. For we might say that if a sea-battle tomorrow is now past stopping but wasn't past stopping yesterday, then the statement "There will be a sea-battle tomorrow" is true today, but yesterday the statement "There will be a sea-battle the day after tomorrow" was not merely neuter but *false.* This sounds almost like a contradiction, but I don't think it is one—we escape contradiction by distinguishing two senses of the phrase "will not", these senses being what I think Miss Anscombe would call the external and the internal negation of the plain "will". We may write down these two senses of "There will not be a sea-battle the day after tomorrow" as follows:

Ext.: It is not the case that
 it will be the case two days hence that
 there is a sea-battle going on.

Int.: It will be the case two days hence that
 it is not the case that
 there is a sea-battle going on.

On the view I'm trying to sketch, as on the three-valued view, the simple statement that it will be the case two days hence that a sea-battle is going on is not *true now, true already,* that is to say *in positive accordance with the present facts,* unless the sea-battle is already in a manner present—present in its causes, to use an old locution—and indeed in such a way that we cannot now prevent it happening. If it is *not* so present, whether because it has already been prevented or merely because it is still preventable, the positive "will" statement is false, and the direct external negation, asserting that it is *not* the case, i.e. not now the case, not yet the case, that there will be a sea-battle in two days' time, is true. On the other hand the *internal* negation of the simple future, which doesn't merely deny the future being but asserts the future non-being of the sea-battle, is only true if the sea-battle is not merely still preventable but has already been prevented; only then is it true now, true already, that it *is going to* not-happen. This way of talking gives us the distinction that we want to make between necessary, contingent, and impossible futures without introducing a third truth-value.

Nevertheless, the way of talking that I have just sketched shares with the three-valued way of talking one big disadvantage, namely that it is grossly at variance with the ways in which even non-determinists ordinarily appraise or assign truth-values to predictions, bets, and guesses. Suppose at the beginning of a race I bet you that Phar Lap will win, and then he does win, and I come to claim my bet. You might then ask me, "Why, do you think this victory was unpreventable when you made your bet?" I admit that I don't, so you say "Well I'm not paying up then—when you said Phar Lap would win, what you said wasn't true—on the three-valued view, it was merely neuter: on this other view of yours, it was even false. So I'm sticking to the money." And I must admit that if anyone treated a bet of mine like that I would feel aggrieved; that just isn't the way this game is played.

What one would like to see is a systematisation of ordinary betting talk that is quite unfatalistic. And this I think can be provided; but only, I would suggest, if one is prepared to deny or qualify the other premiss of the original argument I gave, namely the unpreventability of the past. And to bring this out in detail I shall try to pass on a way of talking that was originally put to me by my New Zealand colleague Mr. Michael Shorter as a kind of gloss on the second chapter of Professor Ryle's *Dilemmas*, from which of course I have pinched the title of this present paper. Basically what must be abandoned, if we are to use betting language correctly and yet indeterministically, is the assumption that the present truth of an assertion must consist in its accordance with something in the non-linguistic world around one at the time the assertion is made. For the whole peculiarity of future tense assertions is precisely that with them this assumption fails. There may be just nothing in the world around us that verifies a statement like "Phar Lap will be the winner in two minutes' time" at the time when it is made; that is to say there may be *no grounds* for making any pronouncement as to its truth-value at that time; there only come to be such grounds two minutes later, and then we can look back and say "That statement *was* true" or "That statement *was* false", as the case may be. But does this mean that when it was made the statement was neither true nor false? Not at all. At all times, including the time when they are made, the two statements

A1. Phar Lap *will* win in two minutes

A2. "Phar Lap will win in two minutes" *is* true

are exactly equivalent and on exactly the same footing; and if A1 is what you might describe as a wait-and-seeish sort of statement, meaning by that that when it is made there are no grounds for judging it true or false, but if you wait and see there will be grounds for saying that it was true or was false—well, if A1 is a wait-and-seeish statement in this sense, so is A2, despite the fact that its main verb is present; and the same also goes for

A3. "Phar Lap will win in three minutes" *was* true a minute ago,

despite the fact that the main verb of *this* one is past. It's about what was the case—the truth-value of a certain statement—a minute ago; nevertheless we have no way of assigning a truth-value to it until two more minutes have gone.

This is a procedure which, Mr. Shorter has pointed out, could be applied to other types of sentences which are sometimes said to be either permanently or temporarily without a truth-value. Imperatives, for example. We are tempted to say that "'Shut the door' is true" must be false or senseless because by the ordinary conventions about the word "true" it ought to be equivalent to the plain "Shut the door", but it can't be because the plain "Shut the door" is an imperative whereas "'Shut the door' is true" is an indicative. But why should we not use the sentence "'Shut the door' is true" as a way of *endorsing* the imperative "Shut the door", and so as another imperative? We *don't*, of course, as our language now is, use the sentence "'Shut the door' is true" in that or any other way, but it is at least arguable that we do use sentences like "He is quite right to tell him to shut the door" in precisely that way, despite their indicative grammatical form. And as with imperativeness, so it could be with futurity or wait-and-seeishness.

Wait-and-seeishness, we might say, is not in this language acquired by statements from their main verb only; let even a subordinate clause, or something in quotes, be of the wait-and-seeish kind, and the wait-and-seeishness *may* be transmitted to the whole. And along with this wait-and-seeishness goes preventableness. An example that Mr. Shorter sometimes used was giving up smoking. "I have given up smoking" is past in form but does it really describe something which I cannot now undo? On any analysis, it contains a compound to the effect that I used to smoke, and that is certainly something that I cannot now undo. But what about the rest of it? Well, there are two possible analyses of this remainder, namely

B1. For some time I haven't smoked, and I shall not smoke any more.
B2. It has been the case for some time that I shall not smoke any more.

On the view I sketched earlier, these could be different in force. On that earlier-sketched view, both B1 and B2 are only true if I have now effectively prevented myself from ever smoking again; but B2 is only true if this effective prevention took place some time ago—B1 would be true, but B2 false, if for some time I haven't smoked but still could have done, though now I can't any more. But on what one might call the Shorterian or perhaps Rylo-Shorterian view B1 and B2 are equivalent forms and in any case they both express something that could still be preventable. If I do prevent my never smoking again by having another smoke, then of course I shall say, looking back, that B1 and B2 were false when said, and that at that time I *hadn't* in fact given up smoking; but on the other hand this may never happen, in which case that B1 and B2 are true will be retrospectively verified.*

Now I want to suggest that the difference between this way of talking and that sketched earlier is *just* a difference in ways of talking and not in what is said. And what shows this is that within either of these languages you can give the basic rules of the other language. Suppose I use capital letters for the tense-forms of the language in which it is important to distinguish the internal from the external negation of the plain future; and small letters for the tense-forms of the betting language. Now I can easily *mention* the small-letter "will" in the big-letter language, but it's a tricky matter to explain how it works when you can only *use* the big-letter "Will". It obviously won't do to say, e.g.

C1. "Phar Lap will win" is true if and only if Phar Lap WILL win.

Nor will it do to say

C2. It WILL be right to say "'Phar Lap will win' was true" if and only if Phar Lap WILL win.

This is true but unhelpful—it only tells us that the future rightness of the thing in quotes is now unpreventable if and only if Phar Lap's winning is now unpreventable, but it's the use of the small-letter "will" and "was" when Phar Lap's win isn't unpreventable that we want to explain. And the way to do it is like this.

C3. If anyone says "Phar Lap will win 2 minutes hence"
then it WILL be the case 2 minutes hence that
"what he said was true" is true if and only if Phar Lap is the winner.

The big WILL in the main consequent of this is justified because although nothing compels Phar Lap to win and nothing compels the man to say he will, once the man *has* said that Phar Lap will win he has in a manner put his hand in the fire and *one* thing cannot now be stopped, namely that when the time comes what he has said will stand or fall under the conditions stated. But note that the big WILL governs the whole "if and only if" statement—we get things that we don't want at all if we

---

*The text in this final clause seems to contain a typographical error in the original, and we have elected to clarify Prior's text in the given way. [Volume editors.]

try to put the big WILL into one or both of the *parts* of the biconditional—we go all wrong if we try to replace "It WILL be that if and only if . . ." by "If and only if it WILL be that . . ." Of course C1 is only the first of a whole series of statements needed to explain the small-letter usages, but it will do for a start.

Conversely, the way to introduce the big-letter language into the other is by supplementing the pure tense apparatus of the betting language with a modal operator "It is inevitable that . . ." "It WILL be the case that . . ." can then be explained as "It is inevitable that it will be the case that . . ." The difference between the internal and external negation of "WILL" then becomes simply that between "It is inevitable that it will not be the case that" and "It is not inevitable that it will be the case that". This makes the rules for "will" in themselves very simple; there's no need, for example, to distinguish different senses of "will-not"—"It *is not* the case that it *will* be" is just the same as, I mean logically equivalent, to "It will be that it is not the case that". And similarly with disjunctive forms—"It either will be that *p* or it will be that *q*" is just the same as "It will be that either *p* or *q*". There's nothing as simple as that with "WILL"; e.g. it WILL be that either *p* or not-*p* even in cases where it neither WILL be that *p* nor WILL be that not-*p*. But in the betting or Shorterian language the complications come in with the relation of "WAS" to the "It is inevitable that" and "was". Let us begin consideration of this by noting that the internal and external negations of "WAS" statements are the same, the big-letter language being designed precisely to give direct expression to the idea that whereas for every *p* it either WAS the case that *p* or WAS the case that not-*p*, at any given time ago, there are *p*s such that it neither WILL be that *p* nor WILL be that not *p*—the clear expression of this felt difference between past and future is the special merit of that system. But if you define "WAS" simply as "It is inevitable that it was", it would seem that you'd only get the required simple bifurcation of the past if you could assume that all "wases" are now inevitable; and that, as we have seen, isn't the case. This is a bit tricky, so let's put up an example. In big-letter language this is a law:

D1. Either it WAS the case yesterday that *p* or it WAS the case yesterday that not *p*.

But the following

D2. Either it is inevitable that it was the case that *p* or it is inevitable that it was the case that not *p*.

is *not* a law in little-letter language, for if *p* is a sufficiently future-tense statement it may be still open to us to prevent or not to prevent its having been the case that *p*;

e.g. it is still open to me to prevent or not to prevent its having been the case yesterday that I would have a smoke two days from then.

I think the position is more or less as follows: Little-letter statements aren't universally translatable into big-letter ones, e.g. simple "will" statements have no exact equivalents in the big-letter language—they're not statements in the big-letter sense. But simple "will" statements preceded by "It is inevitable that" *are* translatable as the corresponding "WILL" ones. *Simple* "was" statements even when not preceded by "It is inevitable that" translate directly as the corresponding "WAS" ones, likewise "was" statements that have no subordinate "wills" except ones preceded by "It is inevitable that". But "was" statements containing unqualified "wills" are no more translatable into big-letter language than the simple "will" ones are. All you can do for these in big-letter language is to explain their syntax in the way I've outlined; so that you *can teach* a big-letter speaker how to talk little-letter, but cannot always supply big-letter translations. And the law D1 only applies where the *p*s stand for statements in the big-letter sense.

We might say briefly that "It WAS the case that *p*", where *p* is a genuine big-letter sentence, *is* always translatable into little-letter language as "It is now inevitable that it was the case that *p*", but the converse translation with *p* a genuine *little*-letter sentence is not always possible. And with regard to the limitations of translating little-letter language into big-letter language, the following generalisation may be made: The only expressions which count as indicative sentences in big-letter language are ones which state what already is or already is not the case, i.e. which state what is now either beyond prevention or—if the sentence is false—already prevented. We can, of course, state in big-letter language that it neither WILL be the case that *p* nor WILL be the case that not-*p*, i.e. we can state in big-letter language *that p is now a future contingency*; but this thing that we state is not itself a future contingency, i.e. it is not now a future contingency *that p* is now a future contingency; on the contrary this present contingency of *p* itself either a fact which it is now too late to prevent or a falsehood which it is now too late to make true. The big-letter language, in other words, can only set forth truly or falsely that which has already come to be the case, in such a sense as to be now beyond prevention, including now unpreventable futures. The future, one might say, is only describable in the big-letter language to the extent to which it is assimilable to the present and the past. There are no wait-and-seeish statements in big-letter language, so no wait-and-seeish statements are translatable into it.

We *can* all the same explain in big-letter language how the wait-and-seeish statements of little-letter language are used. That is, we *can* explain in big-letter language how our ordinary appraisals of bets and guesses work. Bets and guesses don't have present truth-values in the sense in which big-letter statements of all tenses have present truth-values. And this entails that they haven't big-letter past or future truth-values either; for X big-WAS true if and only if X's truth big-WAS present. We can, however, introduce into big-letter language, firstly, *names* for bets and guesses, i.e. bets and guesses in quotes, and secondly, a special unanalysable semantic predicate "(little)-was-true" which attaches to bets and guesses according to rules that can be stated in a pure big-letter way. The paradigm is like this:

(a) It is, always WAS and always WILL be the case that

(b) *if* a man says "Phar Lap will win in two minutes", then

(c) it WILL be the case in two minutes that

(d) if and only if Phar Lap is winning, what the man said was true.

Here the big WILL in (a) is justified because the totality of what follows exemplifies a *law* of the logic of guesses and bets and so is not only now but at all times unpreventable. The big WILL in (c) is justified because once a man has committed himself to the bet or guess recorded in (b), nothing can prevent his bet or guess being appraised, when the time comes, in the manner described in (d). He has, as it were, once he has betted, put his hand in the fire, and *must* now take the consequence of standing or falling, when the time comes, in the manner (d). But note that to convey what we want to do, the big WILL must be placed *before* the whole biconditional (d), and not within it. For if we say instead of (c) –(d), the following:

(e) If and only if it WILL be the case in two minutes that Phar Lap wins, it WILL be the case that what the man said was true,

this will be true enough as far as it goes, but only tells us that the future appraisal was true is now beyond stopping if and only if Phar Lap's win is now beyond stopping, and what we want is a rule for the use of this appraisal that can be applied even when we *aren't* thus betting on a certainty.

I'd like to repeat that this semantic term "was-true" that I have introduced in the above manner is *not* a compound of the ordinary big-"WAS" and the ordinary "true", as that term applies in big-letter semantics to big-letter statements. And I don't mind at all if you put this point, as I think Ryle puts it, by saying that "true" is not *quite* the right word to apply to bets and guesses, and that bets and guesses aren't in the ordinary sense statements. But I would add that you *can* use a language in which bets and guesses and statements are all put in a single box, similar semantic appraisals used for all of them, and the same expression used for the "was" of "was-true" and for the ordinary past tense. My little-letter language is in fact just that: in the little-letter language, one might say, you can't distinguish between a formal *assertion* and a mere bet or guess; while in the big-letter language you can't distinguish between what will be so and what will inevitably be so. But in both of them you can express consistently the hypothesis of freedom—in little-letter language by saying that what will be, and in some cases even what has been, is not always beyond stopping, and in big-letter language by saying that there are some things of which it is not yet true either that they WILL be so or that they WILL be not-so.

Neither big-letter language nor little-letter language, so far as I can see, supplies us with a means of reconciling free power over the future with foreknowledge. For, to take big-letter talk first, it is obvious that if you define foreknowing that p as knowing that it big-WILL be the case that p, and adopt the usual view that what is known is true, then nothing can be foreknown in this sense but what big-WILL be the case, that is, what is unpreventable. With little-letter talk the question is a bit more tricky, but if you define foreknowing that p as knowing that it little-will be the case that p, I cannot see how any such thing can take place if what is said to be known is of a *strictly* wait-and-seeish sort. If one *has to*, in *principle*, "wait and see" whether it will be the case that p—if there is *nothing* presently round about one which decides the matter one way or the other—I cannot see that one can talk of *knowing* that p. And this doesn't seem to me an avoidable defect of either of these languages, for I must confess I can't see that foreknowledge *is* compatible with preventability. And I am *not* now doing anything so silly as to treat foreknowledge as any sort of *cause* of what is foreknown. What is known must be so in order to be known rather than vice versa, so that the knowing is much more like an effect of what is known than a cause of it. But that only makes what is foreknown less preventable than ever; for what has already got so far as to have *effects*, and effects which nothing but that thing *could* have, is surely beyond stopping. Uniformly correct *prediction* compatible with preventability, yes; but foreknowledge is surely more than that.

15

FUTURE CONTINGENTS AND RELATIVE TRUTH

John MacFarlane

I. THE PROBLEM OF FUTURE CONTINGENTS

Suppose that the world is objectively indeterministic. In some possible futures, there is a sea battle tomorrow. In others, there is not. How should we evaluate an assertion (made now) of the sentence "There will be a sea battle tomorrow"?

The question is difficult to answer because we are torn between two intuitions. On the one hand, there is a strong temptation to say that the assertion is neither true nor false. After all, there are possible future histories witnessing its truth and others witnessing its falsity, with nothing to break the symmetry. I shall call this "the indeterminacy intuition". On the other hand, there is a strong temptation to say that the assertion does have a definite truth-value, albeit one that must remain unknown until the future "unfolds". After all, once the sea battle has happened (or not), it seems quite strange to deny that the assertion was true (or false). I shall call the thought that the assertion does have a definite truth-value "the determinacy intuition".

On the face of it, these two intuitions look incompatible. No surprise, then, that standard "solutions" to the problem of future contingents have been able to save only one. Some approaches save the indeterminacy intuition, others the determinacy intuition. In §§II and III I discuss these one-sided approaches and argue that they are all unsatisfactory. A satisfactory account of future contingents must give both intuitions their due.

But how? Are they not incompatible? Only in the presence of the orthodox assumption that truth for utterances is non-relative. I shall call this assumption "the absoluteness of utterance-truth". No one would deny that the truth of sentences must be relativized to a context: "I am cold" has no absolute truth-value, but is true in relation to some contexts of utterance, false in relation to others. But on the orthodox view, no further relativization is called for once the context of utterance has been taken into account: the truth-value of an utterance does not depend on who is asking about it, or when. Thus if we say that an assertion of "There will be a sea battle tomorrow" is neither true nor false when it is made, then we cannot allow that it might acquire a truth-value later; conversely, if tomorrow (in the midst of a sea battle) we say that the assertion has turned out to be true, we cannot say that it was neither true nor false when it was made. The truth-value of an utterance is independent of the context from which the utterance is being assessed.

Given the absoluteness of utterance-truth, then, the indeterminacy intuition and the determinacy intuition are incompatible. But an adequate account of future contingents must respect both these intuitions. In §IV I draw the obvious conclusion: we must reject the absoluteness assumption. We must relativize the truth of utterances to a *context of assessment*, and we must relativize the truth of sentences to both a context of utterance and a context of assessment. This amounts to recognizing a new kind of linguistic context-sensitivity: sentence truth can vary not just with features of the context of utterance (*u-contextuality*) but with features of the context of assessment (*a-contextuality*). It is failure to make room for this kind of context sensitivity that has left us with the traditional menu of unsatisfactory solutions to the problem of future contingents.

In the second half of the paper, I try to remedy this failure. In §V I develop a semantic framework that allows for *a*-contextuality. Within this framework, I give an account of the semantics of future contingents that respects both the indeterminacy intuition and the determinacy intuition. Then in §VI I defend *a*-contextuality against a challenge to its very coherence, first raised (with somewhat less generality) by Gareth Evans. Discharging these tasks should go some way toward convincing philosophers who have grown up with the absoluteness assumption that it is not obligatory.

II. THE INDETERMINACY INTUITION

Suppose that at some moment m_0 there is an objectively possible future history h_1 in which there is a sea battle the next day, and another h_2 in which there is no sea battle the next day (see Fig. 15.1).[1] These alternative histories are both objective possibilities, not just epistemic ones. It is not just that we do not know whether or not there will be a battle, or even that we could not know, but that both courses of events are real possibilities. Whether the world is objectively indeterministic in this sense is,

---

[1] Here I presuppose the metaphysical picture of objective indeterminism articulated in N. Belnap et al., *Facing the Future* (Oxford UP, 2001), pp. 29–32, 139–41. Moments are idealized time-slices of the universe, partially ordered by a causal-historical precedence relation (<) with no backword branching histories; see Belnap, "Branching Space-Time," *Synthese*, 92 (1992), pp. 385–434. Although it is strictly correct to say that moments are *contained in* histories, I shall sometimes talk informally of histories *passing through* moments.

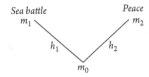

Sea battle — m_1 Peace — m_2

h_1 h_2

m_0

Figure 15.1 Branching Histories.

¬		∧	t	i	f	∨	t	i	f	⊃	t	i	f
t	f	t	t	i	f	t	t	t	t	t	t	i	f
i	i	i	i	i	f	i	t	i	i	i	t	t	i
f	t	f	f	f	f	f	t	i	f	f	t	t	t

Figure 15.2 Łukasiewicz's Three-Valued Semantics.

of course, a substantive scientific (and perhaps metaphysical) question. I do not here presuppose an affirmative answer to this question. All I am presupposing is that talk about the future would not be incoherent in an objectively indeterministic world. Determinism may be true, but it is not for the semanticist to say so.

Now suppose that at m_0 Jake asserts "There will be a sea battle tomorrow". Is his utterance true or false? The utterance takes place at m_0, which belongs to both h_1 and h_2. In h_1 there is a sea battle the day after m_0 while in h_2 there is not. We may assume that nothing about Jake's intentions picks out a particular history (h_1 or h_2). Jake may take himself to be making a claim about "the actual future history", but if this means "the future history that includes this utterance", then it is an improper definite description. There is no such unique history. Given that nothing about the context of utterance singles out one of the histories of which it is a part, symmetry considerations seem to rule out saying either that the utterance is true or that it is false. Thus, it seems, we must count it neither true nor false. This is the indeterminacy intuition.

There are two standard ways to capture the indeterminacy intuition in a rigorous semantics. The first, due to Łukasiewicz, is to introduce a third truth-value for future contingents (*i* for "indeterminate") and give three-valued truth-tables for the basic logical connectives (see Fig. 15.2).[2] But Łukasiewicz's semantics has some implausible consequences. When "There will be a sea battle tomorrow" has the value *i*, so does "There will be a sea battle tomorrow or there will not be a sea battle tomorrow", even though the latter sentence is not a future contingent. It will not help to change the truth-tables or add more values: the culprit is the assumption that the connectives are truth-functional.[3] Suppose that "There will be a sea

[2] J. Łukasiewicz, "On Three-Valued Logic," in S. McCall (ed.), *Polish Logic* (Oxford UP, 1967) 5 pp. 16–18.

[3] See A. N. Prior, "Three-Valued Logic and Future Contingents," *The Philosophical Quarterly*, 36 (1953), pp. 317–26, at p. 326.

battle tomorrow" and "There will be an eclipse tomorrow" both receive the same (indeterminate) truth-value. Then no matter how many truth-values there are, and no matter what truth-tables we use for "not" and "or", the sentences "There will be a sea battle tomorrow or there will not be an eclipse tomorrow" and "There will be a sea battle tomorrow or there will not be a sea battle tomorrow" will be assigned the same truth-value. But the former is indeterminate, while the latter is true.

A more attractive approach is the supervaluational semantics due to Thomason.[4] On this approach, an utterance is counted as true (*simpliciter*) if it is true on all possible future histories, false (*simpliciter*) if it is false on all possible future histories. Future contingents are true on some possible future histories, false on others; so they are neither true nor false. But instances of the law of excluded middle, even those whose disjuncts are future contingents, are true on all histories, and so true *simpliciter*. This approach seems to capture the indeterminacy intuition without the implausible consequences of the truth-functional approach.

III. THE DETERMINACY INTUITION

If we think about how to assign a truth-value to Jake's utterance at m_0, the indeterminacy intuition seems overwhelming. But now what about someone who is assessing Jake's utterance from some point in the future? Sally is hanging onto the mast, deafened by the roar of the cannon. She turns to Jake and says, "Your assertion yesterday turned out to be true." Sally's reasoning seems unimpeachable:

Jake asserted yesterday that there would be a sea battle today
There is a sea battle today
So Jake's assertion was true.

When we take this retrospective view, we are driven to assign a determinate truth-value to Jake's utterance: this is the determinacy intuition.

But how can we give Jake's utterance a determinate truth-value if the future is genuinely open at the time of utterance? Those who have tried to save the determinacy intuition have typically resorted to the following expedient. Out of all the possible futures at the moment of utterance, one is marked out as "the actual future", as if with a "thin red line" (see Fig. 15.3).[5] The thin red line is an objective

---

[4]See R. H. Thomason, "Indeterminist Time and Truth-Value Gaps," *Theoria*, 36 (1970), pp. 264–81.
[5]The metaphor is due to Nuel Belnap and Mitchell Green, "Indeterminism and the Thin Red Line," in J. Tomberlin (ed.), *Philosophical Perspectives* 8: *Logic and Language* (Atascadero: Ridgeview, 1994), pp. 365–88, revised as ch. 6 of Belnap et al., *Facing the Future*.

Figure 15.3 The "Thin Red Line".

feature of the context of utterance, but not an epistemically accessible one: there is no way to know which future is the marked one, except by waiting. Positing such a thin red line looks like a way to eat our cake and have it, too. By supposing that there are many objectively possible future histories, we hang on to objective indeterminism, and by positing the thin red line, we get the determinate truth-values we need for "retrospective" assessments of utterances. We are not forced to say, as the supervaluationist does, that assertions of future contingents are neither true nor false.

My view is that the eating precludes the having. Like Belnap and Green, I hold that positing a thin red line amounts to giving up objective indeterminism. The non-red branches in the tree are supposed to represent objectively possible futures, but their non-redness indicates precisely that they will not be the continuations of the history that includes the utterance in question. Looking down on the tree of branching histories from above, God can see that given the past and the context of utterance, only one continuation remains in play: the one marked with the thin red line. In what sense, then, are the others really "possibilities"? They are possible in an epistemic sense: the utterer does not know which history is marked out with the thin red line. But objectively speaking they are not genuine possibilities at all.

The idea that it makes sense to talk of a thin red line is, I think, an illusion which results from a conflation of "external" with "internal" perspectives in semantics. We do often say that one of two objectively possible outcomes of a past event turned out to have been the actual one, and even that it "was going to be" the actual one. When the coin lands heads up, we can say that heads was the side that "was actually going to land facing up", even if we do not think that the outcome was predetermined. It is this kind of talk that makes the thin red line seem intelligible and even compelling. But such talk makes sense only from some particular perspective within the tree of branching histories. From the point of view of an observer at m_1 (in Fig. 15.1) the actual future at m_0 held a sea battle, while from the point of view of an observer at m_2 it did not. And *qua* semanticists, we do not speak from the perspective of any particular moment on the tree of branching histories; instead we take a God's eye point of view, looking down on the tree from the outside, and try to say how the truth of sentences depends on features of the context of utterance. From this external point of view, there is no sense to saying that one of two histories passing through a moment is "going to be the actual one". It is only if we blur our vision, taking up internal and external perspectives simultaneously, that it can seem to make sense to mark out one of the histories in the tree (as seen from above) with a thin red line.

David Lewis sees this point very clearly. He acknowledges that if an utterance of a future contingent belongs to more than one possible future history, we cannot appeal to "the actual future" to secure it a determinate truth-value. But Lewis does not want to give up the determinacy intuition. His solution is to reject branching altogether.[6] On his view, each utterance takes place at a unique possible world, and each possible world has a unique future history. On these assumptions, the context of utterance always determines a unique "actual future".

Like the "thin red line", however, Lewis's picture saves the determinacy intuition only by sacrificing genuine objective indeterminism. Given a context of utterance, there is only one possible future history that contains it: the future is in that sense determined. Granted, there are other possible worlds that are qualitative duplicates of the actual world up to the present and diverge thereafter, but these worlds contain different utterances (and utterers), mere "counterparts" of the actual ones. Thus the future is open only in the sense that we do not (and perhaps cannot) know what it will bring.

IV. THE ABSOLUTENESS OF UTTERANCE-TRUTH

To sum up, if we focus on m_0 the indeterminacy intuition seems compelling, and we are pushed toward saying that Jake's utterance is neither true nor false. But if we focus on a later moment m_1 or m_2 at which the predicted sea battle is (or is not) happening, the determinacy intuition seems compelling, and we are pushed toward saying that Jake's utterance is determinately true (or false). I have argued that traditional approaches which save only one of these intuitions at the expense of the other are inadequate. But is it possible to do better? On the face of it, there is no way to capture both. If Jake's utterance is neither true nor false, as the indeterminacy intuition demands, it is not true and it is not false. But the determinacy intuition demands that it must be one or the other.

However, this quick argument for incompatibility assumes the absoluteness of utterance-truth. If utterance-truth were relativized to the context at which the utterance is being assessed, then we could accommodate both intuitions easily. We could say that Jake's utterance is true as assessed from m_1, false as assessed from m_2, and

---

[6]See Lewis, *On the Plurality of Worlds* (Oxford: Blackwell, 1986), pp. 206–09. Lewis's arguments against branching are effectively countered by Belnap et al. in *Facing the Future*, pp. 206–09.

neither true nor false as assessed from m_0. In fact this is precisely what I think we should say, and what people unschooled in philosophy naturally will say. What has kept philosophers from adopting this natural solution to the problem of future contingents is their deeply entrenched theoretical commitment to the absoluteness of utterance-truth. So much the worse for absoluteness. If we need to reject it to get a plausible account of our talk about the future, then reject it we should.

I have said that philosophers of language are deeply committed to absoluteness. I have sometimes heard this questioned, on the following ground. According to one dominant paradigm in the philosophy of language, an (assertive) utterance expresses a proposition, and propositions—contingent ones, anyway—are true at some possible worlds or situations, false at others. For example, the proposition Sam expresses when he says "I am cold" on New Year's Eve 2001, the proposition that Sam is cold on New Year's Eve 2001, is true with respect to some possible worlds (including worlds in which Sam, or a counterpart of Sam, is in Norway on New Year's Eve 2001), and false with respect to others (including worlds in which Sam, or a counterpart of Sam, is in Australia on New Year's Eve 2001). The objection goes as follows: to say that an utterance is true is to say that the proposition it expresses is true. But on the standard picture, the truth of propositions is relativized to worlds or situations. So the standard picture cannot avoid relativizing utterance-truth to worlds as well. If this is right, then the standard picture is not committed to absoluteness after all. Even Sam's mundane utterance is true as assessed from some possible worlds, false as assessed from others. But this objection rests on a misunderstanding. Yes, the proposition expressed by Sam's utterance is true with respect to some possible worlds, false with respect to others. But to say that an utterance is true is to say more than that the proposition it expresses is true: it is to say that this proposition is true *with respect to the world at which the utterance occurs.*

A simple example will help. Let w_1 be the actual world and w_2 a world very like the actual world, except that in w_2 the dodo never became extinct. Let u_1 and u_2 be utterances, in w_1 and w_2 respectively, of the sentence "The dodo is extinct in the year 2002"; u_1 and u_2 express the very same proposition p, and truth for p is world-relative: p is true in w_1 and false in w_2. Nonetheless, u_1 and u_2 can be assigned absolute truth-values: u_1 is true *simpliciter*—it accurately describes the world in which it is made—while u_2 is false *simpliciter*. All that matters for the truth of the utterance u_2 is the truth-value of the proposition it expresses at w_2; the truth-value of this proposition at other worlds (including the actual world w_1) is simply not relevant. So relativization of propositional truth to worlds is compatible with the absoluteness of utterance-truth. The relativization of utterance-truth to a context of assessment is a different beast entirely.

V. A FRAMEWORK FOR RELATIVE TRUTH

I have argued that in order to make good sense of future contingents, we must allow the truth of utterances to be relativized to the context from which they are being assessed. The suggestion will raise some hackles: it is widely believed that there is something incoherent about relative truth. My aim in the next two sections is to put this worry to rest. In this section, I shall show how a standard framework for the semantics of indexicals can be modified to allow for relativity of truth to a context of assessment. In the next, I shall show how the modified framework can be integrated with a plausible account of assertion.

In standard indexical semantics, truth for sentences must be relativized to a context of utterance. But for technical reasons, we cannot give a direct recursive definition of "s is true at context of utterance u". Here is a simple proof, adapted from Kaplan.[7] The sentence "I am here" is true at every context of utterance.[8] So is "$2 + 2 = 4$". But "It is always the case that I am here" is false at (nearly) every context of utterance, whereas "It is always the case that $2 + 2 = 4$" is true at every context of utterance. So the truth-at-a-context profile of a sentence s does not contain enough information to determine the truth-at-a-context profile of "It is always the case that s".

For technical reasons, then, the recursive clauses of a semantic theory must define not truth at a context, but truth at a *point of evaluation* (or simply "a point").[9] Points of evaluation are sequences of parameters, for example, speaker, location of utterance, time, and assignment. The recursive clauses for operators can vary these parameters independently: for example, the clause for "it is always the case that" shifts only the time parameter, while that for the universal quantifier shifts only the assignment parameter. So the truth-at-a-point profile of "$2 + 2 = 4$" differs from that of "I am here": the former sentence, but not the latter, is true at a point where *speaker* = Albert Einstein, *location of utterance* = New York City, and *time* = summer solstice, 1387. (There is no context of utterance corresponding to this combination of parameters.) Unlike its truth-at-a-context profile, a sentence's truth-at-a-point profile does determine the sentence's contribution to the truth-at-a-point profile of complex sentences embedding it.

---

[7]See D. Kaplan, "Demonstratives," in J. Almog et al. (eds.), *Themes from Kaplan* (Oxford UP, 1989), pp. 481–563, at pp. 508–10. See also Lewis, "Index, Context, and Content," in S. Kanger and S. Ohman (eds.), *Philosophy and Grammar* (Dordrecht: Reidel, 1980), pp. 79–100.

[8]I ignore complications raised by recorded messages and the like, which need special treatment. See S. Predelli, "I Am Not Here Now," *Analysis*, 58 (1998), pp. 107–15.

[9]The terminology is Belnap's: *Facing the Future*, p. 142. Points of evaluation differ from Kaplan's "circumstances of evaluation" or Lewis's "indices" in that they may include both shiftable and non-shiftable parameters, e.g., both *time* and *time of utterance*.

Semantics proper
⇓
truth at a point
⇓
Postsemantics
⇓
truth at a context

Figure 15.4 Semantics and Postsemantics.

I call the recursive definition of *truth at a point of evaluation* the "semantics proper". Of course it is the truth-at-a-context profile that we are interested in: this tells us how to evaluate assertions and other speech acts. Truth at a point is just a technical device for defining truth at a context. So we need a definition of *truth at a context of utterance* in terms of truth at a point of evaluation; I call this definition the "postsemantics" (see Fig.15.4). Distinguishing these two modules will help me make things clearer when I add contexts of assessment.

Here is an example. Suppose the only operators in our language are tense-operators ("it will be the case that", "it was the case that") and historical modalities ("it is settled that", "it is historically possible that"). For simplicity, suppose we have no quantifiers. Then our points will need just two parameters: moment and history. Our semantics proper will be a recursive definition of "s is true at m/h" (where the slash indicates that m belongs to h), along the following lines:

Semantics proper for "it will be the case that" and "it is settled that":
"Will: ϕ" is true at m/h iff for some $m_1 > m$ on h, ϕ is true at m_1/h
"Sett: ϕ" is true at m/h iff for every h_1 through m, ϕ is true at m/h_1 .

These operators behave just as you would expect they would: "*Will:*" shifts you forward along a history, while "*Sett:*" quantifies over all histories passing through a given moment. But all I have given so far is a definition of truth at a point (here, a moment/history pair). A moment/history pair is not a context of utterance, so I need a further step to define truth at a context of utterance. This step is made in the postsemantics, which mediates between *truth at a point* and *truth at a context of utterance*.

Here is where the controversy begins. Which moment/history pairs are relevant to the truth of a sentence at a context of utterance? Supervaluational postsemantics looks at every point whose moment parameter is the moment of utterance:

Supervaluational postsemantics: ϕ is true [false] at a context of utterance u iff ϕ is true [false] at every point m/h such that
m = the moment of u
h passes through m.

Thin red line postsemantics, on the other hand, supposes that context of utterance determines a unique history parameter, as well as a moment:[10]

> *Thin red line postsemantics:* φ is true [false] at a context of utterance *u* iff φ is true [false] at every point *m/h* such that
> *m* = the moment of *u*
> *h* = the "thin red line" at *u*.

I have already explained why neither of these accounts is acceptable, and I have suggested that an acceptable postsemantics will have to reject the absoluteness of utterance-truth. How, then, can we modify the framework so that utterance-truth can be relativized to the context in which the utterance is being assessed? Plainly we are going to need sentence-truth to be doubly relativized, to a context of utterance and a context of assessment. That is, we need the postsemantics to define *truth at a context of utterance and context of assessment*, instead of merely *truth at a context of utterance*. But this change in the *definiendum* of the postsemantics is the only change that is required. We can leave the semantics proper just as it is. Moreover, although the new framework will allow us to describe sentences that are *a*-contextual—sentences whose truth-values vary with the context of assessment—the framework itself is neutral about whether there *are* any a-contextual sentences. If one's definition of "*s* is true at context of utterance *u* and context of assessment *a*" makes no reference to *a*, no sentence in the language will be *a*-contextual. Thus an advocate of the absoluteness of utterance-truth has nothing to fear from the new framework itself, only from the freedom it gives us.

Taking advantage of this freedom, however, I can give a much more satisfactory postsemantics for the simple tensed language:

> *Double time reference postsemantics:* φ is true [false] at a context of utterance *u* and context of assessment *a* iff φ is true [false] at every point *m/h* such that
> *m* = the moment of *u*
> *h* passes through *m* and (if the moment of *a* > *m*) through the moment of *a* as well.

The essential structural feature of this account is what Belnap calls "double time references".[11] We evaluate φ with respect to the moment of utterance and all of the

---

[10]This proposal is not touched by Belnap and Green's semantic arguments against the use of a thin red line (*Facing the Future*, pp. 160–70). It uses the very same semantics proper as Belnap and Green endorse, and appeals to the thin red line only in the postsemantics.

[11]See *Facing the Future*, p. 175, and "Double Time References: Speech-Act Reports as Modalities in an Indeterministic Setting," in F. Wolter et al. (eds.), *Advances in Modal Logic*, vol. 111 (Stanford: CSLI, 2001), pp. 1–22. There is also an anticipation of double time references in Michael Dummett, *Frege: Philosophy of Language*, 2nd ed. (Harvard: UP, 1981), p. 395.

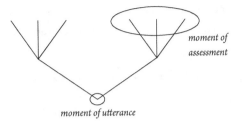

Figure 15.5 Double Time Reference.

histories passing through both it and the moment of assessment (see Fig. 15.5). But my use of double time references to define truth at a context of utterance and context of assessment is different from Belnap's. Whereas I use them to define truth at a context of utterance and context of assessment, he uses them to define when an assertion counts as "vindicated" or "impugned". Thus his account of assertion appeals directly to truth at a point of evaluation, and needs to be retooled when new parameters of points are added. My approach is to interpose another layer, the postsemantics, between the semantics proper (the definition of truth at a point) and the account of assertion. The account of assertion can then appeal to a uniform notion of truth at a context of utterance and context of assessment (for details, see §VI below). Everything specific to the structure of points, and hence to the particular expressive resources of a language, is handled in the postsemantics, and "screened off" from the theory of speech acts, which can then be developed (as it should be) in abstraction from the details of particular languages.

The double time reference postsemantics allows us to say just what we wanted to say about Jake's utterance of "There will be a sea battle tomorrow" at m_0 (see Fig. 15.1). The semantics proper tells us that "There will be a sea battle tomorrow" (s) is true at m_0/h_1 but false at m_0/h_2. Idealizing the context of utterance (u) and context of assessment (a) as moments, the postsemantics yields the following:

At $u=m_0$ and $a=m_0$, s is neither true nor false (because we must look at both points, m_0/h_1 and m_0/h_2)
At $u=m_0$ and $a=m_1$, s is true (because we look only at m_0/h_1)
At $u=m_0$ and $a=m_2$, s is false (because we look only at m_0/h_2).

Since an utterance is true [false] with respect to a context of assessment a iff the sentence uttered is true [false] with respect to the context of utterance and a, this account implies that Jake's utterance at m_0 is true as assessed from m_1, false as assessed from m_2, and neither true nor false as assessed from m_0. This is just the result I said would respect both the determinacy and indeterminacy intuitions. The price is that we must countenance a novel kind of context-sensitivity, *a*-contextuality. I think that this is a small price to pay for an adequate account of future contingents.

VI. MEETING EVANS'S CHALLENGE

The persistence of the problem of future contingents over two millennia attests to the reluctance of philosophers to consider abandoning the absoluteness assumption. Why have we been so unwilling to give it up? Why does *a*-contextuality seem so outlandish?

The best diagnosis I have seen is due to Gareth Evans, who criticizes a view on which "the evaluation of an utterance as correct or incorrect depends upon the time the *evaluation* is made."[12] The particular view Evans criticizes is manifestly implausible, but the grounds on which he criticizes this view are general enough to apply to any view on which the truth of utterances is relativized to a context of assessment, including the view advocated here. Evans argues, in effect, that no such view is consistent with the role played by utterance-truth (or "correctness") in our practice of making assertions. It is incoherent, he says (pp. 349–50), to suppose that a single assertion might count as "objectively correct" at some times but not at others:

> Such a conception of assertion is not coherent. In the first place, I do not understand the use of our ordinary word "correct" to apply to one and the same historical act at some times and not at others, according to the state of the weather. Just as we use the terms "good" and "bad", "obligatory" and "permitted" to make an assessment, once and for all, of non-linguistic actions, so we use the term "correct" to make a once-and-for-all assessment of speech acts. Secondly, even if we strain to understand the notion "correct-at-t", it is clear that a theory of meaning which states the semantic values of particular utterances solely by the use of it cannot serve as a theory of sense. If a theory of reference permits a subject to deduce merely that a particular utterance is now correct, but later will be incorrect, it cannot assist the subject in deciding what to say, nor in interpreting the remarks of others. What should he aim at, or take the others to be aiming at? *Maximum* correctness? But of course, if he knew an answer to this question, it would necessarily generate a once-and-for-all assessment of utterances, according to whether or not they meet whatever condition the answer gave.

---

[12]"Does Tense Logic Rest on a Mistake?," in Evans, *Collected Papers* (Oxford: Clarendon Press, 1985), pp. 343–63, at p. 348. Evans talks of the "correctness" of utterances instead of their truth, reserving the word "true" for the truth of sentences relative to a point of evaluation. This difference is, I think, entirely terminological.

I need to rephrase Evans's criticism using the terminology I have introduced in this paper. When we make sincere assertions, we aim to speak the truth. But if the sentence we assert is *a*-contextual, there is no non-relativized fact of the matter as to whether our assertion is true: it is true relative to some contexts of assessment, untrue relative to others. So how can we aim to speak the truth in asserting? At best we can aim to speak the truth *as assessed from such and such a context*. But the context of utterance (including our intentions in uttering the sentence) does not pick out a uniquely relevant context of assessment. If it did, then we would not need to relativize truth to a context of assessment; the context of utterance alone would provide all the information needed to get a truth-value. Perhaps we should aim at maximum truth, truth at most contexts of assessments? But in that case, too, we would end up with singly relativized truth, because we would be quantifying over contexts of assessment in the postsemantics. As Evans points out, any answer to the question "What should we aim at in assertion?" will provide a way for the postsemantics to avoid serving up doubly relativized truth. The upshot seems to be that (doubly relativized) truth at a context of utterance and context of assessment is not a suitable input to an account of assertion or other speech acts. The postsemantics must tell us in what contexts of utterance a sentence is true (full stop); otherwise we can have no understanding of what someone might be aiming at in asserting it.

I think that Evans's argument neatly articulates a worry many philosophers have had about the very coherence of what I am calling *a*-contextuality, a worry that has no doubt kept the requisite semantic machinery from being developed.[13] But at most Evans's argument shows that *a*-contextuality is incompatible with a particular picture of assertion, on which assertion is like a game one can either win (by speaking the truth) or lose (by speaking falsely). Why should that be our picture? When I was young, my friends and I used to play multi-player Rochambeau. In this game, whether a move counts as winning varies from opponent to opponent. A play of "rock" will win with respect to an opponent who plays "scissors", but lose to one who plays "paper". Though one cannot aim to win *simpliciter*, the game is not incoherent. It is just different from games in which winning is not relativized to opponents. Similarly, I suggest, assertions of *a*-contextual sentences, whose truth varies from one context of assessment to another, are not incoherent: they are just different from assertions of non-*a*-contextual sentences. What we need is an account that does not rule them out from the start.

---

[13]Philip Percival calls Evans's argument "the best available defence of the absolutist's claim that any relativization of token truth is incoherent": "Absolute Truth," *Proceedings of the Aristotelian Society*, 94 (1994), pp. 189–213, at p. 198.

Indeed, it is not obvious that "aiming at the truth" should play any part in an account of assertion. If we aim at anything in making assertions, it is to have an effect on other people: to inform them, persuade them, amuse them, encourage them, insult them, or (often enough) mislead them. Even if we limit ourselves to sincere assertions, truth is only our indirect aim: we aim to show others what we believe, and we aim to believe what is true. If we misrepresent our beliefs but hit the truth anyway (because our beliefs are false), we have failed to make a sincere assertion, while if we miss the truth but accurately represent our beliefs, we have succeeded in making one. Perhaps belief or judgment constitutively aims at truth; assertion does not.[14]

What is it, then, to make an assertion? What is one doing when one asserts a sentence? One must have certain intentions and produce certain noises, but there is no assertion unless one thereby brings about a certain kind of change in normative status. One commits oneself to the truth of the sentence asserted (at its context of utterance).[15] But what kind of a commitment is this? When one commits oneself to the truth of a sentence, what exactly is one committed to *doing*?

I suggest that one is committed to producing a justification, that is, giving adequate reasons for thinking that the sentence is true (relative to its context of utterance and the asserter's current context of assessment), whenever the assertion is challenged.[16] (Not every objection to an assertion will count as a challenge, in the sense at issue here. Ordinarily, the challenger must give reasonable grounds for questioning the asserter's warrant. Thus one may be justified in ignoring objections which are frivolous or unfounded, or which merely repeat challenges to which one has already responded.) If one cannot meet a challenge, whether through lack of resources or because the sentence asserted has been decisively shown to be untrue (relative to its context of utterance and one's current context of assessment), then one is obliged to withdraw the assertion. The act of withdrawal can be formal, as when a scientist retracts a claim in a journal, or informal, as when one says "I take that back." More often there is no explicit act of withdrawal at all, because (given natural expectations) none is needed: the speaker simply stops taking responsibility for the assertion. The norms constitutive of the practice of assertion, as I have

[14]This point of disanalogy between judgment and assertion means that my defense of relative utterance-truth may not generalize to a defense of relative judgment-truth. Cf. J. Campbell, "The Realism of Memory," in R. Heck Jr. (ed.), *Language, Thought, and Logic* (Oxford UP, 1997), pp. 157–81, at p. 165. I plan to address this intricate issue in future work.

[15]Cf. J. R. Searle, "The point or purpose of the members of the assertive class is to commit the speaker (in varying degrees) to something's being the case, to the truth of the expressed proposition": *Expression and Meaning* (Cambridge UP, 1979), p. 12.

[16]The basic structure of this account of assertion comes from R. Brandom, *Making It Explicit* (Harvard UP, 1994), ch. 3, and "Asserting," *Noûs*, 17 (1983), pp. 637–50.

described them, do not include an obligation to withdraw an assertion one believes or even knows to be false. Thus one can lie without violating the constitutive norms of assertion. Of course, one may be violating other, moral, norms, and if one lies too often and too egregiously, one risks no longer being treated as an asserter.[17]

On this account of assertion, a-contextuality poses no special problem. Indeed, the account allows us to describe exactly what is accomplished by the assertion of an a-contextual sentence. In asserting "There will be a sea battle tomorrow" at m_0, Jake comes to be bound by certain obligations. For example, if someone challenges the assertion at m_0, Jake must give adequate reasons for thinking that it is true, relative to context of utterance m_0 and context of assessment m_0. If the challenge takes the form of a conclusive demonstration that it is not yet settled whether there will be a sea battle, Jake will not be able to meet the challenge, and he will be obliged to withdraw his assertion. But if the challenge is weaker, and he meets it, then his assertion can stand. On the other hand, if at m_1 someone challenges his (original) assertion, Jake can meet the challenge by pointing to ships fighting. At this point, a proof that it was not settled at m_0 whether there would be a sea battle the next day would no longer count as a sufficient challenge to Jake's assertion, because it would not show that the sentence Jake asserted is untrue relative to the context of utterance m_0 and his current context of assessment m_1. Some might think it odd that a challenge that would oblige Jake to withdraw his assertion at m_0 should be ineffective at m_1. But if there is any oddity here, it has nothing to do with a-contextuality. Suppose Anne makes a mathematical assertion at m_0 but does not have a proof until m_1. Then she would be in a position at m_1 to meet a challenge she could not have met at m_0. Same phenomenon, no a-contextuality.

Pace Evans, then, we need not accept the absoluteness of utterance-truth in order to make sense of assertion and other speech acts. We can still think of assertions as commitments to the truth of the sentences asserted (at their contexts of utterance), for to be committed to the truth of a sentence (at a context of utterance u) is simply to be obliged, if challenged at any context of assessment a, to give adequate reasons for thinking that the sentence asserted is true (with respect to u and a), and to withdraw the assertion if the challenge cannot be met. It appears, then, that a postsemantics that defines doubly relativized truth can serve as input to a perfectly respectable account of assertion and other speech acts.

VII. CONCLUSION

I have argued that in order to give a satisfactory solution to the problem of future contingents, we need to relativize utterance-truth to a context of assessment,

---

[17]Cf. Brandom, *Making It Explicit*, p. 180.

and sentence-truth to both a context of utterance and a context of assessment. This amounts to recognizing a new kind of linguistic context-sensitivity: in addition to being indexical in the ordinary way, or *u-contextual*, sentences can be *a-contextual*: their truth-values can vary with the context of assessment. I have shown how we can make room for *a*-contextuality in a formal semantic framework, and I have shown how this framework can be integrated with a plausible account of assertion.

Once we have accepted *a*-contextuality in sentences about the future, it is natural to look for it elsewhere. I have found fruitful applications to Lewis's theory of accommodation, epistemic contextualism, evaluative relativism, and the interpretation of our scientific predecessors' theoretical discourse. I do not think that any of these other applications *demand* a-contextuality, as future contingents do. In each case, there are acceptable (even if not optimal) solutions that do not require rejecting the absoluteness of utterance-truth. But once we have abandoned absoluteness and accepted *a*-contextuality in one case, there is no principled reason not to explore its applications to these other cases as well. Future contingents are important because they force us to abandon absoluteness, liberating us from its conceptual bonds elsewhere.[18]

[18]This paper owes much to discussions with Nuel Belnap, Joseph Camp, Jeff King, Lionel Shapiro, and Paul Teller.

16

IN DEFENSE OF OCKHAMISM

Sven Rosenkranz

FUTURE CONTINGENTS

The philosophical debate to which the view here called "Ockhamism" contributes concerns the alethic status of *future contingents* like "There will be a sea-battle tomorrow" or "Two days hence, it will rain". The class of statements that comprises all and only the future contingents is rarely characterized in general, theory-neutral terms, but is instead illustrated by means of examples such as the ones just cited. To get the debate into clear focus, however, such a general characterization proves helpful.

Let "n days from the present, p" be short for "n days hence, p" if n is positive, for "$(-n)$ days ago, p" if n is negative, and for "Presently, p" if n equals zero. Then define *genuinely future-tensed statements* as those statements equivalent to a statement of the form "n days from the present, p" whose numeral refers to a positive number and whose embedded clause is tense-logically simple. Let genuinely past- and genuinely present-tensed statements be defined accordingly. Now let *future contingents* be those statements equivalent to a genuinely future-tensed statement whose embedded clause is contingent and which is such that no collection of genuinely past- and genuinely present-tensed truths implies its present truth, not even in conjunction with whatever lawlike connections can be assumed to hold.

Following Prior (1967), we may now understand *Ockhamism* to be the view that there are truths about what will be the case—true future contingents—which are not also truths about what will inevitably, or now-unpreventably, be the case. Thus understood, Ockhamism seeks to reconcile indeterminism about the future with the present truth of future contingents (Prior 1967: 121–32, Øhrstrøm 2009).[1]

---

[1] As Thomason notes, Prior's formal characterization of Ockhamism is at best incomplete, as it makes truth relative to a history without saying anything about which history, if any, is the one relative to which future contingents ought to be evaluated (Thomason 1970: 269–71). See Øhrstrøm (2009) for arguments showing that the position properly called "Ockhamism" requires such a privileged history—the notorious *thin red line*. If there is such a privileged history, then truth (at a moment) *simpliciter* can be understood in terms of truth (at a moment) relative to that history.

A caveat is in order. Although the view I just called "Ockhamism" is a view that William of Ockham actually held, he made further claims about the future that I do not wish to subsume under that label as I am here using it. For example, the historical Ockham also maintained that God has foreknowledge of the truth of future contingents in the sense defined. However, as Prior (2003: 48–50) has argued, this is highly controversial as long as we think of whatever it is that makes present knowledge *knowledge*, rather than a lucky guess or a pledge to be redeemed *ex post facto*, as something that must presently exist. For then it becomes very tempting indeed to think that the fact presently known must also presently exist, in which case foreknowledge of the truth of future contingents is ruled out. However, I do not here wish to enter the debate about whether divine foreknowledge is possible if indeterminism is true, nor do I pretend to address all of Ockham's claims about the future, let alone aim to defend them all. In fact, some of the things I later say in defense of Ockhamism, as here characterized, might for all I know go against other claims the historical Ockham held. Still, since Ockham did subscribe to the view I labeled "Ockhamism", and since I wish to contrast this view with those held by others in the debate about future contingents, my use of that label is not entirely inadequate.[2]

Ockhamism, as characterized, is opposed by both *Peirceanism* and what we may call "*Supervaluationist Indeterminism*". The Peircean treats the future-tense "will be" as equivalent, in meaning to "will inevitably be" and, by thus driving a wedge between "It is not the case that *n* days hence, it will be the case that *p*" and "*n* days hence, it will be the case that *¬p*" treats all future contingents as being uniformly false (Prior 1967: 128–32, Thomason 1970: 267). The Supervaluationist Indeterminist, by contrast, quantifies over (nomologically) possible histories that overlap in the present and past but diverge in the future, and construes the present truth of a statement as its truth relative to each such history (see Thomason 1970: 273–77 for details). By treating "It is not the case that *n* days hence, it will be the case that *¬p*" and "*n* days hence, it will be the case that *p*" as equivalent, and so denying that "will be" and "will inevitably be" are equivalent in meaning, the Supervaluationist Indeterminist accordingly treats all future contingents as being presently neither true nor false (Thomason 1970: 274, 277, McCall 1976; Belnap et al. 2001, cf. also MacFarlane 2003). Thus, Peirceans and Supervaluationist Indeterminists alike deny the Ockhamist's main tenet that future contingents can be presently true.

Challenges to Ockhamism's main tenet are various, some being of a purely technical nature (see e.g. Belnap et al. 2001; Braüner et al. 2000; and Øhrstrøm 2009).

---

[2] I am indebted to an anonymous referee for calling my attention to the need for this caveat.

Here, I will exclusively be concerned with two challenges of a more metaphysical kind. The first challenge is that Ockhamism is incapable of heeding the *grounding-requirement*, i.e. the requirement that truths be grounded in what facts there are. The second challenge is that, by allowing for the present truth of future contingents, Ockhamism proves after all incompatible with *indeterminism about the future* according to which there is a whole tree of objectively possible continuations of the present and past. Both these challenges can be met, or so I will argue, by exploiting the idea that certain kinds of truths are true only courtesy of other kinds of truths and of what makes the latter true.

It is worthwhile setting the record straight. On the one hand, not only has it become something of a common prejudice amongst philosophers that indeterminism about the future is incompatible with the present truth of future contingents, this contention has also recently been put to heavy-duty use as a *point de départ* of rather extravagant philosophical views, i.e. assessment-relativism and its varieties (MacFarlane 2003, 2008). On the other hand, others who have challenged the Ockhamist's opponents have advanced considerations that are far too concessive to be at the Ockhamist's service. Thus, recently Barnes and Cameron (2009) have argued against Supervaluationist Indeterminism that the openness of the future is quite compatible with future contingents being either true or false, while conceding that, insofar as the future is open, there is no *definite* truth-value future contingents presently have. On one reading, which I take to be the one most faithful to the authors' intentions, this is understood to mean that none of these statements is presently true *rather than* false, in any sense of "rather than" that implies grounding—in which case Bivalence, as applied to future contingents, is treated in a fashion similar to the one in which Supervaluationist Indeterminists treat the Law of Excluded Middle, as so applied. Alternatively, this may be understood to mean that although some future contingents are presently true rather than false, and so are grounded, they are only ever indeterminately so, in some deep non-epistemic sense of "indeterminate" in which it is, say, indeterminate whether an object *a* fissioning into *b* and *c* is identical to *b*. Neither is acceptable to the Ockhamist. After all, the Ockhamist insists that a future contingent may be presently true rather than false, and not just either presently true or false, while its being presently true rather than false in no way compromises the thought that the future is open with respect to the matter to which that statement relates. And that the future is nonetheless open in this respect does nothing to suggest that there is any non-epistemic indeterminacy as to whether the relevant future contingent *is* a grounded truth.

THE OCKHAMIST'S NARRATIVE

Just as, for suitable p, something happening here may make "One mile to the north from here, p" true here, so for suitable p, something occurring at present may make "One day hence, p" true at present. Thus, "One day hence, there will have been a firestorm a day earlier" may be made true by a present firestorm, just as "One mile to the north from here, it rains heavily one mile to the south from there" may be made true by heavy rainfall around here. These examples are trivial because neither is the future-tensed statement really about the future—it is no *genuinely* future-tensed statement—nor is the distant-location statement really about a distant location. But there are also nontrivial examples: a meltdown occurring here may make "One mile to the north from here, people are in imminent danger" true here, just as a meltdown occurring at present may make "Tomorrow, the environment will be infested with radioactive pollution" true at present. The latter examples rely on lawlike connections between what is happening here and now, on the one hand, and what will happen or happens further away, on the other.

According to the Ockhamist, not all present truths about the future need to be made true by what is happening at present, or by what has happened in the past, just as not all truths here about what goes on over there need to be made true by what goes on around here or anyplace other than over there. Arguably, statements like "One day hence, I will either sing a song or none", whose embedded clause is necessary, are present truths of this kind: they may be true at present although nothing in the present or past makes them so, just as "One mile to the north from here, either it rains or it doesn't" may be true here although nothing going on around here, or anyplace other than one mile to the north from here, makes it so.

Both the Peircean and the Supervaluationist Indeterminist may concede that statements about the future whose embedded clause is necessary are presently true without being made true by anything present or past. But for them these are the only statements, if any, meeting that condition. By contrast, the Ockhamist thinks that there are less trivial examples of statements about the future that are presently true without being made true by anything present or past. Thus, she contends that, even where p is contingent and tense-logically simple, "One day hence, p" may be true at present although there is nothing to be found in the present or past that makes it true. Instead, for such p, "One day hence, p" may be true at present solely in virtue of what will happen one day from the present, just as "One mile to the north from here, p" may be true here solely in virtue of what happens one mile to the north from here. Thus, for example, "One day hence, love will be in the air" may be true at present just because tomorrow, something will make "Love is in the air" true although, tomorrow, nothing that will have gone on one day earlier guaranteed that to be so;

and "One mile to the north of here, love is in the air" may be true here just because one mile to the north from here, something makes "Love is in the air" true although, one mile to the north from here, nothing that goes on one mile to the south from there guarantees that to be so.

The Peircean, for one, objects to this narrative: for her, "One day hence, *p*" cannot be presently true unless either *p* is necessary or *p* is contingent but present or past facts, maybe in conjunction with lawlike connections, already guarantee, or make inevitable, that one day hence, *p* is true. In other words, the Peircean only allows those genuinely future-tensed statements to be presently true that are *temporally necessary*, and so denies that *future contingents* can be presently true. And the Peircean is not the only one who thinks so: the Supervaluationist Indeterminist who, unlike the Peircean, regards future contingents not as false but as neither true nor false, objects to the Ockhamist's narrative on the same grounds. But the Ockhamist's narrative sounds like merest common sense. So on what basis can one find fault with it?

Trivially, what is future is not yet. But to infer that, therefore, future contingents are not presently true is to ignore that future contingents are *in the future tense*: their being presently true in no way conflicts with the aforementioned triviality: what will be need not presently be. The Peircean and the Supervaluationist Indeterminist cannot be taken to make *that* kind of mistake. So why reject the Ockhamist's story?

GROUNDING TENSED TRUTHS

It might be suggested, on behalf of the Ockhamist's opponents, that if "One day hence, love will be in the air" was indeed true at present, then it would after all be a *present fact* that one day hence, love will be in the air, and this present fact would then make "One day hence, love will be in the air" true at present. One may talk this way if one so pleases. One should then also say that insofar as "One mile to the north from here, love is in the air" is true here, it is a fact here that one mile to the north from here, love is in the air, and that this fact will then make "One mile to the north from here, love is in the air" true here. But even then, it will still be correct to say that if "One mile to the north from here, love is in the air" is true here, nothing *happening* here need make it true here, and similarly that even if "One day hence, love will be in the air" is true at present, nothing *occurring* at present need make it true at present. A more restricted notion of fact is surely available to the Ockhamist according to which only present happenings or occurrences, and their absences, qualify as (particular) present facts.

Taken at face value, the Ockhamist's account assumes that sometimes facts exist that do not always exist. Otherwise, to say that *n* days hence, some facts will exist that do not exist *n* days earlier would be to say something false. It would then equally be false to say that "One day hence, it will rain" is true in virtue of there going to be, one day hence, some fact that will then make "It is raining" true but does not exist today. It would thus seem that the Ockhamist must both take tensed existence as basic and deny *Sempiternalism*, i.e. the view that always all facts always exist. In the light of the foregoing, this observation may be taken to provide the basis for an argument meant to show that Ockhamism violates the *grounding-requirement* for truth, i.e. that for all *p*, whenever *p* is true, *p*'s truth is grounded in what facts there are.

It is a common complaint against *Presentism* that proponents of this view have trouble accounting for the grounding of present truths about the past: if all that metaphysically matters is what facts presently exist, it seems such truths can only be grounded in the instantiation of quite peculiar, and irreducibly peculiar, properties, e.g. that of *having-been-tired-a-day-ago*. And similarly for present truths about the future and properties of the kind exemplified by *going-to-be-tired-a-day-hence*. Neither the Eternalist who takes the basic notion of existence to be tenseless, nor the Sempiternalist faces any comparable problem. How about the Ockhamist?

The Ockhamist was said to operate with a notion of present fact designed to exclude facts like its being presently the case that one day hence, Giovanni will be tired, and so to deny herself the Presentist's way out. And yet, the Ockhamist insists that statements like "One day hence, Giovanni will be tired" can be presently true. It would now seem that the Ockhamist faces a dilemma. Either she holds that "One day hence, Giovanni will be tired" is presently true, if it is, in virtue of something like Giovanni's taking a caffeine pill in conjunction with lawlike connections that make truths of that form the inevitable consequence of one's taking caffeine pills—in which case she gives up on the idea that the statement is a future contingent. Or else she denies that this statement, if presently true, is grounded in what facts there are—in which case she is guilty of violating the grounding-requirement.

Neither horn of the dilemma is acceptable to the Ockhamist who wants to heed the grounding-requirement and yet leave room for historically contingent truths about the future that are not guaranteed by any present or past facts, be they strange beasts like Giovanni's having the property of *going-to-be-tired-one-day-hence* or more familiar facts and lawlike connections apt to make such truths inevitable. However, it is no good charging one's opponent with a dilemma, if that dilemma rests on a biased account of her theoretical commitments. For all that the Ockhamist has been shown to be committed to, she can coherently contend that a present truth about the future may be grounded in virtue of there going to be, in the future, facts that then make the corresponding present-tensed statement true, just as a truth here about what goes on over there may be grounded in virtue of there being, over there, some facts that make the corresponding "here"- statement true. Facts of those kinds need involve no peculiar properties.

The notion of grounded truth that the Ockhamist appeals to can be defined as follows:

> ϕ is a grounded truth iff$_{df}$ there is a collection of tensed statements Σ and a function δ from the members of Σ to numbers suitable for measuring temporal distances such that, first, for all ψ in Σ, $\delta(\psi)$ days from the present, ψ is made true by some fact, and secondly, necessarily always, if for all ψ in Σ, $\delta(\psi)$ days from the present, ψ is true, then ϕ is true.[3]

This definition will be deemed inadequate by anyone who refuses to countenance negative or universal facts. But this is not the present issue, and we may safely assume that the controversy between the Ockhamist and her opponents will persist even after negative and universal facts have been admitted into one's ontology. So for present purposes at least, the aforementioned definition will do.

The grounding-requirement was said to be the requirement that for all p, whenever p is true, p's truth is grounded in what facts there are. Complications having to do with plural quantification aside, the Ockhamist will now interpret the existential quantifier involved in terms of "for some n, n days from the present, there is", where the latter occurrence of "there is" is tensed. Thus understood, the grounding-requirement amounts to the requirement that whenever p is true, p be a grounded truth in the sense defined. Even if the Ockhamist thus takes tensed existence as conceptually basic, she may still hold that when it comes to metaphysics, it matters that for some positive n, n days from the present, some fact exists that does not exist n days earlier. This is in stark contrast to the Presentist's view, according to which all that metaphysically matters is what facts presently exist. Consequently, although the Presentist is free to introduce the locution "for some n, n days from the present, there is" into her metalanguage, she can only treat it as a genuine quantifier for which a domain is defined by taking it to be equivalent to "0 days from the present, there is", in which case "For some n, n days from the present, some fact exists that does not exist $(-n)$ days from the present" comes out false. If, instead,

---

[3]If all the laws, as well as the claim that they are laws and nothing else is, may be taken to be made true at some particular time, the modality involved may be construed as metaphysical necessity. If this condition is not met, the modality involved may instead be construed as nomological necessity. However, even then one might insist on a reading of "necessarily, A" on which it says that A is metaphysically necessary. It all depends on whether one wishes to account for the nontrivial examples mentioned in the first paragraph of the section entitled "The Ockhamist's Narrative," which is nothing the Ockhamist *qua* Ockhamist is committed to.

the Presentist denies the locution "for some n, n days from the present, there is" the status of a genuine quantifier, she is obliged not to use it in her attempt to meet the grounding-requirement. The Ockhamist, by contrast, can treat that locution as a genuine quantifier for which a domain is defined without thereby being forced to treat it as being equivalent to "0 days from the present, there is". Thus she is free to use it in her attempt to heed the grounding-requirement.

Unlike being made true, being a presently grounded truth, as defined, is not a relation to anything present, as for some ϕ and all ψ in any collection Σ meeting the above conditions, the only δ that fit the bill may be such that $\delta(\psi)$ is without exception positive. Now, the grounding-requirement was meant to ensure that there is some systematic connection between true statements and reality; and one might accordingly wonder how a notion of groundedness that is in this sense nonrelational can at all be suited to formulate that requirement. However, we are already familiar with the idea that truth depends on how things are without truth therefore being relational: on an inflationary conception of truth such as Davidson's, to say that "Snow is white" is true iff snow is white is not just to express that the left-hand side is a notational variant of the right-hand side, as some deflationists would have it, but to express that in order for the sentence "Snow is white" to be true, a certain denizen of reality—snow—has to be a certain way—white. Stating *conditions* for truth can thus be seen as a way to capture the systematic connection between true statements and reality without the need to postulate any *relation* between the two. Likewise, the above definition of groundedness implies that in order for an attribution of grounded truth to be correct, reality must at some times be certain ways—contain certain facts. It is thus hard to see why and how the groundedness of tensed truths, as defined, might be accused of failing to capture any systematic connection between tensed truths and temporal reality.

USE AND MENTION

A rather different complaint against the Ockhamist's attempt to heed the grounding-requirement is that it is ultimately *circular*: if "n days hence, p" is a future contingent, so is "n days hence, there will be a fact that makes "p" true". Accordingly, when the Ockhamist contends that the future contingent "n days hence, p" is presently true because n days hence, there will be a fact that makes "p" true, she uses another future contingent in a way that implies *its* present truth. But the grounded truth of "n days hence, there will be a fact that makes 'p' true" is just as much in need of explanation as the grounded truth of "n days hence, p". This, or so it might be suggested, is already bad enough. But it would seem that things get even worse. Reapplying her own recipe, the Ockhamist must now say that "n days hence, there will be a fact that makes 'p' true" is presently true because n days hence, there will be a fact that makes "There is a fact that makes 'p' true" true. But arguably, n days hence, there is not going to be any further fact, besides the fact, if any, making "p" true, that then makes "There is a fact that makes 'p' true" true: insofar as facts necessitate what they make true and what is necessary is necessarily necessary, whenever there is a fact making "p" true, that very fact will also make "There is a fact that makes 'p' true" true. If this is so, we accordingly arrive at the claim that "n days hence, there will be a fact that makes 'p' true" is presently true because n days hence, there will be a fact that makes "p" true. But in saying this, the Ockhamist presupposes the grounded truth of the very statement whose grounded truth she set out to explain; and this, or so it might be concluded, makes her account unacceptably circular.

One should be suspicious of this pessimistic conclusion, if only because we can reproduce structurally the same reasoning applied to the standard clause for conjunction. Thus, when we set out to explain why a conjunctive statement "p and q" is true by saying, in a first go, that it is true because both "p" and "q" are true, we use a conjunctive statement in order to do so whose truth we thereby imply. It takes little reflection to see that if "p is true" is true, it is true because "p" is true. So, assuming this instance of transitivity for "because", saying that "Both 'p' and 'q' are true" is true because both " 'p' is true" and " 'q' is true" are true, boils down to saying that "Both p and q are true" is true because both p and q are true. And here we use the very statement whose truth we set out to explain. Does this alleged "circularity" confute the proposed explanation? It seems not.

We can be more precise where the objector goes wrong. To begin with, the question with which we started was whether the *Ockhamist* can meet the grounding-requirement. In her attempt to do so, she must accordingly be allowed to use the resources that, according to her view, are available to her. Yet, according to her view, unlike her opponents', "n days hence, there will be a fact that makes 'p' true" *can* be presently true (without there presently being any facts that make it so), and will be presently true whenever "n days hence, p" is. So there is nothing wrong with her using the former future contingent in a way that implies its present truth, in order to state in virtue of what the latter future contingent is presently true, inasmuch as there is nothing wrong with using the conjunction "Both 'p' and 'q' are true" in order to explain why the conjunction "p and q" is true.

Secondly, even in the odd case in which the statement used to effect the explanation is the very statement whose truth needs explaining, nothing goes wrong. For, it is still instructive to say that a statement is true because of things being, or going to be, the way this statement can be used to say they are or are going to be. This applies both to the case in which "Both 'p' and 'q' are true" is said to be true because both 'p' and 'q' are true, and to the case in which "n days hence, there will be a fact that makes 'p' true" is said to be presently true because *n* days hence, there will be a fact that makes 'p' true. Of course, this will not be instructive on any deflationary conception on which the statements either side of "because" are mere notational variants of each other. But any view advocating the grounding-requirement should be hostile to such a deflationary conception of truth.

DISTANT TIMES, DISTANT LOCATIONS

The Ockhamist's narrative capitalized on an analogy between statements about the future and statements about other places. It might now be rejoined, on behalf of her opponents, that this spatial analogy, however intuitive, is highly misleading: while it is determinate what goes on in other places, it is correspondingly indeterminate what will go on in the future.

Whether this complaint has any force depends on what "determinate" and "indeterminate" are taken to mean. Both the Peircean and the Supervaluationist Indeterminist hold that the future is indeterminate in at least the sense that for a relevant class of statements about the future (i.e. the future contingents), nothing to be found in the present or past determines them to be true at present (cf. Prior 1967: 129, Belnap et al. 2001: 162). The Ockhamist agrees. But while her opponents draw the conclusion that statements in that class fail to be true (or are even false), the Ockhamist rejects this conclusion on the grounds that it either mistakes truth for temporal necessity or rests on a questionable conception of grounding.

Note that on this understanding of "indeterminate", it is entirely unclear whether it is in a corresponding sense of "determinate" determinate what goes on in other places. As already indicated, a statement like "One mile to the north from here, *p*" may be true here although there is nothing occurring here, or in fact anyplace other than one mile to the north from here, that makes it true. In this sense of "determinate", it is not determinate what goes on in other places; and the analogy is restored.

However, this may after all not be the relevant sense of "determinate" the objector has in mind when suggesting that it is determinate what goes on in other places. She may, rather, mean that what goes on over there *at present* is determinate in that statements like "One mile to the north from here, it is raining" are made true or false by what is present or past. But this, while true, is not to take the analogy very seriously. It is merely to say that statements about the present are, if true, already made true by what is present or past, never mind whether they concern what's going on over here or what's going on over there, while future contingents are not made true by what is present or past, never mind whether they concern what will go on over here or what will go on over there. On this the Ockhamist agrees with her opponents. The Ockhamist nonetheless insists that "One day hence, *p*" may be presently true although it is not made presently true by anything occurring in the present or past, just as "One mile to the north from here, p" may be true here although it is not made true by anything happening here or anyplace other than one mile to the north from here.

TRUTHS BY COURTESY OF OTHER TRUTHS

The Ockhamist allows, while both the Peircean and the Supervaluationist Indeterminist deny, that for positive n and all p, including contingent atomic ones, either "n days hence, p" is presently true or "n days hence, $\neg p$" is presently true—in other words, that there is a *thin red line* marking out the one and only course of events, of all the possible future ones, that is going to unfold. But, one may ask, if there is a thin red line in this sense, then never mind what makes or will make those statements true, how can the future nonetheless be presently *open*?

If "open" means what "indeterminate" was said to mean above, then by now the answer is clear: even if "n days hence, p" is presently true, its truth may fail to be determined by what has gone on up to the present, and so what has gone on up to the present may leave it open whether that statement is true. On that same conception of indeterminacy, the claim, which is the Supervaluationist Indeterminist's usual stock-in-trade, that it is determinate that a unique future course of events will come to pass, while there is no unique such course of events which determinately will come to pass, is perfectly acceptable to the Ockhamist. By contrast, the Ockhamist will reject this claim as soon as "determinate" is understood in terms of grounded truth.[4] Yet, as we have seen, there is a plausible conception of what it is for a present truth about the future to be grounded in the light of which that claim, as thus understood, can no longer be seen as sanctioned by the existence of future contingents alone.

What else could "open" mean? One likely suggestion is that the future is claimed to be open in the sense that different future courses of events are *consistent with all past and present truths* (see e.g. Markosian 1995: 96). In this sense of "open", the Ockhamist will of course forego any commitment to the future's being open. But how damaging is this?

Once we concede that the present truth of "One day hence, it will rain" may be grounded solely in virtue of there going to be, one day hence, facts that then make "It is raining" true, we can get no more metaphysical mileage out of the finding that

---

[4] . . . or, for that matter, in terms of *determinately* grounded truth, where "determinately" is some primitive non-epistemic notion. This is precisely where the Ockhamist parts company with Barnes and Cameron (2009) (see the section entitled "Future Contingents" above).

this truth is inconsistent with its being sunny tomorrow than out of the finding that there cannot be going to be, one day hence, two facts one of which makes "It is raining" true while the other one makes "It is sunny" true. The present truth of "One day hence, it will rain" rules out tomorrow's being sunny *only because*, first, tomorrow's truth of "It is raining" rules out tomorrow's being sunny *and*, secondly, "One day hence, it will rain", if presently true, is presently true in virtue of there going to be facts tomorrow that then make "It is raining" true. Yet, tomorrow, any facts that then make "It is raining" true may not have been forced into existence by anything that went on, or had been going on, a day earlier, least by the truth a day earlier of "One day hence, it will rain". In that case, it is still, metaphysically speaking, left open by all facts present or past whether tomorrow it will rain or rather be sunny, even if for each p and positive n, either "n days hence, p" or "n days hence, $\neg p$" is presently true.

The point that the Ockhamist here wishes to make is that some kinds of truths are truths only *courtesy of* other kinds of truths and whatever makes the latter true. The point is familiar enough from other contexts. For example, if I father a child, my mother becomes a grandmother and so "My mother is a grandmother" becomes true and, assuming I am an only child, vice versa. But it would be absurd to suggest that just because truths about my mother and my being an only child entail that I father a child, my mother's properties, in conjunction with the fact that I am an only child, make inevitable, or explain, the truth of "I father a child": some truths about my mother are, both in a logical sense and in a metaphysical sense, *consequential upon* my having certain properties, and it is my having these properties which makes certain statements about myself true that may in turn entail others, e.g. about my mother. Similarly in the temporal case: that "One day hence, it will rain" is presently true, if it is, is both a logical and a metaphysical consequence of how things will be tomorrow, and as long as it is not inevitable that it will rain tomorrow, that it will rain tomorrow is not settled by that present truth or any genuinely present fact that might be invoked in the vain attempt to explain it, *even if that truth logically entails that one day hence, it will rain, and so likewise that one day hence, it will be a fact that it rains.*

It is because of the existence of present truths that are truths courtesy of future truths and of future facts accounting for the latter, that consistency with all present and past truths is not a good criterion for the temporally contingent: too many historical contingencies will mistakenly be classified as historical necessities. The same applies, *mutatis mutandis*, to what is, metaphysically speaking, open.

That it is the metaphysical notion rather than the linguistic one that is central to indeterminism also transpires from considerations about freedom, which latter the indeterminist wishes to leave room for. If a statement about the future outcome of my decisions and deliberations is presently true only courtesy of what I will decide, or of where my deliberations will have led me, the present truth of that statement in no way compromises my freedom, as long as the future outcome of my decisions and deliberations is not already made inevitable by facts about the present and past (cf. Dummett 2004: 81).

INDETERMINISM AND THE THIN RED LINE

Adherence to the linguistic criterion would seem to underlie the most common objections to Ockhamism and the thin red line. For example, in defending what he calls the "indeterminacy intuition" according to which present utterances of future contingents presently lack a truth-value, MacFarlane (2003: 325) writes:

> [P]ositing a thin red line amounts to giving up objective indeterminism. The non-red branches in the tree are supposed to represent objectively possible fixtures, but their non-redness indicates precisely that they will not be the continuations of the history that includes the utterance in question. Looking down on the tree of branching histories from above, God can see that given the past and the context of utterance, only one continuation remains in play: the one marked with the thin red line. In what sense, then, are the others really "possibilities"? They are possibilities in an epistemic sense: the utterer does not know which history is marked out with the thin red line. But objectively speaking they are not genuine possibilities at all.

See Thomason 1970: 270–71, for a similar kind of complaint. Contrary to what both Thomason and MacFarlane suggest, however, from there being a particular branch along which history continues from the moment of utterance onward it does not follow that, at that moment, it is objectively impossible for history to continue along a distinct branch. That there is a thin red line merely implies that for every n and p, either "n days from the present, p" or "n days from the present, $\neg p$" is presently true. But insofar as p is both contingent and tense-logically simple, such statements may presently have these truth-values only *courtesy of* what will happen, where what will happen is not made inevitable by what has gone on so far. To be sure, if it will be the case tomorrow that a sea-battle takes place, then relative to what either has been, is, or will be going on, a peaceful tomorrow is objectively impossible. But that is not the notion of positional modality objective indeterminism is concerned with. Rather, objective indeterminism is concerned with what is possible relative to what either has been or is going on. Yet, relative to *that*, a peaceful tomorrow may still be possible, in whatever objective, non-epistemic sense objective indeterminism requires.

It is only if one (mis-)conceives the objectively possible in terms of what is consistent with all present and past truths, that assumption of a thin red line renders all branches marked in non-red impossible. The two conceptions will collapse only if grounding is cast in terms that require the grounds to presently exist. But as we have seen, this is far from mandatory; and as long as it is instead cast in terms that allow for future-tensed statements being true courtesy of what will happen, the linguistic conception of positional modality ought to be resisted.[5]

A similar complaint can be raised against the suggestion, reviewed earlier, that present facts include facts like its being presently the case that one day hence, a sea-battle will take place. Here the spatial analogy again proves instructive. Thus, if one asks whether what goes on over here determines what goes on over there, then a negative answer might seem inadequate as soon as one includes, amongst the things going on over here, things like living in the neighborhood of certain events going on over there. But to invalidate a negative answer in this way betrays a willful misconstrual of the question being asked. Counting facts like its being presently the case that one day hence, a sea-battle will take place, amongst the present facts is equally likely to misconstrue the question, raised and answered in the negative by the objective indeterminist, of whether the present and past jointly determine the future.

Shortly after the passage just quoted, MacFarlane (2003: 326) goes on to say:

> David Lewis […] acknowledges that if an utterance of a future contingent belongs
> to more than one possible future history, we cannot appeal to "the actual future"

---

[5]According to McCall's preferred dynamic account (what he calls "Theory D"), different "universe pictures", displaying forward branching, are adequate representations of reality at different times, with branches falling off, as it were, as time goes by (McCall 1976: 342–43). McCall is adamant that Theory D is not simply a dynamic version of the Everett-Wheeler conception according to which reality is "multiple" and so, as Lewis would put it, "many ways" (McCall 1976: 342; Lewis 1986: 207–08). It thus becomes unclear why, as soon as it is viewed *sub specie aeternitatis*, Theory D does not collapse into the Ockhamist's account (what he calls "Theory B"), according to which there is a thin red line, while at each time there are many historically possible continuations of the present. Faced with the challenge, McCall resorts to semantic considerations (McCall 1976: 350). Once the familiar kind of supervaluationist semantics is in place (McCall 1976: 355–60), the threat of collapse can indeed successfully be averted. However, it is hard to see how this semantic maneuver to define truth as supertruth can carry any metaphysical weight, unless it is being presupposed that there is a metaphysically relevant notion of indeterminacy the Ockhamist fails to capture, viz. that different continuations of the present are consistent with all present and past truths (cf. McCall's discussion of timeless vs. temporal truth on pp. 354–56). As was argued earlier, given the conception of statements about the future as being true courtesy of what will happen, it becomes very doubtful that this *is* a metaphysically relevant notion, or anyway one according to which the future is indeed indeterminate.

to secure it a determinate [i.e. definite, SR] truth-value. But Lewis does not want to give up the determinacy intuition [i.e. the intuition that such utterances have definite truth-values, SR]. His solution is to reject branching altogether. On his view, each utterance takes place at a unique possible world, and each possible world has a unique future history. On these assumptions, the context of utterance always determines a unique "actual future."

Like the "thin red line," however, Lewis' picture saves the determinacy intuition only by sacrificing genuine objective indeterminism. Given a context of utterance, there is only one possible future history that contains it: the future is in that sense determined. Granted, there are other possible worlds that are qualitative duplicates of the actual world up to the present and diverge thereafter, but these worlds contain different utterances (and utterers), mere "counterparts" of the actual ones. Thus the future is open only in the sense that we do not (and perhaps cannot) know what it will bring.

In this passage, there is much distracting noise, echoing Burgess's complaint that according to counterpart theory, what could be going to happen to me, but is not, is really just a future possibility for "someone like me" (Burgess 1978: 173, quoted approvingly by Belnap et al. 2001: 207, from whom MacFarlane takes much of his inspiration). Never mind whether one should at all be swayed by this kind of consideration, MacFarlane's diagnosis is tendentious in a more decisive respect. For, even if the Ockhamist buys into Lewis's counterpart theory, it is entirely unclear why that should force her to reject objective indeterminism and leave her with no more than a range of epistemic possibilities. According to that theory, what will happen to our counterparts in worlds that are qualitative duplicates of our own up to the present *does* matter for whether our future is predetermined by present and past facts. MacFarlane's reasoning is seductive but, mildly put, inconclusive.

FIXING VS. DETERMINING

Belnap et al. (2001) construe future contingents as involving a hidden history-parameter and then argue that given objective indeterminism, the context of utterance fails to fix a unique value for that parameter. Consequently on that view, not only the future contingents themselves but also utterances of them lack a truth-value. Roughly, Belnap et al. (2001) reason as follows. First they argue that according to objective indeterminism, there are many mutually exclusive possible histories including the same utterance. From this they conclude that according to objective indeterminism, the context of utterance itself fails to single out any particular such history. Since for some values of the history-parameter, the uttered future contingent receives the *prima facie* assignment (or proto-value) 1, while for others, it receives the *prima facie* assignment (or proto-value) 0, it is then but a small step to the conclusion that the utterance itself lacks a truth-value.

As Belnap et al. (2001: 156–60) are aware, it is difficult to square this conclusion with the idea that future contingents are ever assertable. Their solution to this problem follows a suggestion made by Prior (1967: 131) and likens assertions to bets. The authors argue that the content of a future contingent "is the sort of thing that can be borne out or not, depending upon what comes to pass" (Belnap et al. 2001: 175). And now, just as "it makes sense to wonder about what history has not yet decided as long as history will decide the matter" (Belnap et al. 2001: 171), betting on a certain future outcome makes sense as long as history will decide the matter. And according to the authors, history *will* decide the matter: "time will tell whether we arrive at a moment at which the truth value (at the moment of assertion) becomes settled" (Belnap et al. 2001: 175), while to claim of two future possibilities that they "will each be realized" is to claim "an absurdity" (Belnap et al. 2001: 207).

But then, if we merely have to sit and wait until history decides the matter, it becomes entirely unclear why the context of utterance fails to fix a unique value for the history-parameter: even if nothing that has come to be the case up to the moment of utterance, including the utterance itself, predetermines what comes to pass thereafter (Belnap et al. 2001: 151), the contention that amongst the equally possible future courses of events, there is a unique such course of events that will unfold after that moment, is enough to vindicate the claim that the identity of that moment uniquely fixes that course of events. Belnap et al. themselves profess that if the history-parameter "can be fixed by the context, then we automatically *do* let the context fix it for stand-alone sentences" (Belnap et al. 2001: 148).

Of course, Belnap et al. (2001) deny that amongst the equally possible future courses of events, there is a unique such course of events that will unfold after that moment, even if they affirm that it will be the case that a unique such course of events unfolds. But such denial is not sanctioned by objective indeterminism which is after all consistent with future contingents being presently true courtesy of what will happen, as long as what will happen will do so contingently. If time will tell whether there is a sea-battle tomorrow, then an utterance of "One day hence, there will be a sea-battle" may presently have a definite truth-value that it has only courtesy of what time will tell. If waiting until tomorrow will be enough for it to be settled whether there will be a sea-battle tomorrow, "One day hence, there will be a sea-battle" may be presently true solely in virtue of there going to be a sea-battle after one's having waited 24 hours. Similarly, the present assignment of a particular value to the history-parameter may be correct courtesy of all that will happen after the moment of utterance, even if nothing that is present or past at the moment of utterance grounds that assignment. A moment of utterance can thus fix a unique future without determining it, just as a shadow can fix a unique object without determining it.

Again, it is only if one thinks that present possession of a definite truth-value cuts down the tree of *possibilities* to just one branch, that one has any reason to deny that Ockhamism is compatible with objective indeterminism. Yet, that thought either presupposes the linguistic conception of positional modality or a notion of presently grounded truth as a relation to something present, neither of which is adequate if there are statements about the future that are presently true only courtesy of what will happen, where what will happen will do so contingently. And this is precisely what the Ockhamist contends.

CONCLUSION

None of the arguments reviewed here suggests that Ockhamism, properly construed, violates the grounding-requirement or proves incompatible with objective indeterminism according to which there is a whole tree of possible continuations of the present and past.

ACKNOWLEDGMENTS

I am grateful to the following colleagues, students, and friends for their critical comments that helped to improve the paper significantly: Fabrice Correia, Manuel García-Carpintero, Carl Hoefer, Dan López de Sa, Giovanni Merlo, Ivan Milic, Nathan Oaklander, Pablo Rychter, Albert Solé, Stephan Torre, and Richard Woodward. The research leading to these results has received funding from the European Community's 7th Framework Programme under grant agreement PITN-GA-2009-238128, and was also partially funded by the Consolider-Ingenio project CSD2009-0056 and the project FFI-2008-06153, both financed by the Spanish Ministry of Science and Innovation (MICINN).

REFERENCES

Barnes, E., & Cameron, R. (2009). The open future: bivalence, determinism and ontology. *Philosophical Studies*, 146, 291–309.

Belnap, N., Perloff, M., & Xu, M. (2001). *Facing the future*. Oxford: Oxford University Press.

Braüner, T., Hasle, P., & Øhrstrøm, P. (2000). Determinism and the origins of temporal logic. In H. Barringer et al. (Eds.), *Advances in temporal logic*, 185–206. Dordrecht: Kluwer.

Burgess, J. (1978). The unreal future. *Theoria*, 44, 157–74.

Dummett, M. (2004). *Truth and the past*. New York: Columbia University Press.

Lewis, D. (1986). *On the plurality of worlds*. Oxford: Blackwell.

MacFarlane, J. (2003). Future contingents and relative truth. *The Philosophical Quarterly* 53, 321–36.

MacFarlane, J. (2008). Truth in the garden of forking paths. In M. Garcia-Carpintero & M. Kölbel (Eds.), *Relative truth*, 81–102. Oxford: Oxford University Press.

Markosian, N. (1995). The open past. *Philosophical Studies*, 79, 95–105.

McCall, S. (1976). Objective time flow. *Philosophy of Science*, 43, 337–62.

Øhrstrøm, P. (2009). In defence of the thin red line: a case for Ockhamism. *Humana.mente*, 8, 17–32.

Prior, A. N. (1967). *Past, present and future*. Oxford: Clarendon.

Prior, A. N., et al. (2003). In P. Hasle (Ed.), *Papers on time and tense*. Oxford: Oxford University Press.

Thomason, R. H. (1970). Indeterminist time and truth-value gaps. *Theoria*, 36, 264–81.

BIBLIOGRAPHY
(COMPILED BY PATRICK TODD)

Adams, Marilyn McCord. (1967). "Is the Existence of God a 'Hard' Fact?," *The Philosophical Review* 76: 492–503; reprinted in Fischer 1989: 74–85.

Adams, Marilyn McCord and Norman Kretzmann. (1969). *William Ockham: Predestination, God's Foreknowledge, and Future Contingents. Translated with an introduction and notes.* New York: Century Philosophy Sourcebooks, Appleton-Century-Crofts.

Alston, William. (1986). "Does God Have Beliefs?," *Religious Studies* 22: 287–306.

Anderson, David J. and Joshua L. Watson. (2010). "The Mystery of Foreknowledge," *Philo* 13: 136–50.

Armstrong, D. M. (2004). *Truth and Truthmakers.* Cambridge: Cambridge University Press.

Arnold, Alexander. 2015. "Knowledge First and Ockhamism," in Jonathan Kvanvig, ed., *Oxford Studies in Philosophy of Religion*, vol. 6. Oxford: Oxford University Press.

Ayer, A. J. (1963). "Fatalism," in *The Concept of a Person and Other Essays*, 235–68. New York: St. Martin's.

Barnes, Elizabeth and Ross Cameron. (2009). "The open future: bivalence, determinism and ontology," *Philosophical Studies* 146: 291–309.

Belnap, Nuel and Mitchell Green. (1994). "Indeterminism and the Thin Red Line," *Philosophical Perspectives* 8: 365–88.

Belnap, Nuel and Michael Perloff and Ming Xu. (2001) *Facing the Future: Agents and Choices in Our Indeterminist World.* Oxford: Oxford University Press.

Bernstein, Mark. (2002). "Fatalism," in Robert Kane, ed., *The Oxford Handbook of Free Will*, 65–81. Oxford: Oxford University Press.

Bradley, R. D. (1959). "Must the future be what it is going to be?," *Mind* 68: 193–208.

Brueckner, Anthony. (2000). "On an Attempt to Demonstrate the Compatibility of Divine Foreknowledge and Human Freedom," *Faith and Philosophy* 17: 132–34.

Byerly, T. Ryan. (2012). "Infallible Divine Foreknowledge Cannot Uniquely Threaten Human Freedom, but Its Mechanics Might," *European Journal for Philosophy of Religion* 4: 73–94.

—— (2014). *The Mechanics of Divine Foreknowledge and Providence: A Time-Ordering Account.* London: Bloomsbury.

Cahn, Steven. (1967). *Fate, Logic, and Time.* New Haven: Yale University Press.

Clark, Michael. (1969). "Discourse About the Future," *Royal Institute of Philosophy Lectures* 3: 169–90.

Craig, William Lane. (1987). *The Only Wise God: The Compatibility of Divine Foreknowledge and Human Freedom.* Grand Rapids: Baker.

Dummett, Michael. (1964). "Bringing about the past," *The Philosophical Review* 73: 338–59.

—— (2004). *Truth and the Past.* New York: Columbia University Press.

Eklund, Matti. (2011). "Fictionalism,"*The Stanford Encyclopedia of Philosophy* (Fall 2011 Edition), Edward N. Zalta (ed.), URL = <http://plato.stanford.edu/archives/fall2011/entries/fictionalism/>.

Evans, Gareth. (1985). "Does tense logic rest on a mistake?," in *Collected Papers*, 343–63. Oxford: Clarendon Press.

Fine, Kit. (1994). "Essence and Modality," *Philosophical Perspectives* 8: 1–16.

Fischer, John Martin. (1983). "Freedom and Foreknowledge," *The Philosophical Review* 92: 67–79; reprinted in Fischer 1989: 86–96.

—— (1985). "Scotism," *Mind* 94: 231–43.

—— ed. (1989). *God, Foreknowledge, and Freedom*. Stanford, CA.: Stanford University Press.

—— (1992). "Recent Work on God and Freedom," *American Philosophical Quarterly* 29: 91–109.

—— (1994). *The Metaphysics of Free Will: An Essay on Control*. Oxford: Blackwell Publishers.

—— (2008). "Molinism," in Jonathan Kvanvig, ed., *Oxford Studies in Philosophy of Religion*, vol. 1, 18–43. Oxford: Oxford University Press.

—— (2012). *Deep Control: Essays on Free Will and Value*. Oxford: Oxford University Press.

Fischer, John Martin and Mark Ravizza, S. J. (1998). *Responsibility and Control: A Theory of Moral Responsibility*. New York: Cambridge University Press.

Fischer, John Martin and Neal A. Tognazzini. (2014). "Omniscience, Freedom, and Dependence," *Philosophy and Phenomenological Research* 88: 346–67.

Fischer, John Martin, Patrick Todd, and Neal Tognazzini. (2009). "Engaging with Pike: God, Freedom, and Time," *Philosophical Papers* 38: 247–70.

Flint, Thomas P. (1998). *Divine Providence: The Molinist Account*. Ithaca, NY: Cornell University Press.

Frankfurt, Harry. (1969). "Alternate Possibilities and Moral Responsibility," *The Journal of Philosophy* 66: 829–39.

Freddoso, Alfred. (1983). "Accidental Necessity and Logical Determinism," *Journal of Philosophy* 80: 257–78; reprinted in Fischer 1989: 136–58.

—— (1988). "Introduction" to Luis de Molina, *On Divine Foreknowledge: Part IV of the Concordia*, tr. Alfred J. Freddoso. Ithaca: Cornell University Press.

Geach, Peter. (1965). "Some Problems about Time," *Proceedings of the British Academy*, Vvol. 11.

—— (1973). "The Future," *New Blackfriars* 54: 208–18.

—— (1977). *Providence and Evil*. Cambridge: Cambridge University Press.

—— (1998). *Truth and Hope*. Notre Dame: University of Notre Dame Press.

Ginet, Carl. (1990). *On Action*. Cambridge: Cambridge University Press.

Hartshorne, Charles. (1938). "Are Propositions About the Future Either True or False?," *Proceedings of the American Philosophical Association—Western Division* (April 20–22): 26–32.

—— (1941). *Man's Vision of God and the Logic of Theism*. Chicago: Willet, Clark & Company.

—— (1964). "Deliberation and Excluded Middle," *The Journal of Philosophy* 61: 476–77.

Hasker, William. (1988). "Hard Facts and Theological Fatalism," *Noûs* 22: 419–36; reprinted in Fischer 1989: 159–77.

—— (1989). *God, Time, and Knowledge*. Cornell: Cornell University Press.

—— (1998). "No Easy Way Out: A Response to Warfield," *Noûs* 32: 361–63.

Heck, Richard. (2006). "MacFarlane on Relative Truth," *Philosophical Issues* 16: 88–100.

Horwich, Paul. (1987). *Asymmetries in Time: Problems in the Philosophy of Science.* Cambridge: MIT Press.

Hoffman, Joshua and Gary Rosenkrantz. (1980). "On Divine Foreknowledge and Human Freedom," *Philosophical Studies* 37: 289–96.

—— (1984). "Hard and Soft Facts," *The Philosophical Review* 93: 419–34; reprinted in Fischer 1989: 123–35.

Hunt, David. (1993). "Simple Foreknowledge and Divine Providence," *Faith and Philosophy* 10: 394–414.

—— (1995a). "Does Theological Fatalism Rest on an Equivocation?," *American Philosophical Quarterly* 32: 153–65.

—— (1995b). "Dispositional Omniscience," *Philosophical Studies* 80: 243–78.

—— (1997). "Two Problems with Knowing the Future," *American Philosophical Quarterly* 34: 273–85.

—— (1998). "What Is the Problem of Theological Fatalism?," *International Journal for Philosophy of Religion* 38: 17–30.

—— (2001). "The Simple Foreknowledge View," in James K. Beilby and Paul R. Eddy, eds., *Divine Foreknowledge: Four Views*, 65–103. Downers Grove: InterVarsity Press.

—— (2004). "Providence, Foreknowledge, and Explanatory Loops: A Reply to Robinson," *Religious Studies* 40(4): 485–91.

Kapitan, Tomis. (1990). "Action, Uncertainty, and Divine Impotence," *Analysis* 50: 127–33.

—— (1996). "Modal Principles in the Metaphysics of Free Will," *Philosophical Perspectives* 10: 419–45.

Knuuttila, Simo. (2011). "Medieval Theories of Future Contingents," *The Stanford Encyclopedia of Philosophy* (Spring 2014 Edition), Edward N. Zalta (ed.), URL = <http://plato.stanford.edu/archives/spr2014/entries/medieval-futcont/>.

Kvanvig, Jonathan. (1986). *The Possibility of an All-Knowing God.* London: Macmillan.

Lehrer, Keith. (1976). " 'Can' in Theory and Practice: A Possible Worlds Approach," in Miles Brand and Douglas Walton, eds., *Action Theory*, 241–70. Dordrecht: Reidel.

Leftow, Brian. (1991). *Time and Eternity.* Ithaca: Cornell University Press.

Lowe, E. J. (1998). *The Possibility of Metaphysics: Substance, Identity, and Time.* Oxford: Oxford University Press.

Lucas, J. R. (1989). *The Future: An Essay on God, Temporality, and Truth.* Oxford: Oxford University Press.

Łukasiewicz, Jan. (1957). *Aristotle's Syllogistic from the Standpoint of Modern Formal Logic.* Oxford: Clarendon Press.

Łukasiewicz, Jan. (1967). "On Three-Valued Logic," in S. McCall, ed., *Polish Logic*, 15–19. Oxford: Oxford University Press.

MacBride, Fraser. (2013). "Truthmakers," *The Stanford Encyclopedia of Philosophy* (Spring 2014 Edition), Edward N. Zalta (ed.), URL = <http://plato.stanford.edu/archives/spr2014/entries/truthmakers/>

MacFarlane, John. (2014). *Assessment Sensitivity: Relative Truth and Its Applications.* Oxford: Oxford University Press.

Markosian, Ned. (1995). "The Open Past," *Philosophical Studies* 79: 95–105.

Mavrodes, George. (1984). "Is the Past Unpreventable?" *Faith and Philosophy* 1: 131–46.

—— (1988). "How Does God Know the Things He Knows?," in Thomas V. Morris, ed., *Divine and Human Action: Essays in the Metaphysics of Theism*, 345–61. Ithaca: Cornell University Press.

McCall, Storrs. (2011). "The Supervenience of Truth: Freewill and Omniscience," *Analysis* 71: 501–06.

Merricks, Trenton. (2011). "Foreknowledge and Freedom," *The Philosophical Review* 120: 567–86.

Montague, Richard. (1960). "Mr. Bradley on the Future," *Mind* 69: 550–54.

Moruzzi, Sebastiano and Crispin Wright. (2006). "Trumping Assessments and the Aristotelian Future," *Synthese* 166: 309–31.

Øhrstrøm, Peter. (2009). "In Defence of the Thin Red Line: A Case for Ockhamism," *Humana.mente* 8: 17–32.

Øhrstrøm, Peter and Hasle, Per. (2011). "Future Contingents," *The Stanford Encyclopedia of Philosophy* (Summer 2011 Edition), Edward N. Zalta (ed.), URL = <http://plato.stanford.edu/archives/sum2011/entries/future-contingents/>.

Pendergraft, Garrett and D. Justin Coates. "No (New) Troubles With Ockhamism," in Jonathan Kvanvig, ed., *Oxford Studies in Philosophy of Religion*, vol. 5, 185–208. Oxford: Oxford University Press.

Perszyk, Ken, ed. (2011). *Molinism: The Contemporary Debate*. Oxford: Oxford University Press.

Pike, Nelson. (1965). "Divine Omniscience and Voluntary Action," *The Philosophical Review* 74: 27–46; reprinted in Fischer 1989: 57–73.

—— (1966). "Of God and Freedom: A Rejoinder," *The Philosophical Review* 75: 369–79.

—— (1970). *God and Timelessness*. New York: Schocken.

—— (1977). "Divine Foreknowledge, Human Freedom, and Possible Worlds." *The Philosophical Review* 86: 209–16.

—— (1993). "A Latter-Day Look at the Foreknowledge Problem," *International Journal for Philosophy of Religion* 33: 129–64.

Plantinga, Alvin. (1986). "On Ockham's Way Out," *Faith and Philosophy* 3: 235–69; reprinted in Fischer 1989: 178–215.

Prior, A. N. (1957). *Time and Modality*. Oxford: Oxford University Press.

—— (1962). "The Formalities of Omniscience," *Philosophy* 37: 114–29.

—— (1967). *Past, Present and Future*. Oxford: Oxford University Press.

Rice, Hugh. (2010). "Fatalism," *The Stanford Encyclopedia of Philosophy* (Spring 2013 Edition), Edward N. Zalta (ed.), URL = <http://plato.stanford.edu/archives/spr2013/entries/fatalism/>.

Rhoda, Alan, Gregory Boyd, and Thomas Belt. (2006). "Open Theism, Omniscience, and the Nature of the Future," *Faith and Philosophy* 23: 432–59.

Rhoda, Alan. (2007). "The Philosophical Case for Open Theism," *Philosophia* 35: 301–11.

Robinson, Michael. (2004). "Divine Providence, Simple Foreknowledge, and the 'Metaphysical Principle,'" *Religious Studies* 40: 471–83.

Ryle, Gilbert. (1954). "It Was to Be," in *Dilemmas*. Cambridge: Cambridge University Press.

Schaffer, Jonathan. (2009). "On What Grounds What," in David Manley, David J. Chalmers & Ryan Wasserman, eds., *Metametaphysics: New Essays on the Foundations of Ontology*, 347–83. Oxford: Oxford University Press.

Seymour, Amy. "The Advantages of All-Falsism," manuscript, University of Notre Dame.

Shields, George W. and Donald W. Viney. (2004). "The Logic of Future Contingents," in George W. Shields, ed., *Process and Analysis: Whitehead, Hartshorne, and the Analytic Tradition*, 209–46. Albany: State University of New York Press.

Shields, George W. (1988). "Fate and Logic: Cahn on Hartshorne Revisited." *The Southern Journal of Philosophy* 26(3): 369–78.

Smart, J. J. C. (1964). "Introduction," in *Problems of Space and Time*. New York: Macmillan.

Smith, Quentin and Nathan L. Oaklander. (1995). *Time, Change and Freedom*. London: Routledge.

Speaks, Jeff. (2011). "Foreknowledge, Evil, and Compatibility Arguments," *Faith and Philosophy* 28: 269–93.

Stump, Eleonore and Norman Kretzmann. (1981). "Eternity," *Journal of Philosophy* 78: 429–58.

—— (1991). "Prophecy, Past Truth, and Eternity," in James Tomberlin, ed., *Philosophical Perspectives 5: Philosophy of Religion*, 395–424. Atascadero, CA: Ridgeview.

Swinburne, Richard. (1977). *The Coherence of Theism*. Oxford: Oxford University Press.

Talbott, Thomas. (1993). "Theological Fatalism and Modal Confusion," *International Journal for Philosophy of Religion* 33: 65–88.

Taylor, Richard. (1963). "Fatalism," *The Philosophical Review* 71: 56–66.

—— (1964). "Deliberation and Foreknowledge," *American Philosophical Quarterly* 1: 73–80.

Todd, Patrick. (2013a). "Soft Facts and Ontological Dependence," *Philosophical Studies* 164: 829–44.

—— (2013b). "Prepunishment and Explanatory Dependence: A New Argument for Incompatibilism About Foreknowledge and Freedom," *The Philosophical Review* 122: 619–39.

—— (2014). "Against Limited Foreknowledge," *Philosophia* 42: 523–38.

—— (forthcoming). "Future Contingents Are All False! On Behalf of a Russellian Open Future," *Mind*.

—— "On Behalf of a Mutable Future," manuscript, University of Edinburgh.

Todd, Patrick and John Martin Fischer. (2013). "The Truth About Foreknowledge," *Faith and Philosophy* 30: 286–301.

Tooley, Michael. (2000a). *Time, Tense, and Causation*. Oxford: Oxford University Press.

—— (2000b). "Freedom and Foreknowledge," *Faith and Philosophy* 17: 212–24.

Torre, Stephan. (2011). "The Open Future," *Philosophy Compass* 6: 360–73.

Thomason, Richard. (1970). "Indeterminist Time and Truth-Value Gaps," *Theoria* 36: 264–81.

Tuggy, Dale. (2007). "Three Roads to Open Theism," *Faith and Philosophy* 24: 28–51.

van Inwagen, Peter. (1983). *An Essay on Free Will*. Oxford: Oxford University Press.

—— (2008). "What Does an Omniscient Being Know About the Future," in Jonathan Kvanvig, ed., *Oxford Studies in Philosophy of Religion*, vol. 1, 216–30. Oxford: Oxford University Press.

Viney, Donald W. (1989). "God Only Knows? Hartshorne and the Mechanics of Omniscience," in Robert Kane and Stephen H. Phillips, eds., *Hartshorne: Process Philosophy and Theology*, 71–90. Albany: State University of New York Press.

Wallace, David Foster. (2011). *Fate, Time, and Language: An Essay on Free Will*, Steven M. Cahn and Maureen Eckert (eds.). New York: Columbia University Press.

Warfield, Ted. (1997). "Divine Foreknowledge and Human Freedom are Compatible," *Noûs* 31: 80–86.

——— (2000). "On Freedom and Foreknowledge: A Reply to Two Critics," *Faith and Philosophy* 17: 255–59.

Westphal, Jonathan. (2011). "The Compatibility of Divine Foreknowledge and Freewill," *Analysis* 71: 246–52.

Widerker, David. (1989). "Two Fallacious Objections to Adams's Soft/Hard Fact Distinction," *Philosophical Studies* 57: 103–07.

——— (1991). "A Problem for the Eternity Solution," *International Journal for Philosophy of Religion* 29: 87–95.

Wierenga, Edward. (1991). "Prophecy, Freedom, and the Necessity of the Past," in James Tomberlin, ed., *Philosophical Perspectives* 5: *Philosophy of Religion*, 425–45. Atascadero, CA: Ridgeview.

Zagzebski, Linda. (1991). *The Dilemma of Freedom and Foreknowledge*. Oxford: Oxford University Press.

Zagzebski, Linda. (2011). "Foreknowledge and Free Will," *The Stanford Encyclopedia of Philosophy* (Fall 2011 Edition), Edward N. Zalta (ed.), URL = <http://plato.stanford.edu/archives/fall2011/entries/free-will-foreknowledge/>.

Zemach, Eddy and David Widerker. (1988). "Facts, Freedom, and Foreknowledge," *Religious Studies* 23: 19–28; reprinted in Fischer 1989: 111–22.

INDEX